LIBRARY OF NEW TESTAMENT STUDIES

617

Formerly the Journal for the Study of the New Testament Supplement Series

Editor
Chris Keith

Editorial Board
Dale C. Allison, John M. G. Barclay, Lynn H. Cohick, R. Alan Culpepper,
Craig A. Evans, Robert Fowler, Simon J. Gathercole, Juan Hernández Jr, John
S. Kloppenborg, Michael Labahn, Matthew V. Novenson, Love L. Sechrest, Robert
Wall, Catrin H. Williams, Brittany Wilson

Saint Thecla

Body Politics and Masculine Rhetoric

Rosie Andrious

LONDON • NEW YORK • OXFORD • NEW DELHI • SYDNEY

T&T CLARK
Bloomsbury Publishing Plc
50 Bedford Square, London, WC1B 3DP, UK
1385 Broadway, New York, NY 10018, USA
29 Earlsfort Terrace, Dublin 2, Ireland

BLOOMSBURY, T&T CLARK and the T&T Clark logo are trademarks
of Bloomsbury Publishing Plc

First published in Great Britain 2020
This paperback edition published in 2022

Copyright © Rosie Andrious, 2020

Rosie Andrious has asserted her right under the Copyright, Designs and Patents
Act, 1988, to be identified as Author of this work.

For legal purposes the Acknowledgements on p. xi constitute an extension
of this copyright page.

All rights reserved. No part of this publication may be reproduced or
transmitted in any form or by any means, electronic or mechanical,
including photocopying, recording, or any information storage or retrieval
system, without prior permission in writing from the publishers.

Bloomsbury Publishing Plc does not have any control over, or responsibility for, any
third-party websites referred to or in this book. All internet addresses given in this
book were correct at the time of going to press. The author and publisher regret any
inconvenience caused if addresses have changed or sites have ceased to exist, but can
accept no responsibility for any such changes.

A catalogue record for this book is available from the British Library.

A catalog record of this book is available from the Library of Congress.

ISBN: HB: 978-0-5676-9176-7
PB: 978-0-5676-9908-4
ePDF: 978-0-5676-9177-4
ePUB: 978-0-5676-9179-8

Series: Library of New Testament Studies, volume 617
ISSN 2513-8790

Typeset by Newgen KnowledgeWorks Pvt. Ltd., Chennai, India

To find out more about our authors and books visit www.bloomsbury.com
and sign up for our newsletters.

For Richard, and our children, Alex and Kirsty Ratcliffe.

Contents

List of figures	x
Acknowledgements	xi
List of abbreviations	xii
Overview	xiv

1	Introduction	1
	Thecla: The state of the question	1
	Women in the Apocryphal Acts	2
	Key issues of authorship, readership and liberation	5
	The *Acts of Paul and Thecla*	9
	Women's resistance	9
	Masculinization	10
	A shift in the hermeneutical field	12
	Evolution in Thecla scholarship	13
	The Apocryphal Acts and the Hellenistic novel	17
	The distinctive nature of the *Acts of Paul and Thecla*	20
	Moving forward	20
2	The *Acts of Paul and Thecla*: Text and context	33
	The question of genre	33
	Classification of the *Acts of Paul and Thecla*	36
	Textual history and dating	37
	Social location of the authorial voice	38
	The question of origins and the Pauline tradition	39
	Relationship to the Pauline tradition	41
	A Pauline tradition empowering to women?	44
3	Methodology	51
	Feminist hermeneutics	51
	Problems of male textuality and women as a vehicle of rhetoric	54
	Gender theory	56

	My approach	57
	The gender specifics of my approach	58
	A word about the author and narrator	59
4	**Female beheadings**	65
	Introduction	65
	Becoming male	66
	Does Thecla cut her hair and become male?	68
	Setting the scene	68
	Textual evidence	70
	Contextual evidence	72
	Alternative traditions?	74
	Thecla: The sexy cross-dresser	76
	Women's hair and heads	80
	Pleasurable viewing and disappearing men	82
	Conclusion	85
5	**Naked truths: Pornography and violence in the *Acts of Paul and Thecla***	95
	Introduction	95
	Defining pornography	96
	Specifics of pornographic representation	98
	Martyrdom and spectacle	99
	Re-reading the *Acts of Paul and Thecla*	104
	Analysis and observations thus far	121
	Conclusion	123
6	**Bewitched and bewitching women: Miracles and magical practices**	133
	Introduction	133
	Defining miracle	133
	Spellbinding thaumaturge and enchanted maiden	136
	A baptism of fire: Miracle 1	139
	Bound together: Miracle 2	143
	Dreams can come true: Miracle 3	145
	Animal magic: Miracle 4	146
	A second baptism: Miracle 5a	147
	Hubble bubble toil and trouble: Miracle 5b	147

	Raging bulls: Miracle 6	149
	Do miracles happen for the female gender?	150
	Conclusion	152
7	Violating the inviolate body	161
	Assessing gender construction in the *Acts of Paul and Thecla*	161
	Picturing female representation	163
	How does ego identification work?	164
	Roman visual representation	168
	Christians versus Empire, really?	174
	Authorial intention: Do I know something others don't?	181
	Conclusion	182
8	Conclusion	189
	Thecla: This is my body	189
	Thecla: The Church	192
	Thecla: A man within and a man on top	194
	Thecla: Imagine my body	196
	Thecla: The myth of the perfect female body	198
Bibliography		201
List of ancient sources		221
Index		223

Figures

4.1	Saint Thecla with wild beasts and angels	75
7.1	'Judaea Capta' coin issued following the destruction of Jerusalem	169
7.2	Emperor Augustus in military dress: marble figure from the Prima Porta	170
7.3	Cuirass of Augustus from Prima Porta, Hispania and Gaul	171
7.4	Relief of Emperor Claudius triumphing over Britannia, from the Sebasteion at Aphrodisias	172

Acknowledgements

This monograph is the result of research undertaken at King's College, London, for the degree of PhD. Perhaps the greatest lesson I learned during my years at King's was that a PhD requires a community for support and sanity. No publication, therefore, is complete without acknowledgement to those who helped to make that journey more enjoyable and bearable than it otherwise might have been.

First and foremost, I would like to thank the scholar and friend, Michelle Fletcher, for her generous and patient support. What would I do without you, my friend?

I also wish to express my deepest gratitude to those who supervised me, Joan Taylor and Edward Adams. Thank you for your insights and expert guidance and for helping me to finish what I started. Thanks are also due to my external examiners, Kate Cooper and Bridget Gilfillan Upton, whose recommendations helped to shape the final version of my thesis.

A word of thanks must go to Judith Lieu who was the initial supervisor of this project and who continued to offer invaluable critique long after her move to Cambridge University as Lady Margaret's Professor of Divinity: you left an indelible imprint on me as a scholar, thank you.

To my publishers T&T Clark and especially to Sarah Blake for her support and understanding kindness.

Of course, nothing is possible without the love and support of my family, to whom this book is dedicated: my children (and teachers), Alex and Kirsty, you fill my heart with joy, pride and laughter, thank you for choosing me; and my soulmate and love of my life, Richard. You always were the 'wind beneath my wings'.

Finally, since they are the reason that I am here, I would like to thank my parents, the truly indomitable Andrious Mama and the most gracious late Victoria Mama, for giving so much.

Abbreviations

Am. Anthropol.	*American Anthrolopology*
ANF	*Ante-Nicene Fathers*
ATR	*Anglican Theological Review*
BDAG	Walter Bauer, Frederick W. Danker, William F. Arndt and F. Wilbur Gingrich, *A Greek-English Lexicon of the New Testament and Other Early Christian Literature*, 3rd ed. (Chicago: University of Chicago Press, 2000)
BibInt	*Biblical Interpretation*
Br. J. Sociol.	*British Journal of Sociology*
BTB	*Biblical Theology Bulletin*
CBQ	*Catholic Biblical Quarterly*
Curr. Anthropol.	*Current Anthropology*
HR	*History of Religions*
HTR	*Harvard Theological Review*
Hugoye JSS	*Journal of Syriac Studies*
JAAR	*Journal of the American Academy of Religion*
JBL	*Journal of Biblical Literature*
JECS	*Journal of Early Christian Studies*
JFSR	*Journal of Feminist Studies in Religion*
JR	*Journal of Religion*
JRS	*Journal of Roman Studies*
JSNT	*Journal for the Study of the New Testament*
JTS	*Journal of Theological Studies*
LCL	Loeb Classical Library
LSJ	G. Liddell and R. Scott, *Greek-English Lexicon* (Oxford: Clarendon Press, 1996)
LTQ	*Lexington Theological Quarterly*
LXX	Septuagint
Neot	*Neotestmentica*
NPNF	*Nicene and Post-Nicene Fathers*
NRSV	New Revised Standard Version
NT	New Testament
NTA	Wilhelm Schneemelcher, ed., *New Testament Apocrypha*, rev. ed., trans. R. McL. Wilson (Cambridge: James Clarke; Louisville, KY: Westminster/John Knox Press, 1992).
NTS	*New Testament Studies*
Oxf. J. Leg. Stud.	*Oxford Journal of Legal Studies*
PGM	Greek Magical Papyri

PH	Hamburg Papyrus
P. Heid.	Coptic Papyrus No. 1 in Heidelberg
PSB	*Princeton Seminary Bulletin*

All English biblical quotations are from the NRSV, unless otherwise stated.

The standard edition for the *Acts of Paul and Thecla* is Richard Adelbert Lipsius and Maximillianus Bonnet, *Acta Apostolorum Apocrypha, Post Constantinum.* Leipzig: Hermann Mendelssohn, 1891–1903. Reprint, Hildenscheim: G. Olms Verlagsbuchhandlung, 1959. Translations are my own.

In citing chapters and fragmentary material of the Apocryphal Acts of the Apostles, I follow the numbering and usage found in Wilhelm Schneemelcher, ed., *New Testament Apocrypha*, rev. ed. Translated by R. McL. Wilson. Cambridge: James Clarke; Louisville, KY: Westminster/John Knox Press, 1992.

Overview

The *Acts of Paul and Thecla* (*APTh*) contains the representation of a woman savagely abused, and yet in modern scholarship it has predominantly been taken as a female-friendly text. But can a narrative which contains sado-erotic representations of a woman be held up as affirming of women? This study demonstrates that the text of Thecla is, in fact, highly androcentric and patriarchal and, even though the text is packaged in a way that focuses on one female protagonist who rebels against society and *polis* and is commissioned by Paul to 'Go and teach the Word of God', it nevertheless takes a highly ambivalent stance towards the female heroine.

Within this monograph, I concentrate on three main areas of the text. First, I look at Thecla's apparent 'manly' transformation. I question the assumption that Thecla undergoes a sexual transformation by way of a haircut and a change of clothing and argue that she very much remains female in form. Second, I consider the representations of sado-erotic violence in order to reveal the structures of power and dominance within the text. Finally, I examine the role of magic and miracles, analysing the rhetorical and ideological dimensions of the text that impact upon constructions of gender. I then move on to summarily consider my findings within the context of Roman Imperial power in the Greek East in the second century CE. Here, advancing the insights of Kate Cooper, who has suggested that texts such as the *Acts of Paul and Thecla* are complex literary entities that represent a power struggle between men, I argue for the ideological function of Thecla as a constructed body who transcends her 'natural' feminine weakness. I conclude that Thecla's inviolate body is linked to the self-identity of male Christians and communicates conceptions of inviolability that speak back to the Roman Empire.

1

Introduction

Thecla: The state of the question

For some thirty years, scholars have focused on the liberating effects of chaste ascetic practice for women in early Christianity. In removing women from the normative world of family life, this practice was thought to provide a means of escape from marriage, maternity and subjugation by men. In this regard, there is the example of Thecla, in a text embedded within the apocryphal *Acts of Paul* (*AP*): the *Acts of Paul and Thecla* (*APTh*). As a young, betrothed virgin who, on hearing Paul preach, decides to pursue the chaste Christian life, Thecla makes up her own mind, spurns her fiancé and rebels against family and societal values in order to follow Paul's teaching. In this respect, many scholars have contemplated her importance as an emancipated model, especially since she is eventually commissioned by Paul to 'go and teach the Word of God' (*APTh*. 41). There has been a strong tendency towards reading this chaste heroine as a positive representation of a woman.

However, is Thecla really such a positive model? In between her decision to follow Paul and his commission to her, Thecla is subjected to horrific public abuse, avoiding martyrdom by divine intervention only after enduring desperate humiliation, which is graphically depicted. Even if the text were intended, in its own distinctive patriarchal second-century way, to convey or propose an alternative way of life for women, why was the message communicated in a manner which degraded the female heroine, with her assailants exposing and attempting to torture her beautiful naked body?

For me, this intriguing text contains many irreconcilable tensions that need closer interrogation. Not least is the need to question any 'female empowering' interpretation of a text that contains within it scenes of a woman stripped, abused and violated. This study thus grew out of my questioning how a narrative which contains sado-erotic and voyeuristic representations of a woman can be held up as female-affirming.

While the heroine Thecla is often seen as a positive representation of a woman and a paragon of female liberation in antiquity, much of the text makes for disturbing reading for women of today and may have done so for women in antiquity whose models of shame and honour were more defined than ours. The fact that Thecla is voyeuristically paraded and subjected to a kind of sado-erotic torture clashes with a notion that she is presented as a positive role model for women. It is also intriguing that, despite the focus of attention Thecla has received from feminist scholars, there has been no comprehensive treatment of the themes of graphic violence and pornography within the text.

There also seems to be an underlying assumption made that rejection of the household is liberating, and – likewise – since Thecla offers to cut her hair and dons a male χιτών at the close of the narrative, that 'becoming male' is, in some way, a good thing. To complicate matters further, there is no certainty that Thecla becomes 'male' by an ascetic renunciation of her gender; she is very much depicted as a beautiful woman throughout the text. Thus, in her journey to 'become male', as many scholars see it, Thecla does not cut her hair to look like a man, despite offering to do so. This has raised serious questions for me in regard to the text. This stalling of Thecla's manly transformation, combined with the explicit portrayal of her naked and abused female body, is something I will explore here in detail.

This thesis, then, considers the *Acts of Paul and Thecla* from various angles in order to probe the complexities of the gender presentation of Thecla it contains. I will begin by situating my discussion within the scholarly context that has gone before, in terms of the Apocryphal Acts as a whole and the *Acts of Paul and Thecla* in particular, and it will be seen that there is a growing tendency to question whether the supposed emancipation of ascetic women read from such texts was a historical reality for women in the first two centuries of Christian history. In reaching an impasse on the historical question, some scholars have focused more on certain liberating models as ideals that texts such as the *Acts of Paul and Thecla* may have provided for women of early Christianity. But, even still, are these literary models and ideals really emancipatory, and do they really provide positive representations of a woman?

Women in the Apocryphal Acts

The Apocryphal Acts have provided a range of influential stories in Christian hagiography, evidenced in art throughout the centuries, but they were not much studied until the second half of the twentieth century. Their popularity as a subject of academic attention was boosted by the translation work of Wilhelm Schneemelcher, who updated the German collection of Edgar Hennecke to produce the *Neutestamentlichen Apokryphen in deutscher Übersetzung* (1959), subsequently translated into English by R. McL. Wilson as *The New Testament Apocrypha*.[1] However, only in 2008 has there been an updated and easily accessible work in English that collects the Apocryphal Acts together as a type of early Christian literature.[2]

With the rise of the women's movement in the 1970s and a concern about women's roles within the church, it is no wonder that the women of the Apocryphal Acts would receive particular attention. One of the first scholars to focus specifically on the female figures of the Apocryphal Acts was Ross Kraemer in an article of 1980 entitled 'The Conversion of Women to Ascetic Forms of Christianity'.[3] While taking into consideration the pseudonymous and legend-like quality of the texts, her project was an act of historical retrieval: of consciously writing women into narratives of early Christian history. Kraemer hypothesized that the legends which arose in Christian circles contained a reflection of actual early Christian practice in which ascetic, celibate women enjoyed new-found freedom and played important roles. For Kraemer, female chaste ascetic practice involved a rejection of traditional socio-sexual roles and reversed societal values.[4]

Following on from Kraemer, three seminal works were published, which were, at the time, remarkable for their groundbreaking approach in advancing the feminist cause to focus on neglected female figures and the part they played in the early church.[5] These works by Stevan Davies, Dennis R. MacDonald and Virginia Burrus, all followed a socio-historical method of inquiry which provided an extensive analysis about the possible folkloric origins of the texts and sought to understand how the Apocryphal Acts reflected actual social situations. Although there were differences among the approaches and methodologies employed by each author, it is clear that they all assumed a shared outlook in terms of viewing the Apocryphal Acts as reflecting a socio-historical reality and evidence of female liberation in antiquity.

In *The Revolt of the Widows* (1980), Stevan Davies argued that the rebellion of second- and third-century celibate Christian women against an increasingly powerful and repressive church led to all-female communities.[6] Using an approach that utilized a sociological method combined with historical critical inquiry, Davies suggested that since the stories contained within the Apocryphal Acts are so exaggerated, it was necessary to concentrate on the relationships reflected in the texts rather than the events they recount.[7] Davies made the methodological assumption that the texts reflect the actual world of the authors and audience, along with the tensions experienced by the community. Guided by Schneemelcher, who argued that the Apocryphal Acts were designed for entertainment, edification and instruction,[8] Davies surmised that women were the target audience, since they predominate in the literature and often emerge as paragons of discipleship outshining the men in the stories.[9] Examining Tertullian's comments and Pseudo-Clementine literature, Davies developed the connection between the narrative and the social world and argued that the predominance of chaste women in the texts, along with the conflict between them and threatening males, reflects just such a community. Davies thus proposed that the original readership community of the Apocryphal Acts was largely female in composition and made up of the two categories of 'widows' and 'virgins'. Davies also argued that it would make psychological sense if the authors of the texts were women since the texts project a positive picture of feminine potential, while at the same time providing an outlet for female resentment toward men who may have tried to repress their initiative.[10]

Similarly, three years after Davies, MacDonald also argued that the Apocryphal Acts are a reflection of a woman's world.[11] MacDonald explored the relationship between the Pastoral Epistles and the *Acts of Paul* in particular. His central thesis was that the Pastoral Epistles were written to counter the representation of Paul presented in the *Acts of Paul* and a female ascetic strain within early Christianity, with different groups battling to show that they preserved the true Pauline legacy. MacDonald noted that, even if in their current form the *Acts of Paul* came from a generation later than the Pastoral Epistles, the stories they contain have oral antecedents and originate from circles of independently minded celibate women within the church.[12]

MacDonald began by establishing the original oral character of the legends through the application of folklore analysis. He supported his thesis further through external evidence from Tertullian and references to the historical Queen Tryphaena of Pontus. He then set out to determine the relationship between the legends and the Pastoral Epistles by arguing that the characteristics of the false teachers in the Pastoral Epistles (1 Tim. 1.5-7; 4.1-7; 6.3-5; Tit. 1.10-11) are akin to those of Paul in the *Acts of Paul*.[13] Furthermore, the support for traditional societal norms promoted in the Pastoral Epistles (1 Tim. 2.7-10; 3.11-15; 5.23; 6.2-3; Tit. 2.1-10) was meant as a corrective to the radical ascetic practice promoted in the legends. Their restrictions on the order of widows (1 Tim. 5.3-16) and on women teachers (1 Tim. 2.11-15) were also intended to circumscribe and control the celibate women who promoted the legends. In highlighting the differences and agreements between the *Acts of Paul* and the Pastoral Epistles, MacDonald asserted that the author of the Pastoral Epistles knew the legends. He explained the relationship in terms of 'a common knowledge of oral traditions'. Due to their inclusion in the canon, MacDonald saw the Pastoral Epistles as the 'victors' of the battle for Paul's memory.[14]

MacDonald, like Davies, believed that social aspects are reflected in the texts. He highlighted the prominence of widows in the Apocryphal Acts, which he argued pointed to the likelihood that widows and female virgins were a distinct chaste group living in established houses together. In line with Davies, MacDonald believed that the predominance and sympathetic treatment of 'all' women, along with the contemptuous portrayal of men, strongly suggested female storytellers.[15] He furthermore interpreted the virginal life as 'rebellion, conscious or unconscious, against male domination'. As for the *Acts of Paul*, MacDonald wrote, '[N]owhere is the relationship between silencing women and returning them to diapers and aprons more apparent than in 1 Tim. 2.11-15.'[16]

In her work *Chastity as Autonomy* (1987), Virginia Burrus argued too that the Apocryphal Acts contain important accounts and evidence of women's religious activity and experiences in early Christianity.[17] Once again, chastity leads to autonomy and freedom from oppressive authority of husband and political ruler. Burrus also employed folkloric methods, which she supported with models from psychology and the sociology of religion, fundamentally seeing these stories as literary adaptations of folk stories. By applying folklorist structural analysis, she noted the particular sequence of functions that represent the basic narrative structure in the five earliest Apocryphal Acts.[18] She argued that this proliferation of variants on a single story type with varying characters and settings is characteristic of folklore. Burrus also argued against the theory that the Apocryphal Acts were originally literary works shaped by the forms and concerns of the Graeco-Roman novel. Rather, she indicated the likelihood that the texts are based directly on oral legends. In this way, Burrus shifted the focus away from male scribes to the oral beginnings of these tales which, she argued, likely originated with female storytellers. Burrus believed that the predominance of women in the 'chastity stories' underscored her conclusions. Her argumentation was further supported by employing evidence from Graeco-Roman cultural and cross-cultural analyses which demonstrate that women produced and transmitted women's stories.[19]

Burrus went on to offer a social historical interpretation, claiming that folk-narrative or 'legends' in their natural inclination to reflect their cultural milieu and community concerns often betray elements of historical information or a 'historical kernel'. In this respect, the chastity stories reflect a distinct 'female sphere' and a conflict between women and the institution of patriarchal marriage. For Burrus, the stories contained in the Apocryphal Acts allowed women to express repressed hostilities and dissatisfaction and to fantasize about defiance of husbands and freedom from marriage.[20]

Along with Davies and MacDonald, Burrus speculated that the women who promoted the 'chastity stories' lived together in self-supporting communities.[21] The named apostle brings in an element of erotic substitution and serves to legitimate the chaste lifestyle and strengthen the identity of the community of women. Burrus interpreted the motif of erotic substitution psychologically, arguing that women were able to project their fantasies onto this 'donor' or auxiliary figure; this allowed the sublimation of sexual energies in their new spiritual relationship with Christ.[22]

Burrus's analysis led her to conclude that the Apocryphal Acts provide us with early documentation of the attraction a life of chastity held for many early Christian women, who were willing to abandon the social status and sexual life of a married woman for the autonomous life of a virgin. While the heroines of the stories may have been fictional figures, their stories point to a historical reality, embodied in the audiences that heard and circulated these women's stories.

Key issues of authorship, readership and liberation

The work of Burrus, Davies and MacDonald created the momentum and impetus in the study of the Apocryphal Acts as a whole, especially as they defined this body of texts as essentially women's literature. To what extent, however, is this really the case? How does this then affect how we read these texts today?

In fact, despite their popularity and influence, the works of Burrus, Davies and MacDonald have not been read without criticism, the most prominent critics being Jean-Daniel Kaestli, Margaret Howe, Peter Dunn and Lynne Boughton.[23] While Kaestli and Willy Rordorf were critical of the methodologies employed, they were, nevertheless, favourable to the idea of a women's liberation movement within the early Church.[24] However, it was also argued that Burrus, Davies and MacDonald failed to take into consideration the fact that the Apocryphal Acts are religious documents with no concern to promote any particular 'militant' female perspective.[25] In regard to MacDonald and Burrus, Dunn observed that it is quite possible for authors to imitate the devices and motifs of folklore; thus, written stories with no oral history may well exhibit oral features.[26] Kaestli also contended that their unity of composition argued against a pre-literary existence of the Apocryphal Acts.[27]

Part of the difficulty for both Burrus and Davies was their attempt to join together a heterogeneous corpus of literature to a common narrative structure.[28] Burrus also neglected to incorporate into her study a number of other stories in the Apocryphal Acts without female heroines but which revolve around the theme of chastity.[29] Such stories include the story of Peter's daughter, found in the Coptic *Acts of Peter* (*APt*), the story of the parricide in the *Acts of John* (*AJ*), the episode of the woman possessed by a demon and a young man who murdered his beloved in *Acts of Thomas* (*AT*).³⁰ These narratives, all excluded by Burrus, would significantly have modified her thesis that chastity leads to female autonomy. While Burrus argued that clear differences between such stories and the 'chastity stories' made it difficult to group them together,³¹ their exclusion left her open to accusations of bias.³²

In her response to Kaestli, Burrus contended that, in part, gender differences accounted for their conflicting views.³³ However, female scholars too could interpret the Apocryphal Acts in a way which is diametrically opposed to Burrus, as evidenced, for example, by Margaret Howe and Lynne Boughton.³⁴ Indeed, Howe warned against seeing the figure of Thecla as a positive role model. She viewed Thecla as a pathetic figure whose obvious devotion to Paul clearly shows that she is not concerned to escape male domination. Far from affirming women, Thecla demeans them. She resorts to wearing men's clothes in order to fulfil her ministry, thereby denying all that is female within her.³⁵ Boughton argued that Thecla's religiosity and conversion is grounded not in the person of Jesus but rather based on her attraction to Paul.³⁶ Mary Lefkowitz also reads the text of Thecla from a more negative perspective and criticizes Thecla for her constant need for approval and acceptance by Paul.³⁷ Furthermore, although working from a more literary perspective, Kate Cooper also reads the texts quite differently to Burrus. For Cooper, despite the seeming centrality of women in the Apocryphal Acts, the real issue at stake in these stories was between men; the challenge is about authority and social order, not women and sexual continence (this will be discussed in more detail below).³⁸ The fact that female scholars can read the text of Thecla in a way that opposes Burrus's interpretation would, therefore, negate her defence to Kaestli that gender differences account for the different readings of the text. Rather, it raises serious issues about how we read female figures in the texts and what criteria we use to judge whether a presentation is 'liberating' or not.

Furthermore, with the exception of the *Acts of Paul and Thecla*, which historically has an independent tradition of transmission and may account for Thecla's prominent role, it is difficult to avoid the fact that the Apocryphal Acts focus very much on the male apostles, and it is they who are portrayed as central characters in the narratives. Cooper also notes that one of the central themes of the Apocryphal Acts is the moral superiority of the apostolic hero.³⁹

In addition, it is hard to get away from the fact that the women in the Apocryphal Acts continued to be defined in terms of men, whether a male divinity or his agent, the apostle.⁴⁰ This aspect further undermined all reasoning (by Davies, Burrus and MacDonald) that resentful and suppressed women sought to rebel and break free of patriarchy. Another issue is whether narrative events really do mirror the real world. Without this mimetic link, the theory that the Apocryphal Acts might be literature authored for women, with women readers, lacks substantial evidence. To what extent do the representations of women in the text bear any relation to real women or their social circumstances? Where women are concerned, there is, as Judith Lieu notes, a need to think of 'politics' at every level of analysis.⁴¹

There is also the fact that these texts have been subjected to extensive redactional influences to reach the forms we possess today.⁴² The question then is whether it is plausible that earlier oral or written traditions of the Apocryphal Acts had origins in female circles. However, even if this is so, it is not quite the female 'authorship' that Davies, Macdonald and Burrus advocated. Furthermore, if these texts passed through various male filters, it would render any attempt to recover a social history of women a hazardous project. There are then real questions about whether the readings of Davies, Macdonald and Burrus may be somewhat hopeful and designed to support the second-wave feminist cause.[43]

Both Sheila McGinn and Elisabeth Schüssler Fiorenza note the general patriarchal and male bias of the *Acts of Paul* as a whole.[44] Indeed, McGinn, in her commentary, has also successfully highlighted the unsympathetic treatment of women in the *Acts of Paul* where, in contrast to the *Acts of Paul and Thecla*, even the animals are male. Here, women are subordinated to Paul; they are either his opponents or the vehicle for men's opposition to him. Indeed, the final message of these sections of the *Acts of Paul* is that women, even women sympathetic to the Christian cause, are dangerous to Christian mission.[45]

Kraemer also highlighted the point that Davies's hypothesis amounted to the assumption that a combination of central female characters and the absence of misogyny points strongly to a woman author.[46] Similarly, Jan Bremmer notes that the simple fact of a sympathetic treatment of women in a piece of writing does not necessarily make the author a woman.[47] Such a hypothesis would make any number of ancient writings contenders for female authorship. A further inference of this view is that women are unlikely to have authored work in which men are the central characters or in which women are portrayed in a negative light.[48] Kraemer, however, observes that feminist research has demonstrated that the majority of women become indoctrinated by the dominant, misogynist values and perspectives of their own cultures; these then become subsumed into their self-understanding.[49]

Mary Rose D'Angelo, in a similar discussion concerning the possibility of whether any of the four gospels could have been authored by a woman, likewise notes that androcentric perspectives in a text would not preclude the possibility of female authorship since ultimately women inculcated societal views and ideology.[50] Lefkowitz also notes that behind the suggestion that texts sympathetic to women were written by female authors lies the assumption that writers put themselves into whatever they write.[51] Thus, directly or indirectly, one writes about what one is. Lefkowitz, however, argues that content is not always a sure or reliable means of determining authorship.[52] Such a notion fails to consider the power of an individual artist to develop or even to break with inherited tradition; neither gender nor race can explain distinctive qualities of style or content. Furthermore, Lefkowitz has demonstrated that in ancient Greek literature, there was 'an established tradition of men writing with sympathy and concern for women's experience', beginning with Homer and continued by the Attic dramatists and lyric poets, Euripides, Stesichorus and Sophocles.[53] From her study of Greek texts in the classical period and beyond, Lefkowitz observes that it would not have occurred to the Greeks that only women could write about women's experience, any more than they found it remarkable that dramatists could write about the conversations of the gods on Mount Olympus. It follows, therefore, that sympathy for women alone, in the absence of other kinds of evidence, does not constitute proof that a text was composed by a woman. A further question is whether or not the Apocryphal Acts ultimately do treat women sympathetically.

It is relevant to note that Lefkowitz concludes in her analysis that since there was no taboo on women publishing in their names, and since the descriptions of the women in the Greek texts do not emphasize or even refer to those aspects of women's life apart from men, it is most unlikely that women did write novels.[54] The author's tendency to describe the heroine's sexuality from a man's point of view leaves the impression that these ancient novels were written by the kind of writers who normally wrote this type of narrative: men. Indeed, judging from poems and epitaphs written by women for women, they can be distinguished from men's writing about women by their tendency to describe women's thoughts about aspects of their lives not connected with marriage or sexuality, or the men in their lives. Male patrons, by contrast, even in poems written for women, tend to call attention to themselves.[55] Lefkowitz, however, does remain open to the fact that it is theoretically possible that some women in antiquity did write novels, and this possibility should certainly not be ruled out.[56] This is especially the case since there is evidence that many women in the Roman period could read and write.[57]

Thus, despite the fact that very few women in antiquity are known to have written prose fiction,[58] as Kraemer rightly highlights, it is important to remain sensitive to the possibility that some of our texts in the Apocryphal Acts may not have been written by men.[59] Kim Haines-Eitzen's close study of ancient manuscripts, for example, reveals that women were involved in the copying of early Christian literature.[60] She points out that the ancient textual sources betray 'hints' of women as authors. Eusebius, for example, comments about Origen's female calligraphers.[61] Although she underscores the fact that we cannot rely on Eusebius's claims uncritically, what is instructive is that Eusebius nowhere suggests that women calligraphers were unusual.[62] Her survey of ancient literature concludes that women were '(occasionally? rarely? sometimes?) involved in the many and various stages of the production, reproduction and dissemination of early Christian literature.'[63]

In his evaluation of MacDonald's work, Dunn observed that, despite Tertullian's resistance, the Church had little difficulty in accepting the conflicting traditions of both the *Acts of Paul and Thecla* and the Pastoral Epistles.[64] Dunn argued that MacDonald considerably overstated the polarity between the Pastoral Epistles and the *Acts of Paul*.[65] Indeed, Paul himself held onto the tension between the ideal of chastity and the remedy of marriage for sexual immorality in 1 Cor. 7.24.[66]

MacDonald's work was important in that it brought to the fore the fact that the Church remembered Paul in diverse ways and consequently opened up the possibility of alternate interpretations of Paul other than those found within the Pastoral Epistles. Moreover, his approach was certainly legitimate, in that the two texts do hold personal names in common and the *Acts of Paul* certainly advocate practices and beliefs which are forbidden within the Pastoral Epistles.[67] Furthermore, MacDonald was not alone in reading back into the Pastoral Epistles from other sources which suggest that virgins might have belonged to the order of widows.[68] However, despite the general correlation between the *Acts of Paul* and the Pastoral Epistles, it is quite another matter to argue for a simple and straightforward trajectory between the situations reflected in each of these texts as MacDonald has done.

In short, the work of Davies, Macdonald and Burrus has been undoubtedly creative and greatly influential. In bringing women to the forefront of the interpretative scene as subject, they paved the way forward in highlighting the fact that history may not have been as clear cut as interpreters had previously claimed. Consequently, these studies had a significant impact upon the reading and interpretation of the Apocryphal Acts. However, there are key issues that have been raised over the past thirty years. To what extent might the Apocryphal Acts be considered the work of early Christian women, presenting images of women that are empowering and liberational? What criteria can we use to assess whether a text is such in terms of its characterization and the actions that are described?

However, while the corpus of the Apocryphal Acts has many stories, each with their own integrity, it is above all the *Acts of Paul* that has been of special interest, not only to MacDonald but also to others looking for key female figures, because it is in this text that we have the important figure of Thecla.

The *Acts of Paul and Thecla*

The *Acts of Paul and Thecla* is a discrete section within the larger narrative of the *Acts of Paul*. Embedded within the *Acts of Paul*, it presents the story of a young betrothed virgin who on hearing Paul preach decides to pursue the chaste Christian life. This decision costs her dearly as she encounters familial and social opposition and persecution. However, she overcomes the many ordeals that are sent to challenge her and she eventually receives Paul's blessing to:

Ὕπαγε καὶ δίδασκε τὸν λόγον τοῦ θεοῦ (*APTh*. 41)

Thecla is depicted as a virgin who ventures out in the public, dons male apparel and eventually assumes the role of teacher and preacher. Her representation, therefore, counters the expected Graeco-Roman norms for women in antiquity: norms which saw a distinction between the female private domain and the male public domain and clearly associated women with the private sphere of the home.[69] Within the *Acts of Paul and Thecla*, a woman receives apostolic blessing to abandon kin, marriage and maternity in order to teach the Word of God. Here, women's procreative ability is negated as virginity reigns supreme.

Given that the writings of Davies, MacDonald and Burrus all emerged at the height of feminist hermeneutics in biblical studies, the possibility of recovering a 'usable history' for women from ancient texts became a tangible reality, and the *Acts of Paul and Thecla*, which featured a lone female protagonist, was seized upon.

Women's resistance

A number of scholars hailed the *Acts of Paul and Thecla* as authoritative evidence of women's lived reality. Here, 'women's resistance' becomes a discernible theme. Luise Schottroff, for example, argued that the *Acts of Paul and Thecla* is an 'outstanding document of women's resistance against patriarchy during early Christianity'.[70] For Maud Burnett McInerney, the *Acts of Paul and Thecla* represents a choice of virginity which is both socially and politically radical in its challenge to the heterosocial norms of marriage and family and to the spiritual and temporal authority of men.[71] The text of the *Acts of Paul and Thecla* thus bears witness to women's own experience in an immediate and provocative way.[72] McGinn, too, offers a very positive reading of the text and notes that Thecla is depicted as a faithful servant of God, while Paul is presented as one who fails her. McGinn goes as far as to argue that the prison scene (*APTh*. 18-19) forms Thecla's 'call narrative', comparative to 1 Kgs 19.19-21, which suggests that Thecla will become the prophet to succeed Paul, as Elisha did Elijah (1 Kgs 19.16). McGinn's admission that the scene is 'unusual', since (1) there is no vision from God or invitation from Paul and (2) Thecla initiates the action, perhaps demonstrates that scholars were, at this time, somewhat overenthusiastic in the interpretations they were gleaning from the text.[73]

However, while more circumspect in her conclusion, Margaret MacDonald also argued that the text reveals the controversy created by women who remain unmarried.[74] Although she conceded that the legend-like quality of the *Acts of Paul and Thecla* makes it difficult to use the text as a straightforward comparison about real-life situations, she went on to argue that the text is a bold promotion of the celibate life. The text may be a fabrication, but the work mirrors the actual experience of early Christian women who rejected marriage and found themselves in violent confrontation with society. In demonstrating Thecla's increasing independence from Paul, the narrative testifies to how early Christian women subverted the traditional Graeco-Roman household and constructed an alternate household community.[75] Beate Wehn also saw the *Acts of Paul and Thecla* as a historically significant source which gives expression to the experiences of women in the interface between early Christianity and Roman-Hellenistic society. She has noted that within the text, we glimpse traces of women's struggle for equality and just relationships in the early Christian communities. The Apocryphal Acts of the Apostles (or the *Acts of Paul and Thecla*) thus offer the beginnings of a critique of patriarchy and a criticism that sometimes deserves the name 'feminist'.[76]

This trend in interpretation has been both popular and prominent within Thecla scholarship, with scholars arguing that virginity and the refusal to marry offered women a liberating alternative and opportunity to gain independence and escape patriarchal confinement, thus lessening female oppression and giving women more control over their lives.[77] The question is whether this women's resistance is clearly indicated in the *Acts of Paul and Thecla* or whether it is a notion that is imposed upon the story. Moreover, if it is indicated in the text, is this done in a way that is actually liberating to women? Is celibate asceticism a model that could be used helpfully for liberating women in churches today?

Masculinization

A further trend in scholarship saw Thecla abandon her femininity and womanhood and 'become male'. Here, the text of Thecla is seen to destabilize and undermine the gender categories of male and female as gender is reconceptualized and reconfigured. Again, this movement in Thecla scholarship reflected a very female-affirming perspective of the narrative and demonstrated a tendency to read for positive female empowerment. Since 'becoming male' was considered a huge achievement for a woman in a culture which generally connected women with corruptible bodies, our heroine Thecla is seen to rise above her limiting female nature.

Such notions that maleness was linked to the heavenly and salvation and that femaleness had a special relationship to the body and sin were perhaps a natural development of concepts regarding gender construction in antiquity. In ancient discourse, masculine and feminine categories were fixed and arranged in a hierarchical dualism of male over female. Greek philosophical thought was grounded in the belief of women's physical inferiority as a sort of 'deformed' male.[78] Thecla, with short hair and a manly χιτών, is the first model of a transvestite saint who is, once again, seen to challenge social models of male authority and female subjugation. Here, not only does Thecla 'decisively' rebuff the male advances of Alexander in Antioch but she also takes measure to 'efface her beauty ... she cuts off her hair'.[79] Thecla then further 'annihilates' the image of the beautiful female by means of a gesture of transvestism.[80]

Although it has been argued that such gestures of transvestism were carried out by women as an act of disguise for reasons of safety against rape,[81] or to prevent suspicion that Thecla's motives for following Paul might be of a sexual nature,[82] or even as a way of dissuading men from initiating sexual advances,[83] Willi Braun argues that these interpretations miss the fundamental point of the story since Thecla does not travel alone. Rather, we should be alert to the fact that the transvestism is a symbolic indicator that Thecla has entered not only the spatial and social spheres of maleness but also the bodily dimension of maleness.[84] Thecla thus takes flight from femininity so that masculinity and all the positive values attached to the masculine would prevail.[85]

Johannes Vorster too has argued along similar lines in regard to Thecla's gender transformation. He noted that to be a person in antiquity is to be a male. Thus, for Thecla to move into a space allocated to the bodies of men requires imitation of their bodies.[86] By redefining her personhood, Thecla undermines 'the value-system of the dominant culture', modifying its social values by proposing an alternative construction of a person. For Vorster, Thecla is an emblem of 'alternate personhood' in which the androcentric component of the person 'has been dismantled and replaced by a personhood that asserts the power of womanhood'. In this way, redefinition of personhood leaves room for the possibility of an emerging alternative culture.[87]

While Gail Corrington Streete interprets Thecla's male guise and vow to cut her hair short as part of the inseparability of women's bodies from their religious commitment,[88] John Petropoulos sees Thecla's 'haircut' as a gesture that may be interpreted as a sign of her step-by-step surrender of the outward trapping of her obvious and highly vulnerable femininity.[89] Her male χιτών serves as 'combative garb' so that she can conduct her ministry without being 'ogled at' as a female. Indeed, the tale of Thecla resembles a 'proto-feminist' fantasy which unmasks and upsets the obvious sexual stereotypes of female inferiority and subordination.[90]

Thecla's 'gender-bending' is understood in this vein by a number of scholars who highlight her haircut and change of garb as effecting a positive transformation and a move away from feminine inferiority to masculinized superiority and control. Thecla is again seen to transgress the more usual cultural codes of femininity in antiquity,[91] although it should be noted that Braun does question the positivist model here and instead sees Thecla's masculinization as an annihilation of womanhood and a collusion with male views of female inferiority.[92]

A shift in the hermeneutical field

It is evident from the survey of literature so far that the majority of commentators on Thecla view her as a heroic example of women's liberation from patriarchal constraints. Rosemary Radford Ruether sums this up well when she argues that Thecla is 'an audacious role model for sweeping disobedience to the established order of family and state'.[93] However, despite the initial optimism of this line of inquiry, the absence of definitive evidence of such women in early Christianity led these scholars to view the sources anachronistically and with a bias that accorded well with contemporary concerns. This was particularly highlighted by a redactional study by D'Angelo on Luke-Acts which demonstrated that many of Luke's stories about women displayed evidence of Luke's emendation.[94] She argued that the stories concerning women served Luke's various agendas including his desire to demonstrate the respectability of Christianity in keeping with Graeco-Roman ideals.[95] D'Angelo's approach emphasized the manifold literary techniques employed by ancient authors along with the complex treatment of women in texts. In this respect, as will be discussed in further detail below, Cooper has also strongly questioned the historical validity of the Apocryphal Acts.[96] This approach underscored the fact that the voices of real women are hard to find in ancient texts. Historical women left little evidence of their daily lives and ideas of self and the world. Anyone attempting to uncover the history of women as subjects rather than as objects of description faces a formidable hermeneutical challenge.

Certainly, from a historical perspective, it is necessary to question how the renunciation and negation of a woman's sexual identity in a fertility-centred age could amount to a positive construct. Such conclusions perhaps reveal that scholars, in their eagerness to trace evidence of empowered women in antiquity, were retrojecting twentieth-century values onto the ancient world. There is no certainty that present-day dissatisfactions were shared by women in antiquity whose experiences and expectations were so different from our own. Did women in the ancient world feel resentful, suppressed and restricted? Were women aggrieved by their culture and society, and is 'rebellion' a concept that could be applied to women in the ancient world? We have little evidence to suggest that women saw themselves as suppressed and marginalized or indeed that they rebelled against the ideology of patriarchy.[97]

Given the lack of evidence for women's independent activity in antiquity, the conclusions reached by some feminists suggested that a certain predilection coloured their reading of texts. This lack of evidence revealed the highly tentative nature of the feminist historical project and led scholars to question whether the texts, that had initially seemed to yield so much in the recovery of women, could be used as historical sources. While Christianity undoubtedly displayed chaste ascetic tendencies from the very beginning, the earliest sources are scarce and fragile. This often led scholars to interpret early ascetic practice in light of how asceticism developed in later centuries where evidence is less fragmentary. However, although asceticism in the fourth century CE and beyond appeared to offer women a form of power, Joyce Salisbury notes that female ascetics did not always have the freedom and autonomy from men they may have desired.[98] Moreover, Elizabeth Clark has demonstrated that ascetic renunciation in later Christianity often attracted women of status and privilege who had 'unimaginable wealth'.[99] What emerges hardly amounts to a picture of downtrodden women who find a sense of worth and value through chastity.[100] Indeed, 'the earth was theirs before their ascetic renunciation, and they appear to have sacrificed less of it than we might have expected in their adoption of asceticism'.[101] Nevertheless, the endeavours of scholars such as Burrus, Davies and MacDonald, among others, enabled a recasting of previously Western male historical paradigms and brought to the fore issues of authority, power and sexuality.

From the perspective of this particular study, it will be patently clear that in their eagerness to interpret the *Acts of Paul and Thecla* as a female-affirming text, scholars disregard important aspects of the text that do not sit well with such a reading. As a result, the sado-erotic violent and pornographic aspects of the narrative are sidelined. Furthermore, where scholars were keen to hold Thecla up as an early manifestation of 'woman becoming male', arguing that she transcends her inferior feminine gender, they omitted to point out that Thecla's gender transformation is, in fact, quite equivocal since Paul prohibits Thecla from cutting her hair (*APTh*. 25).

Evolution in Thecla scholarship

Following the 'heady days' of feminist criticism, Thecla scholarship makes a shift away from historical analysis and readings which see the text as a reflection of women's lived reality.[102] Scholars here begin to employ a more judicious approach in their analysis and are far more tentative in their conclusions. Thus, recovering the lives of women in ancient Christianity evolves and shifts while continuing to play a prominent role in scholarly debate. A more recent contribution to this field sees Susan Hylen citing the *Acts of Paul and Thecla* as a good example of a woman with authority and influence and arguing for women's leadership as a historical reality. Although Hylen upholds the historical theme, she does offer a more balanced approach to earlier scholarship. She acknowledges that Thecla's characterization is fraught with contradiction and tension, noting that Thecla both inhabits and breaks free from patriarchal expectations of women. She acts decisively to shape her own future, yet she does not speak at her own trial. She baptizes herself and is authorized to teach the gospel, but her pursuit of Paul suggests that she remains his subordinate.[103]

Hylen seeks to understand these contradictions against a background of complex social and cultural norms where women exerted influence as civic and religious leaders within a culture with inherent gender biases. Thus, while women in the Roman period were expected to exhibit gendered virtues like modesty, industry and loyalty to family, they pursued these virtues in remarkably different ways, including through active leadership in their communities. However, their roles were always shaped and constrained by social expectations.[104] The demands for traditional feminine behaviour were never cancelled out by a woman's civic and public role. Female modesty alongside leadership for women was then neither incongruous nor radical; the two existed side by side.[105]

Hylen's approach offers a more nuanced view of the historical egalitarian reading of the Thecla narrative. However, while she seeks to point to a new way of understanding women in the early church, one that insists upon the acknowledgement of both women's leadership and the culture's inherent gender bias, her approach fails to probe the deeper complexities of Thecla's gender representation. Although she rightly highlights the many contradictions of Thecla's characterization, she never questions why the text on the one hand seemingly promotes female empowerment/leadership, while on the other – in a culture of honour and shame – it denigrates the heroine through demeaning and debasing sexual exposure.

Hylen does discuss the importance of chastity in the ancient world, noting that it is a 'precious communal possession'; she also references stories where fathers resort to murdering their daughters rather than risk their defilement; however, she fails to discern the more subtle texture of honour and shame societies.[106] Honour and shame were – and for many cultures continue to be – serious commodities that carried an intense charge. Honour existed only in line with the perception that access to honour is limited: this is what made it so valuable. If honour was in bountiful supply, losing a little here or there would carry no consequences.[107] In this respect, Hylen gives little weight to Thecla's excessive naked exposure in a culture which closely guards the female body. In order to yield to an 'empowering' reading of the text, the gender-based, sexualized violence directed at Thecla has to be downplayed and de-emphasized.

In her book *Saving Shame*, Burrus speaks of transcendence bought at the expense of the shaming of the body, above all the sexual body, of which women (along with other minorities) generally carry the lion's share.[108] Within our text, we have an image of a naked woman, her legs akimbo, her feet in restraints, her most intimate parts exposed, portraying woman at her most vulnerable. Is it ever possible to transcend such humiliation in a culture of honour and shame, or indeed, in any culture? By exposing Thecla's body in this way, the text ultimately keeps Thecla's strength in check. Implicit is the message that Thecla will never be able to transcend her sexuality and gender. Within her study, Burrus notes that the 'enormously destructive potentiality of shame is undeniable'.[109] Despite her eventual commissioning to 'go and teach the Word of God', Thecla carries with her the destructive effects of sexual exposure that the text has, shamefully, forced her to bear.

In a further shift away from seeing the text as a 'mirror' through which to read women in antiquity, scholars have also explored the possible 'liberating models' such texts may have provided for women in antiquity. Thus, Bremmer discusses Tertullian's *De baptismo*, which condemns women for following Thecla's example, and notes how women invoked the narrative of Thecla to claim the right to instruct and baptize.[110] Therefore, in texts where women do emerge as autonomous and independent, outshining the men, they may well have inspired women of later generations to follow in their footsteps. In this respect, the most recent feminist compendium on the Apocryphal Acts, where five out of twelve articles focus on Thecla and one other includes a discussion of the text, scholars are not only more moderate about the conclusions they draw about women in early Christianity but they also focus more on the 'inspiration' that the text of Thecla may have provided for its readers.[111] Furthermore, in their analysis, there is a move away from women per se to a more inclusive discussion of gender and its inversions. Richard Valantasis, therefore, circumvents the historical question in his interpretation of the Apocryphal Acts and takes up instead the question of Christian identity.[112] He argues that the Apocryphal Acts proposed a redefinition of social categories by constructing Christian identity as a third *genos*. Although the Apocryphal Acts accept traditional gender constructions and social patterns as normative, they change their meaning by transforming their content. Thus, sexual identity no longer means sexual actions but continence and chastity; marriage no longer unites two people to become one flesh but unites two chaste partners to a heavenly bridegroom, Christ. Categories of identity, gender and social relationships, therefore, no longer hold the meaning maintained in the dominant society. In this way, the texts display a strategy which attempts to create an alternative way of living.[113]

Vorster believes that the ascetic discourse in the *Acts of Paul and Thecla* provides us with what he terms a 'counterculture'.[114] In redefining bodily behaviour, the ascetic discourse contributes to the construction of an alternative society. As such, the *Acts of Paul and Thecla* functions as an example of how culture is constructed through the construction of a person. Vorster concludes that Thecla offered a possibility to women that might have come as a relief to their overburdened bodies, liberating them from the status of being the reproductive containers.[115] In this way, Thecla becomes an exemplum who casts doubt upon the social androcentric values of the period and endorses their negation.

Two more publications, which include discussions on Thecla, also demonstrate the move away from trying to locate independently minded historical women within texts and the interpretative shift towards issues of gender, power and bodies. Thus, Elizabeth Castelli offers a more rhetorical analysis of the would-be martyr Thecla employing 'collective memory' as a theoretical model. She also analyses how authors variously appropriated past experiences of martyrdom for defining Christian self-sacrifice, spectacle and society.[116] The chapter which focuses on the person of Thecla explores the multiple 'layers' of Thecla's life and martyrdom through a comparative discussion of the textual and visual representations of Thecla over the centuries. Castelli highlights how the representation of Thecla is developed and manipulated over time to serve differing rhetorical purposes over the centuries. Eventually, Thecla's 'manly' characterizations are erased as she is feminized more and more.

Corrington Streete also focuses on female martyrs in her book *Redeemed Bodies*.[117] She evaluates the account of Thecla (and Perpetua) through the lens of gender in order to analyse and illuminate the complexity and ambiguity of Christian interpretations of martyrdom. She argues that both representations of these women are ways of constructing identity through the body.[118] They each also demonstrate the ambiguous value of these routes to authority and their relationship to definitions of 'maleness' and 'femaleness'. It is argued that the shaping of their stories responded to specific needs within developing Christianity, functioning as models of and for female authority, both spiritual and institutional.[119] Where Thecla is concerned, she is eventually closed up in a rock. This seems to symbolize permanent divine protection of her chastity and ensures that she remains a model for female ascetic piety.[120]

These more recent approaches demonstrate not only the continuing interest in female figures such as Thecla but also the move away from trying to locate independently minded historical women within texts and the interpretative shift towards issues of gender, power and bodies. The survey of literature so far demonstrates the extent to which the *Acts of Paul and Thecla* has been celebrated by scholarship as a glorious example of female independence and liberation in antiquity. Although, given the shift in the hermeneutical field, scholars are no longer attempting to make a direct link between text and reality, the *Acts of Paul and Thecla* is still consistently read as a female affirming text which reflects favourably on women. This 'positive' reading of the *Acts of Paul and Thecla* continues with the literary approaches; however, here we see scholars begin to question the 'overall' powerful and resolute representation of Thecla within the text.

Elisabeth Esch-Wermeling, for example, notes that Thecla is passive in the first cycle and more active in the second. The audience, therefore, perceives two different Theclas. She goes on to say that the older Antioch cycle is framed by the younger Iconium cycle which restricts the role of women.[121] Esch-Wermeling's approach works to highlight the relationship and dynamics between the two cycles in an attempt to determine the motivation for melding the two accounts together. She contends that the *Acts of Paul and Thecla* refers to, and answers, the issues of female silence and subordination reflected in the Pastoral Epistles. The first Iconium episode shares an understanding with the Pastoral Epistles, but eventually through the second cycle, the text develops a contrasting strategy. Thus, although Thecla is silent in the first episode, having been taught by Paul, she emerges as a theological speaker. However, although Thecla achieves an 'unusual' speaking/teaching role, she still submits to apostolic authority and is, therefore, ultimately 'tamed'. The text thus demonstrates submission but not silence. She notes that Paul's disappearance from the second half of the story is due to the fact that he is simply not a part of that narrative,[122] while the account of Thecla's abandonment by Paul (*APTh.* 26) is composed to join the two narratives together. Esch-Wermeling argues that this approach explains the dramatic change in Thecla from one cycle to the other. The redactor (a presbyter) wanted to ensure the emphasis on men and in order to provide some gender balance framed the Antioch cycle with the newer Iconium cycle which features Paul. A new picture portraying Thecla as Paul's celibate pupil emerges. However, Esch-Wermeling considers that the 'older' Antioch cycle speaks for women and promotes them as the 'true wielders' of power.[123] In essence, therefore, Esch-Wermeling argues that male redaction eventually constrains what was essentially an empowered female representation of Thecla.

Esch-Wermeling is not alone in highlighting the two part structures of the text. Anne Jensen had long noted the two separate tales that had been combined in one text.[124] She also suggested that the Iconium episode, in comparison to the Antiochene episode, represents the presbyter's own invention.[125] Margaret Aymer too underscores the various layers of redaction within the text and posits that the first episode reflects a male-dominant community and presents women as the 'silent' actors, while the second Antioch cycle depicts women as empowered with speaking and acting roles.[126] She argues that ultimately the *Acts of Paul and Thecla* represents the folk tales of two different communities with contrasting membership, agendas and world views. These two folk tales thus represent two constructed, symbolic worlds, and each reinforces the beliefs and practices of the community from which they emerge. In this way, each community constructs its own particular memory of the saint. For Aymer, the *Acts of Paul and Thecla* carries the 'bothness' of the masculinity of Iconium as well as the feminine power of Antioch.[127] Corrington Streete, who has written a number of articles on Thecla, in her more recent book agrees with Aymer's analysis.[128] Diane Lipsett too, drawing on the insights provided by these literary interpreters, offers a reading of the *Acts of Paul and Thecla* that foregrounds the construction of 'desire'. She argues that Thecla emerges 'as a figure who supersedes Paul in authority and masculine license'. Indeed, 'Paul ... repeatedly appears impotent in comparison' (to Thecla).[129] For Lipsett, desire dislocates Thecla from female passivity and, as she is transformed, she moves from feminine desire to masculine control.[130]

Although these literary approaches highlight the passive and submissive elements of Thecla's characterization, these are seen to be contained within the Iconium episode, while the Antioch episode is once again seen to promote an empowered female champion. The Antioch cycle, therefore, overshadows the more conventional elements of Thecla's characterization. However, as will be discussed in more detail below, it is not so certain that the passive and active elements of Thecla's representation can be categorized in such a straightforward way. For example, despite Thecla's passivity within the Iconium cycle, she does venture out in public into the male domain (*APTh.* 18). Furthermore, she becomes dynamic and active in the arena, so much so that she displays a 'power' which intrigues the Governor (*APTh.* 22). In addition, although these approaches argue that Thecla becomes more active and empowered within the Antioch episode, scholars have failed to address the fact that the more active Thecla becomes, the greater the violence she meets.

The Apocryphal Acts and the Hellenistic novel

There remains one further significant area of scholarship to be discussed which, although it does not relate to the *Acts of Paul and Thecla* specifically, does ultimately have an important impact upon Thecla studies. At this point, therefore, it is necessary to momentarily step back to refer, once again, to the entire corpus of the Apocryphal Acts, because this approach argued for a close association between the ancient Hellenistic novel and the Apocryphal Acts. Here, scholars called for a much clearer classification of the Apocryphal Acts in terms of their genre, and although it should be emphasized that there is no agreement among scholars on this question,[131] this area of study is, nevertheless, influential and far ranging.

In 1932, Rosa Söder was the first to highlight a number of similarities between the ancient novel and the Apocryphal Acts. Söder concluded that although there was no direct literary relationship between them, the Apocryphal Acts were the literarily 'fixed' witnesses of ancient folk stories that should be included within the category of the Graeco-Roman novel since they shared similar motifs and novelistic elements.[132] With their common ascetic theme, their narrative form and their emphasis on adventures, trials and travels, scholars were quick to admit the comparative value of the Apocryphal Acts with the Graeco-Roman novel.[133] It was also argued that ancient readers would not have seen any clear distinction between the two groups of works.[134] However, it was Cooper's influential book, *The Virgin and the Bride*, which most adequately accentuated the relationship between the ancient novel and the Apocryphal Acts, highlighting that they are manifestations of the same genre.[135] Cooper argued for a direct literary comparison to the ancient novels, stating that neither genre can be fully understood without reference to the other.[136]

For Jeremy Barrier too, the Apocryphal Acts are a 'special type' of the ancient novel and can be interpreted more appropriately if read with the genre of the ancient novel in mind. Such an approach, he argues, also explains the sexual overtones of the text.[137] Thus, Paul does not abandon Thecla at Antioch (*APTh*. 26), leaving her to die on her own.[138] Rather, in the same manner as witnessed in the ancient novels, this scene 'intensifies' the trials of the young lovers and, following a period of intense persecution, the lovers are finally rejoined. As with the ancient novel, all attempts of the hero and heroine to stay alive at all costs are taken advantage of in the hope that the lovers will eventually reunite.[139] The idea that Paul should have protected Thecla is, for Barrier, inconsistent with the themes of the ancient novel: survival for the sake of love is the key virtue, not dying a noble death.

However, in her book, Cooper moves beyond the question of genre and contrasts the Hellenistic romance, which celebrates the institution of marriage with the Apocryphal Acts, which subvert the social order of society. Cooper particularly emphasized that whereas the novel was meant to uphold the ideal values of society, the Apocryphal Acts aim to be socially disruptive.[140] Cooper devotes an entire chapter to the Apocryphal Acts and argued that these narratives borrow from and invert the ideology of the romances. Here, celibacy is seen to have a political motivation and is a form of protest that challenges the elite ruling class. The Apocryphal Acts thus have an anti-civic purpose and chastity serves as the narrative device which propels the conflict between the apostle and the city's ruling class into motion.[141]

The view that the Apocryphal Acts should be categorized as novels with a subversive message has been supported by other scholars.[142] Judith Perkins, for example, argues that with their rejection of marriage, the Apocryphal Acts are socially disruptive with an antisocial message. They reverse the depiction of marriage and chastity in the romance.[143] Furthermore, she notes that 'the texts are seen relentlessly to construct and to project a world view in conflict with contemporary social structure'.[144] For Perkins, although the literature is fictive, it reflects its readers' social concerns. Indeed, the Apocryphal Acts should be understood as the 'displacement of social problems into an imaginary realm'.[145] Cooper and Perkins thus offer a more astute, cultural and ideological analysis of how the Apocryphal Acts both share and invert the literary motifs of the Hellenistic novels. At this point, these scholars have moved far beyond the comparison of motifs and a discussion of genre to a more complex analysis of the social functions within the text.[146]

Cooper, however, nuances her approach slightly differently. Cooper looks at the motifs of displacement, risk and social aversion, with particular attention to gender. She underscores not only the fact that the Apocryphal Acts reflect 'the challenge by the apostle to the household' but also that, most importantly, the conflict is 'essentially between men'.[147] For Cooper, the Apocryphal Acts represent a conflict between men around issues of authority and social order.[148] The women in the texts are being used to secure Christian male identity over and against pagan counterparts. In this respect, Thecla functions as a type of trope of masculine identity.[149] Thecla, therefore, no longer serves as a representative for patriarchal resistance; rather, she reinforces those patriarchal structures. Cooper argues that the presence of women characters reflect not interest in women but rather a critique of male character; wherever a woman is mentioned, a man is being judged.[150] Thus, despite the fact that Thecla served as a source for ongoing piety in later generations, she is merely an ideological construct and expresses a socially specific representation of sexual difference.[151]

Cooper's point about 'male power brokering' is an important one and will be dealt with more fully in Chapter 3. Nonetheless, here, very significantly, it is evident that the treatment of women in the Apocryphal Acts shifts quite dramatically. The texts have little to do with women; rather, they testify to a contest between men. This methodological principle fundamentally changes the way in which the texts of the Apocryphal Acts are read.

Cooper offers up a new, exciting and original perspective. The interdisciplinary approach that she applies to the study of the Apocryphal Acts is crucial in serving as a warning to anyone who would read female characters in ancient narratives as evidence for real women in antiquity. In this respect, her contribution to the study of gender constructs in late antiquity is invaluable. However, I would tentatively suggest that one of the weaknesses of her approach is the fact that, in her analysis, she joins together the entire corpus of the Apocryphal Acts. This is all part of a bigger problem that has been highlighted by scholars working on these narratives and it relates to the difficulty of trying to join together what is essentially a very diverse and composite corpus of literature.[152] Even though there are similarities between each of the stories, in that they focus on specific apostles and the theme of chastity, they also contain integral differences. Francois Bovon has, for example, drawn attention to the fact that the *Acts of Peter* are concerned with propaganda of the Christian faith through miracles; the *Acts of Paul* with a subversive attitude to political authorities and a claim for female ministry, while the *Acts of John* are concerned with veneration of the Beloved Disciple.[153] Thus, despite the areas of commonality there are also important differences. The problem is also compounded by the fact that the extant sources of the Apocryphal Acts are fragmentary with misplaced information and absent texts. Attempting to group together such contrasting and disparate texts can blind us to important nuances that the individual texts contain.

This problem of divergence is even more acute when it comes to the text of the *Acts of Paul and Thecla*. The radical departure of this text from the other Apocryphal Acts would suggest that the text may, indeed, have a unique and distinct message of its own to tell.

The distinctive nature of the *Acts of Paul and Thecla*

While the elements of social disruption and conflict with society are present within the *Acts of Paul and Thecla* (after all, Thecla disobeys her mother, refuses marriage and is condemned to die as a consequence), the text is, nevertheless, unique among the Apocryphal Acts in a number of ways. To begin with, the narrative focuses on one female protagonist who is, unarguably, the 'star' of the show. Thus, unlike the other Apocryphal Acts, there is far less focus on the male apostle who regularly disappears from the narrative. In addition, although the *Acts of Paul and Thecla* is closely associated with the *Acts of Paul*, it also had its own extensive independent tradition and circulation history.[154] Indeed, McGinn and Schüssler Fiorenza argue that male redaction accounts for what they believe to be the originally independent tradition of the *Acts of Paul and Thecla* being re-conceptualized and subordinated within the wider and more androcentric *Acts of Paul*.[155] Male redaction of the text has also been emphasized by scholars working on the *Acts of Paul and Thecla* from a more literary perspective. This separate circulation tradition is evident in the fact that there is a break in the narrative of the *Acts of Paul* where the *Acts of Paul and Thecla* is inserted.[156]

However, perhaps the most substantive difference between the *Acts of Paul and Thecla* and the other Apocryphal Acts is the fact that Thecla undergoes not one martyrdom, but two, and, quite unlike any other martyrdom account and, in absolute contrast to the martyrdoms of the apostles in the other Apocryphal Acts, Thecla survives. These numerous points of variation and distinctness should alert us to the fact that, despite its semblance and affinities with the other Apocryphal Acts in its focus on female chastity, the *Acts of Paul and Thecla* is a conspicuously distinct text in its own right and, therefore, warrants separate treatment.

Jensen, too, rightly argues that since the text of Thecla is so distinct, it should be studied on its own and not grouped with the other Apocryphal Acts, even the *Acts of Paul*.[157] She notes that, on the one hand, Thecla appears as a typical female figure within the 'Apostolic Novel', in that she is linked to a chastity story, is connected with numerous miracles and her story climaxes with a martyrdom report. On the other hand, Thecla is also atypical, in that the other women remain under the apostle's shadow and she herself is the protagonist of the drama. Thus, Thecla is 'active' in an apostolic manner and experiences martyrdom, unlike the other women in the Apocryphal Acts.[158] What is also interesting is the fact that when it comes to the secondary literature on the Apocryphal Acts, a simply cursory examination will reveal that no other female character in the narratives of the Apocryphal Acts receives even a fraction of the attention given to the heroine Thecla. The *Acts of Paul and Thecla* thus warrants consideration as a unique, distinctive text in its own right.

Moving forward

This chapter began by highlighting how scholars in the 1980s rescued the Apocryphal Acts from oblivion in their mission to retrieve the history of women in early Christianity. They believed that within the Apocryphal Acts, female sexual renunciation provided evidence of women's liberation and autonomy from the constraints of patriarchy, marriage and childbearing. Their approach comprised some of the most progressive and radical exegesis of modern biblical criticism, often challenging and countering customary biblical translations. The writings of Davies, MacDonald and Burrus were particularly influential and emerged at the height of feminist hermeneutics in biblical studies. Despite the critique these works received, the possibility of recovering a 'usable history' for women from ancient texts became a tangible reality. A number of scholars thus followed in the footsteps of Davies, Macdonald and Burrus and hailed the *Acts of Paul and Thecla* as authoritative evidence of women's lived reality. Here, not only did 'women's resistance' become a discernible theme but so did the view that Thecla had to abandon her femininity and womanhood to 'become male' and thereby liberated.

These trends within Thecla scholarship reflect a wholly female-affirming way of understanding the narrative and demonstrate a strong tendency to read for positive female empowerment within the text. Thecla is seen to transgress the more usual cultural codes of femininity in antiquity, with the majority of commentators viewing Thecla as a heroic example of women's liberation from patriarchal constraints.

Given the lack of evidence for women's autonomous and independent activity in antiquity, the highly tentative nature of the 'second-wave' feminist historical project has been revealed. This has led scholars to question whether the texts, that had initially seemed to yield so much in the recovery of women, could be used as historical sources. Consequently, newer approaches have retreated from attempting to make a direct link between text and reality and became far more judicious in the claims they made about women in antiquity. Scholarly opinion, as shown in the feminist compendium of the Apocryphal Acts, focused less on Thecla as representative of women's voices in antiquity and more on the 'inspiration' that the text may have provided for its readers. Other approaches focus on the symbolic meaning of gender and explore how the stories were shaped to respond to specific needs within developing Christianity.

Nonetheless, the *Acts of Paul and Thecla* continues to be read as a female-affirming text which reflects favourably on women. This 'positive' reading is also evidenced in the literary approaches. While Esch-Wermeling and Aymer underscore the contradictory portrayal of Thecla as both passive and empowered in the two different cycles, they, nevertheless, still maintain that Thecla emerges as a strong and powerful woman within the Antioch episode (*APTh*. 26-43). What these approaches fail to account for is Thecla's empowered representation in the first arena scene (*APTh*. 22) and the fact that the violent and sado-erotic treatment of Thecla escalates within the so-called more empowering second episode. Why is there such a focus on the sado-erotic victimization of Thecla and why, unlike most martyr stories, does Thecla's body remain immune from all injury?

This chapter has also highlighted interpreters who seek to interpret the Apocryphal Acts more in line with the Hellenistic novel. Here, there is close attention to the rhetorical use of narratival women in antiquity, and new ways of interpreting these documents, other than as reflections of historical reality and female empowerment, are considered. This approach has opened up new and fresh ways of reading these narratives. However, one of the weaknesses of this approach (which also impacts on the question of genre)[159] is the fact that the Apocryphal Acts are a heterogeneous group of texts with different foci and emphasis. All the same, even though there is no agreement on exactly how the Apocryphal Acts, as a corpus of literature, should be read, what this discussion did emphasize was the fact that the *Acts of Paul and Thecla* is a particularly distinctive text in its own right, with its own separate circulation tradition, and, because of this, it warrants independent treatment.

Although the claims made about Thecla and what she stood for have changed and shifted dramatically over the years, it is evident that Thecla continues to hold an important place in the study of the early churches and the apocryphal gospels and Acts that circulated within them. Thecla allegedly hovers on the threshold between manhood and womanhood (she does at least offer to cut her hair short and dons male apparel) and, thus, from the perspective of gender, she is an intriguing representation of woman. Perhaps this is why she forms a continuous thread in feminist debate and gender critical studies.

However, despite the popularity of the Thecla narrative among scholars and the extensive treatment the text has received, there are a number of significant questions that remain unanswered, not least the fact that Paul himself instructs Thecla to keep her hair long following her offer to cut it short. I believe that, in line with Corrington Streete (*Redeemed Bodies*), there is still more to be gained from a continued exploration on gender, power and bodies, and from reframing the discussion, along the lines of Cooper, who reads the female figures within the Apocryphal Acts as ideological constructs of masculine identity. What more can be learned from this text about male competition and Christian identity in the second century?

Thus, following in the footsteps of many scholars who have been particularly captivated by the heroine Thecla, I too find her fascinating, but within this study I will focus upon aspects of the text that have previously been somewhat neglected or overlooked (perhaps because they do not fit with a pro-'womanist' or pro-feminist reading). Overall, the key question is whether the *Acts of Paul and Thecla* is designed to be a text promoting female empowerment or whether, as Cooper has suggested about the Apocryphal Acts generally, it is a complex literary entity that represents a power struggle between men and that ultimately has very little to do with women at all. In short, what is the message of the text? In order to move forward, to answer some of the questions that have been raised within this chapter, I will consider three main areas of *Acts of Paul and Thecla*.

First, since scholars seem to veer towards reading Thecla as male (despite Paul's refusal of the offer she makes to cut her hair), I reassess Thecla's alleged gender transformation and transgendered nature. As noted above, scholars frequently argue that since Thecla cuts her hair short and sews her cloak in a manly style (*APTh*. 25, 40), she undergoes some kind of gender transformation and becomes male. In this respect, the *Acts of Paul and Thecla* has been regarded as the quintessential text which displays an early manifestation of this notion of the female becoming male. In Chapter 4, I will, therefore, be focusing upon the textual representations within the *Acts of Paul and Thecla* in order to reassess whether sexual difference within the text is truly eradicated. The aim within this section is to question the common assumption that Thecla undergoes a sexual transformation by way of a haircut and a change of clothing and to assess what the implications of Thecla retaining her feminine characteristics may reveal about her representation and the construction of masculinity.

Second, despite the fact that many scholars have given extensive consideration to the text of the *Acts of Paul and Thecla*, much less attention has been focused upon the sado-erotic violence within the text. The text contains graphically depicted scenes where Thecla is stripped naked (*APTh.* 22, 33), forced to 'mount' (ἐπιβῆναι) the pyre (*APTh.* 22), threatened with rape (*APTh.* 26) and paraded through the streets and arena as an object of voyeurism (*APTh.* 22, 28, 33). When Thecla, with God's miraculous help, repeatedly manages to evade death, she is humiliated even further by being tied naked by the feet between two bulls (*APTh.* 35). The physical abuse directed at this female heroine is extreme and debasing. How can a text of this nature be considered liberating or empowering for a woman? The aim within Chapter 5, therefore, is to assess the impact of sexualized representations within a text that is considered 'empowering' and 'liberating'. Is Thecla empowered and liberated or is she exploited and abused?

Third, given that the miracles ensure Thecla's survival to eventually receive Paul's commission to teach the Word of God, I investigate the level to which Thecla is empowered by the miraculous. There is little doubt that since Thecla survives two attempts of painful execution unscathed, the text is trying to say something quite positive about her. It is the miracles that ensure her survival. However, despite her survival, is Thecla truly vested with power? In Chapter 6, I will, therefore, be examining the rhetorical and ideological functions of the miracles to assess whether they impact upon Thecla's representation in a wholly positive way. Is there any tension between the narrative point of view and rhetoric, which seeks to liberate Thecla from the constraints of marriage and childbirth, and a general androcentric or patriarchal point of view, which treats women disdainfully and seeks ultimately to subjugate them? When it comes to the miraculous, where exactly is power located in terms of gender relations?

Finally, what if these texts are male-authored, and women within these texts function as literary creations expressing aspects of male contemplation and problem-solving? The question becomes, what do these texts reveal about male identity, self-definition and masculinity? Chaste ascetic women embodied an ideological contradiction about the nature of female identity and sexuality in antiquity; what type of men might focus, promote and construct gender ambiguously in this way in a fertility-centred age?

Following on from the substantive chapters of this study, I will move on in Chapter 7 to briefly highlight some tentative suggestions of what it may mean to read this text as an expression of a male response to female sexuality. Within this chapter, I will summarily posit what distinctive Christian message is being conveyed within the narrative as this female ascetic Christian clashes with society and *polis*. What we have is a sado-erotic discourse about female 'self-control' and 'chastity' set over against the invasive violence of Rome. The site of engagement is the arena, made famous and popular by Rome. What role does the victimized, voyeuristic female representation of Thecla fulfil for early Christian writers within a Roman Imperial context? Thus, as I begin to draw this study to a close, I go on to consider what function the character of Thecla fulfils in the *Acts of Paul and Thecla*, suggesting a new way of seeing her that re-envisages her as a meaningful symbol for the church, as male authors of texts negotiated gendered concepts of power and agency in the Roman world. In this final analysis, a new perspective on Thecla is suggested. A conclusion in Chapter 8 will summarize and assess the findings of this study and its impact on how we read the figure of Thecla.

This study will, therefore, be focusing on the analysis of gender construction and the meaning of women's bodies in antiquity in order to determine something about men, masculinity and power and in so doing will be looking for signs of female repression and objectification. In doing this, might key issues about authorship and readership be answered more effectively? Can this text truly be 'liberating' to women, or does it use the figure of a woman to enhance Paul and configure masculinity, power and dominance in the era of the Church's conflict with Rome?

Within this study, then, I endeavour to draw out of the shadows those aspects of the text that display little evidence of female subjectivity and empowerment. However, before doing this, it is necessary to consider first some background information that is important for understanding the textual history and reception of the text, including its relationship to the wider Pauline tradition. Chapter 2 will, therefore, take in these primary points. In addition, since genre is widely acknowledged as one of the key conventions guiding both the composition and the interpretation of a text, within Chapter 2, I will also further consider the question of genre of the Apocryphal Acts generally and the *Acts of Paul and Thecla* more specifically. Chapter 3 will look at the primary methodology and approach of this study.

Notes

1. Edgar Hennecke, *Neutestamentlichen Apokryphen in deutscher Übersetzung*, ed. Wilhelm Schneemelcher, 2 vols. (Tübingen: Mohr Siebeck, 1959–64); Edgar Hennecke, *New Testament Apocrypha II*, ed. Wilhelm Schneemelcher, trans. R. McL. Wilson (Louisville, KY: James Clarke, John Knox, 1992), henceforth *NTA*.
2. Hans-Josef Klauck, *The Apocryphal Acts of the Apostles: An Introduction* (Waco, TX: Baylor University Press, 2008).
3. Ross Kraemer, 'The Conversion of Women to Ascetic Forms of Christianity', *Signs* 6 (1980): 298–307; see also Gail Paterson Corrington, 'The "Divine Woman?" Propaganda and the Power of Celibacy in the New Testament Apocrypha: A Reconsideration', *ATR* 70 (1988): 207–20, who explores the Apocryphal Acts for the female equivalent of the 'divine man' paradigm and concludes that women experienced the ascetic life as a new alternative and chosen liberation from expected social roles.
4. Kraemer, 'Conversion', 303.
5. Stevan L. Davies, *The Revolt of the Widows: The Social World of the Apocryphal Acts* (Carbondale: Southern Illinois University Press, 1980), 66; Dennis R. MacDonald, *The Legend and the Apostle, The Battle for Paul in Story and Canon* (Philadelphia, PA: Westminster, 1983); Virginia Burrus, *Chastity as Autonomy: Women in the Stories of the Apocryphal Acts* (Lewiston, NY: Edwin Mellen, 1987); also Virginia Burrus, 'Chastity as Autonomy: Women in the Stories of the Apocryphal Acts', *Semeia* 38 (1986): 101–17.
6. Davies, *Revolt of the Widows*.

7   Ibid., 15.
8   *NTA*, 85.
9   Davies, *Revolt of the Widows*, 51–61.
10 Ibid., 50, 71, 105–8.
11 MacDonald, *Legend*.
12 Ibid., 26–7.
13 Ibid., 9–27, 56–7.
14 Ibid., 57–9, 69, 77.
15 Ibid., 34–6.
16 Ibid., 40, 77.
17 Burrus, *Chastity*.
18 Apostle arrives in town; woman goes to hear the apostle preach; woman vows chastity; husband/fiancé attempts to violate vow; apostle encourages woman; woman resists husband/fiancé; husband/Governor imprisons apostle; woman visits apostle in prison (encouragement; baptism); husband/Governor attempts to kill apostle; apostle dies or is rescued (leaves the scene); husband/Governor persecutes the women; woman is rescued; woman defeats husband/Governor (who may be converted or punished and never succeeds in persuading the woman); woman is freed (allowed to remain chaste). Burrus, 'Chastity', 104.
19 Ibid., 33, 68–72.
20 Ibid., 81–2, 87, 97, 114.
21 Burrus, *Chastity*, 101–2.
22 Burrus, 'Chastity', 116.
23 Jean-Daniel Kaestli, 'Response', *Semeia* 38 (1986): 119–31; E. Margaret Howe, 'Interpretations of Paul in the *Acts of Paul and Thecla*', in *Pauline Studies: Essays Presented to Professor F.F. Bruce on His 70th Birthday*, ed. Donald A. Hagner and Murray J. Harris (Exeter: Paternoster, 1980), 33–49; Lynne C. Boughton, 'From Pious Legend to Feminist Fantasy: Distinguishing Hagiographical License from Apostolic Practice in the Acts of Paul/Acts of Thecla', *JR* 71 (1991): 362–83; Peter W. Dunn, 'Women's Liberation, The Acts of Paul and Other Apocryphal Acts of the Apostles', *Apocrypha* 4 (1993): 245–61; Peter W. Dunn, 'The Acts of Paul and the Pauline Legacy of the Second Century' (unpublished PhD Diss., Queen's College, Cambridge, 1996, online at http://actapauli.files.wordpress.com/2009/01/pwdunn1996.pdf); see also François Bovon and Eric Junod, 'Reading the Apocryphal Acts of the Apostles', *Semeia* 38 (1986); *NTA*, 81–8; Esther Yue L. Ng, '"Acts of Paul and Thecla," Women's Studies and Precedent', *JTS* 55 (2004): 1–29.
24 Jean-Daniel Kaestli, 'Les Actes Apocryphes et la reconstitution de l'histoire des femmes dans le christianisme ancien', *Cahiers bibliques de Foi et Vie* 28 (1989): 71–9; Jean-Daniel Kaestli, 'Fiction littéraire et réalité sociale: que peut-on savoir de la place des femmes dans le milieu de production des Actes apocryphes des Apôtres?', *Apocrypha* 1 (1990): 279–302; Willy Rordorf, 'Tradition and Composition in the Acts of Thecla', *Semeia* 38 (1986): 43–53.
25 See Bovon and Junod, 'Reading the Apocryphal Acts', 164–5; see also Kaestli, 'Response', 121–2; Dunn, 'Women's Liberation', 249 and *NTA*, 81–3.
26 Dunn, 'Women's Liberation', 249.
27 Kaestli, 'Response', 129. See also Jan N. Bremmer, 'Women in the Apocryphal Acts of John', in *The Apocryphal Acts of John*, ed. Jan N. Bremmer (Kampen: Kok Pharos, 1995), 51.
28 Kaestli, 'Response', 123; Dunn, 'Women's Liberation', 247–8.

29 Kaestli, 'Response', 125. Boughton also argues along similar lines that these studies have 'drawn conclusions from too narrow and, therefore, too arbitrary a range of evidence', Boughton, 'Pious Legend', 370.
30 Kaestli, 'Response', 125.
31 Virginia Burrus, 'Response', *Semeia* 38 (1986): 134.
32 See also *NTA*, 82. Bovon and Junod also point out that the feminist perspective issues from a biased reading of the text, 'Reading the Apocryphal Acts', 164–5.
33 Burrus, 'Response', 134–5.
34 See Howe, 'Interpretations', and Boughton, 'Pious Legend'.
35 This point is also made by Mary R. Lefkowitz, 'Did Ancient Women Write Novels?', in *'Women Like This' New Perspectives on Jewish Women in the Greco-Roman World*, ed. Amy-Jill Levine (Atlanta, GA: Scholars Press, 1991), 214–15. See also Howe, 'Interpretations', 39–46.
36 Boughton, 'Pious Legend', 378. Bremmer, however, would contest this point noting that the negative description of Paul is meant to counter any idea that Thecla is physically attracted to him. Rather, her fascination for him lies solely in his message, Jan N. Bremmer, 'Magic, Martyrdom and Women's Liberation', in *The Apocryphal Acts of Paul and Thecla*, ed. Jan N. Bremmer (Kampen: Kok Pharos, 1996), 39.
37 Lefkowitz, 'Ancient Women', 213–15. See also Yue L. Ng, 'Women's Studies', who similarly argues against a positive female liberationist perspective.
38 Kate Cooper, *The Virgin and the Bride: Idealized Womanhood in Late Antiquity* (Cambridge, MA: Harvard University Press, 1996), 19, 54–5.
39 Ibid., 58. An analogous point is also noted by Schneemelcher, *NTA*, 82. Cooper also argues that we see in the *Acts of Paul and Thecla* a direct substitution of the apostle as romantic hero, *Virgin and the Bride*, 50.
40 Kraemer, 'Conversion', 303–4.
41 Judith M. Lieu, 'The "Attraction of Women" into Early Judaism and Christianity: Gender and the Politics of Conversion', *JSNT* 72 (1998): 9.
42 See also Chapter 2.
43 By 'second-wave feminism', I mean the movement that arose in wake of the civil rights movement in the 1960s, when feminist enquiry entered general academic discourse and programmes in feminist and women's studies (and eventually gender studies) began to be created and developed in academic institutions. The main paradigm shift here was the focus on the distinctive experience of women and placing women rather than men in centre stage, see Ahida E. Pilarski, 'The Past and Future of Biblical Feminist Hermeneutics', *BTB* 1, no. 41 (2011): 20–1. See also Chapter 3.
44 Elisabeth Schüssler Fiorenza, *In Memory of Her: A Feminist Theological Reconstruction of Christian Origins*, 2nd ed. (New York: SCM Press, 1994), 175; Sheila E. McGinn, 'The Acts of Thecla', in *Searching the Scriptures*: vol. 2, *A Feminist Commentary*, ed. Elisabeth Schüssler Fiorenza, A. Brock and S. Matthews (New York: Crossroad, 1994), 805–6.
45 McGinn, 'The Acts of Thecla', 820.
46 Ross S. Kraemer, 'Women's Authorship of Jewish and Christian Literature in the Greco-Roman Period', in *'Women Like This': New Perspectives on Jewish Women in the Greco-Roman World*, ed. Amy-Jill Levine (Atlanta, GA: Scholars Press, 1991), 221–42.
47 Jan N. Bremmer, 'Drusiana, Cleopatra and Some Other Women in the Acts of John', in *A Feminist Companion to the New Testament Apocrypha*, ed. Amy-Jill Levine, with Maria Mayo Robbins (Cleveland, OH: Pilgrim, 2006), 85.
48 Kraemer, 'Women's Authorship', 233.
49 Ibid., 233.

50 Mary Rose D'Angelo, '(Re)Presentations of Women in the Gospel of Matthew and Luke-Acts', in *Women and Christian Origins*, ed. Ross Shepard Kraemer and Mary Rose D'Angelo (Oxford: Oxford University Press, 1999), 190-1.
51 Lefkowitz, 'Ancient Women', 201.
52 Ibid., 199.
53 Ibid., 200.
54 Ibid., 207-8.
55 Ibid., 211-13.
56 Ibid., 207-8.
57 See S. G. Cole, 'Could Greek Women Read and Write', in *Reflections of Women in Antiquity*, ed. H. Foley (New York: Gordon and Breach, 1981), 219-45. See also R. Lane Fox, 'Literacy and Power in Early Christianity', in *Literacy and Power in the Ancient World*, ed. A. K. Bowman and G. Woolf (Cambridge: Cambridge University Press, 1994), 126-48.
58 See E. Bowie, 'The Readership of Greek Novels in the Ancient World', in *The Search for the Ancient Novel*, ed. James Tatum (Baltimore, MD: John Hopkins, 1994), 438.
59 Kraemer, 'Women's Authorship', 240, 242.
60 Kim Haines-Eitzen, 'Engendering Palimpsests: Reading the Textual Tradition of the *Acts of Paul and Thecla*', in *The Early Christian Book*, ed. William E. Kingshirn and Linda Safran (Washington, DC: Catholic University of America Press, 2007), 182.
61 Euseb., *Hist. eccl.* 6.23.
62 Kim Haines-Eitzen, *The Gendered Palimpsest: Women, Writing, and Representation in Early Christianity* (Oxford: Oxford University Press, 2012), 31-2.
63 Ibid., 37.
64 Dunn, 'Pauline Legacy', 64; see also Monika Pesthy, 'Thecla among the Fathers of the Church', in *The Apocryphal Acts of Paul and Thecla*, ed. Jan N. Bremmer (Kampen: Kok Pharos, 1996), 164-78.
65 Dunn, 'Women's Liberation', 250-1.
66 Ibid., 252.
67 See e.g. 2 Tim. 1.15; 1.16-18; 3.11; 4.10; 4.14. See also Chapter 2 on Pauline tradition.
68 Ibid.
69 For notions of public and private see Margaret MacDonald, *Early Christian Women and Pagan Opinion: The Power of the Hysterical Woman* (Cambridge: Cambridge University Press, 1996), 30-41. See also the article by Kate Cooper, 'Approaching the Holy Household', *JECS* 15 (2007): 131-42, who highlights the complexity and the blurring of the boundaries behind the notions of public and private.
70 Luise Schottroff, 'Non Violence and Women's Resistance in Early Christianity', in *The Pacifist Impulse in Historical Perspective*, ed. Harvey L. Dyke (Toronto: University of Toronto Press, 1996), 83.
71 Maud Burnett McInerney, *Eloquent Virgins from Thecla to Joan of Arc* (New York: Palgrave MacMillan, 2003), 22-45.
72 Ibid., 17.
73 McGinn, 'The Acts of Thecla', 814.
74 MacDonald, *Early Christian Women*, 172.
75 Ibid., 173, 176.
76 Beate Wehn, 'Blessed Are the Bodies of Those Who Are Virgins: Reflections on the Image of Paul in the Acts of Thecla', *JSNT* 79 (2000): 151.
77 See also e.g. Gail P. C. Streete, 'Authority and Authorship: *The Acts of Paul and Thecla* as a Disputed Pauline Text', *LTQ* 40 (2005): 265-76; Magda Misset-van de Weg, 'Magic, Miracle and Miracle Workers in the Acts of Thecla', in *Women and*

Miracle Stories: A Multidisciplinary Exploration, ed. Anne-Marie Korte (Leiden: Brill, 2001), 29–52.
78 See Marilyn B. Skinner, 'Ego Mulier: The Construction of Male Sexuality in Catullus', in *Roman Sexualities*, ed. Judith P. Hallett and Marilyn B. Skinner (Princeton, NJ: Princeton University Press, 1977), 134; see also the discussion on Aristotle in Aline Rousselle, *Porneia: On Desire and the Body in Antiquity* (New York: Basil Blackwell, 1988), 27–34.
79 Willi Braun, 'Physiotherapy of Femininity in the Acts of Thecla', in *Text and Artifact in the Religions of Mediterranean Antiquity: Essays in Honour of Peter Richardson*, ed. Stephen G. Wilson and Michel Desjardins (Waterloo, ON: Wilfrid Laurier University Press, 2000), 215.
80 Ibid., 215.
81 So McGinn, 'The Acts of Thecla', 828.
82 So Bremmer, 'Magic, Martyrdom and Women's Liberation', 45.
83 Davies, *Revolt of the Widows*, 104.
84 Braun, 'Physiotherapy', 216.
85 Ibid., 222.
86 Johannes N. Vorster, 'Construction of Culture through the Construction of Person: The Construction of Thecla in the Acts of Thecla', in *A Feminist Companion to the New Testament Apocrypha*, ed. Amy-Jill Levine, with Maria Mayo Robbins (Cleveland, OH: Pilgrim, 2006), 111.
87 Ibid., 114.
88 Gail Corrington Streete, 'Of Martyrs and Men, Perpetua, Thecla and the Ambiguity of Female Heroism in Early Christianity', in *The Subjective Eye, Essays in Culture, Religion and Gender in Honor of Margaret R. Miles*, ed. Richard Valantasis (Eugene, OR: Pickwick, 2006), 260.
89 John C. B. Petropoulos, 'Transvestite Virgin with a Cause, The Acta Pauli et Thecla and Late Antique Proto-"Feminism"', in *Greece and Gender*, ed. Brit Berggreen and Nanno Marinatos (Athens: The Norwegian Institute at Athens, 1995), 132.
90 Ibid., 136, 137.
91 John Anson, 'The Female Transvestite in Early Monasticism: The Origin and Development of a Motif', *Viator* 5 (1974): 1–32; Margaret P. Aymer, 'Hailstorms and Fireball: Redaction, World Creation and Resistance in the Acts of Paul and Thecla', *Semeia* 79 (1997): 45–61; Stephen J. Davis, 'Crossed Texts, Crossed Sex: Intertextuality and Gender in Early Christian Legends of Holy Women Disguised as Men', *JECS* 10 (2002): 1–36; B. Diane Lipsett, *Desiring Conversion: Hermas, Thecla, Aseneth* (Oxford: Oxford University Press, 2001), 85, 121–2.
92 Braun, 'Physiotherapy', 221–2.
93 Rosemary Radford Ruether, 'Mother of the Church: Ascetic Women in the Late Patristic Age', in *Women of Spirit: Female Leadership in the Jewish and Christian Traditions*, ed. Rosemary Radford Ruether and Eleanor McLaughlin (New York: Simon & Schuster, 1998), 71–98.
94 Mary Rose D'Angelo, 'Women in Luke-Acts: A Redactional View', *JBL* (1990): 441–61.
95 Ibid., 443–51.
96 Kate Cooper, 'Apostles, Ascetic Women and Questions of Audience: New Reflections on the Rhetoric of Gender in the Apocryphal Acts', *Society of Biblical Literature Seminar Papers*, no. 31 (Atlanta, GA: Scholars Press, 1992): 147–53; see also Kate Cooper, *Virgin and the Bride*.

97 An important point to note is that in portraying Christianity as a 'feminist' liberation movement 'good' for women, scholars at the same time can inadvertently cast a shadow over Judaism which emerged as anti-women and anti-feminist. See Marlene Crusemann, 'Irredeemably Hostile to Women: Anti-Jewish Elements in the Exegesis of the Dispute about Women's Right to Speak (1 Cor. 14.34-35)', *JSNT* 79 (2000): 19–36; Luzia Sutter Rehmann, 'German-Language Feminist Exegesis of the Pauline Letters: A Survey', *JSNT* 79 (2000): 5–18; see also Schüssler Fiorenza, *In Memory*, 106.
98 Joyce Salisbury, *Church Fathers, Independent Virgins* (London: Verso, 1991), 3.
99 Elizabeth Clark, 'Ideology, History, and the Construction of "Woman" in Late Ancient Christianity', *JECS* 2 (1994): 179.
100 Ibid., 193; see also Kate Cooper, 'Poverty, Obligation, and Inheritance: Roman Heiresses and the Varieties of Senatorial Christianity in Fifth-Century Rome', in *Religion, Dynasty and Patronage in Early Christian Rome*, ed. Kate Cooper and Julia Hillner (Cambridge: Cambridge University Press, 2007), 169–71, 182–7.
101 Clark, 'Ideology', 190.
102 Corrington Streete employs this term in her paper 'Of Martyrs and Men', 254.
103 Susan E. Hylen, *A Modest Apostle: Thecla and the History of Women in the Early Church* (Oxford: Oxford University Press, 2015), 1.
104 Ibid., 12–20.
105 Ibid., 73, 74.
106 Ibid., 79–81.
107 See e.g., Zeba Cook, 'Honour, Shame and Social Status Revisited', *JBL* 128, no. 3 (2009): 593.
108 Virginia Burrus, *Saving Shame: Martyrs, Saints and Other Abject Subjects* (Philadelphia: University of Pennsylvania Press, 2008), xi.
109 Ibid., xii.
110 Bremmer, 'Drusiana, Cleopatra', 85–7.
111 See e.g. Cornelia B. Horn, 'Suffering Children, Parental Authority and the Quest for Liberation?: A Tale of Three Girls in the Acts of Paul (and Thecla), the Act(s) of Peter, the Acts of Nerseus and Achilleus and the Epistle of Pseudo-Titus', in *A Feminist Companion to the New Testament Apocrypha*, ed. Amy-Jill Levine, with Maria Mayo Robbins (Cleveland, OH: Pilgrim, 2006), 118–45; Gail P. C. Streete, 'Buying the Stairway to Heaven: Perpetua and Thecla as Early Christian Heroines', in *A Feminist Companion to the New Testament Apocrypha*, ed. Amy-Jill Levine, with Maria Mayo Robbins (Cleveland, OH: Pilgrim, 2006), 186–206; Susan A. Calef, 'Thecla "Tried and True" and the Inversion of Romance', in *A Feminist Companion to the New Testament Apocrypha*, ed. Amy-Jill Levine, with Maria Mayo Robbins (Cleveland, OH: Pilgrim, 2006), 163–85.
112 Richard Valantasis, 'The Question of Early Christian Identity: Three Strategies Exploring a Third Genos', in *A Feminist Companion to the New Testament Apocrypha*, ed. Amy-Jill Levine, with Maria Mayo Robbins (Cleveland, OH: Pilgrim, 2006), 60–76.
113 Ibid., 60–8, 70–5.
114 Vorster, 'Construction of Culture', 105.
115 Ibid., 117.
116 Elizabeth Castelli, *Martyrdom and Memory: Early Christian Culture Making: Gender, Theory and Religion* (New York: Columbia University Press, 2004).

117 Gail P. Corrington Streete, *Redeemed Bodies, Women Martyrs in Early Christianity* (Louisville, KY: Westminster John Knox, 2009), 73–102.
118 Ibid., 26.
119 Ibid., 43–7, 90–5.
120 Ibid., 99–102.
121 Elisabeth Esch-Wermeling, *Thekla – Paulusschülerin wider Willen? Strategien der Leserlenkung in den Theklaakten* (Münster: Aschendorff, 2008), 20.
122 Ibid., 64–5, 145.
123 Ibid., 142, 167, 186.
124 Anne Jensen, 'Die Theklageschichte. Die Apostolin zwischen Fiktion und Realität', in *Compendium Feministische Bibelauslegung*, ed. L. Schottroff and M. T. Wacker (Darmstadt: Wissenschaftliche Buchgesellschaft, 1999), 746–7.
125 Ibid., 83.
126 Aymer, 'Hailstorms and Fireball', 47–8.
127 Ibid., 48, 55–6.
128 Corrington Streete, *Redeemed Bodies*, 42, 45, 87.
129 Lipsett, *Desiring Conversion*, 70–1.
130 Ibid., 85.
131 See e.g., *NTA*, 78, see also the discussion on genre in Chapter 2 below.
132 Rosa Söder, *Die apokryphen Apostelgeschichte und die romanhafte Literatur der Antike* (Stuttgart: W. Kohlhammer, 1932), 187.
133 Judith Perkins, 'The Social World of the Acts of Peter', in *The Search for the Ancient Novel*, ed. J. Tatum (Baltimore, MD: John Hopkins University Press, 1994), 296–307, repr. in Judith Perkins, *The Suffering Self: Pain and Narrative Representation in the Early Christian Era* (London: Routledge, 1995); R. Pervo, 'Early Christian Fiction', in *Greek Fiction: The Greek Novel in Context*, ed. J. Morgan and R. Stoneman (London: Routledge, 1994), 239–54; R. Pervo, 'The Ancient Novel Becomes Christian', in *The Novel in the Ancient World*, ed. G. Schmeling (Leiden: Brill, 1996), 685–711.
134 Pervo, 'The Ancient Novel', 694.
135 Cooper, *Virgin and the Bride*, see especially Chapters 2 and 3.
136 Ibid., 22.
137 Jeremy M. Barrier, *The Acts of Paul and Thecla: A Critical Introduction and Commentary* (Tübingen: Mohr Siebeck, 2009), 1.
138 As argued, e.g., by Davies, *Revolt of the Widows*, 58–9.
139 Barrier, *Acts of Paul and Thecla*, 9–11.
140 Ibid., 66–7.
141 Cooper, *Virgin and the Bride*, 44–6, 50–4.
142 See e.g. Perkins, *The Suffering Self*, 26, 52, 62, 71, 131–2; Judith Perkins, 'The Apocryphal Acts of the Apostles and Early Christian Martyrdom', *Arethusa* 18 (1985): 212–19; Barrier, *Acts of Paul and Thecla*, 1–15; Melissa Aubin, 'Reversing Romance? The Acts of Thecla and the Ancient Novel', in *Ancient Fiction and Early Christian Narrative*, ed. Ronald F. Hock, J. Bradley Chance and Judith Perkins (Atlanta, GA: Scholars Press, 2003), 257–72; see also David Konstan, 'Acts of Love: A Narrative Pattern in the Apocryphal Acts', *JECS* 6, no. 1 (1998): 34–5; Calef, 'Thecla "Tried and True"', 164–5. Burrus has suggested that the less-than-subtle subversions of the Apocryphal Acts do not so much invert as intensify certain aspects of what she calls the 'pagan romances', in terms of *eros* and *gamos*, city and empire. Here, the pagan romances complicate and render more ambiguous the strident social critique

already conveyed by the Apocryphal Acts, Virginia Burrus, 'Mimicking Virgins, Colonial Ambivalence and the Ancient Romance', *Arethusa* 38 (2005): 55.
143 Perkins, 'The Apocryphal Acts', 213.
144 Ibid., 219.
145 Ibid., 212. See also, Perkins, *The Suffering Self*, 46, 59.
146 Perkins continues this comparison of the ancient novel, the Apocryphal Acts and other texts in her book entitled *Roman Imperial Identities*. Although she does not focus on the *Acts of Paul and Thecla* specifically, she examines cultural constructions of Christian and elite imperial identities in relations to themes such as judgement, resurrection and gender. Judith Perkins, *Roman Imperial Identities in the Early Christian Era* (London: Routledge, 2009).
147 Cooper, *Virgin and the Bride*, 27, 55.
148 Ibid., 66-7.
149 Ibid., 66-7, 55.
150 Ibid., 19.
151 Kate Cooper, 'Insinuations of Womanly Influence: An Aspect of the Christianization of the Roman Aristocracy', *JRS* 82 (1992): 150.
152 For difficulties in joining the Apocryphal Acts corpus together, see Kaestli, 'Response', 123; Dunn, 'Women's Liberation', 247-48; Anne Jensen, *Thekla - Die Apostelin: Ein apokrypher Text neu entdeckt* (Freiburg: Herder, 1995), 69; see also Judith Perkins, 'Fictional Narratives and Social Critique', in *Late Ancient Christianity: A People's History of Christianity*, vol. 2, ed. Virginia Burrus (Augsburg, MN: Fortress, 2005), 48. See also *NTA*, 78, and Chapter 2.
153 Francois Bovon, 'Canonical and Apocryphal Acts of Apostles', *JECS* 11 (2003): 193-4.
154 See Chapter 2, Textual history and dating; Schneemelcher also notes that the wide dissemination of the *Acts of Paul and Thecla* shows that this part of the narrative separated off from the *Acts of Paul*, *NTA*, 222.
155 Schüssler Fiorenza, *In Memory*, 175; McGinn, 'The Acts of Thecla', 801-4; see also Dennis R. MacDonald, 'From Audita to Legenda: Oral and Written Miracle Stories', *Forum* 2, no. 4 (1986): 15-26, which discusses the textualized alterations of the Thecla story.
156 See *NTA*, 217, 220 – Schneelemcher argues that the author of the *Acts of Paul* has absorbed independent Thecla traditions into his book and worked them up. See also Rordorf, 'Tradition and Composition', 279.
157 Jensen, *Thekla - Die Apostolin*, 69-70.
158 Ibid.
159 See Chapter 2.

2

The *Acts of Paul and Thecla*: Text and context

The question of genre

This chapter begins by assessing the question of the genre of the Apocryphal Acts generally and the *Acts of Paul and Thecla* more specifically. I will then move on to discuss specific fundamental points about the text and its reception history.

As noted in Chapter 1, the question of genre is of particular concern to scholars interested in aligning the Apocryphal Acts with the ancient Hellenistic novel. The ancient novel is not, however, the only literary model connected with the Apocryphal Acts. In recent years, a number of scholars have suggested that the Apocryphal Acts bear an affinity with the canonical gospels. In what follows, I will explore this suggestion further.

In the previous chapter, I argued that the *Acts of Paul and Thecla* has prompted consideration as a unique and distinctive text in its own right, with the suggestion made that it may have had an independent existence prior to its inclusion with the *Acts of Paul*. In terms of genre too, the *Acts of Paul and Thecla* can be seen as distinctive from the other Apocryphal Acts.

As noted above, the issue of how to categorize the Apocryphal Acts has been variously debated by scholars. However, despite these influential and important approaches that identify a strong association between the Apocryphal Acts and the Hellenistic novels, there is no consensus regarding the genre of the Apocryphal Acts. Due to their varied and disparate nature, both classicists and New Testament scholars have had difficulty in agreeing upon their genre.[1] The problem is that they are in some ways 'historical', in that they use known historical figures such as Paul, Peter and Andrew. However, they are also fictional, in that the style of presentation does emulate that of the Hellenistic novels. Questions have also been raised about the validity of attempting to mould the Apocryphal Acts neatly into, what is thought to be, the anachronistically created designation, 'ancient novel'.[2] Christine Thomas, for example, believes the generic designation 'ancient novel' has obscured the true relationship between early Christian and polytheist literature during the Roman Imperial period. Thomas further highlights that the Apocryphal Acts do not share the stylistic aspirations of the Koine novel fragments or the high-flown self-referential prose of the authors of the Hellenistic novels. She notes that the most elegant of the Apocryphal Acts, the *Acts of Paul*, casts nearly half of its sentences in simple paratactic style.[3]

However, not every literary feature needs to be present in every example of a genre. Tzvetán Todorov rightly observes that genre is 'a principle operative in a number of texts, rather than which is specific about each of them'.[4] Such an approach prevents genres having to adhere to prescriptive rules and allows for flexibility and the omission of one or a number of features.[5] What is important is that the genre presents sufficient features for the family resemblance to be recognized. 'Recognition of genre depends on associating a complex of elements which need not all appear in one work ... Usually there are so many indicators, organized into so familiar a unity, that we recognize the generic complex instantly.'[6]

Such an understanding of genre would negate Thomas's argument in discounting the Apocryphal Acts as novels because of stylistic differences, since not every text within a genre needs to share every single feature. Nevertheless, Thomas is not alone in rejecting the view that the Apocryphal Acts are novels. In regard to the *Acts of Paul*, Ann Graham Brock also disagrees that it is novelistic, arguing that although novelistic elements appear within the text, the genre of novel does not fully encompass the force and motive of the text.[7] She suggests that the *Acts of Paul* (incorporating the *Acts of Paul and Thecla*) is a religious propaganda tract modelled somewhat after the gospels.[8] This idea, that the Apocryphal Acts resemble the genre of the gospels, is also supported by Bovon. Both Bovon and Brock note the recurrent parallels between Paul's and Jesus' ministry in the *Acts of Paul*, such as performance of miracles, preaching, persecution, death and resurrection appearances.[9] Bovon argues,

> It becomes clear, therefore, that the Apocryphal Acts prefer to establish links with the canonical gospels rather than with the canonical acts, and with Jesus' teaching rather than with Jesus' deeds. The authors of the Apocryphal Acts, however, do not seem to feel any need to be literal in the quotations because the content is more important than the form.[10]

This is an interesting angle, especially since it is now widely held that the gospels are to be viewed as biographies of Jesus.[11] Like the gospels, the Apocryphal Acts focus on specific apostolic figures and trace each individual life. Sean Adams writes that any consistent focus on an individual is determinative of *Bios*.[12] Thus, although a number of scholars classify the Apocryphal Acts as novels, there are also a significant number of scholars who recognize dominant biographical characteristics within them.[13] In a similar vein, Eric Junod sees parallels between the Apocryphal Acts and philosophical lives.[14] Tamás Adamik argues,

> The only literary genre in which we can place the Acts is biography ... The Apocryphal Acts always deal with the life and deeds of a single apostle who is the central figure. It is natural that they do not mention the childhood of the apostle since the Gospels and the canonical Acts of the Apostles did not refer to it. It can be regarded as logical, too, that travelling plays an important part in the Acts of apostles, since the conversion of different people and nations to Christianity presupposes a journey. Miracles also form an essential part of the Acts of apostles, because when Jesus sent his apostles away in order to preach, he said that they

would perform miracles ... In addition, several motifs, such as love, teratology, and aretology were taken over from the ancient novel ... When we regard the Apocryphal Acts of the Apostles as biography, we can easily understand why they influenced the lives of the Saints: because the Apocryphal Acts and the lives of the Saints both belong to the literary genre of biography.[15]

Such a range of possible readings in terms of genre underscores the extremely complex problem of classifying the Apocryphal Acts with any certainty.

Quintilian, in the *Institutio Oratoria*, wrote that there are three forms of narrative, *fabula*, *argumentum* and *historia*. *Fabula* is legendary-type literature found in the form of narrative used in tragedy and poetry (it was regarded as remote, not merely from truth (*veritas*), but the appearance of truth); *argumentum*, which is false, can have the appearance of truth, such as the plots of comedy; and *historia* narrates historical events and fact.[16] These rhetorical principles, which were also followed by Aristotle and Cicero, were not, however, definitive.[17] Lyndan Warner states, 'The models of classical rhetoric provided by Aristotle, Quintilian and Cicero allowed for an overlapping of rhetorical categories.'[18] Genre mixing was, therefore, an established concept among ancient writers.[19] It may well be, therefore, that within the Apocryphal Acts, all three genres, *fabula*, *argumentum* and *historia*, are being utilized. The narratives certainly display elements of *fabula* and *argumentum* (in their legendary-like quality and sermonizing) while, at the same time, like the gospels and the canonical Acts, they purport to record and perpetuate historical facts and stories about the followers of Jesus.

Modern literary theory would support such a view of overlapping genres. Alistair Fowler points out that many generic conventions are acquired by authors and reader alike in unconscious ways, as we acquire the grammar of our native language: 'Codes often come to a writer indirectly, deviously, remotely, at haphazard ... So much of genre's operation is unconscious.'[20] In addition, Jonathan Culler observes that both genres and the boundaries between them shift from age to age and according to locality.[21] Indeed, according to Fowler, genre evolves in the way a species evolves.[22] Genres thus extend and amalgamate other existing genres, while developed genres are open to further mixture and modulation.[23] If the acquisition of genres is largely unconscious, and if genres are fluid in nature and also mix in their development, it may help explain why a number of different generic features are present within the Apocryphal Acts.

A further explanation for what appears to be such a commingling of different genres is the level of redaction that these texts have undergone. Thomas argues that the presence of so many translations demonstrates that these works did not circulate as fixed original texts but that they were subjected to multiple redactions by multiple authors.[24] As the title of her article shows, she views the Apocryphal Acts as stories without texts or authors. David Konstan too holds a similar view and because of this labels the narratives 'open text'.[25] Thus, although the framework of these stories may be fairly uniform, their hospitality to inserted episodes allows the several recensions to have a character of their own, depending on the choice and arrangement of the subordinate tales.[26]

As noted in Chapter 1, for example, Bovon has highlighted a number of quite clear distinctions between each of the various acts. He particularly underscores the fact that the primary concerns of the *Acts of Peter* are connected with propaganda of the Christian faith through miracles. Where the *Acts of Paul* are concerned, there is a focus on subversive attitudes to political authorities and a claim for female ministry, while the *Acts of John* are concerned with veneration of the Beloved Disciple.[27] Thus, although there are similarities between each of the stories, they also contain important integral differences. These variations in emphasis and style resist classification. The problem is also compounded by the fact that the extant sources of the Apocryphal Acts are fragmentary with misplaced information and absent texts.

This discussion demonstrates that the question of the genre of the Apocryphal Acts is a complicated and disputed issue. As Schneemelcher points out, while in their aim toward entertainment, instruction and religious propaganda, the Apocryphal Acts cohere enough as a group to provide a unique *Gattung*, on the question of genre, 'There is still no exact and generally recognised definition of the kind of text to which the Apocryphal Acts belong.'[28] It thus becomes evident that the question of genre in regard to the corpus of the Apocryphal Acts remains unsettled.

Again, as noted above, this is all part of a bigger problem that has been highlighted by scholars working on these narratives, and it relates to the difficulty of trying to join together a diverse and composite corpus of literature in an attempt to classify their genre.[29] Richard Burridge contends that genre holds the hermeneutical key to any text.[30] If this really is the case, then there may yet be new light to shed on these texts. However, in the meantime, until a definitive argument in terms of genre is put forward, what this discussion has highlighted is the multiform nature of the Apocryphal Acts and the difficulty of trying to group such disparate texts together.

Classification of the *Acts of Paul and Thecla*

While classifying the genre of Apocryphal Acts as a corpus of literature has proved challenging, where do we stand in terms of the genre of the *Acts of Paul and Thecla* specifically? Although there is no agreement as to exactly how the text should be classified, an important approach is taken by Jensen who, in her attempt to free the *Acts of Paul and Thecla* from the classification of 'novel', contends that the text should be regarded as martyrdom literature. In order to support her argument, Jensen compares the *Acts of Paul and Thecla* with traditions about female martyrs, female apostles and prophetesses, including the martyrdom account of Polycarp and Perpetua.[31] As noted above, a number of scholars have argued that the Apocryphal Acts are biographical and there is, of course, a broad correspondence between biography and martyrology, in that both genres are concerned to preserve the memory of a person. Burridge notes that Graeco-Roman biographies were meant to offer a kind of portrait of a person, and often an author's underlying aim would be didactic while also containing elements of apologetic and polemic.[32] Adams has also pointed out that an author's motive in writing a biography could vary diversely (from encomium to moralistic modelling).[33] Since biographies were used so diversely, Adams believes that their functionality made them ideal candidates for generic experimentation and ingenuity.[34] That martyrology is a derivative of biographical genre and a form of life-writing has been argued by Nikki Shephardson. In tracing the development of martyrology into hagiographical writing, she notes that both genres are related and consist of 'biographical' accounts of Christian saints. However, martyrologies are distinct in that the subject of such accounts is limited to those who witness Christ with their blood; it is their sacrifice that qualifies them as worthy or recognition.[35] In addition, since martyrologies are more concerned with the legendary 'witness' of a saint's suffering, they tended to include vivid descriptions and spectacle.[36]

With its focus on one female Christian protagonist and a story that revolves around two accounts of dramatic and violent persecution by the Roman authorities, it is not difficult to see an affinity between the *Acts of Paul and Thecla* and other female martyrdom accounts. In this respect, unlike the other Apocryphal Acts, there is far less focus on the male Apostle. In fact, as noted above, he regularly disappears from the narrative. Thus, although Jensen's motivation is to find the historical Thecla, there is much to commend her classification of the text. Jensen's categorization of martyrdom literature is, therefore, an important one. Important also is the fact that Jensen is not a lone voice. Even though they offer no formal discussion about genre, scholars writing on early Christian female martyrdom regularly include the *Acts of Paul and Thecla* in their discussions.[37] Of course, there is a problem because Thecla atypically survives persecution and torture unharmed, twice. However, since, as noted above, genre categories are flexible and texts do not have to contain every single feature to be classified as belonging to a particular genre, it may still be possible to effectively argue, along with Jensen, for martyrdom literature.[38] Of course, ultimately a far more detailed examination, beyond the scope of this study, is needed in order to establish this more conclusively.

Textual history and dating

The title *Acta Pauli et Theclae* was given to the text by its first modern editor, Ernestus Grabe, in 1698. Its use is continued in the critical edition of the *Acts of Paul* published by Richard Lipsius and Maximillianus Bonnet in 1852, as a translation of the Greek title Πράξεις Παύλου καὶ Θέκλης found in the eleventh-century codex Parisinum Graecus (Paris. Gr.) 520. More common, however, among the codices cited by Lipsius, is the title μαρτύριον τῆς ἁγίας πρωτομάρτυρος Θέλης (or some variation thereof). The title *Acta Theclae et Pauli* appears in the *Decretum Gelasianum* 5, where it is listed among the apocryphal works.[39]

In comparison with the other Apocryphal Acts, there are good textual witnesses for the apocryphon of the Greek text of the *Acts of Paul and Thecla* and for the *Acts of Paul* as a whole, testifying to their popularity.[40] Ancient translations are found in Latin, Coptic, Slavic, Ethiopian as well as a Syriac version, three Russian codices and an Arab version; the Syriac versions date from the sixth to the twelfth centuries.[41] However, while the Lipsius-Bonnet edition was based on eleven Greek manuscripts,[42] there are now more than eighty extant manuscripts, papyrus fragments and ancient translations of the *Acts of Paul and Thecla*. The discovery of the fragmentary sixth-century Coptic manuscript, Papyrus No. 1, in Heidelberg (P. Heid.) in 1894, along with the Hamburg Papyrus (PH) of the third and fourth centuries, have hugely contributed to a greater knowledge of the *Acts of Paul*.[43] There are other manuscripts that also need to be included in a new edition, such as the fourth-century Antinoopolis fragment, the small fragment of the Fackelmann papyrus and the fourth- to fifth-century Oxyrhynchus papyrus. Of the Greek manuscripts employed by Lipsius-Bonnet, six are considered superior (E Vatican, of the eleventh century; 1 Paris, from the twelfth century; K Paris, from the thirteenth century; L Palatine at the Vatican, from the thirteenth century; F Vatican, of the eleventh century; and H Oxford Huntingdon, of the twelfth century).[44] The Syriac is also considered to be a good manuscript, even though Lipsius notes that it does not always render the Greek word for word, especially in the sermons and speeches.[45] The Latin versions also tend to paraphrase rather than translate accurately, and by far the best is considered to be the Mombritian, which is closely related to Codex E.[46] However, the stemmata are not yet completely clear.[47] Important is the critical discussion and translation done previously by Rordorf,[48] and the critical commentary, with discussion of manuscript variants and reconstruction, produced by Barrier.[49]

Social location of the authorial voice

Although MacDonald, Burrus and Davies have hypothesized that the Apocryphal Acts originate from oral folk traditions of women, very little is known for certain about the actual circumstances of their production. Just like the ancient novels, our understanding of the Apocryphal Acts is frustrated by lack of information in regard to authors, date and audience.[50] Where the novels are concerned, scholars have been forced to focus on internal evidence as a way of determining their implied social location.[51] Since we know so little of the circumstances of those who produced the Apocryphal Acts, here again the social location for the most part has to be deduced from the texts themselves.[52] Of course, the possibility of later redaction and the fact that more than one authorial hand may be at work in the texts clearly adds yet another complicating dimension to the interpretation of these stories.[53]

What we can say with some certainty is that the *Acts of Paul* (like the other Apocryphal Acts) heavily reflects the circumstances of a popular form of second-century Christianity in Asia Minor which included the practice of continence. In this respect, the narratives were an important influence on female piety in the centuries that followed. In their focus on female chastity and virginity, the narratives thus left quite a theological imprint in their own right in the emerging institution and practices of the early church.[54] This influence on female piety is evidenced quite early in Tertullian (*De bapt.* 17.5) towards the end of the second century, where he mentions not only Thecla's influence on women but also a suggested author and location for the *Acts of Paul*. However, this reference is not without its difficulties (for a fuller discussion see below).

Of course, this focus on female chastity very much influenced theories that women were the intended audience of these narratives.[55] However, when it comes to the Apocryphal Acts, Kim Haines-Eitzen argues against the claim that they were written by women and for women. Noting the physical features of the textual papyri of these books – the handwriting, quality of papyrus and parchment – she believes that it is far more likely that members of the upper echelons of society, who enjoyed poetry, history and philosophy, were the probable and likely readers of the Apocryphal Acts.[56] This corresponds to theories about the inferred readership of the ancient novels: that the educated classes were the likely readers.[57] Larry Hurtado also argues strongly against the fact that the Apocryphal Acts are a corpus of literature intended for women and read by women.[58] Ultimately, Thomas and Hurtado contend that the narrative fluidity and multiple renditions evidence for a variety of audiences over time and place.

Looking at the internal evidence of the *Acts of Paul and Thecla*, it is quite evident that the narrative focuses almost entirely on the preservation of the virginity of one particular female. Understanding how virginity functions rhetorically may, therefore, help to illuminate questions of authorial intent and audience.

The question of origins and the Pauline tradition

As noted, the *Acts of Paul and Thecla*, despite being the earliest extant text presenting the Thecla tradition, is part of the larger apocryphal *Acts of Paul*, expanding on Paul's travels and preaching throughout Asia Minor. It is contained in Books Three and Four of this larger work. The P. Heid. text, discovered in 1894, contained the *Acts of Paul* in its entirety and appeared to form a coherent whole, incorporating the *Acts of Paul and Thecla*, *3 Corinthians* and the *Martyrium Pauli*.[59] The relationship of the *Acts of Paul and Thecla* to this other material concerning Paul is unclear. While the discovery of the P. Heid. demonstrates conclusively that, at least by the sixth century, the *Acts of Paul and Thecla* circulated as one section of the longer *Acts of Paul*, there is also evidence of the work circulating independently.[60]

Unusually for the Apocryphal Acts, there is ancient testimony to a specific author. Tertullian, writing in Carthage in North Africa around the year 200 CE, provides a key external reference to it. In his text *De baptismo*,[61] Tertullian mentions a work on Paul, which provides the example of Thecla as one who baptizes and teaches, used by women to argue a case for leadership (*De bapt.* 17.5). However, there is considerable debate about whether this testimony provides an actual author, which also impacts the issue of dating. Based on this reference, most scholars subscribe to a second-century date for the *Acts of Paul and Thecla* (185–200 CE),[62] with the absolute terminus generally held to be around 200 CE.[63] However, the text of Tertullian is the subject of some dispute. Up to 1916, *De baptismo* was only known through the 1545 edition of the now lost Mesnartius manuscript, which was reproduced in Oehler's critical edition published in 1853.[64] Within this manuscript, 17.5 reads,

> But if wrongly they read the writings on Paul with the example (or possibly 'the writing') of Thecla to defend women's licence to teach and immerse, let them know (*sciant*) that the presbyter in Asia who constructed that writing, adding

enrichments of his own to Paul's reputation, was found guilty and confessed that he did it for a love of Paul, [so] left the place.⁶⁵

There is a variant, *exemplum* instead of *scriptum*, mentioned in the margin of Mesnartius's edition. In 1916, however, a twelfth-century manuscript, *Codex Trecensis* 523, came to light, and this explicitly refers to the discredited writings as *Acta Pauli* but still does not specify who exactly is intended by the verb *sciant*.⁶⁶ The fact that *Acta Pauli* is mentioned explicitly in *Codex Trecensis* suggests that what is being referred to in the Mesnartius manuscript is the story of Thecla and not the entire text of the *Acts of Paul*. It is uncertain whether Tertullian or a copyist included both *Acta Pauli* and *exemplum Theclae*. Schneemelcher holds fast to *Acta Pauli* and questions *exemplum Theclae*.⁶⁷ However, his discussion significantly antedates Anthony Hilhorst who has argued that the inclusion of *exemplum Theclae* makes for a smoother reading and that, apart from *De baptismo* 17.5, *Acta* does not occur in Tertullian's works as a reference to the Apocryphal Acts.⁶⁸ The question is whether Tertullian knew the whole of the *Acts of Paul* or only the *Acts of Paul and Thecla*. Schneemelcher argues that there is much in favour of the view that Tertullian knew the whole of the *Acts of Paul* since he states that the presbyter's purpose in writing was to add to Paul's reputation (*De bapt.* 20), and yet the *Acts of Paul and Thecla* focuses almost exclusively on the person of Thecla. This would suggest that Tertullian is referring to the whole of the *Acts of Paul* and not merely the *Acts of Paul and Thecla*.⁶⁹

In regard to the textual problem relating to the verb *sciant*, Hilhorst has attempted to solve it by utilizing Gelenius's 1550 edition of the manuscript no longer extant. This edition corrects *sunt* to *legunt* and, therefore, reads, 'But if those *women* who read the falsely named writings about Paul', thus supplying a feminine plural subject, *quae* (those women) for the various verbs in the passage, which previous editions lacked. Hilhorst highlights the fact that Gelenius had no manuscript evidence for this reading; nevertheless, he regards it a plausible conjecture that solves many of the problems of the prior readings.⁷⁰ However, the manuscript evidence for *De baptismo* is far too inadequate to argue the case with complete certainty.

Although Tertullian allows us to roughly fix the dating for the *Acts of Paul*, it does not, of course, give us the earliest starting point, but suggestions have been made by Bremmer and James of a date as early as *c*. 160 CE.⁷¹ Bremmer bases this early dating on a Roman inscription of a certain Pompeia Sosia Falconilla, daughter of Pompeius Susius Priscus, whose husband was Consul in 163 CE. He argues that the author of the *Acts of Paul* borrowed Tryphaena's daughter's name, Falconilla, from this woman.⁷² This early dating is, however, a minority view.

As noted in Chapter 1, it has been suggested that the text of the *Acts of Paul and Thecla* existed in some form independently, either written or oral, before the composition of the *Acts of Paul*, and that it was included in the earliest form of the larger text.⁷³ Brock and McGinn also contend that the author of the *Acts of Paul* substantially reworked the source material of the *Acts of Paul and Thecla*.⁷⁴ Indeed, Rordorf maintains that the style and vocabulary of the Greek of the *Acts of Paul* so resembles that of the *Acts of Paul and Thecla* that the identity of the author of the two narratives can 'hardly be doubted'. Rordorf, nevertheless, concludes that the Thecla narrative, introduced into the *Acts of Paul* by the presbyter of Asia Minor, has 'retained some particularities of the oral narrative'.[75] The extent to which this pre-existing oral tradition may have been worked over to reach the form it appears in the *Acts of Paul* is, however, a matter of conjecture.

Relationship to the Pauline tradition

Although there is no reference to Thecla in any of Paul's letters, the narrative of the *Acts of Paul and Thecla* shows Thecla as a converted student and temporary companion of Paul; thus, whatever its origin, the text is considered to form part of the Pauline tradition. This Pauline legacy is also reflected in the fact that the *Acts of Paul and Thecla* displays a development of Paul's teaching found in 1 Cor. 7.8: 'To the unmarried and the widows I say that it is well for them to remain unmarried as I am.' Here, inspired by eschatological conviction and an anticipation of the imminent return of Jesus,[76] Paul suggests an avoidance of marriage for those who are able to endure. With Paul preaching chastity (*APTh*. 5-6), Thecla's refusal to marry (*APTh*. 20) and the widow Tryphaena taking Thecla under her wing (*APTh*. 27, 30), the *Acts of Paul and Thecla* is seen to be an intensification of the teaching found in 1 Cor. 7 and considered to provide an opening for the expression of ascetic fervour in which women exercised a particular freedom and independence.[77] This ascetic fervour is eventually seen to give way to communities of widows and virgins. As Davies suggested, it was believed that these female communities, which began as a form of organized charity, reflected the ideal of Christian virginity.[78]

Subsequent to Davies, the idea of communities of widows which helped to support and advance the practice of asceticism among women has been popular.[79] The assumption has been that the ascetic life was made possible for women through a network of financially independent widows who supported others less well off. However, as the expectation of the *parousia* begins to fade, the Pastoral Epistles, written in Paul's name, are seen to react against such a development. The linguistic and theological dissimilarities from the seven undisputed Pauline letters, as well as the difficulty of situating the letters in the chronology of Paul's ministry, has raised serious questions about the accuracy of an ascription to Paul. Furthermore, since the epistles contain a more developed sense of church structure, authority and leadership, this has also suggested that they were written after the death of Paul. For the majority of scholars, the letters are, therefore, seen to be pseudepigraphal and dated towards the end of the first and beginning of the second century.[80]

The Pastoral Epistles are considered to have the converse view to that reflected in the *Acts of Paul and Thecla*. Here, provisional church orders are considered necessary, and they look to construct a fixed masculine church hierarchy (see e.g. 1 Tim. 2.1-3.12). Although Christian communities are still to assume responsibility for widows, there is at the same time a strong desire to restrict these female communities (1 Tim. 5.3-16). The Pastoral Epistles, therefore, suggest that the widows of each community should be enrolled on an official list (1 Tim. 5.9-10). In addition, 1 Tim. 2.15 also reacts against female chastity by stating that women will be saved through τεκνογονίας (childbearing).

MacDonald, Burrus and others have held up the Pastoral Epistles as a point of conflict within some early Christian communities where the emerging patriarchal hierarchy was attempting to restrict the activities and leadership of women; they were seen as a voice of containment.[81] The Pastoral Epistles thus cut across any development concerning gender found in the Apocryphal Acts as women were exhorted to embrace marriage and maternity.[82] A reference to 'virgins called widows' in Ignatius, *Smyrna.* 13, and to a young virgin, who was placed within the order of widows, in Tertullian, *De virg.* 9.4A, have been read back into the situation of the Pastoral Epistles and taken as evidence for the official status of widows and unmarried younger women. Consequently, the Apocryphal Acts have been seen as the fictive element of this celibate life, while the widows of the Pastoral Epistles were seen as embodying the realistic, historical element.[83]

While it is certainly the case that external sources suggest that widows formed a recognized group in the church (see e.g. Polycarp, *Phil.* 4.3, where widows are said to be God's altar and are people of blameless lives engaged in intercession) and that caring for widows was a major priority in early Christianity (see e.g. Acts 6.1 and 6.6), there were reactions against such views.[84]

It has regularly been argued that within the Pastoral Epistles there is evidence that the community was experiencing some kind of threat, probably from within the community itself, and that this was contributing to divisiveness and opposition.[85] Although the precise nature of the difficulties experienced has given rise to a great deal of speculation, this has often been seen as relating to the activity of Christian women.[86] That this opposition was of a nature that reflected the kind of teaching advanced in the *Acts of Paul and Thecla* has frequently been contended.[87] For example, Karen Jo Torjesen, Margaret MacDonald and others hold that women's leadership roles were diminished as the church endorsed a move back to conventional gender roles and the male-orientated conditions of Graeco-Roman society, in which leadership, public authority and office were the province of men.[88] The inclusion of the Pastoral Epistles in the canon demonstrated the winning faction of the debate concerning women's autonomy and leadership within the early church.

The Pastoral Epistles (e.g. 1 Tim. 2.11-12) were also seen to react to Paul's commission to Thecla to teach and preach.[89] That some factions of the early church responded adversely to women teaching is evident from Tertullian, who strongly disapproves of women imitating Thecla in teaching and baptizing, as noted above.[90] Indeed, it has been suggested by Gordon Fee and others that 1 Cor. 14.34-35,[91] which uses language very similar to that of 1 Tim. 2.11-14, and which also contradicts 1 Cor. 11.5 (which stipulates that women can pray and prophesy in congregations as long as their heads are covered), was added to Paul's letter in the second century.[92] It is evident from Tertullian's reference to Thecla and the *Acts of Paul* that the example of Thecla was being used by some as an authority for women to teach and baptize, and, in this respect, the text is seen to provoke a reaction by some who objected to such roles for women in the early church. Women teachers and baptizers were obviously not thought to be consistent with aspects of the more conservative teaching found in the canonical Pauline corpus, involving the subjugation of women to men, as found in Eph. 5.22 and Col. 3.18, but these texts too have been considered pseudepigraphal.[93]

As noted in Chapter 1, MacDonald's position is that the Pauline tradition in the second century bifurcated into two distinct interpretative streams, both originating from Paul's preaching and letters. The more conservative one found expansion and elaboration in the Pastoral Epistles, while the *Acts of Paul and Thecla* supposedly represents the more progressive side of Paul's teaching. These two opposing traditions, regarded as a kind of 'conflict model', where conservative forces are contending against radical elements in the church, marked by openness to women, demonstrate that the church remembered Paul in diverse ways and consequently opened up two alternative interpretations of Paul.[94]

However, to what extent is the depiction of Paul's teaching in the Pastoral Epistles substantively different from that presented in the *Acts of Paul and Thecla*? Although many scholars continue to endorse the perspective that 1 Timothy and the *Acts of Paul of Thecla* represent two distinct and conflicting viewpoints on the role of women, in contrast to many interpreters, Hylen argues that both texts emerge out of, and share, a common cultural framework. Thus, even when holding leadership roles, expectations for women's modest behaviour continued unabated. As noted in Chapter 1, Hylen holds Thecla up as such an example and maintains that traditional feminine modest behaviour was always expected of women who were civic and religious leaders.[95] Therefore, modesty and leadership for women was neither incongruous nor radical but a consistent and familiar pattern through which active, virtuous women served their communities.[96] While I may disagree with aspects of Hylen's interpretation of Thecla's characterization, her point that culture can produce a complex and conflicting mix of messages around gender is valid.

Dunn too has observed that despite Tertullian's resistance, the church had little difficulty in accepting the conflicting traditions of both the *Acts of Paul and Thecla* and the Pastoral Epistles. Indeed, Paul also held onto the tension between the ideal of chastity and the remedy of marriage for sexual immorality in 1 Cor. 7.24.[97] The fact that many of the same personal names and localities appear in *Acts of Paul* and the Pastoral Epistles is striking: for example, 2 Tim. 4.17 ('so I was rescued from the Lion's mouth') is paralleled by the story of Paul's encounter with the lion in Ephesus in *Acts of Paul* (PH, pp. 1–5); 2 Tim. 2.18 (the notion that the resurrection has already taken place) is also stated in the *APTh*. 14. The two traditions also hold place names in common, for example, Lystra, Antioch and Iconium (2 Tim. 3.11); as well as personal names, for example, Demas (2 Tim. 4.10), Hermogenes (2 Tim. 1.15) and Onesiphorus (2 Tim. 1.16-18); and the job title of 'coppersmith' (2 Tim. 4.14). Might these elements have been taken from the Pastoral Epistles? It is possible that both the Pastoral Epistles and the *Acts of Paul* (including the *Acts of Paul and Thecla*) drew upon older material in Paul's letters to argue for their particular perspectives, and they may also have drawn on oral tradition.

To claim that the Pastoral Epistles were written specifically to oppose the Apocryphal Acts is, therefore, to assert more than our sources allow. Furthermore, it needs to be borne in mind that the *Acts of Paul and Thecla* and the Pastoral Epistles are quite distinct texts and serve very different purposes. The legend-like quality of the Apocryphal Acts makes it very difficult to compare these texts with the Pastoral Epistles, which serve very specific purposes and circumstances, and which also have a vastly different, authoritative nuance and focus in their firm life directives.

The fact is that in the early church through to the Middle Ages, the *Acts of Paul*, including the *Acts of Paul and Thecla*, were read widely by Christians who read the Pastoral Epistles as authoritative, as the numerous surviving manuscripts of the *Acts of Paul* indicate, and has been demonstrated by both the popular cult of Saint Thecla (in western Asia Minor, and which spread to Egypt, Syria and elsewhere)[98] as well as by ecclesiastical art and iconography.[99] Thecla is also defined as an apostle in the hagiographical writing *The Life and Miracles of Saint Thecla*, dated to the fifth century.[100] The first volume of this is a different version – often considered a paraphrase – of the *Acts of Paul and Thecla*, and the second is a collection of forty-six healing miracles of Thecla, otherwise not extant in earlier texts.[101] It is, therefore, *not* a presupposition of this study that the Pastoral Epistles and the *Acts of Paul and Thecla* were opposed, but rather this is something that will be left open; also left open is the attribution of Tertullian – what if there was an author who wished to give more honour to Paul by writing the *Acts of Paul*?

A Pauline tradition empowering to women?

In order to determine how much the *Acts of Paul and Thecla* represents a woman-empowering stream of the Pauline tradition, I will, therefore, endeavour to draw out of the shadows those aspects of the text that display little evidence of female subjectivity and empowerment. An appreciation of the ideology and rhetorical techniques that shape the representation and construction of gender within the text will, I believe, help us to perceive how gendered imagery communicates perceptions about power, supremacy and dominance in a patriarchal society. Can female liberation ever truly emerge from a patriarchal and androcentric context or does female liberation from such a context simultaneously 'cast a shadow' of female repression and objectification? Before considering these questions, we will first move on to give a brief overview of the method that will be used to discern whether Thecla is an empowered and liberated woman or whether her representation is, in fact, utilized as an instrument of patriarchal power.

Notes

1 A full discussion of this may be found in Barrier, *Acts of Paul and Thecla*, 2–7.
2 Christine M. Thomas, 'Stories without Texts and without Authors: The Problem of Fluidity in Ancient Novelistic Texts and Early Christian Literature', in *Ancient Fiction and Early Christian Narrative*, ed. Ronald F. Hock, J. Bradley Chance and Judith Perkins (Atlanta, GA: Scholars Press, 2003), 273–4, 278.
3 Ibid., 273–6.
4 Tzvetán Todorov, *Introduction à la literature fantastique* (Paris: Swuil, 1970), trans. Richard Howard into *The Fantastic: A Structural Approach to Literary Genre* (New York: Cornell University Press, 1975), 3.
5 Richard Burridge, *What Are the Gospels: A Comparison with Graeco-Roman Biography* (Grand Rapids, MI: Eerdmans, 2004), 42–3.

6 Alistair Fowler, 'The Life and Death of Literary Forms', in *New Directions in Literary History*, ed. Ralph Cohen (London: Routledge & Kegan Paul, 1974), 80–1; see also Burridge, *What Are the Gospels*, 42.
7 Ann G. Brock, 'Genre of the Acts of Paul: One Tradition Enhancing Another', *Apocrypha* 5 (1994): 133.
8 Ibid., see also 122–3.
9 Bovon, 'Canonical and Apocryphal Acts', 188, 190; Brock, 'Genre of the Acts of Paul', 133.
10 Bovon, 'Canonical and Apocryphal Acts', 191.
11 The work of Richard Burridge, *What Are the Gospels*, is seen as the definitive study in this field.
12 Sean A. Adams, *The Genre of Acts and Collected Biography* (Cambridge: Cambridge University Press, 2013), 114.
13 See also Pieter J. Lalleman,*The Acts of John: A Two Stage Initiation into Johannine Gnosticism* (Leuven: Peeters, 1998), 46; Jean Marc Prieur, 'Le genre Littéraire du récit biographique', *Acta Andreae II: Praefaitio – Commentarius* (Brepols: Turnhout, 1989), 882; David W. Pao, 'The Genre of the Acts of Andrew', *Apocrypha* 6 (1995): 179–202.
14 Eric Junod, 'Les vies des philosophes et les actes apocryphes: Un dessein similarie?', in *Les Acts Apocryphes de Apôtres: Christianisme et Monde Paien*, ed. F. Bovon (Geneva: Labor et Fides, 1981), 209–19.
15 Tamás Adamik, 'The Influence of the Apocryphal Acts on Jerome's Lives of the Saints', in *The Apocryphal Acts of John*, ed. Jan N. Bremmer (Kampen: Kok Pharos, 1995), 174–5.
16 Quint., *Inst.* 2.4.2.
17 Arist., *Rh.*; Cic., *Inv. Rhet.* and *De or.*
18 Lyndan Warner, *The Ideas of Man and Woman in Renaissance France, Print, Rhetoric and Law* (Surrey: Ashgate, 2011), 192; this point, about ancient writers generally, is also noted by Adams, *The Genre of Acts*, 58.
19 This point is also made by Bruno Gentili and Giovvani Cerri, *History and Biography in Ancient Thought*, trans. L. Murray (Amsterdam: Gieben, 1988), 68, 84.
20 Alistair Fowler, *Kinds of Literature: An Introduction to the Theory of Genres and Modes* (Oxford: Oxford University Press, 1982), 43, 52.
21 Jonathan Culler, *Structuralist Poetics: Structuralism, Linguistics and the Study of Literature* (London: Routledge & Kegan Paul, 1975), 129.
22 Fowler, 'The Life and Death', 83–8; Fowler, *Kinds of Literature*, 164–7.
23 Burridge, *What Are the Gospels*, 47.
24 Thomas, 'Stories without Texts', 288–9.
25 Konstan, 'Acts of Love', 34; see also the related argument concerning 'Open Biography', in *The Art of Biography in Antiquity*, ed. Thomas Hagg (Cambridge: Cambridge University Press, 2012), 99–101.
26 Konstan, 'Acts of Love', 34.
27 Bovon, 'Canonical and Apocryphal Acts', 193–4.
28 *NTA*, 78.
29 For difficulties in joining the Apocryphal Acts corpus together see, Kaestli, 'Response', 123; Dunn, 'Women's Liberation', 247–8; Jensen, *Thekla –Die Apostelin*, 69; see also Perkins, 'Fictional Narratives', 48.
30 Burridge, *What Are the Gospels*, 51.
31 Jensen, *Thekla – Die Apostelin*, 70, 81–2, 110.
32 Richard A. Burridge, *Four Gospels, One Jesus?* (London: SPCK, 1994), 7.

33 Adams, *The Genre of Acts*, 113–14; Gentili and Cerri, *History and Biography*, also argue along similar lines, 68, 84.
34 Adams, *The Genre of Acts*, 113–14.
35 Nikki Shepardson, *Burning Zeal: The Rhetoric of Martyrdom and the Protestant Community in Reformation France 1520–1570* (Cranbury, NJ: Rosemont, 2007), 18.
36 Cynthia White, *The Emergence of Christianity* (Westport, CT: Greenwood, 2007), 59. See also Chapter 5 below.
37 See e.g. Castelli, *Martyrdom and Memory*, 134–71; Corrington Streete, *Redeemed Bodies*, 73–102; Corrington Streete, 'Of Martyrs and Men: Perpetua, Thecla and the Ambiguity of Female Heroism in Early Christianity', in *The Subjective Eye, Essays in Culture, Religion, and Gender in Honor of Margaret R. Miles*, ed. Richard Valantasis (Eugene, OR: Pickwick, 2006), 254–66. See also Kate Cooper, *Band of Angels: The Forgotten World of Early Christian Women* (London: Atlantic, 2013), 87–91.
38 See also Adams, *The Genre of Acts*, 117.
39 On the date and place of origin of the *Decretum Gelasianum* 5 see S. Döpp and W. Geerlings, eds, *Lexikon der antiken christlichen Literatur* (Vienna: Herder Verlag, 1998), 160, who suggest an origin of part of the document in Gaul in the late fifth or early sixth century. However, a later date of origin has been argued by Rosamond McKitterick, *The Carolingians and the Written Word* (Cambridge: Cambridge University Press, 1989), 202–4.
40 Richard Adalbert Lipsius and Maximillianus Bonnet, eds, *Acta Apostolorum Apocryphra, Post Constantinum* (Hildesheim: Georg Olms, 1852; repr. 1990).
41 Lipsius and Bonnet, *Acta Apostolorum*, xcix–ci; see also Léon Vouaux, *Les Actes de Paul et ses Lettres Apocryphes* (Paris: Letouzey et Ané, 1913); *NTA*, 217; Hans-Josef Klauck, *The Apocryphal Acts of the Apostles: An Introduction* (Waco, TX: Baylor University Press, 2008), 49–51.
42 Lipsius and Bonnet, *Acta Apostolorum*, xiii–xvi.
43 See *NTA*, 216–7; J. K. Elliott, *The Apocryphal New Testament* (New York: Oxford University Press, 1993), 352–3.
44 Lipsius and Bonnet, *Acta Apostolorum*, ci–cii.
45 Ibid.
46 Ibid.
47 See Ross Shepard Kraemer, *Unreliable Witnesses, Religion, Gender and History in the Greco-Roman Mediterranean* (New York: Oxford University Press, 2011), 121, n. 15.
48 Willy Rordorf, in collaboration with Pierre Cherix and Rudolphe Kasser, 'Actes de Paul', in *Écrits apocryphes chrétiens*, vol. 1, ed. François Bovon and Pierre Geoltrain (Bibliothèque de la Pléiade; Saint Herblain: Gallimard, 1997), 1115–77.
49 Barrier, *Acts of Paul and Thecla*.
50 On the implied social location of the novels, see Cooper, *Virgin and the Bride*, 22–3. For an illustration of the problem of understanding the readership of ancient texts, see Barrier, *Acts of Paul and Thecla*, 12–15.
51 Cooper, *Virgin and the Bride*, 22–3.
52 In addition to the witness of Tertullian, Jeremy Barrier does discuss the witness of Origen (*Princ.* 2.3) who quotes from a section of the *Acts of Paul* which is now lost but, nevertheless, suggests that readers in Alexandria and possibly Caesarea Maritima, were aware of the *Acts of Paul* by the early to middle third century. Barrier, *The Acts of Paul and Thecla*, 16–17.
53 McGinn, 'The Acts of Thecla', 801, 805.

54 See e.g. Pesthy, 'Thecla among the Fathers'. See also the next section, 'The question of origins and the Pauline tradition'.
55 See Chapter 1 above and also Barrier, *Acts of Paul and Thecla*, 15–21.
56 Haines-Eitzen, *Gendered Palimpsest*, 54, 63–4.
57 Bowie, 'Readership of Greek Novels', 443, 451. Barrier also concludes in his discussion on the *Acts of Paul* that there is a strong possibility that the readers of the ancient novel are the same readers of the Christian novel, Barrier, *Acts of Paul and Thecla*, 19.
58 Larry W. Hurtado, 'Who Read Early Christian Apocrypha?', in *The Oxford Handbook to Early Christian Apocrypha*, ed. Christopher Tuckett and Andrew Gregory (Oxford: Oxford University Press, 2015), 153–66; Christine M. Thomas, *The Acts of Peter, Gospel Literature, and the Ancient Novel* (New York: Oxford University Press, 2003).
59 Klauck, *The Apocryphal Acts*, 50; Willy Rordorf, 'Tradition and Composition in the Acts of Thecla', *Semeia* 38 (1986): 43–53.
60 See Rordorf, 'Tradition and Composition', 44, 52; Brock, 'Genre of the Acts of Paul', 120–1.
61 The dating for this text is around 198–200 CE, see discussion by A. Hilhorst, 'Tertullian on the Acts of Paul', in *The Apocryphal Acts of Paul and Thecla*, ed. Jan N. Bremmer (Kampen: Kok Pharos, 1996), 150.
62 E.g. Schmidt (190–200 CE), Carl Schmidt and Wilhelm Schubart, Πράξεις Παύλου, *Acta Pauli nach dem Papyrus der Hamburger* (Glückstadt and Hamburg: Staatsund Universitäts-Bibliothekm 1936), 127; Schneemelcher (185–195 CE), *NTA*, 235; Peter M. Peterson, *Andrew, Brother of Simon Peter* (Leiden: Brill, 1963), 25–6; M. R. James, *The Apocryphal New Testament* (Oxford: Clarendon Press, 1924), 270; Bremmer, 'Magic, Martyrdom and Women's Liberation', 57.
63 James, *Apocryphal New Testament*, 270; *NTA*, 235; Bremmer, 'Magic, Martyrdom and Women's Liberation', 57; Schmidt, Πράξεις Παύλου, 127.
64 Hilhorst, 'The Acts of Paul', 151–2.
65 *Quodsi quae Pauli perperam scripta sunt, exemplum Theclae ad licentiam mulierum docendi tinguendique defendunt, sciant in Asia presbyterum qui eam scripturam construxit quasi titulo Pauli de suo cumulans, convictum atque confessum id se amore Pauli fecisse, loco decessisse.* I am grateful to Joan Taylor for the Latin translation of this passage.
66 Hilhorst, 'The Acts of Paul', 151.
67 *NTA*, 214.
68 Hilhorst, 'The Acts of Paul', 153–5. It should be noted that the title *Praceij Paulou* is confirmed for the whole of the *Acts of Paul* by PH and P. Heid.
69 *NTA*, 215; this debate is given more depth in the discussion between Steven L. Davies and Thomas W. MacKay. Davies argues that Tertullian is referring to a lost pseudepigraphal letter and not the *Acts of Paul* as we now have it. MacKay, on the other hand, rejects this claim on a text critical basis. Steven Davies, 'Women, Tertullian and the Acts of Paul', *Semeia* 38 (1986): 139; Thomas W. MacKay, 'Response', *Semeia* 38 (1986): 148–9. It should be noted that Schneemelcher argues the assumption that Tertullian's remark relates to lost pseudo-Pauline letter is pure speculation, *NTA*, 215.
70 Hilhorst, 'The Acts of Paul', 155–6.
71 Jan N. Bremmer, 'Aspects of the Acts of Peter: Women, Magic, Place and Date', in *The Apocryphal Acts of Peter: Magic, Miracles and Gnosticism*, ed. Jan N. Bremmer (Leuven: Peeters, 1998), 17; James, *Apocryphal New Testament*, 270; Dunn also argues

that a date near the middle of the second century is by no means unreasonable: Dunn, 'Pauline Legacy', 9–11.
72 Bremmer, 'Aspects of the Acts of Peter', 17.
73 See Chapter 1. See also MacDonald, *Legend*, 7–33; Davies, 'Women, Tertullian', 141–2; see also Rordorf, 'Tradition and Composition', 43–53.
74 Brock, 'Genre of the Acts of Paul', 119, 125–30; McGinn, 'The Acts of Thecla', 801–2.
75 Rordorf, 'Tradition and Composition', 44, 52. Rordorf basis his argument on MacDonald's folklorist finding in his book *Legend* and also on Schneemelcher's work which highlights clumsy redactional activity within the *Acts of Paul and Thecla*. For example, (i) although Paul bears responsibility for the conversion to chastity of many women in Iconium, he is merely cast out of the city while Thecla, an innocent victim, is condemned to die (*APTh.* 21); (ii) on surviving persecution, Thecla then has to seek Paul out as he has disappeared without leaving her any message of his whereabouts (*APTh.* 23); (iii) the enigmatic disappearance of Paul when Thecla faces difficulty in Antioch (*APTh.* 26); (iv) Thecla having to once again seek Paul out at the close of the narrative (*APTh.* 40), Rordorf, 'Tradition and Composition', 48–51; see also Brock, 'Genre of the Acts of Paul', 120–1.
76 See e.g. 1 Thess. 5.2 and 1 Cor. 7.26-27.
77 Jo Ann McNamara, *A New Song: Celibate Women in the First Three Centuries* (New York: Hamworth Press, 1983), 37; Turid Karlsen Seim, 'Ascetic Autonomy? New Perspectives on Single Women in the Early Church', *ST* 43 (1980): 128.
78 Davies, *Revolt of the Widows*, 50, 71.
79 Schüssler Fiorenza, *In Memory*, 311; Susanna Elm, *Virgins of God: The Making of Asceticism in Late Antiquity* (Oxford: Clarendon, 1994), 137–83. It has also been argued that widows ranked among the clergy, see e.g. Karen Jo Torjesen, *When Women Were Priests: Women's Leadership in the Early Church and the Scandal of Their Subordination in the Rise of Christianity* (San Francisco, CA: Harper, 1993), 146. Karen Jo Torjesen, 'Reconstruction of Women's Early Christian History', in *Searching the Scriptures: A Feminist Commentary*, vol. 2, ed. Elisabeth Schüssler Fiorenza, with Ann Brock and Shelly Matthews (New York: Crossroad, 1994), 290–310; Howard I. Marshall, *A Critical and Exegetical Commentary on the Pastoral Epistles* (London: T&T Clark, 2004), 492–5; MacDonald, *Early Christian Women*, 27–40, 154–65.
80 The Pastoral Epistles were written in Paul's name and accepted as Pauline by the early church and the majority of nineteenth-century scholarship. However, despite the fact that some scholars still argue for Pauline authorship, this is no longer the majority view. See Jouette M. Bassler, *1 Timothy, 2 Timothy, Titus* (Nashville, TN: Abingdon, 1996), 17–21; William D. Mounce, *Pastoral Epistles* (Nashville, TN: Thomas Nelson, 2000), xlvi–xlvii; James W. Aageson, *Paul, the Pastoral Epistles and the Early Church* (Peabody, MA: Hendrickson, 2008), 4–7; see also Margaret Y. MacDonald, *The Pauline Churches: A Socio-Historical Study of Institutionalization in the Pauline and Deutero-Pauline Writings* (Cambridge: Cambridge University Press, 1988), Part 3, 'The Pastoral Epistles'; Wayne A. Meeks and John T. Fitzgerald, eds, *The Writings of St. Paul* (New York: Norton, 2007).
81 See, e.g., MacDonald, *Legend*, 55–77; Burrus, 'Chastity', 114–15; see also Lucinda A. Brown, 'Asceticism and Ideology: The Language of Power in the Pastoral Epistles', *Semeia* 57 (1991): 88–94; Jouette M. Bassler, 'Limits and Differentiation: The Calculus of Widows in 1 Timothy 5.3-16', in *A Feminist Companion to the Deutero-Pauline Epistles*, ed. Amy-Jill Levine with Marianne Blickenstaff (Cleveland, OH: Pilgrim Press, 2003), 122–46.

82 See, e.g., 1 Tim. 2.11-15; 1 Tim. 4; 1 Tim. 5.14; 2 Tim. 3.6-8; Tit. 2.4-6.
83 See e.g. Charlotte Methuen, 'The "Virgin Widow": A Problematic Social Role for the Early Church?', *HTR* 90 (1997): 285–98; see also Elm, *Virgins of God*, 137–83, 169; Carolyn Osiek, 'The Widow as Altar: The Rise and Fall of a Symbol', *JECS* 3 (1983): 159–69; Brown, 'Asceticism and Ideology', 77–94; Bassler, 'Limits and Differentiation', 122–46; Jouette M. Bassler, 'The Widows' Tale: A Fresh Look at 1 Tim 5.3-16', *JBL* 103 (1984): 23–41.
84 See e.g. Ross Kraemer, *Her Share of the Blessings: Women's Religions among Pagans, Jews and Christians in the Greco-Roman World* (New York: Oxford University Press, 1992), 140; Roger Gryson, *The Ministry of Women in the Early Church*, trans. Jean Laporte and Mary Louise Hall (Collegeville, MN: Liturgical Press, 1976), 109–12; Mounce, *Pastoral Epistles*, 275; Lilian Portefaix, ' "Good Citizenship" in the Household of God: Women's Position in the Pastorals Reconsidered in the Light of Roman Rule', in *A Feminist Companion to the Deutero-Pauline Epistles*, ed. Amy-Jill Levine and Marianne Blickenstaff (London: T&T Clark, 2003), 148; Amy-Jill Levine, 'Introduction' to *A Feminist Companion to the Deutero-Pauline Epistles*, ed. Amy-Jill Levine and Marianne Blickenstaff (London: T&T Clark, 2003), 13.
85 Bassler, *1 Timothy*, 25–31; Gordon D. Fee, *1 and 2 Timothy, Titus* (Peabody, MA: Hendrickson/Paternoster, 1995), 8–10; Marshall, *Pastoral Epistles*, 41–6.
86 Bassler, *1 Timothy*, 30; Fee, *1 and 2 Timothy*, 8; Marshall, *Pastoral Epistles*, 42.
87 See e.g. MacDonald, *Legend*; Burrus, *Chastity*; Methuen, 'Virgin Widow', 285–98; Bassler, 'Limits and Differentiation', 122–46; Bassler, 'The Widows' Tale', 23–41.
88 See e.g. Torjesen, 'Reconstruction', 290–310; Torjesen, *When Women Were Priests*, 40, 143, 152; MacDonald, *Early Christian Women*, 27–40, 154–65. It is also attested that Christian groups which endorsed women's leadership came to be labelled as heretical, see Kraemer, *Her Share*, 157–73; Karen King, 'Prophetic Power and Women's Authority: The Cast of the Gospel of Mary Magdalene', in *Women Preachers and Prophets through Two Millennia of Christianity*, ed. Beverly M. Kienzle and Pamela J. Walker (Berkeley: University of California Press, 1998), 21–41.
89 For scholars who hold this view, see n. 81 above.
90 Tert., *De bapt.* 17.5.
91 'Women should be silent in the churches. For they are not permitted to speak, but should be subordinate, as the law also says. If there is anything they desire to know, let them ask their husbands at home. For it is shameful for a woman to speak in church' (1 Cor. 14.34-35 NRSV). In this verse, we find both the word γὒνή (woman/wife) and ἀνήρ (man/husband). Most English translations render the word ἀνήρ as husband and γὒνή as wife. However, the counterpart of husband is 'wife', not 'woman'. Schüssler Fiorenza argues that the injunction does not pertain to all but solely to wives of Christians. Since 1 Cor. 7.32-35 makes it clear that not all women in the community were married or had Christian spouses, they could not, therefore, ask their husbands at home. Schüssler Fiorenza, *In Memory*, 230–1.
92 Among the textual variants a number of Western manuscripts place 1 Cor. 14.34-35 after 14.40, while the mid sixth-century Codex Fuldensis puts the verses in the margins after 14.33. See B. M. Metzger, *A Textual Commentary on the Greek New Testament* (New York: United Bible Societies, 1971), 565; however, no manuscript omits the verses. A number of scholars have concluded that the verses are a post-Pauline interpolation, see e.g. G. D. Fee, *The First Epistle to the Corinthians* (Grand-Rapids, MI: Eerdmans, 1987), 699–708; H. Conzelmann, *I Corinthians*, trans. James W. Leitch (Philadelphia, PA: Fortress, 1975), 246; Philip B. Payne, 'Fuldensis, Sigla for Variants in Vaticanus and in 1 Corinthians 14.34-5', *NTS* 41 (1995): 240–62.

93 For recent treatments of the pseudepigraphal character of these Pauline letters, see Jörg Frey, Jens Herzer, Martina Janssen and Clare K. Rothschild, eds, *Pseudepigraphic und Verfasserfiktion in frühchristlichen Briefen* (Tübingen: Mohr Siebeck, 2009).
94 MacDonald, *Legend*, 54–77.
95 Hylen, *A Modest Apostle*, 4, 17.
96 Ibid., 74.
97 Dunn, *Women's Liberation*, 250–2.
98 Stephen J. Davis, *The Cult of Saint Thecla: A Tradition of Women's Piety in Late Antiquity* (Oxford: Oxford University Press, 2001). The site near Ephesus is called Meriemlik or Ayatekla and is just south of Silifke (Seleucia). See MacDonald, *Legend*, 92–3; Kate Cooper, 'A Saint in Exile: The Early Medieval Thecla at Rome and Meriamlik', *Hagiographica* 2 (1995): 1–23. Late in the fourth century the pilgrim Egeria (*Itin.* 23.1-6) visited the site, where both men and women lived as cave anchorites, and read a work she calls the *Acts of Holy Thecla*. John Wilkinson, *Egeria's Travels*, rev. ed. (Warminster: Aris and Philips, 1981), 121–2, 288–92.
99 See Davis, *Cult of Saint Thecla*, esp. his appendix A, 195–220, and for illustrations, see figures 7–32; see also David R. Cartlidge and J. Keith Elliott, *Art and the Christian Apocrypha* (London: Routledge, 2001), 134–71; and Claudia Nauerth and Rüdiger Warns, *Thekla. Ihre Bilder in der frühchristlichen Kunst: Göttinger Orientforschungen, Studien zur spätantiken und frühchristlichen Kunst*, Bd. 3 (Wiesbaden: Harrassowitz, 1981).
100 Manuscript copyists originally attribute this text to the fifth-century bishop, Basil of Seleucia. However, Gilbert Dagron has contested this ascription on the basis of internal evidence within the text. In *Miracle* 12, the anonymous author actually attacks Basil, making it unlikely that Basil himself authored the text, see Gilbert Dagron and Marie Dupré de la Tour, *Vie et Miracles de Saint Thècle. Texte Grec. Traduction et Commentaire* (Brussels: Société des Bollandistes, 1978), 13–15. For the dating of the text see Dagron, *Vie et Miracles*, 17–18.
101 MacDonald, *Legend*, 92–3; Corrington Streete, *Redeemed Bodies*, 93–4. For the text see, Dagron, *Vie et Miracles*.

3

Methodology

Feminist hermeneutics

How can we assess whether a text is liberative, or empowering, for women? Given that Thecla's renunciation of sexuality and donning of male clothing has been construed as constituting evidence of female agency and independence, we need to be clear about what assumptions we use in making assessments.

In her seminal work on the subject, Schüssler Fiorenza has highlighted how the biblical decrees and depictions of women reflect the historical overlay of patriarchy in which the texts were written rather than a legitimate theological expression.[1] As a challenge to this male-centred perspective, Schüssler Fiorenza has developed one of the most comprehensive hermeneutical frameworks which utilizes a historical-critical method to reconstruct early Christian origins, from the gender-inclusive nature of the Jesus movement to the more patriarchal culture of the New Testament period.[2] She offers a fourfold procedure which consists of (1) a hermeneutic of suspicion, (2) a hermeneutic of remembrance that uncovers women's agency in foundational Christian tradition, (3) a hermeneutic of proclamation that relates this reconstruction to the Christian community and (4) a hermeneutic of creative actualization that expresses feminism in ritual, prayer, hymns, banners and art. These four different parts are outlined in her book *Bread Not Stone*.[3] Each of these approaches constitutes for Schüssler Fiorenza a different perspective. However, while the final three elements of her hermeneutic are extraneous to this project, it is her groundbreaking 'hermeneutics of suspicion', a tool which has effectively revolutionized biblical scholarship and, perhaps, her greatest contribution to feminist theology and biblical studies, which is most intrinsic to this study.[4]

The 'hermeneutics of suspicion' is a term coined by Paul Ricoeur to describe the practice of reading texts 'against the grain' to expose their repressed hidden meaning. The premise of this hermeneutic is that we must 'look upon the whole consciousness primarily as "false" consciousness'.[5] This approach is championed by Schüssler Fiorenza; she too highlights how interpretation is occasioned by a gap between the real meaning of the text and its apparent meaning, and she advocates questioning the surface construction of the text and becoming a 'resistant reader'.[6] However, while this aspect of the hermeneutic of suspicion, of reading against the grain of the text, is an important facet of Schüssler Fiorenza's approach, it is important to bear in mind that resistance to the text does not encompass the entire hermeneutic of suspicion. Rather, it recognizes that the biblical texts and their interpretations have been written by men, about men and, predominantly, for men. It, therefore, cautions anyone who reads such texts to be wary of the fact that they can be oppressive for women. This hermeneutic thus calls into question the traditional, or 'malestream', position within scholarship, which overlooks the fact that the historical process of interpreting the content and scope of the canon was charged with androcentric bias.[7] Schüssler Fiorenza argues that

> [a] hermeneutic of suspicion does not presuppose the feminist authority and truth of the Bible, but takes as its starting point the assumption that biblical texts and their interpretations are androcentric and serve patriarchal functions. Since most of the biblical writings are ascribed to male authors and most of the biblical interpreters in church and academy are men, such an assumption is justified.[8]

Schüssler Fiorenza underscores the fact that the biblical text is not an unclouded window to the historical reality of women. Rather, 'the Bible is a perspectival rhetorical discourse constructing theological worlds and symbolic universes in particular historical-political situations'.[9] Starting from this premise, the hermeneutics of suspicion then seeks to identify the androcentric and patriarchal discourse embedded within the text. The hermeneutic of suspicion, therefore, aims

> to explore the liberating or oppressive values and visions inscribed in the text by identifying the androcentric patriarchal character and dynamics of the text. Since biblical texts are written in androcentric language within patriarchal cultures, a hermeneutic of suspicion does not start with the assumption that the Martha and Mary story is a feminist liberating text just because its central characters are women. Rather it seeks to investigate *how and why* the text constructs the story of these women as it does.[10]

What is of extreme importance here is Schüssler Fiorenza's point that a hermeneutic of suspicion 'does not start with the assumption' that a text is feminist just because its 'central characters are women'. As the discussion in Chapter 1 highlighted, because the *Acts of Paul and Thecla* focuses on one female protagonist and because she is eventually commissioned by Paul to 'go and teach the Word of God' (*APTh*. 41), there has been a real tendency among scholars to promote the text as a female-affirming narrative. It does, therefore, seem that because of the text's single-minded focus on the figure of Thecla, scholars have either been blinded to or, perhaps more aptly, willing to 'turn a blind eye' to the more androcentric elements of the text. This particular hermeneutic, however, insists that we question and investigate *how* and *why* texts are presented to us as they are, and, it is not simply about highlighting the negative, it investigates both the liberating *and* oppressive elements of the text. We must be vigilant and consistently conscious that, when it comes to biblical texts, we are dealing with a distorted record from which much has been omitted, and much that is included is unreliable because historically, until recently, all influential biblical scholars have been men who were steeped in a patriarchal Church and tradition.

A hermeneutics of suspicion would thus prompt a reader to question why it is that a text, such as the *Acts of Paul and Thecla*, which is held up by scholars as empowering and affirming to women, contains sado-erotic representations of a woman. Previously, in its concern to emphasize an empowered and liberated Thecla, scholarship has marginalized or ignored this material. A hermeneutics of suspicion calls for more incredulity and scepticism where male-authored texts are concerned. It prompts a much deeper analysis of texts which contain female representations which denigrate women, even if they do appear to have a 'happy ending' for women.

Any text which portrays a woman as a beautiful object of lust, and includes voyeuristic sado-erotic treatment, demeans her worth and reduces her to the level of her sexuality. Although Thecla is admired for her δύναμις (power, *APTh*. 22), the text does very little to develop and underscore this quality. Rather, the most vivid and memorable descriptions are in terms of her sexuality.[11] When a woman is objectified to this degree, the hermeneutic of suspicion immediately asks, 'Whose gratification is being served by this picture?'

Additionally, in Schüssler Fiorenza's view, we all carry certain biases. There is no purely objective or neutral interpretation of any text. Schüssler Fiorenza challenges the alleged objectivity of positivism and insists that history is best figured not as an accurate record of the past but as a 'perspectival discourse that seeks to articulate a living memory for the present and the future'.[12] Each and every interpreter is affected by social location, interests and commitments. Perhaps the most unbiased approach is to be self-aware, conscious of our bias and social location, as well as the historical consciousness. Nevertheless, as a woman reading male-authored texts, female interpreters hold certain advantages. Sandra Schneiders notes that

> [i]t is characteristic of ideology that it is invisible to the one whose bias it underwrites. Usually only those who do not participate in the power system … are aware that what seem to be simply 'the way things are' is actually an oppressive conceptual, cultural and social system. The 'hermeneutical advantage' of the oppressed is precisely this ability to see, from the margins of social reality, what is second nature to the beneficiaries of the social system.[13]

Thus, as women, we come to a male-authored text with a certain edge; our distinctive viewpoint from the margins enables new perceptions and interpretations to surface. Schneiders goes on to argue that feminist interpreters must, therefore, 'suspect both the text and the history of its interpretation of anti-woman bias … At the same time they must propose an alternative stance to the false objectivity whose existence (and even possibility) they deny.'[14] Schneiders's approach serves to underscore Schüssler Fiorenza's hermeneutics of suspicion, which provides us with a heightened awareness that the surviving texts of early Christianity are distilled through androcentric and patriarchal perspectives, perspectives which regularly sought to silence and disparage the endeavours and experiences of women.

In the present study, the hermeneutic of suspicion will be rigorously applied in terms of the detailed examinations of the three subjects identified for review. The sex of the author itself may not make a difference to whether the text is essentially androcentric, instilling patriarchal values, as noted above.[15] It is assumed that since a text was popular and utilized in numerous churches imbued with patriarchal values for many centuries, it is appropriate to employ this hermeneutical strategy in its analysis.

Problems of male textuality and women as a vehicle of rhetoric

In addition to using the hermeneutic of suspicion, this project is also shaped by methodological theories concerning women's social roles in antiquity, which see women in literature as constructs by which men could work out their views on sexuality and gender. Following the work of Peter Brown and others, it is now believed that Greek writers sometimes used women in a manner that bore little resemblance to the lives of actual women who struggled to understand, express, criticize and experiment with the problems and contradictions of their culture.[16] Brown writes,

> The girl who found herself among the 'brides of Christ' was spoken of by the clergy as a human *ex voto*. She was no longer a woman; she had become 'a sacred vessel dedicated to the Lord' … To her male admirers, the consecrated virgin stood for continuity in its most pure state … Her physical integrity came to carry an exceptionally high charge of meaning (*for males*) … A sense of the uncanny stability of the life of the virgin, and of the sacred nature of the integrity of her physical body, tended to link the virgins of the church, by association, to all that was most immovable and sacred in the midst of the cities.[17]

Where Thecla, in particular, is concerned, he notes of her male and female followers, 'the Thecla of the day-to-day miracles eluded the precise and radical definition of her person … Her human attributes swallowed up in an "angelic" shimmer.'[18] Women were then often merely mouthpieces for their male authors, whose obsessions or interests they frequently expressed. This artistic license exercised by male authors was a dominant characteristic of classical Greek high culture; it means that distinguishing the voice or perspective of historical women, against those of the author, presents a daunting challenge to the historian. Women in literature are now often viewed as signs or metaphors in conversations that male authors are having with one another. Here the female in the text becomes a representative figure that is used to negotiate male concerns, interests or identity. The hermeneutical climate, therefore, shifts increasingly away from historical 'reconstruction' to an appreciation of the ideology and rhetorical techniques that shape representations of women in ancient texts.[19]

Since women in antiquity were thought to embody a peculiar and undefined nature, they provided a convenient literary tool with which to express and develop ideas. Their peculiar nature was, at times, seen to create a vulnerable link in the world, allowing destructive forces to enter society, an idea which quite clearly finds its expression in Tertullian's description of women as the 'Devil's Gateway'.[20] For Tertullian, women represented a weakness in the defences of the Church against a pagan society and its corrupting influence.[21] As far as Christianity was concerned, however, this gateway that women represented was not always negative and could be utilized for Christianity's advancement. Since women's natural domain was that of the private sphere, they could easily influence not only members of their direct family but also those of pagan households.[22] Women also had easier access to prisons, which enabled them to act as messengers and intermediaries between communities and Christian martyrs.[23] Men, on the other hand, would often remain in hiding for fear of persecution. A woman's undefined nature, on the one hand, and her usefulness, on the other, meant that women soon provided the perfect literary tool for Christian men grappling with issues of strength and loyalty in a pagan environment.

Brown argues that it was an exploration of both women's vulnerability and resilience, and the Church's struggle in an often hostile society, which prompted the writings of the Apocryphal Acts.[24] Consequently, these texts may be seen to reflect this tendency of males in the ancient world to use women to think with. The focus at this point has shifted to questions of textual representation and construction where women are viewed as the literary creations of men. This approach seeks to avoid a simplistic portrayal of viewing women represented in the texts as tangible women, as well as a hypothetical reconstruction based on assumptions of women's historical reality.

Averil Cameron demonstrates that this literary process, of appropriating women's low status as a means of attacking one's enemies, is greatly evidenced in the polemic between pagan writers and Christians.[25] The narrative treatment of women thus served to symbolize aspects of tensions to be found among men. Cameron also discusses how women stood as agents of rhetoric between men in an earlier essay, where she traces this development into the third and fourth centuries. Although her evidence is taken from a later period, she highlights the fact that this representation of women was present in the earliest beginnings of Christianity.[26] Clark similarly examines this rhetorical development in the works of female Christian *vitae*, where again women function as a trope or mouthpiece for the male authors themselves.[27]

As noted in Chapter 1, Cooper employs this approach in her book *The Virgin and the Bride*.[28] The ancient rhetoric of gender and sexuality is here seen as a metaphor for power relations between males. Cooper argues that, from this perspective, ancient writings tell us little about women and gender relations and more about the power dynamics between men. For Cooper, women are used as rhetorical or conceptual devices in a male arena.[29]

Cooper highlights how this rhetorical use of women provided an indirect and polite way by which lower status ascetic bishops dictated and moderated the behaviour of more powerful and eminent men. These 'marginal' Christians had their own civic status and standing, which meant they might balk at deferring in matters of religion to men whose credentials were not always so distinguished as their own, hence the usefulness of the rhetoric of womanly influence. The success of a vision of Christianity which privileged ascetic claims over civic standing would depend on how delicately the celibate handled this tension. At issue was the forging of a powerful new mode of male authority, which challenged a long-held consensus on the nature of the common good.[30]

Cooper says, therefore, that the use of this *topos* should be viewed as an element of cultural continuity with the empire. What distinguishes the Christian use of *topos* is its ability to veil change in terms of the social order.[31] These texts were, therefore, often the result of competition between two groups of late Roman men. On the one hand, there were married men in positions of civic or cultural importance (some married to baptized women, some themselves baptized, others strictly polytheist) and, on the other, celibate men (usually of a lesser rank) who wished to advise the married. In an impasse between men, the introduction of a third, female element diffused the ever-present consciousness of ranking among males.[32] The rhetoric of womanly influence made it possible to gain an advantage over these men while avoiding alienation and confrontation, a destabilizing move which favoured the man who wished to undermine the status.[33]

Overall, then, the current concern is to read the *Acts of Paul and Thecla* on the level of representation and not historical reality.[34] The key issue is whether the representation of Thecla may be construed as empowering; if Cooper is right, then Thecla is a woman that men used 'to think with'.

Having determined that this project will be engaging with the hermeneutics of suspicion, as pioneered by Schüssler Fiorenza, and that the text will be read with an appreciation of the ideology and rhetorical techniques that shape representations of women in ancient texts, it remains for me to explicate the gender specifics of my approach.

Gender theory

There are many modern theorists writing in regard to sex and gender in antiquity, and while most contemporary critiques of sexuality have their origins in the work of Michel Foucault and his three-volume *History of Sexuality*,[35] it is the work of David Halperin that is particularly relevant to this project.[36] Halperin has contrasted the modern construction of 'sexuality' with that of the classical Greek period, arguing that Greeks viewed intercourse as a gendered sociopolitical act, and explained sex acts by using the gender binary: masculine-penetrative-active and feminine-receptive-passive.[37] Halperin's pioneering study underscored the important insight that ancient Greek sex acts, 'active' and 'passive', were gendered 'masculine' and 'feminine', respectively. This view was strengthened further by the now classic study *Before Sexuality: The Construction of Erotic Experience in the Ancient Greek World*, a collection of essays that reaffirmed his stance regarding the gendered and social nature of Greek sex.[38] Although some scholars continue to use the term 'sexuality' and even 'homosexuality' to describe Greek and Roman sexual ideologies, the majority of scholars now acknowledge the modern development of 'sexuality' and the gendered nature of the ancient penetrator-penetrated framework for sexual identity.[39]

Foucault's work has also received further elaboration in the work of classicists such as Jonathan Walters and Holt Parker.[40] These scholars also highlight models of gender, particularly the male dominator/penetrator models in antiquity which consider performance to be an essential. Parker has strengthened the view about the gendered nature of sexual acts by arguing that in Roman sexual ideology, 'active' is by definition male and 'passive' female.[41] For Romans, the names given to sexual actors identified their gender status. Parker introduces the model of the 'Teratogenic Grid' upon which Romans identified sexual actions as person penetrated (*pathicus* or 'passive, not man'; *femina* or 'woman') or penetrator (*vir* or 'Roman citizen male').[42]

It should be pointed out that these theories and paradigms are not intended to provide a historically accurate 'handbook' of knowledge of sex and gender identity in antiquity. Since the theories in question are based on elite perspectives, we should remain cautious as to just how widespread such conceptions and practices in the ancient world were. Nevertheless, we can at least work on the premise that at least some of these notions were of relevance to writers in antiquity. These models, therefore, provide a useful framework for understanding how differently gender, sex and sexuality were understood within the ancient context and will be utilized in my examination of elements in the text of *Acts of Paul and Thecla*.

However, as with all models and paradigms that are put forward, there are always exceptions to the rule. For example, scholars have drawn attention to the fact that some women in antiquity, in particular elite, economically advantaged women, were not always passive and could, therefore, be active in terms of their gendered and sexed performance.[43] Of course, within the *Acts of Paul and Thecla*, aspects of Thecla's representation, such as preaching and teaching, breaking away from family and the prospect of marriage, display characteristics which are gendered masculine. In addition, the practice of asceticism (ἐγκράτεια, self-control) and cross-dressing, which again form part of Thecla's representation, could also be read as woman becoming 'active' in terms of gender performance. Moreover, in regard to Walter's Teratogenic grid, Maud Gleason has demonstrated how an effeminate orator, displaying very feminine traits, could employ a culturally shameful performance to win an audience's approval. Much like parody, the orator reversed the normal patterns of masculinity.[44] Such exceptions must always be taken into account. In this respect, while models and trends are useful to work with, we should remain alert to the fact that no model can be taken as being relevant to the whole of society.

My approach

In the past, in trying to view Thecla in terms of her impact on and for women, important aspects of the text were neglected, de-emphasized and even excused. However, by coming to the text with a hermeneutics of suspicion and by interrogating the complex strands that inextricably link gender and power relations, I hope to create a new and radical reading of the text. The focus then is to move beyond simply concentrating on aspects which are liberative (aspects which see Thecla as liberated from the arena and from marriage) and instead to look at the whole; to bring to light facets of the text that have previously been neglected or taken for granted, these include a reassessment of the heroine's alleged gender transformation and her voyeuristic sado-erotic treatment.

Textual readings in terms of gender also help to define power relationship and to challenge those aspects of social 'realities' which appear 'natural' or 'given'. In focusing upon the male and female representations I will also be deconstructing the gendered and sexed categories in order to examine how they interrelate with other aspects of the gendered norms of the period and how they sustain power over women. From a purely literary perspective, what do the gender representations reveal about power and social ideology? With a view to exposing the underlying ideologies operative within the text, I will be exploring how the construction of representations and the language employed persuades readers and orients them to a particular world view. Thus, within this study, a significant emphasis will also be placed upon where the concepts of power and domination are situated within the discourse. In this respect, my methodology follows on the trajectory of earlier feminist and liberationist approaches, in that I seek to expose areas of masculine domination and consider how they function. This study is thus positioned on the intersection of three major forms of analysis: literary representation, gender studies and feminist analysis. These are the basic analytical tools I use to read and interpret the text.

The gender specifics of my approach

While I have expounded the primary methods and theories that inform and influence my argumentation above, this chapter does not, however, provide an exhaustive list of the theorists with whom I engage. Within this project, I will be making use of a varied number of methodologies that will help to inform my perspective, interpretation and reading of the text. For example, in Chapter 5, I engage with broader, modern feminist perspectives and methods. Here theorists such as Susanne Kappeler, Andrea Dworkin, Catherine MacKinnon and others that have framed my thinking come to the fore.[45] Engaging with modern theories in this way permits multiple intersections between ancient texts and our own modern interpretations of them, and allows for rich and varied readings, such as those found within the volume edited by Amy Richlin, entitled *Pornography and Representation in Greece and Rome*.[46] This collection of essays applies modern feminist theorizing to ancient Greek and Roman texts. Here, too, ancient Graeco-Roman rhetoric and modern interpretations converge and crossover at many points. Engaging with modern theories in this way allows for an analysis which exposes the underlying ideologies and values embedded in the text and helps to elucidate and expound ancient texts.

The feature of Thecla 'becoming male' also forms an important component in the discussion about gender. Thus, in Chapter 4, 'Female Beheadings', alongside the models put forward by Halperin, Walters, Parker and Gleason, I will also be looking at ancient conceptions of sex-distinction which deemed the ideal body to be that of a man. The female body thus represented an inferior version of the normative male body. Beginning with Aristotle, this predominant model for conceptualizing the body in the ancient world was significantly different from our own. Since males were seen to be perfection, it allowed for the notion of women having to become men in order to achieve salvation.[47] I will, therefore, elucidate some particular methodologies I employ within the relevant chapters themselves, to better address the various facets of the text and to shift the attention more overtly from method to text, allowing a more natural conversation between text and theory to develop.

As this conversation between text, method and interpreter evolves, it will become necessary, throughout the chapters that follow, to refer to, and speak of, the 'author' and/or 'narrator' of the text. The relationship between author, reader and audience is a complex one and has been complicated further by elements of narrative and literary criticism. Before proceeding, therefore, it will be necessary to clarify certain ambiguities that are inherent within those terms. Thus, although the short discussion which follows departs somewhat from the feminist emphasis of the project, it is, nevertheless, important to delve, albeit briefly, into the realms of narrative criticism which complicates a simplistic notion of an 'author' and 'narrator'.

A word about the author and narrator

To begin with, as noted above, undoubtedly the *Acts of Paul and Thecla* has been subjected to an extremely long and complex editorial process before reaching its final form. Since the story has undergone many revisions and alterations by any number of redactors, how do we legitimately speak of an 'author' of the text? And secondly, how do we distinguish between the 'narrator' and the 'author' of the text, because there can be a distinct difference between the two?

At the outset, modern concepts of authorship may not be helpful at this point, and our own presuppositions are tested as we try to formulate a likely alternative. If there was a historical Thecla, and there were oral stories about her in circulation, then any original 'author' would have deliberately selected these to record, but if the origins of the *Acts of Paul and Thecla* are essentially in fictional stories, then the author may be seen more as a novelist composing a tale. Of course, there may well have been some middle path between these two. In terms of either, the text of the *Acts of Paul and Thecla* may essentially have been considered one that could be modified for a long period of time. 'Closed' texts, like scriptural books of the Old Testament or the classics of Graeco-Roman literature, are quite different from many of the texts in circulation within early churches, which can show extreme variables in the manuscript tradition, allowing for copyists to make small or large alterations; these are then 'open'.[48] Thomas argues that in the transmission of an 'open' text, the copyist 'approaches the freedom and autonomy that we generally associate with a performer or an author. Their relationship to an original creator is not that of redactor to author, but of author to author.'[49] Thomas notes that, despite the long process of evolution many texts undergo, ultimately there is a creative process (much like that undertaken by an original author) which shapes the final version of a text. The malleability and multiformity of such texts admit the hermeneutical 'space' for adjustment for the predilections and interests of an author.

This is helpful in terms of understanding the comment by Tertullian (*De bapt.* 17.5) that an Asian presbyter, keen to add to Paul's reputation, wrote the *Acts of Paul and Thecla* for his own particular purpose.[50] Whatever traditions he was working with, he was an individual author that could be identified by Tertullian: either he created a fictional text or he compiled and shaped traditions for a particular purpose, with an understanding that these were 'open' to his creative development. Even if we disregard this evidence from Tertullian regarding the *Acts of Paul and Thecla*, when it comes to texts such as the Apocryphal Acts as a whole,[51] the fluidity of the stories allow for innovation and the manipulation or shaping of the received tradition by a single author. The fact that these texts permit a particular stylization of narrative elements that we would normally associate with an author means that we may, in keeping with Thomas's views, properly and legitimately speak of an 'author' of the *Acts of Paul and Thecla*. The text of the *Acts of Paul and Thecla*, as we possess it, thus bears the final imprint of a probable male author/creator or composer. Fundamentally, then, even if stories of Thecla were preserved in women's circles, the final form of the text or story was shaped by a male person and this version of the story eventually influenced subsequent generations of Thecla devotees. Having concluded that we can legitimately speak of an 'author' of the *Acts of Paul and Thecla*, broadly conceived, how then do we distinguish between the author and the narrator of a text?

Contemporary models of narrative criticism distinguish between 'author', 'implied author' (the author's second self: the character a reader may attribute to an author and which may differ from author's personality) and the 'narrator' (the teller of the story). The author is the historical person who does the actual writing or creates a given piece of literature, whereas a narrator is a fictional entity within a text that communicates and transmits information between the text and reader, forming a link between author and reader. Within this process, the real author sometimes creates a literary version of her/himself which the reader comes to know through the medium of the narrative, called the 'implied author'. Both the 'implied author' and the 'narrator' are, therefore, concepts that refer to entities constructed on the basis of textual features; while the 'author' refers to some real historical agent. The introduction of the 'implied author' concept is linked to work with the notion of an unreliable narrator where the narrator's values diverge strikingly from those of the implied author.[52]

However, where the *Acts of Paul and Thecla* is concerned, the readers encounter a 'reliable' narrator. That is, since the story is being told from a Christian perspective, the narrator is in accord with the values and beliefs which undergird and inform the story. There is, therefore, a close identity of values between author and narrator, and no conflict exists between the values and norms of the author and those of the narrator. Since the narrator may be assumed to be the author's spokesperson, the distinction between the two is negligible. As a Christian retelling of a story, the literary goals of both narrator and author are the same; they both have a shared attitude, standpoint and values to the events that are taking place and wish to communicate these to the reader. Thus, although it is important, at times, to distinguish between author and narrator, in this instance, the 'narratorial' voice present in the text can be seen to be indistinguishable from the 'authorial' voice, since there is no 'fictional' narrator at odds with the values of the real author. It is, therefore, not so essential here to distinguish between the narrator and author.

Having concluded that it is perfectly legitimate to refer to an 'author' of the *Acts of Paul and Thecla*, and that, given both author and narrator speak with 'one' voice, it is possible to use both terms interchangeably, I will now proceed to examine the extent to which the *Acts of Paul and Thecla* provides an empowering and female affirming representation of a woman.

Working with a hermeneutics of suspicion, I will consider how gender is constructed within the text and to assess how the gender politics illuminates the structure of narrative. Is Thecla a liberated, winning woman in a 'feminist' drama, or is her representation, from a feminist perspective, quite flawed?

Notes

1. Schüssler Fiorenza, *In Memory*.
2. See ibid., 68–95, for a discussion of her historical-critical method.
3. Elisabeth Schüssler Fiorenza, *Bread Not Stone: The Challenge of Feminist Biblical Interpretation* (Boston, MA: Beacon, 2002), 15–22. See also, Schüssler Fiorenza, *In Memory*, especially chapters 1–3. Schüssler Fiorenza has now developed this fourfold hermeneutic into a multidimensional approach, see Elisabeth Schüssler Fiorenza, *Wisdom Ways: Introducing Feminist Biblical Interpretation* (Maryknoll, NY: Orbis, 2001).
4. See, e.g., Schüssler Fiorenza, *In Memory*, 3–40; Schüssler Fiorenza, *Bread Not Stone*, 93–115; Elisabeth Schüssler Fiorenza, 'Text and Reality – Reality as Text: The Problem of a Feminist Historical and Social Reconstruction Based on Texts', *Studia Theologica* 43 (1989): 19–34.
5. Paul Ricoeur, *Freud and Philosophy: An Essay on Interpretation*, trans. Denis Savage (New Haven, CT: Yale University Press, 1970), 33.
6. Elisabeth Schüssler Fiorenza, *But She Said: Feminist Practices of Biblical Interpretation* (Boston, MA: Beacon, 1992), 35–7, 215; Schüssler Fiorenza, *Wisdom Ways*, 175–7, 183–6.
7. Schüssler Fiorenza, *Bread Not Stone*, 15–16.
8. Ibid.
9. Schüssler Fiorenza, *But She Said*, 47.
10. Ibid., 57.
11. See, e.g., *APTh*. 22, 25-26, 29, 33-35, 38, where Thecla is depicted as naked, beautiful, stripped and exposed.
12. Schüssler Fiorenza, *In Memory*, xxii.
13. Sandra M. Schneiders, *The Revelatory Text: Interpreting the New Testament as Sacred Scripture* (Collegeville, MN: Liturgical Press, 1999), 351.
14. Ibid.
15. See Chapter 1.
16. Peter Brown, *The Body and Society: Men, Women and Sexual Renunciation in Early Christianity* (London: Faber, 1990), 153–5. See also Lawrence M. Wills, *The Jewish Novel in the Ancient World* (New York: Cornell University Press, 1995), 132–57; Sandra R. Joshel, 'Female Desire and the Discourse of Empire: Tacitus's Messalina', *Signs* 21 (1995): 50–82; and also Sandra R. Joshel, 'The Body Female and the Body Politic: Livy's Lucretia and Verginia', in *Pornography and Representation in Greece and Rome*, ed. Amy Richlin (New York: Oxford University Press, 1992), 112–30; Shelly Matthews, 'Thinking of Thecla, Issues in Feminist Historiography', *JFSR* 12 (2002): 46–50.
17. Brown, *The Body and Society*, 260, 270–1.
18. Ibid., 328.
19. E.g., as noted in Chapter 1, D'Angelo reads women's portraits in Luke-Acts from an ideological perspective. Her thesis is that the representation of women in Luke-Acts represents less about historical women per se and more about the author and his

desire to promote an image of Christianity that conformed to Roman civic ideals and values. D'Angelo, 'Women in Luke-Acts'.
20 Tert., *De cul. Fem.*, 1.1.5 (*ANF* 4.14).
21 Ibid., 2.11.13 (*ANF* 4.22-25). Concerning women's 'true' nature and the need to conceal and control it, see H. R. Hays, *The Dangerous Sex: The Myth of Feminine Evil* (London: Methuen, 1966); Rene Girard, *Violence and the Sacred*, trans. Patrick Gregory (Baltimore, MD: John Hopkins University Press, 1977); see also Averil Cameron, 'Virginity as Metaphor: Women and the Rhetoric of Early Christianity', in *History as Text: The Writing of Ancient History*, ed. Averil Cameron (London: Duckworth, 1989), 181.
22 MacDonald, *Early Christian Women*, 45.
23 Brown, *The Body and Society*, 154.
24 Ibid., 153-5.
25 Cameron, 'Virginity as Metaphor', 188-99.
26 Averil Cameron, 'Early Christianity and the Discourse of Female Desire', in *Women in Ancient Societies: An Illusion of the Night*, ed. Leonie S. Archer, Susan Fischer and Maria Wyke (Basingstoke: Macmillan, 1994), 152-68.
27 Elizabeth A. Clark, 'Holy Women, Holy Words: Early Christian Women, Social History and the "Linguistic Turn"', *JECS* 6 (1998): 420-7.
28 Cooper, *Virgin and the Bride*, 19, 54-5.
29 Ibid., 55.
30 Cooper, 'Insinuations', 163.
31 Ibid., 155.
32 Ibid., 163.
33 Cooper, *Virgin and the Bride*, 55.
34 I would like emphasize that despite the fact that this particular project is not focused upon history, and although texts cannot be regarded as open windows affording glimpses of women in antiquity, I do believe that it is still possible to find traces of historical kernels within highly rhetorical and ideological texts. See, e.g., the work of Joan E. Taylor, 'The Women "Priests" of Philo De Vita Contemplativa: Reconstructing the Therapeutai', in *On the Cutting Edge: The Study of Women in the Biblical World*, ed. Jane Schaberg, Alice Bach and Esther Fuchs (New York: Continuum, 2004), 102-3; Maxine L. Grossman, 'Reading for Gender in the Damascus Document', *Dead Sea Discoveries* 11 (2004): 212-39. Castelli also highlights the importance of understanding how writings that appear on the surface not to relate to women or to women's history actually do. See Elizabeth Castelli, 'Romans', in *Searching the Scriptures*, ed. Elisabeth Schüssler Fiorenza, with Ann Graham Brock and Shelly Matthews (New York: Crossroad, 1994), 280-1.
35 Michel Foucault, *The History of Sexuality*, vol. 1: *An Introduction*, trans. Robert Hurley (New York: Vintage Books, 1990); Michel Foucault, *The History of Sexuality*, vol. 2: *The Use of Pleasure*, trans. Robert Hurley (London: Penguin Books, 1984); Michel Foucault, *The History of Sexuality*, vol. 3: *The Care of the Self*, trans. Robert Hurley (London: Penguin Books, 1984).
36 See David M. Halperin, *One Hundred Years of Homosexuality and Other Essays on Greek Love* (London: Routledge, 1990), 15-40.
37 Ibid., 21, 32-3.
38 David M. Halperin, John J. Winkler and Froma I. Zeitlin, eds, *Before Sexuality: The Construction of Erotic Experience in the Ancient Greek World* (Princeton, NJ: Princeton University Press, 1990).

39 Marilyn B. Skinner, *Sexuality in Greek and Roman Culture* (Oxford: Blackwell, 2005), 18; see also Holt N. Parker, 'The Teratogenic Grid', in *Roman Sexualities*, ed. Judith P. Hallett and Marilyn B. Skinner (Princeton, NJ: Princeton University Press, 1997), 47–65.
40 Jonathan Walters, 'Invading the Roman Body: Manliness and Impenetrability in Roman Thought', in *Roman Sexualities*, ed. Judith P. Hallett and Marilyn B. Skinner, 29–43; Parker, 'Teratogenic Grid'.
41 Parker, 'Teratogenic Grid', 48.
42 Parker, 'Teratogenic Grid', 49.
43 See e.g., Lin Foxhall, 'Pandora Unbound: A Feminist Critique of Foucault's *History of Sexuality*', in *Rethinking Sexuality: Foucault and Classical Antiquity*, ed. D. H. J. Larmour, P. A. Miller and C. Platter (Princeton, NJ: Princeton University Press, 1998), 122–37, who offers numerous examples from other ancient texts to demonstrate that women were not always passive in terms of their gendered performances.
44 Maud W. Gleason, 'The Semiotics of Gender: Physiognomy and Self-Fashioning in the Second Century CE', in *Before Sexuality: The Construction of Erotic Experience in the Ancient Greek World*, ed. David M. Halperin, John D. Winkler and Froma I. Zeitlin (Princeton, NJ: Princeton University Press, 1990), 389–415.
45 See Chapter 5 below.
46 Amy Richlin, ed., *Pornography and Representation in Greece and Rome* (New York: Oxford University Press, 1992).
47 Arist., *Gen. an.*, 728a18-20; 737a25-35; 775a15; Pl., *Ti.*, 69c-81c. On the gender spectrum, see Thomas Laquer, *Making Sex: Body and Gender from the Greeks to Freud* (Cambridge, MA: Harvard University Press, 1990); Ann Ellis Hanson, 'The Medical Writers' Woman', in *Before Sexuality: The Construction of Erotic Experience in the Ancient Greek World*, ed. David M. Halperin, John D. Winkler and Froma I. Zeitlin (Princeton, NJ: Princeton University Press, 1990), 309–38; Anne Carson, 'Putting Her in Her Place: Women, Dirt and Desire', in *Before Sexuality: The Construction of Erotic Experience in the Ancient Greek World*, ed. David M. Halperin, John D. Winkler and Froma I. Zeitlin (Princeton, NJ: Princeton University Press, 1990), 135–69; Gleason, 'The Semiotics of Gender'; Bernadette J. Brooten, *Love between Women: Early Christian Responses to Female Homoeroticism* (Chicago, IL: University of Chicago Press, 1996), 167, n. 65; Dale B. Martin, 'Heterosexism and the Interpretation of Romans 1.18–32', *BI* 3 (1995): 193.
48 The *Handbook for Biblical Interpretation* defines 'closed' texts as texts that 'demand relatively few decisions on the part of the reader'. Examples of 'closed' texts include the New Testament Epistles and the book of Proverbs from the Old Testament. 'Open' texts, on the other hand, include texts such as the gospels (or Genesis) and use devices and strategies associated with storytelling (such as plot, characterization, setting, point of view, etc.), W. Randolph Tate, *The Handbook for Biblical Interpretation: An Essential Guide to Methods, Terms and Concepts*, 2nd ed. (Grand Rapids, MI: Baker, 2012), see under 'Closed Texts'. This is in line with Konstan who defines an 'open' text as 'a particular kind of artistic entity' which 'admit a degree of variation or indeterminacy', Konstan, 'Acts of Love', 16. However, it should be borne in mind that the NT Epistles and even the gospels may not have been considered 'closed' for a long time. The evidence of numerous significant textual variants testify to this.
49 Thomas, *The Acts of Peter*, 80. See also Thomas, 'Stories without Texts'.
50 For a more detailed discussion on this reference in *De bapt.*, see Chapter 2.
51 For a discussion of the Apocryphal Acts as 'open' texts, see Chapter 2.

52 See, e.g., Wayne C. Booth, *The Rhetoric of Fiction* (Chicago, IL: University of Chicago Press, 1983), 70–6; Seymour B. Chatman, *Story and Discourse: Narrative Structure in Fiction and Film* (New York: Cornell University Press, 1978), 147–51. See also David Rhoads, 'Narrative Criticism of Gospel of Mark 9–11', *JAAR* 50 (1982): 411–34.

4

Female beheadings

Introduction

The motif of a woman 'becoming male' has been seen as a recurring literary theme of female chaste ascetic practice in early Christian discourse.¹ By 'becoming male', women apparently transcended their inferior gender status. This concept has become one of the central signifiers of women's piety and has been associated with the development of transvestism.² The denunciation of women who dressed as men, at the Synod of Gangra (340 CE), certainly indicates that female transvestism was frequent enough in antiquity to elicit reproach.³ Jerome is also known to have strongly attacked the practice.⁴ However, meaning of the practice is not easy to determine. While some have recognized that early Christian transvestism may have been seen by ascetic women as a very practical means of safeguarding themselves against sexual threats while travelling (in the *Acts of Paul and Thecla*, for example, Thecla is forced to defend herself against the threat of rape when she ventures out in public on the road to Antioch with Paul, *APTh*. 26),⁵ the practice was also strongly associated with female religiosity.⁶

There are echoes of this motif to be found within a number of stories contained in the Apocryphal Acts.⁷ However, the quintessential text which has been regarded as an early manifestation of the notion of the female becoming male is the *Acts of Paul and Thecla*. Within the text, Thecla offers to cut her hair short (*APTh*. 25), and, at the end of the story, having triumphantly survived her trials and ordeals, she sews her χιτών after the fashion of men in order to set upon her travels (*APTh*. 40). These audacious gestures have regularly been interpreted by scholars as reflecting Thecla's transformation from dependent, subordinate woman to charismatic, independent, preacher and teacher.⁸ The text has, therefore, been seen as supporting the liberation of women who overcome the limitations of their inferior gender status.⁹ However, a number of questions need to be raised at this point; not least among them is the question of whether a manly transformation is inherently female-affirming. Second, even if we choose to read 'becoming male' as female affirming, does Thecla actually undergo a sexual transformation by way of a haircut and a change of clothing and, if Thecla does turn out to be 'all woman', what are the implications of her retaining her feminine characteristics? What does a womanly, feminine Thecla reveal about masculinity? Below, therefore, I will problematize the reading of Thecla as male and assess what is 'liberating' for women within the text.

Becoming male

Castelli notes that the *vitae* of many ascetic women in antiquity were preserved simply because these women were esteemed for having transcended the 'bonds of their feminine nature'.[10] Indeed, in a number of cases the women are referred to as ἡ ἄνθρωπος, employing the feminine article with the generic/masculine noun. Within Christianity, from as early as the second century, the Stoic virtue of ἀνδρεία (courage or manly virtue) came to be associated with virgins.[11] The term ἀνδρεία is of course related to the Greek word ἀνήρ, 'man', and when used in relation to women, it is difficult to escape the 'masculine' nuance of the word.[12] It is the essential virtue of manliness.

There is little doubt that from the very earliest period Christian piety could be expressed by reference to breaking down the sexual distinctions of the human body.[13] This can be seen early on in Paul's letter to the Galatians: 'there is no longer Jew or Greek, there is no longer slave nor free, there is no longer male and female' (Gal. 3.28 NRSV).[14] In a groundbreaking article, Wayne Meeks argued that Gal. 3.28 expressed a notion by Paul and the Pauline Churches that Christ was an androgynous saviour figure and that baptized Christians understood themselves to be returning to the original androgynous state.[15] Thus, in pronouncing that there is now 'no male and female', a reference to Gen. 1.27,[16] the statement would suggest that 'in Christ' believers had been re-created and sexual differentiation reversed; there is now an equality between the sexes, an equality that was initially lived out functionally and practically within the Pauline Churches.[17] However, Jouette Bassler argues that this original unity was not regarded as asexual or bisexual but as male.[18] Although Schüssler Fiorenza contends that Gal. 3.28 does not extol maleness but rather an egalitarian oneness of the body of Christ,[19] she also seems to suggest that distinctive femaleness is indeed sacrificed, in that Schüssler Fiorenza herself highlights the development, within certain Christian circles, of the idea of an anthropological unification that speaks of woman relinquishing her powers of procreating to become male. This is because the male principle was thought to stand for the divine realm and the female for human weakness.[20] We shall explore the evidence for this below.

The notion that maleness is linked to salvation and, the underside of that notion, that femaleness has a special relationship to sin, was not, however, distinct to Christianity. Hellenistic men could express their thankfulness to the gods because they were fortunate enough to be born a human being and not a beast, a Greek and not a barbarian, a free man and not a slave, a man and not woman.[21] For example, Plato in the *Timaeus* considers the possibility of wicked men being punished with reincarnation as women.[22] In his hierarchy of beings, women are considered to be situated below men and just above beasts.[23] This cultural positioning was also adopted by Judaism. Sometime around the middle of the second century CE, the synagogue developed a prayer where Jewish men thanked God that they were not created a gentile, a slave or a woman.[24] For Philo, the categories of male and female are not balanced but rather represent superior and inferior states; the movement from femaleness to maleness is understood to be a progressive movement to a higher state of virtue.[25] Philo, writing on early ascetic practice, speaks favourably and with admiration of female ascetics; for him, such women were female in form only. Like good philosophers who aspire to mystical union with the divinity, they had purged their souls of their female elements and become male.[26]

Such theories were perhaps a natural development of concepts regarding gender in antiquity where masculine and feminine categories were arranged in a hierarchical dualism of male over female. Greek philosophical thought was grounded in the belief of women's physical inferiority as a sort of 'deformed' male. For Aristotle, for example, the female was a kind of sterile or castrated male (*Gen. an.* 1.20), who is, therefore, impotent; a simple passive recipient of sperm (*Gen. an.* 728 a). Although a human being, a woman was less perfectly formed than man (*Gen. an.* 737 a 28).[27] Dale Martin notes that when ancient writers talk about the difference between female nature and male nature, they are referring to a difference in degree on a spectrum. In such a system, any androgyny that is taken to be salvific must be oriented towards the higher end of the spectrum, the male.[28] This understanding was basically a 'one-sex' model where women were considered incomplete or deformed males. Within this line of thought, the elimination of sexual differentiation would mean that the feminine was swallowed up by the masculine, the weaker by the stronger. Such thinking was certainly quite evident in later Christian writing, which expressed a clear disdain for the feminine gender as woman was imagined to represent a fleshly imperfection.[29]

Given the widespread acceptance of notions of female inferiority, Christian piety would then develop this notion of women perfecting themselves through 'becoming male', and in certain instances, it is likely that transvestism was an expression of this concept. The condemnation women received in pursuing this practice perhaps reveals not only how women absorbed this understanding within their own thinking and piety but also shows men's ambivalence towards the female sex. Such a visible and tangible blurring of gender boundaries was deemed threatening by men in antiquity. Nevertheless, however this worked out practically, the significance of the notion is that women must somehow endeavour to transcend their sex and seek masculine perfection.[30] This idea is clearly illustrated in the late first- or early second-century text of the *Gospel of Thomas*:[31]

> Simon Peter said to them (the other disciples), 'Let Mary go away from us, because women are not worthy of life'. Jesus said, 'Look, I will draw her in so as to make her male, so that she too may become a living male spirit, similar to you. Every woman who makes herself male will enter the kingdom of heaven'.[32]

However, Logion 22 in the same gospel appears to undermine this quest for maleness, eradicating gender altogether:

> Jesus said to them: 'When you make the two into one and when you make the inside like the outside and the outside like the inside and the above like the below, that is, to make the male and female into a single one, so that the male will not be male and the female will not be female.'[33]

These texts may be reconciled when the understanding of salvation as a return to the singular state comes to the fore, a concept that imagined the male as the higher state to attain to.[34]

From the Nag Hammadi library, the *Gospel of Philip* demonstrates that a return to the singular state heals the rift of gender created by the 'Fall': 'when Eve was in Adam, there was no death; but when she was separated from him death came into being. Again if <she> go in, and he take <her> to himself, death will no longer exist'.[35] The Gospel of Mary also reflects the understanding that the male is superior to the female and suggests that women should aim to become male. Mary is depicted as saying to the disciples, 'Praise his (Jesus') greatness, for he has prepared us and made us into men.'[36]

Similar concepts may also be found in two further early Christian texts. The anonymous homily known as *2 Clement* recommends that believers leave behind this inferior world, this lustful body: 'For the Lord himself was asked by someone when his Kingdom would come, he said: "When the two are one, and the outside like the inside, and the male with the female is neither male nor female."'[37] So too the *Gospel of the Egyptians*, as quoted in Clement of Alexandria, reads, 'When Salome asked when she would know the answer to her question the Lord replied, "When you trample underfoot the garment of shame, and when the two become one and the male is one with the female, and there is no more male and female."'[38]

Although a number of these texts appear to be advocating an eradication of gender (or sexuality) altogether, or even a notion of androgyny which incorporates both genders, as noted above, there needs to be a clear differentiation between the notion of 'oneness' (where sexual or gender identity is erased) and a notion of an androgyny where genders are blended. Concepts of a 'blended' androgyny were seen as monstrous and problematic.[39]

Clearly, then, women can only have access to holiness through the manipulation of conventional gender categories, but this is conceptualized as essentially pursuing 'masculine' perfection of the soul and avoiding procreation. It makes sense, therefore, that texts containing representations of female piety demonstrate this manifestation of woman becoming male, not only in terms of the soul but also in terms of the body. In this respect, much has been made of Thecla cutting her hair and donning male apparel. However, has a desire to 'see what is not there' led interpreters to overlook crucial details within the text?

Does Thecla cut her hair and become male?

Setting the scene

Many contemporary commentators have remarked how Thecla transcends her female gender and becomes male by cutting her hair.[40] For a number of scholars, Thecla's haircut is simply mentioned in passing and is not central to their argument. Thus, Aymer argues that since Thecla's hair is cut, she is no longer a woman and, therefore, no longer a threat to Paul's continence: her identity is changed, and she has become a man.[41] McGinn similarly states that Thecla's adoption of a man's dress and hairstyle may mean that a woman must become 'manly' to be allowed to refuse marriage and pursue a public career as Thecla did.[42]

However, for other scholars, Thecla's haircut forms a fundamental part of their thesis. Thus, Willi Braun focuses on what he terms the 'Christian salvation myths' of reconstituted masculinity and the female becoming male and discusses the *Acts of Paul and Thecla* as his main example of masculinized femininity. Braun explicitly states that his locus is the Greek text of *Acts of Paul and Thecla* in Lipsius and Bonnet and its presentation of Thecla's conversion 'as a process of altering her "gender temperature" ... from female to male'.[43] He notes how the story renders Thecla's transformation from feminine to masculine in three interlinked movements: first, in her relationship to men (her conversion breaks the proprietary relationship of male over female); second, through her transgression of spatial boundaries; and, finally, by taking measures to efface her beauty, in cutting off her hair and rebuffing the advances of Alexander. Since long hair was a naturally required sign of female adornment, Braun notes that this final gesture is full of physiognomic significance as Thecla symbolically renounces her gender. Indeed, her transvestite measures should be seen as a symbolic indicator that she has entered not only spatial and social spheres of maleness but also the bodily dimension of maleness. It represents the 'metamorphosis of a woman into a man'. In sum, Thecla's conversion entails a transformed self-definition and public persona in which femininity increasingly fades out to reveal a masculinized self. The metamorphosis takes her from male custody and control to manly independence, from the womanly space of the household enclosure to the public arenas of male discourse and politics, from female 'bodiliness' to male 'bodiliness'.[44]

Petropoulos too focuses on the *Acts of Paul and Thecla*.[45] According to Petropoulos, transvestism and female chastity remove the assumption that a woman is operatively female and therefore de-sexualizes her; it assigns to her a liminal state between masculine and feminine, with a pronounced bias towards the masculine. In regard to Thecla's haircut, he notes that Paul 'demurs' at Thecla's offer to 'shave her hair'. However, in the very next paragraph, he goes on to say that Paul 'does not actually object ... to her cutting off her hair, but rather to her premature, as he sees it, baptism'.[46] Exactly how Paul 'demurs' at Thecla's offer of a haircut on the one hand and then 'not actually object' to it on the other is not explained by Petropoulos.

Petropoulos argues that short hair in a nubile woman is symbolically equated with restricted sexuality, and Thecla's act makes excellent sense as an attempt at sexual renunciation. Paul has warned her that her beauty may lead her to temptations worse than the trial of martyrdom. If she succumbs to her own sexuality, she will be less of a man. She must, therefore, 'camouflage' her sexuality.[47] However, as will be discussed in more detail below, if Thecla has camouflaged her sexuality, why does Alexander immediately fall in love at first sight?

For Petropoulos, the narrative reads as a story of a 'virgin's progress ... into a (sacred) androgyne. At the same time the tale may resemble a proto-"feminist" fantasy', since it unmasks, 'if only temporarily, the obvious sexual stereotypes of female inferiority and subordination'.[48] Thecla's haircut is thus a part of her permanent transvestism, together with her un-stereotypical behaviour and her transformation in the direction of the male gender. Petropoulos's conclusion thus relies on Thecla having short, masculine hair with male clothing. However, has his desire to read Thecla as an empowered woman throughout the narrative clouded his (and other scholars') reading of the text?

Textual evidence

Despite the common view that Thecla masculinizes herself with a self-imposed haircut, there is, in fact, no textual evidence to support it. Indeed, there is strong evidence to the contrary. The arguments put forward by scholars regarding Thecla's haircut and masculinization are based on the following text:

> καὶ εἶπεν Θέκλα τῷ Παύλῳ Περικαροῦμαι καὶ ἀκολουθήσω σοι ὅπου δἂν πορεύῃ. Ὁ δὲ εἶπεν Ὁ καιρὸς αἰσχρός, καὶ σὶ εὔμορφος· μὴ ἄλλος σε πειρασμὸς λήψεται χείρων τοῦ πρώτου, καὶ οὐχ ὑπομείνῃς ἀλλὰ δειλανδρήσῃς (*APTh*. 25)
>
> [And Thecla said to Paul, 'I will cut my hair and follow you wherever you may go.' But Paul said, 'The time is inappropriate and you are beautiful. Beware lest any other temptation, worse than the first, overtake you and you cannot endure but play the coward.'][49]

This verse follows the section where Thecla, having been rescued from the fire, goes in search of Paul, only to find him praying for her rescue in a tomb (*APTh*. 24). The verse containing the discussion regarding Thecla's haircut follows and begins by describing what could, only very loosely, be construed as a Eucharistic 'type' scene. There is 'much love' and 'exultation' when the group, which includes Onesiphorus and his household, share five loaves, during which they 'make glad over the holy works of Christ' (*APTh*. 25). It is at this point that Thecla says to Paul, 'I will cut my hair and will follow you wherever you may go' (*APTh*. 25). The verb here, περικαροῦμαι, is the future, indicative, middle form of περικείρω, meaning 'to shear or clip all around'. The only difference between the active and middle voices is that the middle calls especial attention to the subject. In the active voice, the subject is merely acting; in the middle, the subject is acting in relation to himself/herself somehow.[50] Thus, Thecla offers, as a *future* possibility, to cut her own hair. The offer then to follow Paul, ἀκολουθήσω, is also set as a future possibility. The use of the future verbs in this sentence draws attention to the fact that Thecla does not carry out any actions immediately but rather suggests that a haircut and following Paul are acts that *may* be carried out in the *future*. This is also reflected in the conditional clause involving the present (middle/passive) subjunctive πορεύῃ with the particles ὅπου δἂν.[51] These particles belong to the verb and denote that the assertion made by the verb is dependent on a condition. Following Paul wherever he goes is conditional upon a haircut and is set as a future possibility, as if Paul might expect that. Is there an assumption that this is normative for women who follow Paul? Thecla's entire pronouncement is, therefore, a future conditional sentence. She is simply suggesting a possible way forward to Paul.

Paul then responds,

> Ὁ δὲ εἶπεν Ὁ καιρὸς αἰσχρός, καὶ σὶ εὔμορφος. (*APTh*. 25)
>
> [But he said, 'the time (καιρὸς) is inappropriate[52] and you are beautiful.']

δὲ is one of the most common Greek particles used to connect one clause to another, either to express contrast or simple continuation.[53] When a contrast between clauses is needed, the most common translation is 'but'; when a simple connective is desired, without contrast being implied, then 'and' is sufficient. In some instances, the marker may be left untranslated. Although here it could be translated 'and', in view of Paul's objection to Thecla's proposal, there is more in favour of an adversative 'but'. The use of καιρός rather than χρόνος is an important distinction to make. Καιρός is especially associated with the eschatological end time.[54] Is Paul suggesting that 'woman becoming male' is associated with eschatological end time and that to enact a haircut in the present time would be shameful, since it counters all current codes of society? Can we read Thecla's offer of a haircut and of masculinization as inappropriate for the current time? Is there resonance here with the non-canonical texts mentioned above which link female salvation and the eschaton with a return to the singular (male) state? Καιρός also frequently has the implication of being especially fit for something and without a precise chronology,[55] thus having the sense of a 'right' or 'favourable' time.[56] This may explain Wilson's translation 'the season is unfavourable'.[57] However, his interpretation does not reflect the full force of the noun αἰσχρός which follows. This is strong language: αἰσχρός is a forceful noun that pertains to being socially or morally unacceptable, shameful, and is a term especially significant in honour-shame-oriented society.[58] Generally it is used in reference to that which fails to meet expected moral and cultural standards.[59] Barrier argues that Thecla is accused of having made a shameless and 'ugly' suggestion when Paul is implying that this is such a shameless time.[60] Corrington Streete translates the phrase as 'Times are ugly (shameful) and you are beautiful'.[61] Why would it cause 'shame' or 'dishonour' if Thecla were to cut her hair? Undoubtedly, this woman's physical beauty is of consequence as is her womanly sense of 'shame' which she was earlier accused of abandoning (*APTh*. 10). The author's choice of words invites thought-provoking questions. One cannot help but speculate on the reasons why Thecla's haircut would bring such dishonour. Does this refusal of a haircut betray a strong element of orthodoxy and conventionality within a text that has regularly been associated with a rebellious unorthodox woman?[62] After all, Paul's prohibition against Thecla's haircut is in line with Canon 17 of the Synod of Gangra (340 CE):

> If any woman shall, under pretence of religion, cut off her hair, which God gave her as the reminder of her subjection, let her be Anathema, as one who annuls the ordinance of subjection.[63]

It also mirrors his words in 1 Cor. 11.6 where he uses the same verb to speak of women's shaven heads being a cause of shame (αἰσχρὸν γυναικὶ τὸ καίρασθαι). In this regard, it is interesting to note the consistency between what have often been regarded as two disparate Pauline traditions.[64]

The term αἰσχρός ('ugly') is also the complete opposite of the noun καλός ('beautiful'), and the contrast between these two nouns is especially telling, particularly since the only time an emphatic pronoun (σὺ)[65] is used in this exchange between Thecla and Paul is in relation to the adjective εὔμορφος. There is, therefore, particular emphasis and significance placed on Thecla's womanly beauty. The text is drawing attention to her beautiful appearance. It is important that such nuances of meaning are not overlooked in a text where a woman's physical beauty is repeatedly stressed.

Paul then goes on to give Thecla a further reason for delaying her masculinization via a haircut:

μὴ[66] ἄλλος σε πειρασμὸς λήψεται χείρων τοῦ πρώτου, καὶ οὐχ ὑπομείνῃς ἀλλὰ δειλανδρήσῃς. (*APTh.* 25)

[Beware, lest any other temptation, worse than the first, overtakes you and you cannot endure but play the coward.]

The noun πειρασμός, 'temptation', occurs here and in the next sentence and highlights a key theme concerning Thecla's trials.[67] It links what has gone before (the first arena scene, *APTh.* 22) with what lies ahead (a further arena scene, *APTh.* 33) and gives a sense of simultaneity. This focus on possible future trials sees the author hinting of more to come. The term δειλανδρήσῃς is also used to denote Thecla's possible reaction to the trials that are to follow. Just as αἰσχρός is the opposite of καλός so δειλανδρήσῃς is the polar opposite of ἀνδρεία (courage). At this point, Paul does not consider Thecla to have proven her worth, and this may well be because it was made patently clear that Thecla's first rescue was due to Paul's fervent prayer and intercession (*APTh.* 24). Thecla's response to his doubt is to demand (employing the imperative δός) 'the seal in Christ' (ἐν Χριστῷ σφραγῖδα, *APTh.* 25), the seal is baptism.[68] If she is baptized, then she will be protected from temptation. However, Paul answers her imperative with his own, μακροθύμησον, and insists that she remains patient.[69] Paul's final imperative puts an end to the discussion and the following verse ensues: Onesiphorus and his household are sent back to Iconium; Thecla and Paul travel to Antioch (*APTh.* 26). Textually, nothing indicates that Thecla disobeys Paul and cuts her hair.

Overall, very little is made of the haircut itself. Thecla suggests it and Paul dismisses it. For the most part, the focus remains on the temptations and Thecla's strength or lack thereof. Thus, the structure of the verse, with Thecla offering to cut her hair, Paul's refusal and concern about her weakness, her demand for baptism and Paul's command for patience, supports the view that, at this point, Thecla's hair remains long. The request is dealt with there and then with an explicit refusal of the offer because she is beautiful and the time is shameful. No haircutting action has taken place since the verbs are set as a future condition.

Of course, it could be argued, in line with Petropoulos, that since, in the next verse, Thecla immediately accompanies/follows Paul on his journey to Antioch, she may well have disobeyed him and cut her hair anyway.[70] However, as we shall see below, contextually there is evidence to show otherwise.

Contextual evidence

The discussion regarding Thecla's hair and future trials provides the context for the reader to understand the ensuing narrative, and this provides a very clear contextual indicator which supports the fact that Thecla does not cut her hair in the very next verse. As soon as they reach Antioch, Alexander, setting eyes on Thecla, instantaneously falls in love (ἠράσθη) with her (*APTh.* 26). Alexander's attraction is immediate and physical; the verb ἠράσθη is associated with sexual lust.[71] Thus, Alexander's reaction is a direct result of her physical beauty (*APTh*. 26). The skirmish that ensues between them then provides the reason for her second trial. Ensuring that Thecla remains beautiful is, therefore, integral to the plot and supports the development of the narrative. It is not said that he finds her beautiful despite her having a shaved head or short hair. In addition, as the narrative develops, there is further substantiation that Thecla remains a beautiful-looking woman. Both Tryphaena and the Governor mourn the potential loss of such a beautiful woman (κάλλος, *APTh*. 29; 34). A woman's hair was (and still is) taken to be an essential part of her beauty. Would a woman who had cut her hair remain conventionally beautiful and elicit such powerful magnetism? Thus, quite contrary to Petropoulos who argues that the narrative's logic requires Thecla to cut her hair because she can only travel with Paul disguised as a man,[72] I would argue she keeps her hair uncut. The narrative logic demonstrates that Thecla must have retained her long hair because she continues to look beautiful. Indeed, Petropoulos undermines his argument when he says that in order to guard against succumbing to temptation, Thecla must camouflage her sexuality.[73] If Thecla has camouflaged her sexuality, why does Alexander immediately fall in love at first sight?

Although admitting it is a complex issue, Ross Shepard Kraemer notes that a woman with short/shorn hair was a sign of social stigma.[74] Indeed, Paul in 1 Cor. 11.6 also underscores the fact that a woman communicated her status and social standing by the length and styling of her hair. When Thecla fights off Alexander, she cries out, 'I am one of the first of Iconium' (*APTh*. 26).[75] Later in the narrative, as a high-status virgin, she is given over to Tryphaena's care in order for her purity to be preserved (*APTh*. 27). If Thecla had cut her hair, surely there would be some comment on how people reacted to a high-born woman having short hair. It would indicate that she had been shamed. Since Thecla's beauty and high status is overt within the narrative, it leaves little room for the conclusion that she cuts her hair and is thus presented as shamed.

It is evident, therefore, that Thecla did not appear manly or 'transformed' into a man. If she had cut her hair, along with donning male clothing at the same time, and actually appeared like a man, it would have provided her with some level of disguise and protection from male attention. After all, there is evidence to show that Christian women who were intent on disguising themselves as men were very successful in their endeavours. For example, Eugenia of Alexandria, martyred in Rome around 257 CE, disguised herself as a man and joined a monastic community of men where, after some years, she was elected Abbott.[76] In a similar vein, Pelagia, a prostitute from Antioch, in the late fourth century, converted to Christianity and then secretly ran away to Jerusalem, where she disguised herself as a male eunuch and lived in a monastery. Her identity was only discovered on her death.[77] However, as far as Thecla is concerned, Alexander's reaction, the repeated claims that she is beautiful and the underscoring of her high status all work to assure readers that Thecla remains a beautiful and, obviously, high-status woman unshamed by her hair.

It is, therefore, quite evident from both a textual and contextual point of view that Thecla communicates high status and remains conventionally (for the period) beautiful with long hair, which would have been arranged in tied-up style. However, despite the use of the future tenses and the conditional clause, which express a possible action to come, and the contextual evidence, which continually asserts that Thecla's beauty attracts attention, the majority of scholars writing on Thecla take Thecla's haircut for granted and choose to interpret this verse as definitive of a haircut. We need to question this assumption.[78] Since Thecla dons a male χιτών only at the end of the narrative (*APTh.* 40) and not at the time that she suggests that she cuts her hair, there is no masculinizing.

In short, the temptation among scholars has been to read more into the hair cutting dialogue than is there. In addition, when she does don male clothing, the assumption has been that she has also cut her hair, but this narrative does not assert that at all – in fact, it asserts quite the opposite. Within this section, and in line with 1 Cor. 11. 6 (and the prohibition in the Synod of Gangra 17), the text quite clearly states that Thecla should follow cultural codes of practice and continue to look womanly, attractive and submissive. Even though it could be argued that the adjective εὔμορφος (well-formed/comely) is both masculine and feminine and could perhaps serve to emphasize a certain ambiguity in regard to Thecla's gender construction, there is no other indicator, either textually or contextually, to support the view that Thecla disobeys Paul and cuts her hair.

In her more recent publication, Kraemer is more judicious in her approach to the text and speaks of Thecla's 'intention' to cut off her hair; although she sees this as signifying her rejection of the sexuality associated with women's hair, as well as male authority, she notes that Thecla's intention to follow Paul wherever he goes somewhat blunts this rebellion.[79]

Alternative traditions?

While the *Acts of Paul and Thecla* does not contain an explicit indication that Thecla cuts her hair, and indicates in fact that she did not, parallel traditions did have Thecla cut her hair and physically masculinize herself in this way. Here it is worthy of note that the adjective εὔμορφος, was amended by later scribes to γυνὴ εὔμορφος ('a comely woman') in order to emphasize Thecla's womanhood.[80] This suggests that alternative Thecla traditions, in which Thecla does cut her hair and masculinize herself, did exist. Indeed, a short-haired, masculinized Thecla is attested in the *Life and Miracles of Saint Thecla*. Within the *Life and Miracles*, although Paul initially rejects Thecla's offer to cut her hair, reasoning that she is too beautiful and too weak to endure like a man, she argues back and insists that she is strong enough to withstand any trials. Paul, therefore, responds, '[S]ince you are resolved, it will be so: now you will participate in my travels and, after some time, you will also receive holy baptism.'[81]

However, the Greek text of the *Acts of Paul and Thecla* aligns itself with an 'uncut' portrayal of Thecla, insisting that no gender transgression in the Thecla tradition is to be expected among churches that subscribed to the Synod of Gangra, and the *Acts of Paul and Thecla* was an extremely popular text.[82] While there were clearly other traditions about Thecla, there is little doubt which tradition came to predominate.

In later centuries, following the development of her cult, it is Thecla's female gender which is most acutely stressed.[83] In the longer ending of the fourth-century manuscript, for example, it describes how 'lawless men' approaching her cave attempted to tear off Thecla's (womanly) veil (μαφορίου).[84] Thecla's femininity also predominates in the iconography of her cult. Later portraits overwhelmingly preserve an image of Thecla as a bound and sexualized condemned female prisoner. An excellent example of this iconography may be seen in Figure 4.1.

This fifth- to eighth-century medallion pictures Thecla in a flowing skirt with her upper torso naked and with her hands tied behind her back.[85] She is bound with ropes to lions that flank her on either side. Her breasts, hips and pelvic area are accentuated and her hair is braided in a womanly way. The sculpture preserves Thecla's femininity and vulnerability.[86]

Stephen Davis lists a total of sixteen representations of Thecla on Egyptian pilgrimage ampullae, where Thecla is paired with the Egyptian saint Menas.[87] Within these images, the representation of Thecla is stylized and formulaic and depicts Thecla bound to a stake, flanked by beasts.[88] Much like the image in the medallion, her hair, nude upper body and captured status all work to draw attention to both her vulnerability and femininity. Claudia Nauerth and Rüdiger Warns note that out of thirty-five genuine representations of Thecla, seven represent Thecla as nude or partially nude with her breasts always distinct.[89] Among the representations listed there, is only one notable exception of a relief that represents Thecla with short hair, looking very 'boyish'.[90] In this case then, it is an anomaly that draws on the alternative Thecla tradition. Later Romanesque carvings and images of Thecla similarly preserved much of the earlier iconography of Thecla, representing her as a beautiful woman with a full figure and with her upper body naked.[91]

Figure 4.1 Saint Thecla with wild beasts and angels.

Egyptian, fifth century CE. Limestone, 3.75 × 25.5 inches (9.5 × 64.8 cm).

Image courtesy of the Nelson-Atkins Museum of Art, Kansas City, Missouri. (Purchase: William Rockhill Nelson Trust, 48-10; photo: Jamison Miller)

Castelli, in discussing the role of memory and identity in early Christianity, points out that the dimensions of the Thecla narrative which are preserved, interpreted and disseminated artistically overwhelmingly represent Thecla as bound and exposed with an explicitly female body. Part of this is to show her with feminine, braided long hair. The memory preserved in these images emphasizes Thecla's feminine sexuality.[92] Strikingly, any narrative elements from the *Acts of Paul and Thecla* (and even the fifth-century *Life and Miracles of Thecla*) that emphasize Thecla's rejection of gender conventions are 'absent and replaced by clothing and coiffure that emphasize the conventional, upper-class femininity of the figure'. Castelli argues that in focusing on Thecla's physical struggle and the violence she experiences Thecla's femininity is 'amplified'.[93]

This examination of later iconography and imagery helps to underscore the more feminized representation of Thecla within the Greek text of the *Acts of Paul and Thecla*. There is little doubt that this early textual tradition left the way open for later interpreters to construe Thecla's gender as untrangressively female, and it is undeniable that the majority of iconographers considered her to be feminine with long hair tied up in the usual way.[94]

Thecla: The sexy cross-dresser

Thus, even though Thecla is prepared to masculinize herself, the male protagonist in the story, Paul, clearly wants her to retain her feminine characteristics and remain a beautiful-looking virgin. Unlike the fifth-century *Life and Miracles of Thecla*, which states quite clearly that Thecla cuts her hair,[95] within the text of the *Acts of Paul and Thecla*, the notion of a masculine transformation via a haircut is simply suggested, and this is *de facto* refused by Paul. Paul dissuades Thecla from cutting her hair, and it cannot be assumed that she does so. Thecla does, however, don male apparel at the end of the narrative as she sets off on her missionary work. Here, Thecla 'sews' (ῥάψασα) her *chiton* (χιτῶνα) in the form (σχήματι) with men (ἀνδρικῷ) (*APTh.* 40).

McInerney has argued that the choice of Thecla's garb has nothing to do with the rejection of femininity. Rather, what Thecla is doing is assuming the τρίβων or the mantle of the philosopher. The mantle is an identifying mark, a provocation and invitation to disputation and philosophical discourse, the polar opposite to the virgin's veil that separates her from society and symbolically muffles her voice as it hides her body.[96] However, the fact that the text employs the word χιτῶνα would make this assumption unlikely. Had the author had in mind the philosopher's τρίβων, it is reasonable to assume, then, that this would have been made explicit since the specific word, along with all its connotations, was freely available for use.

A χιτών, although eventually worn by women too, was originally a man's tunic, worn along with an ἱμάτιον, which is an outer wrap or cloak.[97] The χιτών was similar for men and women, except women wore a floor-length garment of this type, while men's were usually shorter.[98] Indeed, the short skirt or dress was specifically regarded as a sign of masculinity.[99] Occasionally, men of certain occupations, such as priests in certain ritual settings and some musicians, did wear full-length versions.[100] But the fact that this is not specified here and that there is only mention of a general 'manly' *chiton*, presumably Thecla takes her tunic and remodels it in a usually (short) manly fashion, thus revealing her legs. By the end of the narrative, with her long hair and short tunic, Thecla is now transformed into a 'sexy' cross-dresser, an object of voyeurism, vulnerable to the male gaze. The notion that Thecla would be looking quite sexy is perhaps strengthened by the fact that prostitutes were sometimes known to wear the shorter masculine style dress in order to make an impression.[101]

Thecla's gender construction is, therefore, quite unequivocal. It should be noted that this is not in line with the fifth-century *Life and Miracles of Thecla*, where at Antioch Paul not only disowns Thecla but also pretends not to know whether she is male or female.[102] In the *Acts of Paul and Thecla*, her femininity is retained, as discussed above, and so the short *chiton* creates a certain dissonance.

Thecla's femininity is also emphasized in the narrative through her submissiveness. For example, within the Iconium episode, Thecla is presented as a passive virgin with a male owner, and she is properly ensconced and cloistered away within her mother's house (*APTh*. 7). Transfixed to the window by Paul's voice, she is compared to an insect that has been captured by the apostle (*APTh*. 8).[103] Thecla is very much represented as owned, passive, given over to desire for a strange man and is also forced to resort to bribery and deception in order to leave the house (*APTh*. 18). When Thecla is brought before the Governor, she knows her place as a woman and remains silent (*APTh*. 20). Within the arena she is described as a lamb (*APTh*. 21), a weak and vulnerable follower of Paul.

Thus, Thecla's masculine attire comes as some surprise and confuses her gender construction. However, already we find the Iconium episode infused with subtle masculinized innuendo in regard to her actions. This is hinted at right at the beginning when Thamyris accuses Thecla of losing her (womanly) shame (*APTh*. 10), thus suggesting that she may be shedding aspects of her femininity. Thecla also transgresses physical boundaries in leaving the household and stepping out into the male public domain (*APTh*. 18).[104] Once in the arena, Thecla displays strength and bravery as she prepares to be burned making the sign of the cross (*APTh*. 22). Even the Governor is taken by surprise by the power in her (ἐν αὐτῇ δύναμιν, *APTh*. 22). Within the arena, Thecla could have yielded to self-pity and been cowardly or unmanly. At this point, however, her actions demonstrate masculine courage as she remains firm in her resistance to state and power. Thecla's rebellion and bravery merge and coalesce with her beautiful feminine body and her, at times, passive behaviour.

The Antioch episode similarly demonstrates this strange mix of feminine and masculine gender construction. When Alexander falls in love with Thecla at first sight, the text clearly underscores the fact that Thecla is still 'all woman' (from a patriarchal perspective): a beautiful and desirable object to be owned. Her actions initially reinforce this representation. When she is attacked by Alexander, she looks about for her male protector Paul (*APTh*. 26). However, she is left to fend for herself, and, in fighting off Alexander, she demonstrates the masculine virtue ἀνδρεία. Margaret MacDonald notes that here Thecla assumes the offensive stance of the male guardian and protects her own honour. In displaying strength and courage, Thecla appropriates the traditional role of the male in the public honour context.[105] Philo similarly notes in *De specialibus legibus* that women 'unsex' themselves in displaying bold and angry behaviour.[106]

Nevertheless, having masculinized Thecla through her actions, on the one hand, when Thecla asks for protection of her chastity, her feminine bodily status is once again emphasized, on the other (*APTh*. 27). Tryphaena and the Governor also underscore Thecla's object-like status when they simply mourn the death of someone so beautiful (*APTh*. 29, 34). Thus, despite elements of masculinization, Thecla remains trapped in a woman's body. This is also highlighted in the second arena trial. For example, the only action Thecla takes in that trial is to throw herself into a pit of water in an act of self-baptism (*APTh*. 34). For the remainder of the time, Thecla is passive and 'done to'. First, she relies on the lioness to protect her (*APTh*. 33) and then the women's herbal magic (*APTh*. 34). Even at the end of all her trials, and after donning male apparel, she still 'desires' Paul and 'seeks' him out (*APTh*. 40). Thecla is strongly affiliated to Paul and continually seeks his company and approval. This is clearly a predominant discursive setting within the *Acts of Paul and Thecla*. However, as noted above, it is not the only discursive setting. Despite her feminine representation and her strong attachment to Paul, Thecla, nevertheless, still, at times, displays masculine ἀνδρεία, and she also dons a male χιτών. Long hair, a female body, feminine behaviour, masculine dress and masculine courage fuse and blend together in a curious mix.

It is undeniable that a beautiful woman with long hair tied up and a shorter male garment is likely to look alluring and appealing, a pleasurable object for the male gaze.[107] It would seem that the author has simply transformed Thecla from one beautiful feminine object to another. While aspects of Thecla's characterization display signs of masculine ἀνδρεία and perhaps offer a degree of reparation in terms of her objectified representation, Thecla never completely transgresses her feminine role; she is not completely constructed as male. She is still passive at times, she never tires of seeking after Paul and she is also fair of form with feminine locks. There is thus no radically defined alternative identity – of woman progressing to male on her path to autonomy and authority. Instead, Thecla seems to undergo only a partial transformation. It would seem that the text is merely playing tantalizingly with the idea of a manly gender transformation. Thecla remains a complex representation of wo/man.[108]

This 'flirting' with gender boundaries may also be seen in other Christian texts of this period. In *The Martyrdom of Saints Perpetua and Felicitas*, Perpetua has a vision where she finds herself in the arena preparing to fight an Egyptian gladiator.[109] Within this vision, she is stripped naked and her body becomes a male body (*et facta sum masculus*).[110] Burrus rightly suggests that we should pause to take note of the visual impact of the scene as we 'watch with bated breath as a woman is shamefully and shamingly stripped of her clothes'.[111] She goes on to say that our gaze is immediately confounded by the fact that instead of a female body, we see a 'masculine' body. The moment of visual confusion lingers as we watch the apparent male body being rubbed down with oil by handsome youths. Burrus initially states that in this way the female body is shielded from shame and humiliation by exposure to the public eye, and we see instead the shameless display of the oiled body of a male athlete.[112] However, Burrus then immediately admits that we do, in fact, 'see both'.[113] Ultimately, then, the female martyr's naked body is neither shielded from public view nor saved from shame.

This complex confounding and confusing of gender boundaries is further underscored by McInerney who highlights how most translations mask the oddity of the Latin phrase *et facta sum masculus*, generally rendered as 'I had become a man'. In the English, the feminine gender of the word *facta* is entirely faded out of the phrase. This confusion is enhanced by the words of the *lanista* since he refers to the dreamer with the feminine pronouns *hanc* and *illam*.[114] Thus, in spite of the fact that Perpetua has become *masculus*, she is recognized by the authority figure of the dream as female and, perhaps more importantly, presented to the crowd as such. Far from being a rejection of her femininity, even in a male body, Perpetua is still fundamentally and essentially feminine; her transformation was both partial and temporary.[115] Perpetua's feminine nature is again emphasized in the arena as she fights the beasts. Not only is she matched in her sex with a heifer (20) but the narrator also remarks on her dress, comportment and the condition of her hair. After being tossed by a heifer, she rearranges her tunic to cover her thighs, 'thinking more of her modesty than of her pain', and she also asks for a pin to fix her dishevelled hair, 'for it was not right that a martyr should die with her hair in disorder, lest she might seem to be mourning in her hour of triumph'.[116]

Although the narrator provides us with an explanation as to why, in the midst of her ordeal and torture, Perpetua's attention turns to matters of coiffure, there may be an alternative explanation for the martyr's rather bizarre request. Sue Blundell notes that in antiquity, women who let their hair down demonstrate that they are released from normal societal constraints.[117] Perhaps the focus here is to ensure that Perpetua's representation accords well with social and ideological models of femininity. That this is the case has also been argued by McInerney who contends that although Perpetua redefines herself as a Christian, she does not deny or reconfigure her femininity, or even renounce proper feminine behaviour. Rather, these are translated from a pagan to a Christian context, thus ensuring that Perpetua remains an ideal Roman matron even as she dies in the arena.[118] Stephanie Cobb also argues along similar lines, noting that the contradictory nature of Perpetua's representation includes both masculinizing and feminizing elements.[119] On the one hand, Perpetua performs masculinity by showing herself capable of self-control; she even exhibits authority over her father. At other times, however, Perpetua exhibits traditional feminine characteristics such as fear (3.5) and concern for her child (3.9). Furthermore, after her vision, the judge also describes her as 'daughter' (*filia*), underscoring her femininity and legal status as a dependent (4.1; 5.2).

Although readers should be sensitive to the different voices within the text, that of the narrator and that of Perpetua herself, McInerney and Cobb are correct in calling attention to Perpetua's traditional female representation within the martyrdom story.[120] Perpetua is shown to be a woman resistant to imperial but not masculine control; she remains a woman very much concerned about her father, brother and son in this world and about her spiritual fathers and brothers in the next.[121]

The *Martyrdom of Perpetua* thus resonates with the *Acts of Paul and Thecla*, where Thecla offers to cut her hair but is dissuaded from doing so (*APTh*. 25), where she transgresses boundaries and ventures into the male public domain only to kiss Paul's fetters (*APTh*. 18) and then roll about on the floor where he taught (*APTh*. 20). Vorster argues that such erotic overtones which pervade the narrative may be regarded as traces of a dominant culture emphasizing the necessity of the female body to attach itself in one way or the other to the male body.[122] It therefore becomes evident that through literary mechanisms such as this the text maintains a sort of 'duality' in regard to Thecla's gender construction. Apart from her masculinized dress, Thecla is female in body and her behaviour mirrors this confused gender mix. She displays traditional womanly behaviour, but this is at times infused with masculine courage.

So what kind of a gender bender is Thecla exactly? What might be the significance of Thecla's partial transformation? Since one of the major impediments toward Thecla's manly transformation is her long hair, below I focus in more detail on what particular significance may be attached to Thecla's offer to cut her hair and Paul preferring her comely or fair of form.

Women's hair and heads

At this point, we will return to the issue of hair. Hair is particularly associated with femininity and sexuality, and Thecla's offer to cut her hair has been interpreted as a clear sign of her renunciation of female sexuality and a willingness to embrace maleness. As I have discussed, Thecla does not cut her hair in the *Acts of Paul and Thecla*. This gesture is incontrovertibly rejected by Paul. What are the implications of Thecla retaining her feminine characteristics? What might they reveal about her representation and the implied construction of masculinity in the *Acts of Paul and Thecla*?

To begin with, it is worthwhile considering further the meaning of Thecla's suggestion that she cut off her hair, and the reasons why Paul does not want her to do so. Why is this such an important interaction?

In the past, in seeking a deeper understanding of femininity, scholars have tended to concentrate on the representation of women's bodies. Far less attention, however, has been focused upon women's hair. Although hair might be considered a superficial part of the human body, it does, in fact, carry a deep and meaningful significance in many societies and communicates a great deal about sexuality and gender, both unconsciously and non-verbally. In particular, the representation of the female head is especially expressive of femininity and female sexuality: female hair carries a kind of erotic allure. The female head is, therefore, a particularly rich and important site in the symbolization of gender and the values of specific cultural or religious systems.[123] The myth of Medusa, the monster with snakes for hair, perhaps demonstrates that when women are demonized, it is their hair and heads that seem to embody power and potency. For authors of secular love poems too, women's sexual attractiveness is signalled by their beautiful, fair hair.[124] It stands to reason, then, that in a number of different contexts, cutting the hair is associated with asceticism.[125] Shaved heads frequently signify that the person is expected to have no sexual relations, while long, unkempt hair signifies unrestrained sexuality.[126]

Karen Lang explores the treatment of hair among female practitioners in the Buddhist tradition. For the Buddhist nun, her shaved head signifies a rite of separation, a turning away from the heat of sensual desire. By shaving the head, the individual ritually and symbolically separates herself from the world of familial relationship and reorients the self towards another world.[127] For the nun, the continuing commitment to shaving her head indicates her control over her sexuality and her potential fertility. By altering her appearance with the shaving off of her hair, a secular symbol of sexual attractiveness, the nun renders herself sexually unattractive and unavailable.[128]

We can also see an association between hair and sexuality in both Tertullian and Paul. These authors both emphasize the sexual character of women's heads. In 1 Cor. 11.2-16, Paul attempts to justify why women who pray and prophesy in worship must either be veiled or have particular hairstyles. For Tertullian, a woman must cover herself otherwise she announces her own sexual availability.[129] That the text of 1 Cor. 11.2-16 is difficult to interpret is an understatement.[130] Primarily scholars are divided on the issue of whether or not Paul is referring to hairstyles or head coverings.[131] Scholars are also divided on the question of whose behaviour Paul is addressing: that of the women only or that of both the men and the women. Scholars working from both a feminist and conservative perspective tend to assume that the text is dealing solely with women.[132] However, it has been suggested that the behaviour of the Corinthian men is equally at issue.[133]

Whatever it was that the Corinthian women, and possibly men, were doing with their hair or head coverings, while praying and prophesying, it was something that seemed to give Paul reason to be greatly concerned.[134] However, his response to behaviour within the Corinthian Church raises fundamental questions of gender and sexuality.[135] What is significant for our purposes is that this passage discusses women's hair or heads in a way that sexualizes them: 'Does not nature itself teach you that if a man wears long hair it is degrading to him but if a woman has long hair, it is her glory? For her hair is given to her for a covering' (1 Cor. 11.14-15 NRSV). This assumption that long hair is a dishonour to men but a glory to women would have been widely shared by the Romanized society of Corinth.[136] D'Angelo argues that this statement makes some sense if Paul sees an analogy between the woman's head, on which hair grows profusely, and the genitals of men and women, where hair also grows more abundantly, and which in Paul's view must be covered in public. Men's heads are different, in that they can be shaven or go bald without causing shame (1 Cor. 11.4-6).

Tertullian's writing on the veiling of virgins also demonstrates a pairing of women's hair and heads with sexuality. Tertullian wants to eliminate any distinctions between woman and virgin, a distinction which has the effect of exempting virgins from the rulings of 1 Cor. 11.3-16. He therefore makes a case that Paul clearly included virgins among women when he required women to cover their heads (ch. 4); it is shameful for virgins, he claims, as well as for wives to be 'shorn' (ch. 7). Perhaps more importantly, Tertullian's tract reveals an explicit correlation between women's heads and their genitalia: 'Let her whose lower parts are not bare have her upper likewise covered' (ch. 12).[137]

Molly Myerowitz Levine too brings together a wealth of evidence from the ancient Greek, Roman and Jewish traditions and argues that the Mediterranean developed a kind of grammar or language of hair in antiquity. She notes that writing of Spartan marriage customs, Plutarch tells us that after the bride had been carried off by her future husband, her hair was shorn off close to the skin.[138] Her study of first-century Roman poetry also reveals that marriage was seen to transform women, and this transformation was enacted both literally and symbolically through women's hair.[139]

Although these examples are diverse in dating and traditions, they surely help demonstrate the universal and powerful significance of hair and its association with female sexuality across different cultures and periods.

Pleasurable viewing and disappearing men

So what is the significance of Thecla standing before Paul, offering to cut her hair and having that offer rebuffed? By refusing Thecla's haircut, Paul ensures that Thecla remains in a state of sexual attractiveness and the focus of the male gaze. With her long hair, Thecla remains a beautiful and desirable woman – which is why Alexander falls in love with her (*APTh*. 26). Paul's (and the author's) preference seems to veer towards a sexually 'comely' woman. Do we see here a religious and patriarchal insistence on female sexuality? With her hair and head intact, and feminine sexuality preserved, has Paul prevented Thecla's (and subsequently woman's) metaphoric decapitation?

Although this may initially appear to be the case, Howard Eilberg-Schwartz notes the more subtle forms of female beheadings. He argues that it is in the eroticization of the female head that woman is metaphorically beheaded, since it reduces woman to a mere objectified body available for male pleasure.[140] Jennifer Glancy also notes that a key component in the representation of gender is the construction of femininity as 'to be looked-at-ness' and masculinity in terms of voyeurism.[141] The male gaze defines woman as object and man as subject. In retaining her feminine locks, therefore, Thecla remains a sexualized object and is symbolically beheaded.

Of course, the alternative would have been to have given Thecla a haircut. This would have meant that Thecla would have relinquished her sexuality along with her object status and she would have symbolically become male. However, the problem is that, in a transformed state of maleness, Thecla's womanly head would have been removed. It would, therefore, seem that the woman within this text remains in a double bind; either with her hair or without it, Thecla loses her head.

The head is also the anatomical part of the female body that gives women a voice and an identity. As Eilberg-Schwartz points out, it is the voice that threatens to unmake and disrupt the classic gender distinctions that have linked men to speech, power, identity and the mind.[142] Interesting, then, that Thecla in the first two-thirds of the narrative is silent and passive, even when she stands accused before the Governor: 'she stood there looking steadily at Paul. And … she did not answer' (*APTh*. 20).[143] Here too is another form of beheading: a woman without a voice, without identity.

The text symbolically relieves woman of both identity and voice and reduces her to a mere sexual body, albeit one that is not expected to fulfil the biological function of reproduction. By turning the female head into a symbol of desire, rather than a symbol of identity with a capacity for speech and language, woman is beheaded. It is specifically those aspects and features that draw attention to women's heads (their hair, their looks and their voice) that appear to provide the means by which women lose their heads. Thecla, therefore, is not quite the gender bender she was initially taken for. By not allowing her to cut her hair, Paul impedes and resists Thecla's pursuit of religious perfection. There is, therefore, no countercultural subversive narrative of an audacious woman becoming male, overturning gendered hierarchies and norms.

In her book *Dying to Be Men*, Cobb very much focuses on the paradoxical gender constructions of masculinized female martyrs in both male and female martyrologies, noting the regularity with which they are imbued with this complex mix of both feminizing and masculinizing attributes.[144] Her work offers a welcome redress in the balance of scholarship which, as noted above, has generally downplayed the more feminizing aspects of masculinized female martyr representations. It is, however, only by attending equally both to the feminizing and masculinizing imagery that will we fully understand the role these representations play within the texts. Cobb herself acknowledges that modern interpreters have had a tendency to gloss over the more seemingly banal feminized descriptions of women as daughters and mothers who are modest and beautiful. She therefore broadens the scope of her study to consider more carefully the complexity of female representations in ancient martyrdom texts.

Cobb argues that martyrdom accounts are, to some extent, literary creations designed to meet particular communal needs. Utilizing social identity theory, she argues that the paradoxes within masculinized female representations serve an important purpose in the formation of Christian group identity. However, the attributes of Christian identity differ for women in inter- and intra-communal situations. In the former, the female martyr must be more masculine than her non-Christian opponents; in the latter, she must be appropriately feminine when compared to her Christian brothers.[145]

Thus, Cobb argues, the contradictory depictions of female martyrs as both masculine and feminine serve as models for appropriate group identities for women in two distinct social encounters.[146] On the one hand, the stories of female martyrs allow authors to develop Christian social identity through external power negotiations (i.e. the martyr or Christian community against the Roman, Jew or Pagan 'other'). On the other hand, depicting women as feminized displays the more 'socially conservative' side of Christianity. The masculinization and feminization in these narratives thus illustrates a communal concern over appropriate roles for women in two distinct situations, inter- and intra-communal. Feminine characteristics such as modesty and submissiveness continued to be valued within the Christian communities that produced these texts. The authors thus eased the gender tension by illustrating the women's femininity alongside their masculinity.[147]

It is unfortunate that within her study Cobb omits to discuss the explicit eroticization of female martyrdoms, since this forms a central motif in many of the stories. She also fails to discuss what is surely the pertinent text of the *Acts of Paul and Thecla*. One can only speculate on her reasons for doing so: perhaps the fact that Thecla survives her trials and technically never achieves martyrdom? Whatever the reason for this omission, it is evident for our purposes that the underlying thrust of Cobb's argument is that the feminizing aspects of masculinized female martyrs was a way of ensuring that women maintained their socially accepted positions in Christian communities. Thus, while within the context of the amphitheatre, Christian women can endure torture and punishment and 'take it like a man', when it came to their status within the Christian community, they had to firmly know their place. The feminizing aspects of the masculinized female representations thus serve their purpose: a place for everything and everything (read 'woman') in its place. However, Thecla aside, the reality of martyrdoms was that women were unlikely to ever emerge alive from an amphitheatre. They were, therefore, equally unlikely to destabilize the Christian community status quo. Given, as maintained by Cobb (and others), that martyrdom accounts were largely literary creations, why then were the authors of these highly stylized texts so reluctant to permit female martyrs full masculine virilization in the face of their enemies?

As a tentative hypothesis, I would suggest that ancient constructions of masculinity, and the way in which gender was perceived in antiquity, may well have played a hand in impeding the full virilization of the woman in the *Acts of Paul and Thecla*. Julia Epstein and Kristina Straub underscore the fact that since distinctions between male and female bodies are delineated by cultural politics onto an only 'apparently' clear biological foundation, it permanently renders sex/gender systems as unstable constructions.[148] Peter Brown also highlights the fear in antiquity of the male body collapsing into a state of primary undifferentiation. Although no normal man might actually become a woman, men carried with them a constant fear and dread of becoming 'womanish'. Men's fluctuating 'heat' was an uncertain force, and, if it was to remain effective, its momentum had to be consciously maintained. Indeed, 'it was never enough to be male; a man had to strive to remain "virile"'. Thus men had to learn to exclude from their character, poise and temper, all tell-tale traces of 'softness' that might betray in them the half-formed state of woman.[149] The male state, supposedly secured by the laws of nature, is actually revealed as a precarious performance: sexual differentiation had to be maintained by force.

Maud Gleason, in a study comparing two rival rhetoricians, has highlighted how masculinity in the ancient world was perceived as an achieved state, radically underdetermined by anatomical sex.[150] The polarized distinctions, smooth/hirsute, high voice/low voice, panther-like/leonine, that were supposed to characterize the gulf between men and women instead divided the male sex into legitimate and illegitimate players. For individuals, these stereotypes facilitated a process by which the self was projected through certain highly stylized forms of self-display. Thus, manliness was not a birth right; it was something that had to be won.[151] These findings are also borne out by other studies on masculinity. Roman sexual protocol that defined men as impenetrable penetrators was part of a much wider understanding that regarded men of high social status as being able to defend the boundaries of their body from invasive assaults of all kinds. However, some males, because of their low status, were vulnerable to penetration and were, therefore, not full men. Consequently, they lacked the 'manly' characteristic of impenetrable bodies.[152] Although in normal circumstances the body of a Roman citizen male was inviolable, an adulterer lost that inviolability and, if caught by the aggrieved husband, could be subjected to the punishment of rape, thus emasculating him and lowering his status from full man (*vir* – that is full citizen manhood) to something less.[153] Ancient masculinity is then always provisional and contingent, always intrinsically at risk from any sexual 'slippage'.

With such unstable constructions of masculine gender, it is quite possible that a woman becoming fully male could easily serve as a stark reminder of the truly precarious condition of masculinity, its real ephemeral nature. Thus, Thecla must preserve aspects of her femininity and sexuality in order that masculinity retain its constructed power. Thecla's partial transformation gives voice to fears of a brittle masculinity. She challenges the established authority of that sexuality and reveals an incipient threat to heterosexual male dominance. The spectacle of a woman so easily imitating men would undoubtedly have conjured up the foreboding picture of a non-dominant, impotent masculinity, a threat to man's virility. A frightening imitation of the castrated male, she would jeopardize the apparent naturalness of the dominant gender ideology and instead represent a 'failed' masculinity, impinging dangerously upon male subjectivity and male control.[154] Thecla, therefore, cannot become fully male because as fully male, Thecla would threaten to unmake men.

Castelli notes that the martyr's death is a masculine death, even when, or perhaps especially when, it is suffered by a woman.[155] In surviving her martyrdom, Thecla is also denied a masculine death. Thus, despite leading a chaste spiritual life, Thecla is not removed from the challenges of being a woman in the world of men. The beautiful Thecla, with her long hair and legs revealed, remains a pleasurable (and anxiety-provoking) object of the male gaze. Despite never being permitted to gaze at Paul for any length of time, the reader's gaze is repeatedly invited to rest upon the beautiful, desirable, often naked Thecla: there is no veiled voyeurism here.[156] In his book *Foucault's Virginity*, Simon Goldhill asks the provocative question, 'How like a man can a woman be?'[157] The *Acts of Paul and Thecla* would direct us to reply, 'Not very much like a man at all'.

Conclusion

Within this chapter, I have focused upon the motif of woman becoming 'male' as a pathway to spiritual perfection. One of the central signifiers of this concept was the development of traits of female transvestism. Thus, cutting one's hair or resorting to wearing male clothing became associated with the idea of woman 'becoming male'. However, although the *Acts of Paul and Thecla* has regularly been regarded as the quintessential text which displayed an early manifestation of this motif (*APTh*. 25, 40), approaching the text with a hermeneutic of suspicion which takes at its starting point the identification and dynamics of the androcentric, patriarchal character of the text, a close reading has revealed that, despite donning male apparel at the end of the narrative, Thecla's gender transformation is, in fact, only partial because she never cuts her hair (*APTh*. 25). As fully male, Thecla would evoke, within men, a deep anxiety and threaten to unmake their gender. She exposes a fragile masculinity. Her long hair and a short masculine χιτών, therefore, ensure that she remains feminine, objectified and in her proper place: the focus of the male gaze. A sexy cross-dresser and female icon is displayed for the voyeuristic delight and enjoyment of men: the active controllers of the look.

Thecla began the narrative as (to use a modern turn of phrase) 'eye candy', and she remains so by the close of the narrative. Is this a positive representation of a woman? How does such a construct serve to affirm the representation of Thecla and women generally? Is the text empowering for women? Even if becoming male could be seen as a positive construct for women, it is clear that Thecla never fully becomes male.[158] A haircut may well have helped to consolidate her transformation but such an action is considered shameful: in body, Thecla must remain a woman, and one that pleasures the male gaze.

Nevertheless, it is not all bad news for Thecla (and women). Although Thecla is never fully masculinized, and although she is denied a *supposed* 'advancement' into the 'All Men's Club', there is little doubt that there are aspects of virility and, therefore, traces of subjectivity within her representation. She displays manly courage in fighting off Alexander, transgressing spatial boundaries and showing bravery in the arena. This manifestation of ἀνδρεία within the text is important. Furthermore, in cloaking Thecla in a manly χιτών as she sets off to find Paul, the author is undoubtedly working to convey something positive about this female, but, at this point, it is not evident exactly what that positive message is.

Since long hair is one of the foremost markers of Thecla's femininity and womanliness, and since the explicit detail of a haircut could quite easily have been added to complete her masculine transformation, one has to assume that it is obviously essential that Thecla remains female in form. Indeed, in preserving her hair intact and in revealing her legs with her masculine garb, the text appears to emphasize the importance of preserving Thecla's womanly form. Furthermore, the fact that her body remains impenetrable, unmarred and untouched is also of consequence. Masculine virtue is important, but so is Thecla's female virgin body. Thus, although Thecla may be framed as sexual object, the manly traits she exhibits and the masculine χιτών with which she is cloaked ensure complex gendered meanings are assigned to her representation. Thecla must not only contend with the powerful forces of city and state, along with the civic gaze, but she must also contend with her female body: a virgin body which, through miraculous intervention, heroically overcomes and endures in the arena. It is to those very bodily and physical trials in the arena to which we now turn.

Notes

1 Margaret R. Miles, *Carnal Knowing: Female Nakedness and Religious Meaning in the Christian West* (Eugene, OR: Wipf & Stock, 1989), 35; Elizabeth Castelli, 'Virginity and Its Meaning for Women's Sexuality in Early Christianity', *JFSR* 2 (1986): 75; Elizabeth Clark, *Ascetic Piety and Women's Faith, Essays on Late Ancient Christianity* (New York: Edwin Mellen, 1986), 43; Sebastian P. Brock and Susan Ashbrook Harvey, *Holy Women of the Syrian Orient* (Berkeley, CA: University of California Press, 1987), 24; Schüssler Fiorenza, *In Memory*, 276–9; see also e.g. *Acts of Thomas* 114 where Mygdonia cuts her hair and the Codex Vaticanus fragment of *Acts of Andrew* in which the Apostle Andrew addresses Maximilla as 'the wise man' (ὁ φρομινος ἀνηρ, Codex Vaticanus 808, *AA*. 9). Translation taken from *NTA*, 131; the Greek is cited in Daniel Boyarin, *A Radical Jew: Paul and the Politics of Identity* (Berkley: University of California Press, 1994), 321, n. 41.
2 Transvestism here is used to refer to women who don male apparel and cut their hair.
3 'If any woman, under pretence of asceticism, shall change her apparel and, instead of a woman's accustomed clothing, shall put on that of a man, let her be anathema'

(Canon 13), taken from John Fulton, *Index Canonum: The Canons Called Apostolical, the Canons of the Undisputed General Councils, and the Canons of the Provincial Council of Ancyra Neo-Caesarea, Gangra, Antioch and Laodicea* (New York: Pott, Young, 1872).

4 Jer., *Ep.* 22.27; see also Ross Shepard Kraemer, ed., *Women's Religions in the Greco-Roman World: A Sourcebook* (Oxford: Oxford University Press, 2004), particularly 391.
5 See also Davis, *Cult of Saint Thecla*, 33–4; Brown, *The Body and Society*, 268; McGinn, 'The Acts of Thecla', 827, n. 81.
6 Castelli, 'Virginity', 76.
7 See n. 1 above.
8 See e.g. Davis, *Cult of Saint Thecla*, 31; Castelli, 'Virginity', 75–6; McGinn, 'The Acts of Thecla', 827, n. 81.
9 See Chapter 1, esp. Burrus, *Chastity*; Davies, *Revolt of the Widows*, 66; MacDonald, *Legend*.
10 Castelli, 'Virginity', 75.
11 Ibid., 77, 74; for a later fourth-century development of this tradition, see Elizabeth Clark, *Jerome, Chrysostom and Friends: Essays and Translations* (New York: Mellen, 1979), 15, 19, 55–6.
12 Castelli, 'Virginity', 77.
13 See Judith Lieu, *Christian Identity in the Jewish and Graeco-Roman World* (Oxford: Oxford University Press, 2004), 178–210; see also Miles, *Carnal Knowing*, 54.
14 Although the dating of Galatians is contested, MacDonald dates the Epistle around 53 CE, see Dennis R. MacDonald, *There Is No Male and Female: The Fate of a Dominical Saying in Paul and Gnosticism* (Philadelphia, PA: Fortress, 1987), 128.
15 Wayne A. Meeks, 'The Image of the Androgyne: Some Uses of a Symbol in Earliest Christianity', *History of Religions* 13 (1974): 165–208. It should be noted that more recently some scholars argue against any reading of the text that relates Gal. 3.28 to the notion of androgyny. Douglas Campbell, e.g., believes that Paul's rationale of 'oneness' is explicitly Christological and that Paul is speaking of the oneness of sonship in the sense that we are all now 'sons' in Christ. Paul's main emphasis in Gal. 3.28 is that the distinction between Jewish and non-Jewish is superseded within Christ. Douglas A. Campbell, *The Quest for Paul's Gospel* (London: T&T Clark, 2005), 99, 101.
16 That Paul is referring to Gen. 1.27 is recognized by the linguistic shift he makes from the nouns, Jew, Greek, slave and free, to the adjectives ἄρσεν and θῆλυ rather than employing the expected ἀνήρ and γυνή. In addition, the use of καί in place of οὐδέ further highlights that this section mirrors the text of Gen. 1.27 within the LXX.
17 Meeks, 'Image of the Androgyne', 197–202; see also MacDonald, *No Male and Female*. MacDonald is, however, more circumspect in his approach, arguing that although Paul does have a vision of sexual equality, Gal. 3.28 is not a manifesto to the feminist cause. Rather, Paul is more concerned about unity in the Christian community (128–30). It should also be noted that Meeks's interpretation has been seriously challenged on the grounds that the wording of the baptismal formula refers to sexual differentiation rather than to gender equality, see e.g. Dale B. Martin, *The Corinthian Body* (New Haven, CT: Yale University Press, 1995), 229–49, esp. 199.
18 Bassler, 'Limits and Differentiation', 126; see also her n. 15 where she highlights that this point is contested by Phyllis Trible, *God and the Rhetoric of Sexuality* (Philadelphia, PA: Fortress, 1978), 15–21. Trible argues that האדם should not be

understood as a single androgynous creature but as two creatures, one male and one female.
19 Schüssler Fiorenza, *In Memory*, 218.
20 Ibid.
21 These three pairs of oppositions are well attested in Hellenistic ideology and attributed to Plato in Plutarch's *Marius* (46.1) and to Thales and Socrates in Diog. Laert., *Vitae Philosophorum* (1.33) and Lactant. *Div. inst.* (3.19.17). Betz also highlights possible influence from the Sophists, Hans Dieter Betz, *Galatians* (Philadelphia, PA: Fortress), 192, n. 87, and 193, n. 95 – he also notes a Persian parallel on p. 185, n. 26.
22 Pl., *Ti.* 90 e, John M. Cooper and D. Hutchinson, eds, *Plato: Complete Works* (Cambridge, IN: Hackett, 1997).
23 Ibid., 91 d.
24 This text is attributed to R. Judah ben Elai (c. 150 CE) in *t. Ber.* 7.18 and *y. Ber.* 13b, but to his contemporary R. Meir in *b. Menah.* 43b. The thanksgiving was related to male responsibility for the Law, which women, Gentiles and slaves did not inherit, see Schüssler Fiorenza, *In Memory*, 217.
25 Philo, *Quaest. in Exod.* 1.8, 46.
26 Philo, *Vit. Cont.* 68–9. See also Joan E. Taylor, *Jewish Women Philosophers of First-Century Alexandria: Philo's 'Therapeutae' Reconsidered* (Oxford: Oxford University Press, 2003), where she argues that the women described point to the presence of other Jewish women philosophers in Alexandria in the first century CE.
27 See the discussion in Skinner, 'Ego Mulier', 134; Carson, 'Putting Her in Her Place', 153–6; see also Rousselle, *Porneia*, 5–23, esp. 14–15; Diana M. Swancutt, 'Still Before Sexuality: "Greek" Androgyny, The Roman Imperial Politics of Masculinity and the Roman Invention of the Tribas', in *Mapping Gender in Ancient Religious Discourses*, ed. Todd Penner and Caroline Vander Stichele (Boston, MA: Brill, 2007), 11–61, 28–9.
28 Martin, *Corinthian Body*, 230. See also Szesnat who discusses Philo's fear of gender transgression towards the female end of the spectrum. Holger Szesnat, 'Mostly Aged Virgins, Philo and the Presence of the Therapeutrides at Lake Mareotis', *Neot* 32 (1998): 191–201.
29 See e.g. Tert., *De cul Fem.* 16-23 (*ANF* 4.14); Clem. Al., *Paed.* 2, 12, these authors demonstrate a deep distrust of the female body and gender. See also R. Howard Bloch, *Medieval Misogyny and the Invention of Western Romantic Love* (Chicago, IL: University of Chicago Press, 1991), esp. Chapters 2 and 3; Carson, 'Putting Her in Her Place', 135–69.
30 For later examples of chaste ascetic piety among women, see Castelli, 'Virginity' and Clark, *Ascetic Piety*.
31 For dating, see Stephen J. Patterson and James M. Robinson, eds, *The Fifth Gospel: The Gospel of Thomas Comes of Age* (Harrisburg, PA: Trinity, 1998), 40; see also Richard Valantasis, *The Gospel of Thomas* (London: Routledge, 1997), 12–21.
32 *Gos. Thom.*, Logion 114, translation taken from Patterson and Robinson, *The Fifth Gospel*.
33 Ibid., Logion 22.
34 See Martin, *Corinthian Body*, 32, 229–31; see also the discussion in Elizabeth Castelli, 'I Will Make Mary Male: Pieties of the Body and Gender Transformation of Christian Women in Late Antiquity', in *Body Guards, The Cultural Politics of Gender Ambiguity*, ed. Julia Epstein and Kristina Straub (London: Routledge, 1991), 29–49, 32–3.
35 *The Gospel of Philip* 116 (71), Robert McLachlan Wilson, *The Gospel of Philip: Translated from the Coptic Text, with an Introduction and Commentary* (London: Mowbray, 1962).

36 *The Gospel According to Mary* (18–20), Robert McLachlan Wilson and George W. MacRae, *The Coptic Gnostic Library, Nag Hammadi Codices V, 2–5 & VI with Papyrus Berolinensis 8502, 1 and 4*, ed. Douglas M. Parrott (Leiden: Brill, 1979), 461.
37 *2 Clem.* 12.2, Bart D. Ehrman, ed. and trans., *The Apostolic Fathers I, I Clement, II Clement, Ignatius, Polycarp, Didache* (Cambridge, MA: Harvard University Press, 2003). *2 Clem.* is usually dated from the beginning of the second century or the end of the first, see MacDonald, *No Male and Female*, 18, n. 6.
38 Clem. Al., *Strom.* 3.13.92, John Ferguson, *Clement of Alexandria: Stromateis, Books One to Three* (Washington, DC: Catholic University of America Press, 1991), 314.
39 Castelli, 'I Will Make Mary Male', 32; see also the discussion by Swancutt, 'Still before Sexuality', who discusses ancient views of the tribades (or lesbians) who were viewed as a monstrous 'third' sex, 11–61.
40 See e.g. Brittany E. Wilson, *Unmanly Men: Refigurations of Masculinity in Luke-Acts* (New York: Oxford University Press, 2015), 47; Castelli, 'Virginity', 76; Castelli, 'I Will Make Mary Male', 44; Miles, *Carnal Knowing*, 55; MacDonald, *Legend*, 20; MacDonald, 'Corinthian Veils and Gnostic Androgynes', in *Images of the Feminine in Gnosticism*, ed. Karen L. King (Philadelphia, PA: Fortress, 1988), 276–92, 291; McGinn, 'The Acts of Thecla', 820, see also n. 81; Boyarin, *A Radical Jew*, 198; Aymer, 'Hailstorms and Fireball', 53, 57; Kraemer, 'Conversion', 305; Seim, 'Ascetic Autonomy', 136; Howe, 'Interpretations', 40, 45; Mary Rose D'Angelo, 'Veils, Virgins, and the Tongues of Men and Angels: Women's Heads in Early Christianity', in *Off with Her Head! The Denial of Women's Identity in Myth, Religion and Culture*, ed. Howard Eilberg-Schwartz and Wendy Doniger (Berkeley: University of California Press, 1995), 143; Dunn, 'Women's Liberation', 246, n. 6; Jensen, 'Die Theklageschichte', 745; Petropoulos, 'Transvestite Virgin', 132–3; Braun, 'Physiotherapy', 215.
41 Aymer, 'Hailstorms and Fireball', 53. Aymer also argues that Thecla's haircut is a means to fictive kinship and she wishes to follow Paul as a brother, 53.
42 McGinn, 'The Acts of Thecla', 820; see also Castelli, 'Virginity', 76; Miles, *Carnal Knowing*, 55.
43 Braun, 'Physiotherapy', 210, 212.
44 Ibid., 215–16.
45 Petropoulos, 'Transvestite Virgin', 125.
46 Ibid., 127, 131.
47 Ibid., 132.
48 Ibid., 136–8.
49 See note 58 below for an explanation of the translation.
50 A. T. Robertson, *A Grammar of the Greek New Testament in the Light of Historical Research* (New York: Hodder & Stoughton, 1914), 804.
51 Usually spelt as one word in Greek, ὅπουδἄν: see under ὅπου in H. G. Liddell and R. Scott, *Greek-English Lexicon* (Oxford: Clarendon Press, 1996), henceforth, LSJ. See also pp. 717 and 56 in Walter Bauer, Frederick W. Danker, William F. Arndt and F. Wilbur Gingrich, *A Greek-English Lexicon of the New Testament and Other Early Christian Literature*, 3rd ed. (Chicago, IL: University of Chicago Press, 2000), henceforth, BDAG.
52 Or ugly/shameful αἰσχρός.
53 LSJ 371; BDAG 213.
54 See e.g. Mk 13.33; Lk. 21.8; Mt. 8.28; Rev. 1.3; 22.10, BDAG, 498 3 a and b.
55 BDAG 497.
56 BDAG 497 b 1.

57 NTA, 243. αἰσχρός, when paired with καιρός, is translated 'ill-suited', see LSJ 3.43.
58 Although a translation using the words 'shameful' or 'ugly' would be more accurate, I have chosen to nuance my own translation of αἰσχρός as 'inappropriate' because when paired with καιρός, it gives the sense that this is an 'inappropriate time'. This translation would also make more sense to a contemporary reader.
59 BDAG 29.
60 Barrier, *Acts of Paul and Thecla*, 133–4.
61 Corrington Streete, *Redeemed Bodies*, 85.
62 See Chapter 1; see also Chapter 2, on the Pauline tradition.
63 Taken from J. Fulton, *Index Canonum*.
64 See Pauline tradition, Chapter 2.
65 Although the apparatus does not show any variants for this σὶ form, there is no evidence for the existence of this form of pronoun, and it is possible that this is just a scribal error for σύ (nom. of 2nd pers. pronoun sing.). In the remainder of the verse, the pronoun forms σοι and μοι are used. Since these are in the dative and not the nominative, they are not emphatic, cf. J. W. Wenham, *The Elements of New Testament Greek* (Cambridge: Cambridge University Press, 2003), 79.
66 μὴ must here be used like ὅπως μὴ, which is itself an abbreviated idiom. See, LSJ 1A b. Here it is used in a prohibitive sense expressing a warning, see BDAG 645 1 c.
67 BDAG 793.
68 See Robin M. Jensen, 'Baptismal Rites and Architecture', in *Late Ancient Christianity: A People's History of Christianity*, ed. Virginia Burrus (Augsburg, MN: Fortress, 2005), 120–2; Barrier, *Acts of Paul and Thecla*, 134.
69 BDAG 612.
70 Petropoulos, 'Transvestite Virgin', 132.
71 LSJ 680.
72 Petropoulos, 'Transvestite Virgin', 132.
73 Ibid. Although Petropoulos switches between the *Acts of Paul and Thecla* and the *Vita*, here he is specifically referring to APTh. 25.
74 See Shepard Kraemer, *Unreliable Witnesses*, 136–7, see also her n. 76 where she admits that there is no easy correlation between hair length and social status in classical Greek sources as even female slaves adopted the hair style of the Empress Livia.
75 See also APTh. 11, where Thecla is engaged to a high-status man.
76 According to the *Acts of Eugenia* 2, Eugenia was said to have taken Thecla as her model; see Frederick C. Conybeare, *The Apology and Acts of Apollonius and other Monuments of Early Christianity* (London: Swan Sonnenschein, 1894), 158; Laura Swan, *The Forgotten Desert Mothers: Sayings, Lives and Stories of Early Christian Women* (Mahwah, NJ: Paulist Press, 2001), 81–2.
77 Brock and Harvey, *Holy Women*, 25, 40–62.
78 See n. 40 above.
79 Shepard Kraemer, *Unreliable Witnesses*, 137–8.
80 F Codex (Vaticanus Graecus 866; Rome; eleventh century CE); G Codex (Barocciano Graecus 180/Codex Grabe/Recension G, Bodleian Library; Oxford; twelfth century CE), see Lipsius-Bonnet, *Acta Apostolorum Apocrypha*, 253.
81 Dagron, *Vie et Miracles*, 14 (pp. 226–7). My own translation.
82 See e.g. Pesthy, 'Thecla among the Fathers'.
83 On the development of the Thecla cult, see Davis, *Cult of Saint Thecla*; see also Dagron, *Vie et Miracles* and Cooper, 'A Saint in Exile'.

84 For dating and translation of the longer ending, see Shepard Kraemer, *Women's Religions*, 298, 306–8.
85 Nelson-Atkins Museum of Art in Kansas City (48.10), *Age of Spirituality: Late Antique and Early Christian Art, Third to Seventh Century. Catalogue of the Exhibition at the Metropolitan Museum of Art, November 19, 1977, through February 12, 1978*, ed. Kurt Weitzmann (New York: Metropolitan Museum of Art in association with Princeton University Press, 1979), 574–5, figure 512. See also the description and discussion in Claudia Nauerth and Rüdiger Warns, *Thekla. Ihre Bilder in der frühchristlichen Kunst: Göttinger Orientforschungen, Studien zur spätantiken und frühchristlichen Kunst* (Wiesbaden: Harrassowitz, 1981), 31–4, figure 14.
86 This 'Eastern style' representation of Thecla is typical of a number of pilgrims' souvenirs in the form of flasks and oil lamps. See e.g. Cartlidge and Elliott, *Art and the Christian Apocrypha*, 155.
87 See Davis, *Cult of Saint Thecla*, 117–19, also his appendix A, 195–200, and for illustrations, see figures 7–12.
88 The object is also discussed in Nauerth and Warns, *Thekla*, 35–42. See also Davis, *Cult of Saint Thecla*, Appendix A, no. 12, his figure 10. (The date of this object is uncertain.)
89 Nauerth and Warns, *Thekla*, 93–9, Tables I–XVI.
90 Nauerth and Warns, *Thekla*, Panel II (4) Relief in Etschmiadzin (zu S.11).
91 Cartlidge and Elliott, *Art and the Christian Apocrypha*, 158; Cartlidge and Elliott also discuss one exception to this rule; a painting of Thecla from the eighteenth century which represents Thecla as nimbed, with short hair and dressed in monk's cloth tunic, 160.
92 Castelli, *Martyrdom and Memory*, 171.
93 Ibid.
94 The fifth-century *Vita* of Thecla which makes her haircut explicit is obviously an exception to this later development of a more feminized Thecla.
95 Dagron, *Vie et Miracles*, 14 (p. 227).
96 McInerney, *Eloquent Virgins*, 43.
97 LSJ 1993; see also Simon Hornblower and Antony Spawforth, eds, *The Oxford Companion to Classical Civilization*, 2nd ed. (Oxford: Oxford University Press, 2014), 252.
98 See Larrisa Bonfante and Eva Jaunzems, 'Clothing and Ornament', in *Civilization of the Ancient Mediterranean: Greece and Rome*, ed. Michael Grant and Rachel Kitzinger (New York: Charles Scribner, 1988), 1390, 1398, 1403–4; see also Nigel Guy Wilson, ed., *Encyclopedia of Ancient Greece* (New York: Routledge, 2006), 245.
99 Sue Blundell, 'Clutching at Clothes', in *Women's Dress in the Ancient Greek World*, ed. Lloyd Llewellyn-Jones (London: Duckworth and the Classical Press of Wales, 2002), 153.
100 D'Angelo, 'Veils, Virgins', 154, n. 25; Blundell, 'Clutching at Clothes', 15.
101 Hans Herter, 'The Sociology of Prostitution in Antiquity in the Context of Pagan and Christian Writings', in *Sex and Difference in Ancient Greece and Rome*, ed. Mark Golden and Peter Toohey, trans. Linwood DeLong (Edinburgh: Edinburgh University Press, 2003), 88–9. See also Kelly Olson, *Dress and the Roman Woman: Self-Presentation and Society* (New York: Routledge, 2008), 47–9, 127–8.
102 Dagron, *Vie et Miracles*, 15 (p. 231).

103 See Chapter 5, n. 84, for an explanation of Thecla's description as an insect caught in a spider's web.
104 For an understanding of notion of public and private and the complexity of these two terms, see references cited in Chapter 1, n. 69.
105 MacDonald, *Early Christian Women*, 175-6.
106 Philo, *Spec. Leg.* 3.169-75.
107 Thecla would here resemble the goddess Athena or an Amazon warrior with a short manly tunic. This will be discussed further in Chapter 6.
108 This is certainly an 'upgrade' in her characterization and will be discussed further in Chapter 6 since here we are concerned with the extent of her masculine transformation.
109 Musurillo places the dating of the text in the first decade of the third century, Herbert Musurillo, *The Acts of the Christian Martyrs: Introduction, Texts and Translation* (Oxford: Clarendon Press, 1972), xxvi.
110 *The Martyrdom of Saints Perpetua and Felicitas*, 10.6-7, 7 in Musurillo, *Acts of Christian Martyrs*.
111 Burrus, *Saving Shame*, 30.
112 Ibid., 30-1.
113 Ibid., 31.
114 'et expoliata sum et facta sum masculus ... et petiit silentium et dixit: Hic Aegyptius, si hanc uicerit, occident illam gladio', *The Martyrdom of Saints Perpetua and Felicitas*, 7-9, in Musurillo, *Acts of Christian Martyrs*.
115 McInerney, *Eloquent Virgins*, 26-7. Cooper argues that despite the suggestion that Perpetua is a highborn Roman matron a number of points in the text undermine this assertion, Kate Cooper, 'A Father, a Daughter and a Procurator: Authority and Resistance in the Prison Memoir of Perpetua of Carthage', *Gender and History* (2011): 685-6. For our purposes, however, the focus is not so much on Perpetua's status as a woman but more on her gender transformation.
116 Ibid., 20.3-6.
117 Blundell, 'Clutching at Clothes', 161.
118 McInerney, *Eloquent Virgins*, 21.
119 L. Stephanie Cobb, *Dying to Be Men: Gender and Language in Early Christian Martyr Texts* (New York: Columbia University Press, 2008), 94-113.
120 For a discussion of whether the text is autobiographical and the different 'voices' reflected within the text, see Cooper, 'A Father, a Daughter', 685-6, nn. 2 and 3.
121 McInerney, *Eloquent Virgins*, 21-3. Cooper, however, highlights the important point that in refusing to accept the subordinate role of daughter, Perpetua does break free from familial gender hierarchy, Cooper, 'A Father, a Daughter', 697-8.
122 Vorster, 'Construction of Culture', 110.
123 Howard Eilberg-Schwartz, 'Spectacle of the Female Head', in *Off with Her Head! The Denial of Women's Identity in Myth, Religion and Culture*, ed. Howard Eilberg-Schwartz and Wendy Doniger (Berkeley: University of California Press, 1995), 1.
124 Hom., *Il.* 7.355-8.82.
125 Karen Lang, 'Shaven Heads and Loose Hair: Buddhist Attitudes toward Hair and Sexuality', in *Off with Her Head*, ed. Howard Eilberg-Schwartz and Wendy Doniger, 33-4.
126 Eilberg-Schwartz, 'Spectacle', 4.
127 Lang, 'Shaven Heads', 33.
128 Ibid., 35, 46.

129 Tert., *De virg.* (this text is dated *c.* 211 CE, see D'Angelo, 'Veils, Virgins', 131).
130 See e.g. Richard B. Hays, *First Corinthians* (Louisville, KY: John Knox Press, 1997), 190; MacDonald, 'Corinthian Veils', 276.
131 For the view that Paul is referring to loose hair see e.g. Schüssler Fiorenza, *In Memory*, 226-30. For the opposing view see MacDonald, 'Corinthian Veils', 276-92 and the literature there.
132 For further feminist perspectives, see Schüssler Fiorenza, *In Memory*. See also Joan Taylor, 'The Woman Ought to Have Control over Her Head Because of the Angels, 1 Corinthians 11.10', in *Gospel and Gender: A Trinitarian Engagement with Being Male and Female in Christ*, ed. Douglas A. Campbell (London: T&T Clark, 2003), 37-57. For the conservative view see Thomas R. Schreiner, 'Head Coverings, Prophecies and the Trinity', in *Recovering Biblical Manhood and Womanhood*, ed. J. Piper and W. Grudem (Wheaton, IL: Crossway, 1991), 117-32.
133 See especially Jerome Murphy-O'Connor, 'Sex and Logic in 1 Corinthians 11.2-16', *CBQ* 42 (1980): 483-8. For the opposing view that women only are at issue here, see MacDonald, 'Corinthian Veils', 286-92.
134 On the head-covering as a norm for women in antiquity, see the discussion in Molly Myerowitz Levine, 'The Gendered Grammar of Ancient Mediterranean Hair', in *Off with Her Head*, ed. Howard Eilberg-Schwartz and Wendy Doniger, 76-130; see also MacDonald, 'Corinthian Veils', 277, 282-3, 287.
135 A point of contention among scholars is whether Paul's use of κεφαλή in 1 Cor. 11.3 should be translated 'source' or 'ruler'. It is not possible to enter into this discussion here, however, for proponents of the 'source' theory, see Stephen Bedale, 'The Meaning of κεφαλή in the Pauline Epistles', *JTS* 5 (1954): 211-15. For the more conservative position that κεφαλή means *ruler*, see e.g. Wayne Grudem, 'Appendix I: Does kephale ("head") Mean "Source" or "Authority Over" in Greek Literature? A Survey of 2,336 Examples', in *The Role Relationship of Men and Women: New Testament Teaching*, ed. George W. Knight (Chicago, IL: Moody, 1985), 49-80.
136 D'Angelo, 'Veils, Virgins', 135.
137 Tert., *De virg.* (*ANF* 4.27-37).
138 Myerowitz Levine, 'Gendered Grammar', 76-81.
139 Ibid., see also pp. 85, 102.
140 Eilberg-Schwartz, 'Spectacle', 1-2.
141 Jennifer A. Glancy, 'Unveiling Masculinity: The Construction of Gender in Mark 6.17-29', *BI* 1 (1994): 39.
142 Eilberg-Schwartz, 'Spectacle', 1.
143 Although it may be argued that here Thecla may be replicating the model of the 'silence of Christ' before his accusers, I believe that this is unlikely to be the case. Christ was depicted as passive throughout his passion and crucifixion. Thecla, on the other hand, at times, becomes animated in the arena and escapes her trials and ordeals unscathed due to God's miraculous intervention. The two models of suffering would, therefore, appear to comprise quite distinct motifs. See Chapter 6 where this is discussed in more detail.
144 Cobb, *Dying to Be Men*.
145 Ibid., 7-8.
146 Ibid.
147 Ibid., 92-3.
148 Julia Epstein and Kristina Straub, 'Introduction' to *Body Guards: The Cultural Politics of Gender Ambiguity*, ed. Julia Epstein and Kristina Straub (London: Routledge, 1991), 2.

149 See above references to Aristotle, pp. 67–68. See also Brown, *Body and Society*, 11; Swancutt, 'Still before Sexuality', 29–30. On the volatility of gender and the importance of self-control in maintaining masculinity see also Kate Cooper and Conrad Leyser, 'The Gender of Grace: Impotence, Servitude and Manliness in the Fifth-Century West', *Gender and History* 12 (2000): 537–9.
150 Maud W. Gleason, *Making Men, Sophists and Self-Presentation in Ancient Rome* (Princeton, NJ: Princeton University Press, 1995), xxiv, 59, see also her n. 17 and references there; Gleason emphasizes that masculinity is similarly constructed in many tribal societies today.
151 Ibid., 161.
152 Walters, 'Invading the Roman Body', 30. See also Skinner, 'Ego Mulier', particularly 134–5.
153 Walters, 'Invading the Roman Body', 33, 39.
154 See the discussion in Kristina Straub, 'The Guilty Pleasures of Female Theatrical Cross-Dressing and the Autobiography of Charlotte Charke', in *Body Guards*, ed. Julia Epstein and Kristina Straub, 142–66.
155 Castelli, *Martyrdom and Memory*, 61.
156 That Thecla never fixes her gaze on Paul for any length of time is evidenced in *APTh*. 8 (where Thecla hears Paul preach but does not see him) and *APTh*. 22 (where Thecla sees the Lord sitting in the form of Paul but as she looks steadily at him he 'departs' into the heavens).
157 Simon Goldhill, *Foucault's Virginity, Ancient Erotic Fiction and the History of Sexuality* (New York: Cambridge University Press, 1995), 132.
158 Willi Braun e.g. questions the positivistic model of woman becoming male as a model of rebellion against patriarchy. He argues that in attempting to become male, women collude with an androcentric model of perfectionism which seeks to eradicate the female. See Braun, 'Physiotherapy', 209–29.

5

Naked truths: Pornography and violence in the *Acts of Paul and Thecla*

Introduction

Within the *Acts of Paul and Thecla*, Thecla refuses to submit to patriarchal marriage; consequently, she becomes the recipient of violent punishment that is meted out to her in the hope of bringing about her demise, thus setting an example for all women who would dare attempt to assert their subjectivity and autonomy.

The text contains graphically depicted scenes where Thecla is stripped naked (*APTh.* 22, 33), forced to 'mount' (ἐπιβῆναι *APTh.* 22) the pyre, threatened with rape (*APTh.* 26) and paraded through the streets and arena as an object of voyeurism (*APTh.* 22, 28, 33). When, with God's miraculous help, Thecla repeatedly manages to evade death, she is humiliated even further by being tied naked by the feet between two bulls (*APTh.* 35). However, scholars focused on the liberative and empowering perspectives of the text rarely pay heed to Thecla's objectification and the violence to which she is subjected.

Although it may be argued that by present-day standards there is no explicit pornography within the *Acts of Paul and Thecla*, if we were viewing this story rather than reading it, these pornographic elements would become more overtly apparent. Nancy Sorkin Rabinowitz rightly notes that we tend to overlook the more brutal aspects within tragic plays in part because we often read the plays rather than see them; once on stage, these become more apparent.[1] In this respect, although there are no overtly sexual scenes within the *Acts of Paul and Thecla*, one need only conjure up the image of a naked Thecla tied by the legs between two bulls in the middle of an arena of fully clothed spectators. If this were a contemporary scene depicted in pictures or in a film, how might the image be defined or interpreted? It is my contention that such an image could easily be classified as pornographic. A good-looking woman is laid bare and completely exposed before a gathering of fully clothed spectators.

The bodies of chaste women were usually concealed; in being stripped naked and displayed in public, Thecla suffers the humiliation and torment usually reserved for shameless women who transgress sexually.[2] These often pornographic and violent elements within the story display a complete lack of tolerance for women and female subjectivity. Furthermore, they have with depressing regularity been glossed over by scholars. Perhaps the most perplexing aspect in regard to the violence meted out to Thecla is the fact that women collude in punishing her for attempting to assert her independence. Here again, interpreters have focused upon aspects of the text which demonstrate female solidarity and have overlooked the women who aid and abet the civic male authorities to bring about Thecla's demise.[3] Indeed, it is Thecla's mother who initiates the call to burn the 'lawless one' (*APTh.* 20). Moreover, the 'maidens' come along with the young men to bring wood and straw that Thecla may be burned (*APTh.* 22). We are also told that women are included in the baying crowd that demands Thecla is thrown into the arena (*APTh.* 32). The text thus clearly depicts women as collaborators in misogynistic practices.

Such representations raise profound questions especially within a text that has been seen to affirm women and women's leadership. What will the analysis of these aspects of the text reveal about the discourse of gender and women in particular? Can such representations ever truly result in empowerment for a woman? Motivated by these questions, I will explore below if anything is affirming for women in the representations of violence and pornography within the text.

Defining pornography

Before moving on to the interpretation of the text itself, it is necessary to first define exactly what is meant by the highly contentious term 'pornography'. Furthermore, we also need to determine how modern theories of pornography can legitimately be applied to ancient texts.[4] It is beyond the remit of this study to become embroiled in the various contemporary political arguments concerning pornography, which range from arguments of morality to concerns that practices portrayed in pornography may become practices in our lives, or to assertions that pornography leads to violence against women.[5] My primary concern is to examine the structures of representation in order to determine the underlying sexual politics played out in the text. In looking at the text's rhetorical effect, what we find is a notion of sexuality that objectifies women and demonstrates a great chasm of inequity between the male and female. By utilizing contemporary feminist theory on pornography, I hope to show that, despite modern technology and its use in producing very graphic pornography, modern conceptions of what constitutes pornography are not so distant from certain scenes depicted within the text.

There is no unequivocal definition or consensus of exactly what constitutes pornography; commentators are divided on both its definition and significance.[6] Difficulties tend to focus around feminist and non-feminist debates concerning the separation of 'erotica' from pornography and exactly what constitutes 'sexually explicit' materials.[7] Andrea Dworkin focuses in particular on the objectification of women by men in a hierarchy of domination.[8] Catharine MacKinnon follows Dworkin closely in focusing on this same male hierarchy and the objectification of women.[9] For MacKinnon, pornography goes beyond its content; it eroticizes hierarchy and sexualizes inequality; it makes dominance and submission into sex. In this way, pornography institutionalizes the sexuality of male supremacy, fusing the eroticization of dominance and submission with the social construction of male and female.[10]

MacKinnon also asserts that whereas law and society attempt to draw a line between sex and violence, these cannot so easily be separated. Examples cited by MacKinnon include materials which are not overtly sexual, for example, women hanging from trees without exposing their genitalia and not engaging in sexual acts, and pictures of women's bodies which are scarred or women being hunted down and shot.[11] In this way, MacKinnon broadens the popular definition of the pornographic to include what are primarily representations of violence that are not explicitly sexual, noticing how often these involve a reinforcement of patriarchal institutions. MacKinnon would go as far as to argue that the way in which sexuality itself has been constructed is violating and abusive of women. She believes that pornography does not work sexually without gender hierarchy. If there is no inequality, no violation, no dominance, no force, there is no sexual arousal.[12]

In delineating the issue of pornography in this way, Dworkin and MacKinnon have in turn enabled theorists to develop correlations between the pornographic and the process of representation itself. Starting from John Berger's dictum that 'men look at women: women watch themselves being looked at', feminist scholars questioned the way in which the spectator is engendered by the experience of watching.[13] They defined the gaze, or the process of looking, as male. In this way, the concept of the pornographic provides a paradigm for all representation and comes to refer to much more than the common meaning of the word, thus allowing a broadening of scholarly inquiry into areas such as film, narrative and representational art.[14]

Helpfully, theorist Susanne Kappeler asserts that representation (word- or image-based), or representational practices, rather than sexual practices or 'real-life sex', should form the context or basis of any study of pornography, since pornography is not a special case of sexuality but rather a special case of representation and that this needs to be foregrounded.[15] Kappeler is right to insist on this focus since representation is a powerful mechanism. Kappeler gives the example of a white Namibian farmer who instigated the torture and death of a young black worker while his friends took pictures. The picture eventually served as evidence to convict him of the crime of murder. Kappeler argues that the killing and torture done before the camera, that is the artistic composition or representation itself, was integral to the crime. Her example of the Namibian farmer demonstrates that representation does not imitate reality but creates it. For Kappeler, all representation constructs reality in this way.

Kappeler's discussion is very useful in terms of addressing presentations in ancient literature that requires our imagination to work with the words of a text. In drawing a correlation between the process of representation and the process of pornography in this way, Kappeler has brought to light the strong and permeating mechanisms of power latent within both processes. Images and texts are also manifestations of power relationships that affect concepts of gender and culture. Therefore, it becomes evident that feminist insights on pornography can be applied to much more in antiquity than explicitly sexual art and literature.[16] Pornography includes all sexist representation, thus abrogating the necessity to distinguish between pornography and erotica in terms of low or high art, violent or non-violent, or hard or soft content.[17] Broadening the term 'pornography' beyond its much more common usage allows for its wider application in regard to ancient texts which include representations of women. When applied to ancient male-authored texts, such theories will help to unveil the underlying ideology and also help toward defining the cultural construction of the masculine as well as the feminine.

Working from this premise, building on Kappeler, it is my intention to reflect on what I consider to be the – until now – little discussed, pornographic elements within the *Acts of Paul and Thecla*. These elements are pornographic in the feminist sense of the term, as discussed above, not in the sense that they are too obscene or too explicit (although, in regard to the incident with the bulls, this is the case) but rather in the way that they debase women. They are full of objectification, violence, pain and violation.

Specifics of pornographic representation

Framing pornographic representation in a way that focuses on male power enables interpreters to distil the subtle elements of domination and supremacy at play in a text. As Dworkin notes,

> male power ... is discernible in discrete but interwoven, reinforcing strains: the power of self, physical power over and against others, the power of terror, the power of naming, the power of owning, the power of money and the power of sex. These strains of male power are intrinsic to both the substance and production of pornography; and the ways and means of pornography are the ways and means of male power.[18]

In order to see more clearly the pornography at work within the text of *Acts of Paul and Thecla*, it is, therefore, necessary to look at how power and power relations are played out in the narrative and whether the subordinate position is marked as female. Examining where the text produces and preserves the pattern of male domination, particularly in relation to the theme of violence, will highlight how, and in what ways, the text marks a retreat from the endorsement of women in order to preserve male power and bolster masculinity.

The elements of male power and dominance, which are central to pornography, turn the powerless, in this case, women, into mere objects of possession and violence. In fact, it is power that makes the objectification of women possible. Thus, as noted above, the objectification of women becomes a further leitmotif deeply embedded within the pornographic representation of women. Just as hierarchy produces polarity between genders, so too does the objectification of women. MacKinnon speaks of the objectification of women as 'the primary process of the subjection of women'.[19] When women are objectified as a gender, the subject, the objectifier, the surveyor of women is invariably of the male gender. Thus, the objectification of women means the simultaneous subjectification of men.[20] This perception of women as other reduces women to mere commodities to be manipulated for male voyeuristic pleasure.

If we apply this, then, to the *Acts of Paul and Thecla*, Thecla is a chaste, beautiful and desirable woman who is continually exposed to the public gaze. Her body and sexuality play an important part in the drama that unfolds in the narrative. Such representation leaves little space for female empowerment and subjectivity. Discussing the scenes which contain features of objectification, spectacle and power will, therefore, help to elucidate the nature and structures of pornographic representation utilized in the text and ultimately expose how what Helen Elsom terms the 'political economy of sex' operates. [21]

Martyrdom and spectacle

Before proceeding to discuss the violent and pornographic elements within the *Acts of Paul and Thecla* in detail, it is important to first situate the discussion within the wider subject of martyrology and the very graphic sexual violence that regularly accompanies the description of a martyr's death: either male or female. Sado-erotic spectacle and brutal sexual violence was very much part and parcel of the events that took place in Roman arenas. The Roman games contained, in the words of Cooper, 'the despicable pleasure of the pagans'.[22] Tacitus, for example, makes reference to the 'exemplary punishments' suffered by Christians and remarks that 'derision' of every sort 'was added to the death of Christians'.[23] The systematic cruelty and violence in the arena was all part of a planned public celebration of imperial power, and the sexual degradation of women formed part of the spectacle.[24] Clement of Rome comments on how women 'suffered terrible and impious indignities'.[25] Brent Shaw points out that, where women were concerned, witnessing the public violation and mutilation of otherwise protected and honoured female bodies gave a special edge, a sharper culmination of the display.[26]

Death in the arena was a political as well as a judicial ritual which served to reinforce the existing power of Rome. The process of such execution was calculated to debase victims as completely as possible, and sometimes this involved evoking scenes from mythology.[27] Authors of Christian martyrdoms, in recounting the horrific scenes of violence, were on one level, aiming to expose the full horrors and ungodly nature of the Roman pagan authorities. They were also concerned to depict the steel-like endurance and bravery of the Christian martyrs within the arena. Martyrdoms became opportunities for Christians to stand with and alongside Christ. Thus, in public executions where audiences expected to see penitence and terror in the faces of the condemned, martyrdom presented a unique opportunity for those Christians, whom David Potter terms 'over achievers', to demonstrate their piety through the destruction of their bodies.[28]

Burrus argues that martyrdom is the initial site at which shame is converted into shamelessness, giving rise to a performatively queered Christian identity that retrieves dignity without aspiring to honour.[29] These 'queerly – spectacularly – marked by shame' events demonstrated Christian defiance of political authorities. According to Burrus, Christians thus smuggled their witnessing bodies onto the ancient equivalent of the '"prohibitive airwaves" of network television'. In this way, ancient martyrs transform shame into the source of an oddly pure identity politics.[30]

Martyrologies were then a useful rhetorical tool to inspire resilience in the face of suffering among Christian readership. However, although martyrdom stories were an important and formative part of Christianity, there was, at the same time, an awareness of the un-salutary effects of the spectacle involved.[31] Tertullian, for example, while arguing that the blood of martyrs was the 'seed' of the church, at the same time raged against the culture of Roman displays and spectacle.[32] For example, Tertullian begins *De spectaculis* by framing his discussion around 'pleasure' and 'idolatry'.[33] He speaks of the psychological disturbance that comes from being a spectator and argues that there is no spectacle without violence to the spirit.[34] For Tertullian, it is the arousal of pleasure and emotions that makes spectacle so worrying, even for those that attempt to approach spectacle in a more controlled way.[35] A similar argument is employed in *De virginibus velandis*, where he draws a correlation between 'seeing' and 'being seen'.[36] In addressing Christians who attended the arena, Tertullian asks whether it is right to look on what it is disgraceful to do.[37]

An interesting feature in Tertullian's writing is that, despite his censure on spectacle, which he harshly maintains for twenty-nine chapters, when he finally concludes in ch. 30, he employs the very language and imagery of spectacle to describe the events of Judgement Day.[38] An unappeasable gaze watches the torments of those who rejected Christ. Tertullian is as widely excited a spectator of the Judgement Day events as his own portrayal of the baying crowd at the games.

However, Tertullian was opposed to the violent spectacles for good reason. Joyce Salisbury notes that amphitheatres were constructed in such a way as to ensure maximum visual and emotional impact among the crowd. Spectators were not simple voyeurs but were emotionally drawn into the unfolding drama, like participants.[39] Excitement and mass hysteria was intended to erode the individual will and 'sweep away' spectators.[40]

Clement of Alexandria similarly believed the spectacle of the arena encouraged lasciviousness and inflamed desire; so too Cyprian, bishop of Carthage, who highlighted the dangers and scandal nurtured by the act of looking.[41] Pagan observers and writers in antiquity were, therefore, very aware of the damaging psychological and emotional effects of the games. Although some may have believed they could attend the show and avoid the emotional involvement, it is clear that many among the audience were swept into the collective bloodlust of the crowd.[42] Castelli, in her discussion on modern-day uses of martyrdom imagery, underscores the fact that the vivid (violent) imagery of martyrdom can 'compromise' the viewer, thus drawing them into 'complicity with the persecution'.[43] Along similar lines, Gillian Clark highlights that martyrdom accounts may well have evoked a certain 'pleasure in torture' for readers. Even though the narrative was intended to 'correct' the reader's desire, redirecting it toward God, she concedes that it remains 'possible' that some of those who composed or listened to martyr-acts were engaged in fantasies of punitive repression, in which recalcitrant bodies were slashed, burned and amputated.[44] However, Clark believes that such people might imagine themselves as 'enduring' rather than 'inflicting' pain.[45]

This analysis of the more negative consequences of spectacle is significant. It brings to the fore the fact that Christians were aware of the power of spectacle to brutalize and corrupt. In fact, it was this very awareness, of the capacity that spectacle has to engage the viewer, which led them to consciously appropriate the model for their own ends. In reinterpreting stories of persecution, Christians thus privileged the realm of the visual.[46] This conscious creation of sado-erotic spectacle inscribed the horrific details of a martyr's suffering into the imaginations of readers and hearers, forming what Castelli terms, a 'genre of performance'. Indeed, Burrus points out that since ancient 'readers' were far more likely to have heard the text read aloud, it left the 'eyes of the imagination free to wander'.[47] Both Chrysostom and Augustine drew a strong correlation between hearing/reading and seeing in regard to liturgical texts. In a fourth-century homily, Chrysostom writes,

> For as soon as the tongue has uttered the name of the dancer, immediately the soul has figured to itself his looks ... Another again fans the flames in another way by introducing some harlot into the conversation, with the words, and attitudes and glances, her languishing looks and twisted locks, the smoothness of her cheeks and her painted eyelids. Were you not somewhat affected when I gave this description.[48]

As Cobb underscores, Chrysostom's argument relies on a correlation between hearing and visualizing, between knowing and seeing.[49]

Augustine also notes that those who pay attention to what is being said will create a visual image in their mind's eye: 'When these things are read of in the church, you behold them with pleasure with these eyes of the heart, for if you were to behold nothing, you would hear nothing.'[50] Indeed, in a homily on the *Martyrdom of Perpetua and Felicitas*, Augustine writes, 'as it was all being read; and all those things, recounted in such glowing words, we perceived in our ears, and actually saw in our minds.'[51]

In her discussion on Greek drama, Nicole Loraux highlights the importance of visual imagination in Greek Tragedy, which very much relied on this correlation between text and vision. She writes, 'Everything starts by being spoken, by being heard, by being imagined.'[52] Indeed:

> One should not underestimate the real benefit in terms of imagination that these deaths and the fact that they were only described must have brought to an audience of citizen ... Death by report lends itself to conjecture vastly more than does violence exposed to the public view.[53]

It would appear that the narratival spoken word, as opposed to an enacted performance, was so powerful for an audience that it created what Richard Hawley terms a 'gaze of the imagination'.[54] Ancient texts it seemed were effective in that they relied on this imaginative gaze.[55]

It thus becomes clear that forming some sort of picture was crucial in the hearing of a martyrdom; it was a sign of good listening skills and proper attentiveness.[56] The audience of the martyr's *passio* was, therefore, meant to graphically 'picture' in their mind's eye the public, humiliating, cruel treatment of men and women as their bodies were sexualized, torn, broken, dismembered, devoured and burned. However, in the telling and retelling, in the picturing and visualizing of the horrors of martyrdom, Christians were not merely inverting persecution experiences; they were simultaneously producing, perpetuating and mirroring the much-despised Roman values of horror and spectacle, leaving audiences vulnerable to the less than favourable outcomes of complicity, participation and prurience. As Burrus highlights, the literature of martyrdom 'zooms in with all the sensationalizing voyeurism of a news camera'.[57]

Of course, the authors of martyrdoms were presupposing a certain type of reader and they were aiming to produce a certain type of viewer. Here, how you 'look' is meant to depend on whether you are Christian or pagan; but how do you guard against voyeuristic and erotic stimulation through the visual/auditory? Is sado-erotic violence acceptable because listeners do not carry out the acts but only hear/imagine/picture them? Although audiences were meant to 'see' the violators and perpetrators of these crimes as 'other', did audiences not collude, in some way, with those very perpetrators, by imagining and 'looking'? I borrow from Tertullian's *De spectaculis* and ask: is it right to look upon what it is disgraceful to do?[58]

It is my contention that audiences listening to martyr stories engage in precisely the voyeurism that Tertullian condemned. Castelli also makes this point in her discussion of early Christian martyrdoms. She notes that voyeurism is an inevitable part of a martyrdom's retelling and, while spectacle in female martyrdoms functioned in complex ways, it can implicate the reader in the spectacle itself. Thus, the voyeurs are not only those who watch from the crowd but also those who read the text, *however piously*.[59] By inviting the reader to identify with those who watch, the genre of martyrology turns its reading or hearing audience into voyeurs.

Castelli goes on to argue that in providing the graphic details of a martyr's suffering, the narratives appeal to the desire to 'see for oneself, positioning the reader in alliance with those who look in the narrative'. Although 'written, in part, to condemn the prurient interest of the unrestrained mob, the texts of martyrdoms re-inscribe the desire to look denounced implicitly in the text'. Readers and audience, therefore, become implicated in what Castelli calls 'the economy of looking' and contribute to reducing the martyr to a spectacle. [60]

The next question I ask is: was any 'violence' perpetrated by the author in writing the text? Once again, it is my contention that in writing violent and graphic martyr stories, Christians lapse into the same violent self-contradiction that Tertullian displays within his text *De spectaculis*.[61] Throughout Imperial Rome, a culture of display linked spectacle to power.[62] By reinterpreting the violence and spectacle of persecution, Christians were meaning to, somehow (psychologically), wrest control of that power away from Rome. However, in appropriating the model and using it for their own ends, the interpretation of the model may have differed, but the violence and spectacle were exactly the same. Furthermore, appropriation of the model left Christian viewers exposed to the dangers of spectacle.

David Frankfurter argues along similar lines by noting that audiences of martyrdoms cannot help but engage in the sado-erotic violence of spectacle. [63] He contends that, in martyrdoms, the erotically charged bodies of Christians are imaginatively put through sexual display and graphic torture for a prurient gaze. Frankfurter places the sado-erotic voyeurism in historical and performative continuity with the Roman spectacle, literary ambivalence over female chastity and fantasies about the sexual and cultural predilections of the 'Other'. The spectacle of sado-erotic violence allows the enjoyment of erotic display at the same time as the disavowal of that enjoyment, which is projected onto the violent punitive actions of Roman authorities. As martyrs are remembered and their martyrologies are read, this becomes an exercise in viewing and imagining, of vicarious participation.

Frankfurter observes that in framing graphic, explicitly sexualized, scenes of violent atrocity within the context of Roman judicial savagery, early Christian martyrologies allowed their audiences to contemplate, in safe form, scenes that could not otherwise, legitimately, be enjoyed. However, the erotic engagement involved in the voyeuristic experiences is always repudiated and translated into a rage against the source of arousal: the martyr.[64] This means that the rage is really against themselves, for taking illicit pleasure in the scene, but they cannot own that rage. Therefore, it is displaced and projected toward the persecutor. It is, of course, an unconscious process, and the aggressor comes to represent that rage. Thus, the relationship between the eroticized voyeurism of martyrologies and the framing of sexualized violence becomes the work of some monstrous 'Other': Roman, barbarian, or heretic. The 'outsiders' are the heathens/pagans and 'our' victims are the cloistered virgins. Such legends function both to demonize the 'Other' and to provide that voyeuristic confusion of disgust and arousal.

In line with Frankfurter, surely the sado-erotic spectacle of martyrdom nurtures favourable circumstances for the prurient gaze. Along with Frankfurter, I would credit the authors, redactors, and transmitters of these texts with full imaginative agency. As the *Acts of Paul and Thecla* demonstrates, an eroticized heroine depicted along with graphic details of her torture comes to function as pornographic spectacle. There is no question that we should not gaze at Thecla. Indeed, her treatment is sanctioned as legitimate, even pious, and the ones who are responsible for these monstrous acts are the civic (Roman) authorities.

Although it could be argued that such categories of fantasy and its psychodynamic implications impose an anachronistic grid on ancient martyrology, Frankfurter underscores the scholarly emphasis on 'spectacle' in Roman public culture and in the texts which critiqued that public culture. The Roman arena consisted of a world of mimesis and staging, linked to fantasy and myth. Conceptualizing martyrology as spectacle allows us to place the performance of martyr accounts (their public reading and homiletic commentary) in historical and cultural relationship with the experience of the Roman arena. In this way, martyrologies are heirs to the same prurient desires that the arena stimulated.[65]

In asking whether some ancient readers could refuse the voyeurism of these texts, Frankfurter argues that martyrologies carried a persistently didactic meaning which was not conducive to multiple readings. Audiences are literally told, '*this* is why you should glory in her torture and *this* is what you should gaze upon as he suffers; *this* is how you should view her death; *this* is what you should remember of his time on earth.'[66] In this way, the Roman Christian reader is primed to enjoy the sado-erotic testing of the virgin martyr.

As a literary character, the female martyr may be trying to exercise subjectivity and power by reframing her nakedness, for example, as ideological rather than shameful or erotic, but the effort is inevitably drowned out in the voyeurism of the spectacle itself. In his conclusion, Frankfurter returns to Tertullian's question, 'Why is it lawful to see what it is shameful to do?' Frankfurter responds with 'in texts all things are lawful as long as they are properly set-off as Roman brutality'.[67]

These considerations, of the erotic and prurient impact of graphic and violent spectacle, are important in framing the discussion of violence and pornography within the *Acts of Paul and Thecla*. For, although it may be argued that the text of Thecla is merely representing the violence done to her (and other Christian women) and, thus, not partaking in it, the discussion demonstrates that in relating Thecla's experiences in such graphic sado-erotic detail, the author engages in every aspect of the spectacle and becomes complicit in her persecution. Furthermore, although the author attempts to assert a particular gaze or way of reading and interpreting the material (i.e. readers take the side of the victim and see Rome or State as the violent and debased 'other'), as audience/readers and author/narrator engage in the spectacle (by means of reading or description), they too partake in Rome's state-sponsored violence and are, therefore, at risk of inviting the prurient gaze and of being snared or lured into colluding with Thecla's victimization.

The telling and retelling of a martyr's story, involving vivid imagery, forces the audience to look and to see: they cannot (indeed they are not meant to) avert their gaze. The words form powerful erotic pictures and the images become central. The process of 'looking' is stimulated, for the author makes vivid the victims and means of torture. He brings it before their very eyes; the eyes of the hearers and listeners. How do the author and audience then guard against the pleasure that may be derived from the gaze? Do the authors of such spectacles risk turning the audience into scopophiliacs? Each telling of a martyr's story involves a viewer's gaze, a gaze which is charged with a voyeuristic dimension. Readers and audiences of martyrologies were not meant to 'turn a blind eye' or a 'deaf ear' to the horrors of a martyr's suffering. They were meant to *look* and *hear* the gruesome sado-erotic details. However, in so doing, audiences then became enforced voyeurs, susceptible to (to borrow from Simon Goldhill) the 'erotic eye'.

An extraordinary Victorian painting, 'A Christian Dirce', by Henry Siemiradzki (dated 1897) and held at the National Museum in Warsaw, visually displays this process of spectacle and the prurient gaze.[68] The dead, female martyr lies sprawled naked over a dead bull, her arms spread eagled to give a good view of her body. The sophisticated, well-dressed spectators look on voyeuristically and with interested curiosity. They cannot avert their eyes from the naked woman who looks alluring even in death. The painting is a good example of this tradition of erotic spectacle that continued into modern times.

Re-reading the *Acts of Paul and Thecla*

McInerney argues that in surviving her martyrdom, Thecla submits to no-one, not even to death.[69] Indeed, she gains an 'independent and authoritative voice'.[70] Burrus too, in her more recent book *Saving Shame*, argues that Thecla's arena performance was so spectacular that her failure to die hardly mattered. Indeed for Burrus, the shameful exposure of a female body, conveying threats of sexual aggression, despite being 'vividly depicted', results in the woman's shamelessness enduring beyond the arena.[71]

This view of Thecla as an empowered woman who asserts her own will and desire by rejecting the societal norms of marriage and motherhood is held by a number of scholars.[72] However, although Thecla at times takes centre stage and survives the various torturous trials that men put her through, at the same time this heroine is exposed, sometimes in quite degrading ways, to the gaze of not only her persecutors but also readers.

Furthermore, in the narrative, her inferior and chattel-like status is confirmed over and over as she is passed around from man to man (Thamyris, Paul, the Governor, Alexander and soldiers) as an object of exchange. Such treatment affirms male subjectivity and power (*APTh*. 27, 29, 30, 31, 32). Elsom argues that such conduct demonstrates that women always serve as a sign, as something unreal which can be passed around in place of the intangible real: wealth, male sexuality (a symbol of the phallus) or power.[73]

What has often been neglected by scholarship in the case of Thecla is the portrayal of a heroine who is in fact herself overpowered: by her desire for Paul and by the violent forces of masculinity and patriarchy. In the first half of the narrative, Thecla is not accorded any inherent value as a woman, nor does she speak anything of real consequence; rather, her fundamental worth lies in her physical allure. Twice her prospective death is lamented purely because she is a beautiful object (*APTh*. 29, 34). In this respect, the text sets up an ambivalent presentation of Thecla as someone who, on the one hand, is obstinate and rebellious, a thinking acting subject who – despite persistent attempts to execute her, survives – and, on the other hand, as one who presents as a silent, powerless victim/object.

However, from the onset, the narrative constructs the representation of Paul quite differently. He is introduced as a man small in stature with meeting eyebrows and a bald head; his nose is long and thin (hooked) and his legs are crooked. Nevertheless, he is 'healthy' looking and at times his face appears like that 'of an angel' (*APTh*. 3). Both Ben Witherington and Abraham Malherbe have argued that, as far as Greek physiognomy is concerned, such a bodily description of a man in antiquity was intended to be flattering in terms of establishing strength and masculinity.[74] In a number of instances, we find that identical features were regularly attributed to gallant leaders in ancient texts.[75] Witherington contends that Paul's description asserts that he is firm in conviction and values. Indeed, the description of Paul can be compared with the description of the great Graeco-Roman hero figure Heracles (also known as Hercules).[76] Malherbe too points out that the author of the *Acts of Paul and Thecla* derived his description of Paul from ancient sources which were intended to depict Paul as a hero.[77] In this respect, it could be argued that the author is merely invoking a physical stereotype in order to portray Paul in the best possible light.

However, it is not at all certain that Paul's description can be interpreted in such a straightforward, positive way. Malherbe, for example, appears to contradict himself when he notes that while the ancient sources depicting strong, gallant men draw attention to the men's hair, Paul is presented as bald. Malherbe attempts to deal with this anomaly by asserting that it is not impossible that this description of Paul contains some historical truth since there are hints in Paul's letters that 'he was not an outstandingly robust physical specimen'.[78] Translations of the *Acts of Paul and Thecla* also seem to have been sensitive to this aspect of Paul's description. Accordingly, the Armenian translation gives him 'curly' hair, the Syriac 'scanty' and the Latin a 'shaven head'. Obviously, Paul's baldness represented an 'image' problem. Malherbe argues that two possibilities suggest themselves: either Paul was bald and the *Acts of Paul and Thecla* are faithful to that memory or the baldness may have been suggested by the reference to the shaving of heads in Acts 18.18 and 21.24.[79] Malherbe is struggling to hold two very opposing concepts together.

These contradictions of Paul's characterization from the perspective of physiognomy are confirmed by János Bollók.[80] He highlights that a number of Paul's physical characteristics listed in *Acts of Paul and Thecla* evidence weakness, unintelligence and cowardice, while those that concentrate on his spirit and nature emphasize the perfection of the apostle.[81] Thus, despite Paul's unfortunate presentation, Bollók argues that in describing Paul's appearance as that of an angel (*APTh.* 3), the author is praising his hero in the highest way possible, drawing attention to his inner beauty.

Paul's physical description was obviously important to the author, or he would not have included it in such detail within the story. Looking at the narrative function of Paul's description, Bollók's assessment is revealing. In line with his argument, it is also possible to argue that the rhetorical aim is to ensure that Paul could not be perceived as an object of physical desire, as a woman would be (and as Thecla is). This resistance to objectifying Paul's physical body is intensified because when it comes to Paul's character, his nature and his spirit, the audience are left in no doubt as to his perfection. According to Bollók, Paul's angel-like appearance was meant to prove that nothing other than an angel lived in the body of the apostle.[82] We are also informed right at the beginning of the story that Paul is full of the 'goodness of Christ' (*APTh.* 1). Indeed, 'he did no evil', even to those who deserved it (*APTh.* 1).

The author has worked shrewdly with Paul's representation. Rather than reducing Paul to a vacuous physical object that gratifies a lustful gaze, the body instead serves as a vehicle to communicate what a righteous, beneficent and virtuous man Paul is. It is the difference between a body full of essential substance, a powerful combination of honourable, exemplary, moral characteristics, and the body as a thing to be gazed at and lusted after. Contrast this with his later abandonment of a woman threatened by rape (*APTh.* 26). Nevertheless, the physical description of Paul immediately establishes his subject status and guards against physical objectification.

Furthermore, shortly after the introduction to Paul, the narrative endows him with the power of speech as he begins preaching in the house of Onesiphoros.[83] Paul gives an elegant and eloquent sermon in the form of μακάριοι statements (*APTh.* 5-6). This power of rhetoric is demonstrated once again when Paul is brought before the Governor for questioning. His response impresses the Governor so much that he has him led back to prison so that 'he could, at his abundant leisure, give him a more attentive hearing' (*APTh.* 17). During the second hearing, despite the crowd shouting 'He is a Magician! Take him away!' the Governor persisted in listening to him (*APTh.* 20). He emerges as a skilful master of language, easily able to persuade and influence others with his words. Indeed, 'all' (πᾶσαι) the women and young men go in to listen to him (*APTh.* 9).

This representation of Paul is in stark contrast with that of Thecla, who is initially presented as a silent, immovable object (*APTh.* 7, 8) who is 'bound' (δεδεμένη) and held captive (κρατεῖται, ἑάλωται, *APTh.* 9) as if in a 'spider's web' by the power of

Paul's words.[84] Janet Spittler notes that the description of Paul's words as 'deceptive and wily', and their comparison to a web would have been associated by the ancients with weaving and women's work. Weaving was particularly associated with the snares of women. The use of such a feminine-gendered metaphor in regard to Paul may reflect Theocleia's thoroughly negative assessment of him. Here is a man who is stooping to use a woman's method to snare her daughter. Similarly, in antiquity, the spider was regarded as a noxious creature to be avoided and despised. On the surface, such a reading may appear to be portraying Paul negatively; however, when it comes to the categories of power and weakness, it is very clear where strength and dominance is located in the use of the metaphor. Paul emerges as the powerful predatory creature (the spider) and Thecla the entrapped and tangled prey (a gnat or fly is suggested by Spittler[85]).

Thecla's object status is thus assured not only through the description of her as a beautiful woman (εὔμορφος, κάλλος, *APTh*. 25, 29, 35) but also through the description of her as an insect entrapped in a web spun by Paul. Furthermore, her silence reinforces that objectification (*APTh*. 10, 20). Thecla is consistently cast as the object of the discourse of others (*APTh*. 7-20). We are told that although this beautiful woman has never set eyes on Paul (*APTh*. 7), she is completely mesmerized by his preaching. The author repeatedly uses verbs of 'looking' and 'seeing' (ἀτενίζω, βλέπω, *APTh*. 7-10) to describe Thecla; she is a woman who gazes and stares. However, despite the use of these verbs and Thecla's constant gazing, the male is *almost* always protected from the woman's sight (*APTh*. 8, 9, 10, 21).

Here I disagree with Melissa Aubin, who argues that Thecla 'herself frames Paul with her gaze'. Although 'looking' and 'gazing' are active verbs, Thecla is described as someone who is transfixed, and she never actually sets eyes on Paul until she is in prison with him (*APTh*. 18).[86] Furthermore, when she is in the arena in Antioch, she has a vision of Paul, but as soon as her eyes fix upon him he disappears from view (*APTh*. 21). In veiling Paul from Thecla's sight, his authoritative words are given sovereign importance, not his image.

Berger, in his discussion concerning ways of seeing, writes that the reciprocal nature of vision is more fundamental than that of spoken dialogue.[87] However, there is no reciprocity within this text. Thecla listens and hears, but, unlike the other virgins and young men who go into the house to be with Paul, she is not permitted to see. A mere passive object, she listens intently to Paul's word: 'night and day … she did not turn away from the window' (*APTh*. 7). This maiden is seized by a new desire (ἐπιθυμία) and fearful passion (πάθει, δεινῷ), and hangs upon the things Paul says. In this way, she is taken captive (ἑάλωται, *APTh*. 9). Her deep passion for this man leaves her deranged and paralysed (ἔκπληξιν, παραπλήξ, *APTh*. 10).

The power at play is the power of a man's word over a woman, and, apart from her desire for Paul and his words, Thecla's representation appears lifeless: a motionless figure held captive by a man whom she has never seen (*APTh*. 9). Words alone have the capacity to enslave this woman. When she does finally become animated, it is in order to silently follow Paul into prison. Aubin argues that when Thecla gives away her bracelets and silver mirror, in order to escape the house and bribe her way into the prison, she is revoking her traditional gender signifiers and former identity. She says that while shackles bind Paul in prison, with the removal of Thecla's bracelets, a 'reversal' takes place between Paul and Thecla. For Aubin, Thecla is now liberated while Paul is in bondage. In this way, Thecla emerges as a figure that supersedes Paul in authority and masculine license. Indeed, Aubin argues that, from this point on, Paul repeatedly appears impotent in comparison to Thecla.[88]

However, although the bracelets and mirror may be functioning on a symbolic level, it is also the case that, from a practical point of view, Thecla is unlikely to have had access to money, or anything else of value, with which to bribe the doorkeeper and jailer. Furthermore, Thecla's actions in prison, her behaviour at the trial as well as its outcome (which will be discussed in more detail below) would also negate Aubin's interpretation.

In prison, Thecla sits at Paul's feet and hangs onto his every word (*APTh*. 18). Cooper notes that where speech was concerned, a woman was understood to be at her most temperate when 'listening attentively to good'.[89] In prison, sitting at his feet, listening to Paul, Thecla is presented as the model of female temperance. However, Thecla's actions do not stop at listening; she also kisses the chains which keep him bound (*APTh*. 18). Burrus notes that 'shamelessly' kissing Paul's chains is a sign of Thecla's 'humiliation' as she sheds her modestly like an unwanted garment (33).[90] Such adulation hardly displays a liberated and empowered woman; rather, Thecla's adoration and fawning adds an erotic appeal to the scene. Once again, a striking inequity between the two characters sets up a seductive allure in the narrative. Even when the Governor interrogates her, she does not have any words of her own to speak, she simply gazes intently (ἀτενίζω) at Paul (*APTh*. 20).

In a prison, bound by chains, the themes of enslavement and bondage come to the fore. However, there is no hint of a masterful woman punishing or vilifying a male sex object. Rather, here the female serves to strengthen male subjectivity while her own subjectivity is muted. Indeed, although Paul is physically bound, it is Thecla who is the real captive. Her femininity is passive and non-threatening as she accedes to her enslavement. When Paul is taken before the judgement seat for a second time, Thecla remains in prison where Paul had been sitting, not because anyone restrained her, but simply so that she could 'roll' (ἐκυλίετο) herself upon the place where Paul taught as he sat in prison (*APTh*. 20).

It is noteworthy that while Onesiphoros is deeply devoted to Paul and the Christian faith (*APTh*. 2, 4, 5, 23), there is no evidence of him acting in a like manner towards the apostle. Sorkin Rabinowitz, in her study of pornographic representations within Greek tragedy, notes that in tragedy as in pornography, women are either desiring predators or passive victims.[91] Here too, as a silent beautiful object who slavishly devotes herself to a man, Thecla's dominant presentation is that of a passive victim. Thecla may have rejected Thamyris, marriage and childbirth, but this does not leave her free to become an independent and autonomous subject. Her insubordination and little uprising are ultimately insignificant and ineffectual. She merely transfers her affection and desire from one male (Thamyris) to another (Paul).

Berger discusses ways in which people in the contemporary Western world view animals, thereby distancing them from themselves in zoos and art. He notes that although animals can be tamed by people, they remain differentiated. Because we lack a common language with them, their silence guarantees their distance, their distinctness and their marginalization. As noted by Kappeler, historically, a woman's silence was always considered her greatest virtue.[92] As a woman, Thecla's public silence guarantees her distance and distinctness from the world of men and subjectivity, and, in this way, her characterization in the first half of the narrative stands in complete opposition to that of Paul. Unlike Paul, she does not utilize language, an exclusively male privilege.

Historically, of course, men have always had the power of public language and the power to name, and the power to name is the power to control.[93] Language and naming enable men to define experience, to articulate boundaries and values and to determine what can and cannot be expressed, and this power is a force that is denied to Thecla. She is a woman who is predominantly dumb and mute.

Berger goes on to argue that in the accompanying ideology, animals are always the observed.[94] The fact that they can observe us has lost all significance, and however we look at these animals, we are looking at something that has been rendered absolutely marginal.[95] Thecla's marginalization as a woman is secured through her silent devotion to a male who is predominantly shielded from her gaze. Unseeing and speechless, the woman is rendered 'other'. Like the animals in the zoo, she is only looked upon and described. We have the unfailing action of the male authorial voice. The female has no voice and she acts only out of love for a man. Even though this story ultimately concerns the heroine, Thecla, it becomes evident how the structures of representation within the text empower Paul and disempower Thecla. She is a silent object of the gaze. The pornographic features are located within the objectification and silencing of this woman.

McInerney argues that Thecla's docility forms part of the motif which connects physical passivity and verbal authority so common in the Apocryphal Acts. She maintains that in order for the heroine to become a witness to divine truth, she must be transformed. The transformation is a social one, marked by initially presenting her as a passive listener. After her trial by fire, there is active movement from silence to speech; Thecla then passes through martyrdom. In this way, Thecla is shown to be a verbal participant in her own destiny. The incident with Alexander in Antioch emphasizes this verbal autonomy. Here, Thecla claims an identity for herself as stranger and handmaid of God, and this establishes her as a missionary. Thecla is then able to go on to assert her power to choose her own destiny ('I did not wish to marry Thamyris'), and she draws from this assertion the power to physically assault Alexander. According to McInerney, this power to define herself in words is immediately linked to the ability to defend herself from the threat of assault.[96] Thecla then goes on to make her longest speech, after she has been recalled from the arena, as though her sufferings there have authorized it. For the first time, in response to the Governor's question as to who and what she is, her words take the form of something more than prayer. Indeed, Thecla is beginning to preach, beginning to use language designed to move and affect her hearers, using metaphor to make her point.[97]

However, in comparison to Paul, Thecla's speeches are moderate and limited in scope. Corrington Streete highlights that one of the most striking features of the *Acts of Paul and Thecla* is that, unlike Blandina, Thecla does not 'speak' a martyrdom sermon; indeed, she does not even confess to being Christian.[98] Cooper also notes that the martyr was the 'quintessential Christian preacher', whose word served 'as the medium of what might be called divine ventriloquism' and was intended to influence conversion.[99] The author could have chosen to represent Thecla speaking a poignant and powerful martyrdom sermon. This would indeed have helped to endow Thecla with the characteristics of subjectivity and power. However, as it is, the narrative represents Thecla in a way that is more akin to the 'ideal, silent' woman presented in 1 Cor. 14.34, and, when Thecla does speak, her words appear to have little impact on those around her. Thus, unlike Paul, Thecla's words do not have any particular sway or influence upon the Governor: he does not ask to hear more. The Governor is not converted by her utterance when she is released from the arena (or even after her miraculous escape). In fact, unlike Paul's meritorious speech at the beginning of the text, which is designed to fortify and reassure, Thecla's short speech ends by assuring eternal death to all who do not believe (ἀποθανεῖται ... ἀιῶας, APTh. 37). Thecla's words only appear to have an impact upon the women at the end of the narrative, and so 'Thecla went in with her (Tryphaena) and rested in her house for eight days, instructing her in the word of God, so that the majority of the maidservants also believed' (APTh. 39). Thecla's missionary work takes place within the household and she can only count the female gender among her converts. The author, however, does not allow us to hear Thecla's instruction or sermonizing. We cannot, therefore, compare what she says to Paul's sermon at the beginning of the text. In this way, Thecla's verbal authority, verbal power and influence are clearly circumscribed.

This representation is in complete contrast to Thecla traditions which saw her extolled as a brilliant teacher. For example, Methodius, the fourth-century bishop of Olympus and Patara in Lyria, Asia Minor, wrote a *Symposium*, in which Thecla provides the most impressive philosophical speech.[100] Similarly, Gregory of Nyssa applauds the renowned teacher Macrina the Younger as a 'second Thecla' who was also a 'Christian Socrates'.[101]

As Sorkin Rabinowitz, in her essay 'Tragedy and the Politics of Containment', argues, we need to remain cautious of the occasional subject status awarded to women within plays written by men, for all the characters are created by the male playwright. As such, there is no representation of the woman's voice but only subjects of the playwright's discourse and ultimately of the discourse of his culture.[102] Firmly within the domain of women, barely utilizing any language, Thecla in the *Acts of Paul and Thecla* has not disrupted the patterns or balance of male power or social dominance. She clearly represents the discourse of patriarchal culture.

The jealousy of Thamyris that results in Thecla's persecution is similarly a part of the ideological structure that proclaims Thecla as an object to be owned and desired. It reinforces the system and ideology of male propriety over women; even Thecla's mother, Theocleia, endorses this view. This treatment of Thecla as object intensifies following the Governor's hearing. Paul is merely flogged and set free to leave the city (APTh. 21), while Thecla is condemned to die.

Strictly speaking, as a Roman citizen, Paul should not have been flogged.[103] Would the author (and readers) have been aware of his Roman citizenship? Either the author was aware of the fact or he chose to ignore it. One can only speculate, but if the author knew of Paul's citizenship, then we can surmise that to have Paul released at this point, without any punishment at all, while Thecla (the heroine) is condemned to death, may have resulted in readers losing sympathy for Paul completely. The author thus assures the audience/readers that Paul has to contend with some unpleasant consequences. However, his punishment is not narrated in any detail. In this way, the text spares him from any humiliation. Instead, the violence and the harsher treatment are focused upon the woman.

At this point, Thecla's own mother shouts, 'burn the lawless one' (APTh. 20) and so 'the young men and maidens brought wood and straw in order that Thecla might be burned' (APTh. 22). Perkins notes that judicial penalties were legally calibrated to social status, whereby the 'more humble' became liable to harsher judicial treatment than the 'more honourable'.[104] Despite Thecla being one of the 'first' of the city (APTh. 26) and Paul simply being a wandering preacher and suspected magician (ξένῳ, APTh. 8; μάγον, APTh. 15), Thecla is condemned to die and Paul is set free. The reality of who is endowed with more status and importance within this text is made amply clear. Castelli notes that 'if there were no difference between a man and woman they would do and suffer the same things'.[105] In the male construction of the passive victim, Thecla provides the necessary counterpart to the active aggressor.[106] The pornographic elements once again come to the fore in Thecla's objectification and victimization, and even women, her own gender, collude with powerful males in her persecution.

We are informed that, once in the arena, 'Thecla looked around for Paul, as a lamb in the wilderness looks for the shepherd. Then, looking to the crowd, she saw the Lord sitting in the form of Paul' (APTh. 21). However, as 'she looked intently (ἀτενίζω) at him ... he disappeared into the heavens' (APTh. 21). Even though Thecla merely sees an apparition of Paul, as soon as her gaze is fixed steadily upon him, he disappears. The text does not risk a prolonged viewing of Paul by Thecla since, in becoming the object of the woman's gaze, his own subjectivity would be nullified. The subject function of looking is preserved and reserved for the male.[107] Indeed, 'viewing is ... an act of male supremacy'.[108] Although the woman in the arena may be gazed at, her own gaze is ultimately ineffectual.

Laura Mulvey, in looking at the way that cinematic film reflects and plays on the socially established interpretation of sexual difference in its control of images and erotic ways of looking, confirms this active male gaze. She notes that, in a world ordered by sexual imbalance, pleasure in looking has been split between active/male and passive/female. In their traditional exhibitionist role, women are simultaneously looked at and displayed and their appearance is coded for strong visual and erotic impact.[109] With a sexy female cross-dresser and pornographic violence as key images within the narrative, the *Acts of Paul and Thecla* presents Thecla for a strong and erotic impact.

Mulvey also underscores how, despite the fact that in normal narrative film, the presence of a woman is an indispensable element of spectacle, her visual presence tends to work against the development of a story line. It freezes the flow of action in a moment of 'erotic contemplation'. This interruption forces the audience to mentally pause in order to visualize the spectacle of the female body. Mulvey goes on to write that traditionally, women in film function on two levels: as erotic object for the characters within the screen story and as erotic object for the spectator within the auditorium, with a shifting tension between the looks on either side of the screen.[110]

Although the legitimacy of utilizing feminist film critique to read ancient texts may be questioned, Mulvey points out that this process of the gaze is not intrinsic only to film.[111] Furthermore, as noted above, ancient authors very much relied on a correlation between hearing and visualization: reading stimulated imaginative visualization, and within the arena stands Thecla, a beautiful naked woman.

Ultimately, all of this means that women are there merely to provoke erotic reactions, both within the audience and within the other characters of the narrative – they are largely marginal to the plot and are simply there to give the main character a reason to act and drive the story. Women are, therefore, presented in order to trigger emotional reactions in the dominant male characters and to provide titillation for the audience. Thus, although Thecla is the main protagonist in the narrative, her strong visual erotic impact detracts from the plot itself. The sexy vision she presents 'freeze-frames' the action as she is contemplated as an erotic object. Despite being the heroine of the story, Thecla's gaze is ultimately passive. She is an object subjected to the controlling and curious gaze of others, of both characters and audience, and she satisfies the male wish for pleasurable looking.

Ann Kaplan asks what the male gaze does to women in films on the screen and whether women can resist sexual objectification by merely reversing the gaze and staring back. She reveals the many difficulties in establishing women as active viewers with their own subjective power to name and control the meaning of an image. She notes that screen images of women are sexualized no matter what the women are doing literally, or what kind of plot may be involved. Kaplan goes on to assert that if women were simply eroticized and objectified, things might not be too bad, since objectification may be an inherent component of both male and female eroticism. However, she argues that things in this area are not symmetrical. To begin with, men do not simply look; their gaze carries with it the power of action and of possession that is lacking in the female gaze. Women receive and return a gaze but cannot act on it.

This point is borne out in the *Martyrdom of Saints Perpetua and Felicitas*. When Perpetua is marched into the stadium she 'went along with shining countenance and calm step ... putting down everyone's stare by her own intense gaze'.[112] Kaplan concludes that the gaze is not necessarily male (literally), but to own and activate the gaze, given our language and the structure of the unconscious, is to be in the masculine position.[113] Although Perpetua appears to activate a gaze in staring everyone down, ultimately, the narrative demonstrates that her gaze has little impact as she is imminently scourged, stripped naked and thrown to the beasts.[114]

Of course, caution must be observed in the application of modern analytical principles to ancient texts. However, as noted by Berger, the essential way of seeing women and the essential use to which their images are put has not changed. Women are depicted in quite different ways from men, not just because the feminine is different from the masculine, but also because the 'ideal' spectator is always assumed to be male and the image of the woman is designed to flatter him.[115] Like Perpetua, Thecla does not own an empowered gaze, nor does her gaze possess any mutuality, such as that between lovers. Such interaction would signify subjectivity. As an object, Thecla's gaze is inhibited and ineffectual; it lacks exchange and communication. As underlined by Bella Zweig in her study of Aristophanes' plays, he who looks maintains social and political domination by his very presumed authority to gaze as subject at another who is cast in the role of object.[116] Persistently casting the woman as an object of the gaze is, as Kappeler argues, a structural feature of pornographic representation.[117] The gaze is, therefore, typically gendered as male. (It is interesting to observe that one well-known representation of a female with an empowered gaze is the gorgon of Greek myth, the Medusa. In her ability to turn heroes to stone simply by a 'look', her gaze is both active and destructive: a mythologizing image of a fear that an active female gaze is inherently emasculating.)

After Thecla is brought naked into the arena, the executioner commands (κελεύω) her to 'mount' (ἐπιβῆναι) the pyre (APTh. 22). It is difficult to ignore the sexual undertones of the word ἐπιβαίνω which may also be used to describe the mounting actions of male animals as they cover the female.[118] Interestingly, the *Martyrdom of Saints Perpetua and Felcitas* is also highly sexualized as Perpetua and Felicitas are stripped naked and placed in nets (APTh. 20). Like wild animals that have been ensnared, these women are paraded in the most degrading way. In addition, one can hardly miss the nuance of the final scene as the sword, a masculine phallic symbol, is consciously and actively directed by Perpetua to her throat (APTh. 21).[119] Of course, in our text it is Thecla who is taking the dominant position and doing the mounting. Nevertheless, the fact that she is being urged on and commanded by a man adds an erotic and voyeuristic appeal.[120] Kaplan notes that voyeurism, linked to disparagement, has a sadistic side and is involved with pleasure through control or domination.[121] It also confirms the power of the male gaze in demonstrating that masculine desire carries with it the capacity for action. In this way, it clearly positions the woman as object.

At this point, Thecla makes the sign of the cross (APTh. 22) and climbs onto the pyre. In raising her arms out to the sides Thecla not only replicates the position of the crucified Christ but opens herself up to a clear, unobstructed full frontal view of her naked body.[122] In the words of the text, Thecla is now ἀνάγκην τῆς θεωρίας (APTh. 21). Thecla in the arena literally becomes 'compulsive viewing'. While the term ἀνάγκην may be translated as 'compulsion' or 'necessary', it also has the sense of 'violence', 'punishment' and 'torture'.[123] This torturous spectacle is unavoidable, and this is why the Governor and all (πᾶς) the crowd are in the theatre (APTh. 21). With Thecla naked in the arena, objectification, violence and nakedness interweave for a dramatic female display. Richlin notes that the most striking examples of objectification are those that present a naked woman to an audience; the woman here is both nude and for the most part mute.[124] On the symbolic level, this is the establishment of gender through the exposure of a woman to a public gaze.[125]

Cooper notes that in antiquity, the power to shield oneself from the gaze of others was a luxury. On the other hand, visibility on one's own terms was an asset well worth cultivating.[126] Thus, being able to control when and how one would be on view to others served among other things as a status indicator.[127] Such controls were the luxury of high status. Within this narrative, Thecla's nakedness emphasizes her lowliness, vulnerability and lack of control.

Thecla's naked representation thus demonstrates the power of the male gender over the female.[128] The scene mirrors the intimate privacy of a virgin woman's domain, a domain normally cloistered away from male prying eyes. The central features of this scene unmistakably characterize modern pornography: a nude or partially dressed female is exposed to the gaze, commentary and manipulation of others, especially men who are all dressed.[129] Underscoring this difference between active subject and passive object are not only vocalization and discourse (the man speaks, the woman is silent) but also clothing and nakedness: the spectators, the Governor, Thamyris, the executioners are all dressed, the woman is naked. In her book *The Beauty Myth*, Naomi Wolf notes that 'to live in a culture in which women are routinely naked where men aren't is to learn inequality in little ways all day long'.[130] Thecla is divested of the clothing necessary to maintain her σωφροσύνη and prevent her shame. She is also deprived of speech and, as Zweig argues of the Mute Nude Females in Aristophanes' plays, being denied the distinctly human form of communication, women are denied any claim to human status and their objectification is complete: 'Objectification, humiliation, and abuse of women are the lessons of pornography, which ever tries to render women and the female as passive, mute, nude, obedient, and available ... at the whim of the male.'[131]

In his treatise *De virginibus velandis*, Tertullian states that the virgin body has phenomenal erotic and sexual appeal.[132] Is this perhaps one of the reasons why Thecla, the beautiful nude virgin, is offered up to the audience, for aesthetic and erotic contemplation? Berger, in discussing the nudity and nakedness of women, highlights the difference between a woman who is naked and one who is nude.[133] He says that to be naked is to be oneself. However, to be nude is to be seen naked by others and yet not recognized for oneself. A naked body has to be seen as an object in order to become a nude. Indeed, the sight of it as an object stimulates the use of it as an object. Nakedness reveals itself whereas nudity is placed on display. In this way, the nude is condemned to never being naked.[134]

This distinction does seem to be exemplified in the *Acts of Paul and Thecla*: in parading Thecla naked in the arena, the text transforms her into a nude as described by Berger. Her womanhood is embodied in her physical appearance as she becomes available to the audience as an alluring object. She is stripped not only of clothing but also of subjectivity and personhood. Furthermore, according to Tertullian (admittedly an extreme and arguably minority view), her very exposure is tantamount to rape. 'Every public exposure of a good virgin is (to her) a suffering of a rape. And yet the suffering of carnal violence is the less (evil) because it comes of natural office.'[135] For Tertullian, a virgin revealed is no longer a virgin:

> But when the very spirit itself is violated in a virgin by the abstraction of her covering, she has learnt to lose what she used to keep ... You have denuded a maiden ... and forthwith she wholly ceases to be a virgin to herself; she has undergone a change![136]

On the basis of Tertullian's view and understanding, by way of the male gaze and a metaphorical rape, Thecla's virginity is negated and sullied.[137] However, despite Thecla's objectification and (according to Tertullian) her symbolic rape, the text informs us that 'the Governor wept and marvelled at the power that was in her' (*APTh*. 22). Thecla, the object, becomes more than her body, more than her beauty; she is admired for her manly virtue, ἀνδρεία: praise indeed! She does not speak, but, in making the sign of the cross with her body, she acts (*APTh*. 22). Here, as the audience are given a full unobstructed view of a naked Thecla, we see a confluence of objectivity, female action and courage. Do we have a glimmer of female subjectivity? Bearing in mind Sorkin Rabinowitz's precept to remain cautious of female subjectivity portrayed within male authored texts, it needs to be underscored that Thecla at this moment is nude, exposed and accessible to the male gaze.[138] As a beautiful nude woman who merely acts and does not speak, her representation remains erotic in tone and content. The masculine audience can, therefore, enjoy watching her act.

Although Thecla is saved from death by fire, her ordeal in the arena does not deter her from her devotion to the apostle and she dutifully goes after (or pursues, διώκω, *APTh*. 23) Paul and speaks her first full sentence in prayer. However, somewhat disappointingly, she thanks God for saving her from the fire that she 'might see Paul' (*APTh*. 24). Once again, Thecla is represented as deferring to the male, thus bolstering Paul's dominant representation.[139]

Petropoulos argues that within the tomb, Paul is hiding and afraid to venture to the city. Indeed, from the moment of his public humiliation and expulsion from Iconium, the saint becomes a passive and impuissant figure. The glory of martyrdom and simultaneous mastery over the elements is reserved for the heroine.[140] However, this interpretation is inaccurate, for as soon as Thecla is saved from the fire, readers are transported to the tomb where Paul is shown to be fasting (*APTh*. 22-23). Furthermore, on entering the tomb, Thecla finds Paul on his knees praying for her safety (*APTh*. 24). The miracle in the arena is clearly attributed to Paul's prayer, not to Thecla's 'power' as thought by the Governor.[141] Furthermore, Paul does not exhibit fear in any way; he does not hesitate to leave the tomb and travel with Thecla to Antioch (*APTh*. 26).

Before they venture to Antioch together, however, Thecla offers to cut her hair short and follow Paul (*APTh*. 25), as we have seen. The verb ἀκολουθέω generally means 'to follow' someone else who takes 'the lead' and also has the connotation of 'to obey'.[142] Although Thecla is willing to break with conventions of the period by refusing to marry and suggesting she cut her hair short, she is, nevertheless, still operating within the conventions of patriarchy by offering to be Paul's subordinate: to follow *and* obey him. Her fidelity and reverence for the male is complete and unquestioning. Furthermore, while the offer to cut her hair might suggest that Thecla is gaining some level of subject status (for by cutting her hair Thecla would be renouncing a feminine symbol which sexualizes her), the text immediately impedes this development through Paul's objectifying response, 'the time is shameful and you are beautiful' (*APTh*. 25).[143] Paul also at this stage refuses to baptize Thecla, fearing that she 'may play the coward' (δειλανδρήσῃς) if faced with further temptations. Paul has no real regard for Thecla other than as a beautiful woman who is prone to weakness. Furthermore, in using the words πειρασμὸς and χείρων, Paul hints that seduction, moral weakness and inferiority come into play.[144]

Paul's disdain for Thecla is further underlined as they travel together to Antioch. Alexander, a powerful and important man (*APTh*. 26) falls 'in lust' with Thecla immediately upon seeing her (ἠράσθη suggests sexual passion, *APTh*. 26).[145] When Alexander tries to bribe Paul with money and gifts if only he will let him have Thecla,

Paul disowns her completely, 'I do not know the woman of whom you speak, and she is not mine' (*APTh*. 26). The irony of his unmanly and cowardly behaviour in failing to protect Thecla is remarkable, especially given Paul's fear in the previous verse that Thecla may herself play the coward and the fact that the author depicts Paul as a divine and angelic man.

This negative aspect of Paul's characterization has been variously explained. For example, Dunn has argued that the author's intention is not to malign Paul's character but rather to show Paul providing Thecla with an opportunity to test her faith and vow of chastity.[146] Burrus, however, notes that here Paul's credibility with the reader is damaged. Paul comes precariously close to alliance with Thecla's villainous opponents, and we begin to suspect that he is not, in fact, Thecla's helper but is, like the other males in the story, part of her problem.[147]

However, this incident, revealing Paul's sudden loss of courage, signals that a significant (albeit temporary) shift, or displacement of gender boundaries, is about to take place in the narrative. Thus, while in public without a male 'owner' Thecla is vulnerable to the very real threat of rape as the 'powerful' (δυνάμος) Alexander embraced her on the street (*APTh*. 26), she suddenly becomes effectual and dynamic and once again demonstrates ἀνδρεία, manliness: the very opposite of δειλανδρήσης. Thecla resists Alexander's advances and fights back, 'she tore off his cloak and took away the crown from his head and made him a spectacle' (ἔστησεν αὐτόν θρίαμβον, *APTh*. 26). The masculine quality of her actions is quite unmistakable as she unexpectedly gains the upper hand in the skirmish: in a sudden turn of events, a powerful and important man now becomes the object of 'spectacle'.

The text, of course, takes for granted that men have the power of leading women, guarding them and – essentially – owning them. In this respect, it is natural that Thecla should be reckoned as part of Paul's estate, as if she were his wife, a mere chattel of exchange. As Dworkin highlights, to be a chattel, even when human, is to be valued and used as property, as a thing.[148] And so a lascivious, wanton man, supported by the laws of the land, tries to obtain and use Thecla sexually. The theme of rape once again becomes prominent, but this time the threat is of a physical rape.[149] Since Thecla has been marked as 'beautiful' (εὔμορφος, *APTh*. 5, κάλλος, *APTh*. 29), any audience would understand that desire and lust overcame Alexander and rendered him uncontrollable. What he did, he did because the female was 'beautiful'.

As noted earlier, Glancy highlights that an essential component of gender construction involves women being looked at, while masculinity is understood in terms of voyeurism.[150] According to this maxim, things happen not because women are subject and act but because they are looked at by men. This is borne out within the *Acts of Paul and Thecla*. Thecla as an object of desire is responsible for the unhappiness of Thamyris and Alexander. They look at her, they desire her, and because they cannot have her, it results in their misery and negative consequences for her. Glancy rightly observes that the male gaze defines woman as object and man as subject, and women incessantly impact negatively on men. The paradox is that although women are represented as objects, they are held responsible for male behaviour. The principle implies that women who are looked at somehow cause the actions of the men who see them.[151] Men externalize and project their desire onto women; consequently, women are always a source of anxiety and a trap for men. Wolf expresses this perfectly: 'Beauty provokes harassment, the law says, but it looks through men's eyes when deciding what provokes it.'[152] The law, created by men, with a male perspective, ultimately decides whether a woman deserves to be harassed.

When Thecla fights Alexander, it makes no difference that the one constituent element of rape, sex, is missing in the encounter. Although Thecla escapes literal rape, the consequences of her resistance bring down upon her the full force of masculine power, and we are soon shown graphic details of her social rape, as she is tied naked by the feet between two bulls. Rape, whether literal or threatened, is about the power of the male over the female. Although Thecla successfully resists Alexander's physical advances, masculine power and strength is not a subjective phenomenon; laws and customs protect it.[153] Thecla is thus condemned to the beasts for resisting rape and emasculating a powerful man.

Berger notes how when we look, we are always looking at the relation between things.[154] Thus, visualizing a woman being passed around from man to man and violently abused for attempting to defend herself firmly sets in the minds of the audience the gender ideology of society. The violence that is directed towards Thecla reflects this dominant ideology; it establishes her (and other women's) place in the world. Within this text, violence against women is legally sanctioned and condoned.

Before being flung into the arena, Thecla is stripped and given a 'διαζώστραν' to wear (APTh. 33). A διαζώνη would denote a band, usually a waist sash, although sometimes it referred to a loincloth.[155] Such an item could be placed around the waist or the bosom. However, whichever way the 'διαζώστραν' was worn, it would invariably leave Thecla's body partially exposed. Once again, Thecla's naked body is paraded voyeuristically before a gathering of fully dressed men and women. Nevertheless, once she is in the arena, Thecla continues to assert her subjectivity. After the demise of the lioness, which protects her, she stretches out her hands and prays and then throws herself into a pit of water in an act of self-baptism (APTh. 34). Here, the narrator informs us that there was about her 'a cloud of fire' (νεφέλη πυρός) which protected her from the beasts and ensured she could not be seen naked (μήτε θεωρεῖσθαι αὐτὴν γυμνήν, APTh. 34). Thecla provocatively oscillates between being covered and uncovered, thus tantalizing and titillating the audience with her nakedness.

While the text plays interchangeably with Thecla's nakedness, the female chorus, which began in APTh. 27 and raised a protest in regard to the judgement against Thecla, begins to predominate (APTh. 34). This chorus forms a component of the motif of 'women supporting women', for example, Tryphaena who takes Thecla under her wing (APTh. 27) and the lioness who protects her in the arena (APTh. 33). Jensen has placed a question mark on this supposed female coalition, pointing out that the lioness has to fight off a she-bear, a point not evident in English translations. She also offers a number of parallels which show that women in antiquity became involved in protests against state decisions.[156] Jensen's point needs to be borne in mind. It is important not to overstate the female solidarity within the text, especially since the Iconium episode shows women colluding with Thecla's persecution. In addition, it was also probably a custom to send female beasts at condemned women.[157]

As women come forward in this section to consolidate their resources and take centre stage, the violence in the narrative also appears to dissipate (albeit fleetingly) as they utilize heavy scents and fragrances, female-associated products, to overpower the wild beasts and help rescue Thecla (*APTh.* 35). They protect Thecla without resorting to aggression or savagery. McInerney contends that the author, at this point, sets up a veritable battle between the sexes.[158] However, this is hardly the case. This gentle picture of women working together, non-violently, to neutralize masculine force and violence does not prevail for very long. Just as the women gain some level of control, masculine hostility reappears with even greater force to overcome all trace of feminine empowerment and advancement, thus demonstrating that women have no real power as such. Alexander said to the Governor, 'I have some very fearsome bulls, let us tie her to them.' The Governor, 'looking gloomy' (στυγνάσας), gave consent (*APTh.* 35), and they 'bound her by the feet between the bulls and placed burning-hot irons onto their genitals that being the more agitated they might kill her' (*APTh.* 35).[159] The third-person narration shifts the focus to the events and characters in the story itself, thus giving the reader an 'eagle eye' view of the events taking place. The reader's gaze is thus effectively manipulated as we are forced to look upon this pornographic sado-erotic spectacle: we become active voyeurs, along with the narrator and spectators in the arena.

Of course, Thecla does not need to be tied by the feet to these bulls; she could have, just as easily, been tied by the hands. But in doing so, the author categorically tailors the text towards a prurient gaze. The scene is pornographic to the extent that it is gratuitous, completely unnecessary to the plot. Given the indeterminate state of Thecla's nakedness, this amounts to a lewd and obscene attack on a woman. It could, of course, be argued that Thecla here is not naked, for we are soon told that although the bulls leaped forward, 'the flame that was around her (περικαιομένη φλὸς) burned through the ropes (διέκαυσεν τοὺς κάλους) and she was as if she were not bound' (*APTh.* 35). Presumably, this is the same flame/fire mentioned in *APTh.* 34, which veiled Thecla's naked body from view. However, the narrator fails to reassure the audience at this stage that Thecla's nakedness is covered, and this gives the sense that the fire is mentioned at this point purely to help provide the heroine with a means of escape.

Spittler also notes that the phenomenon of the fire which blazed around Thecla must have been of limited duration since the women in the crowd have to act to save Thecla from the beasts. Furthermore, if Thecla is permanently surrounded by a cloud of fire capable of burning through rope, it is difficult to understand how anyone managed to tie her to the bulls in the first place.[160] This confusion over the source of the flames/fire also manifests itself both in the Greek and Latin texts which reveal extensive textual variations.[161] Spittler argues that it seems better to understand this 'scorching flame' as a product of the 'burning irons' used to goad the bulls.[162] For our purposes, however, it seems quite reasonable to assume that if there is a fire around Thecla, it is a mere flickering presence, and at times, when it matters, the flame is not protecting Thecla's body from view. Thus, Thecla is laid bare, with her legs apart, in the middle of the arena.

Berger tells us that when someone is naked, the focus of perception shifts from eyes, mouth, shoulders and hands to the sexual parts. At this point, the other is reduced to their primary sexual category: male or female.¹⁶³ The equivocal state of Thecla's dress/ undress leaves her sexuality exposed before our very eyes. The display is overt and salacious in tone. Just like the victim in pornography, Thecla is exhibited to those who watch and reduced to a body.

In a society in which women and girls of elite citizen status were rigorously segregated, where sexual and social mores were controlled by strict notions of etiquette and propriety, and where a very sharp distinction was drawn in respect of public and private,¹⁶⁴ such exposure is particularly hostile and serves only to degrade its object. As Zweig argues, any public exposure of 'respectable' women, whether visual or verbal, leads to shame. She notes that such exposure deliberately plays on shameful undertones and serves as an instrument of male control over women and their sexuality: a realm designated as women's greatest vulnerability.¹⁶⁵ Thecla's bondage, objectification and degradation are complete. Her treatment and representation demonstrates the masculine power to tyrannize women and amounts to a form of pornography that contributes to the prurient gaze, male dominance and masculine subjectivity.

In her book *Torture and Truth*, Page duBois examines how, in the ancient world, the testimony of the slave under torture was always believed to be true, whereas a slave testifying without torture was assumed to lie.¹⁶⁶ The slave's body was thus viewed as a mere container of words that required extraction. Relating classical Greek juridical practices to the torture of slaves in antiquity, duBois argues that the tortured slave body is the site of the production of truth and that a goal of torture is to obtain truth. Burrus develops the principle of linking truth with torture in the ancient world and argues that it persists in martyrdom texts (including the gospels).¹⁶⁷ The juridical context highlighted by duBois remains decisive for her interpretation. However, whereas classical Greek practice frames the slave as the passive container of a truth that another can claim, the ideology of Christian martyrdom assigns truth to the tortured subject herself. Thus, within martyrdom texts, the tortured bodies of slaves, women and men come to be privileged in their capacity to give visual witness to Christian truths. Traditionally, a slave is tortured to divulge evidence concerning his or her master, but within martyrdoms, the master is Christ. In the figure of the martyr, the eloquence of body and word converge in order to testify against the torturer and witness for Christ: the tortured body is itself rendered eloquent. For Burrus, martyrdom witness testifies at once to his or her own identity as a true Christian, the truth of Christ and the wrongdoing of the torturers.¹⁶⁸ The context of Roman Imperial rule, together with the public spectacles of violence through which imperial power is performed, is highly relevant. Indeed, it is precisely these Roman contextual features that not only invite but also enable the resistance staged by Christian martyrdom texts.

In short, Burrus argues that since the goal of torture is truth, the torture of martyrdom is the ultimate witness to the truth of Christ. However, if tortured martyr bodies are the site of the production of truth, I am compelled to ask whether all martyr bodies, male, female and slave, are rendered equal in the business of 'truth making'. When taking account of gender, there remain stark differences in the way male and female martyrs are depicted. Despite inscribing truth onto male, female and slave bodies, it remains the case that female martyrs continue to be sexualized through sado-erotic torture. Inscribing truth onto the body of a sexualized woman is just another way of turning women into another particular type of 'body' (read 'object'). Thus, even as Thecla's tortured body gives birth to the truth of Christ, her body continues to sustain androcentric regimes of truth (and power) regarding women. Sado-erotic torture ensures the oppressive forces of patriarchy maintain control over female bodies and female subjectivity.

Pornography, pain and violence cannot, then, be excised from the *Acts of Paul and Thecla*. Such graphic, vivid description forms powerful erotic images of representation that force readers to 'look' and to 'see' what is being described, and, even if they wanted to, the reading audience cannot turn away from the spectacle.[169] In this way, readers/listeners are forced to collude with the arena audience. Whether the image invokes enjoyment or abhorrence, ultimately, we cannot avert our eyes from the display.

In discussing the themes of nudity and clothing in the *Acts of Paul and Thecla*, Margaret Miles argues that public nakedness is clearly conceived by the anonymous author as part of Thecla's punishment and torture. However, she argues that Thecla at the end of the story reinterprets her nakedness, removing it from the Governor's power and aligning it with her strength as a confessor of Christ: 'The one who clothed me while I was naked among the beasts shall clothe me with salvation on the day of judgement' (*APTh.* 38). Miles contends that Thecla insists that her body is not ultimately at the disposal of the Governor to cover or strip but is an aspect of her religious integrity, incorporated and included in her salvation.[170] However, despite Thecla's words and the interpretation proposed by Miles, the point is that the text has demonstrated, incontrovertibly, that Thecla's body is very much at the disposal of the Governor and all the other men, to do with exactly as they pleased. Even while Thecla makes this statement, the text leaves us in little doubt that she stands naked and exposed before the powerful Governor (*APTh.* 38). We return to Wolf's axiom: for a woman to be naked where men are not is 'to learn inequality in little ways all day long'.[171] If, as Thecla asserts to the Governor in her speech, she really was clothed by God in the arena, then she was done so only intermittently.

Burrus also reads this scene as an act of defiance and argues that 'shame' is a test that Thecla has passed 'with flying colors'.[172] Arguing for 'shame' as a kind of 'performativity' that allows Christians to establish a new identity, Burrus asserts that Thecla is '[b]oth shamed and unashamed – splendidly shameless'.[173] However, although Burrus is highly conscious of the fact that the figure of the martyr has been domesticated,[174] to argue for the construction of a positive female Christian identity through sexualized violence runs the risk of further normalizing the gendered violence written into female martyrdoms. Sexual violence against women is a consequence of a dehumanized perception. Burrus is astutely aware that shame is enormously powerful and destructive.[175] Secretly, shame wounds; it creates an inner blemish, an invisible wound. Can such a painful and visceral emotion be so easily silenced and miraculously erased?

Jennifer Wright Knust, speaking about the long history of the intersection of sex and politics, notes that there has rarely been a time when 'sex itself was not also about power'.[176] Within martyrdoms, sexualized violence is used as a sign of male domination and power from which women rarely, if ever, truly escape. Thus, despite her speech to the Governor, Thecla's nakedness has served its purpose in making a spectacle of her, exposing her to the prurient gaze and utilizing her as a pornographic object of voyeurism. Commensurate with this treatment, there is no apology from the Governor that she had to endure such a debasing ordeal. No male (not even she) objects to the violence and humiliation she had to bear.

It thus becomes evident that the scenes discussed within the text contain a whole range of disparaging and humiliating representations of Thecla. They parallel elements of contemporary pornography in that they reflect unequal social dynamics and portray Thecla as an object of degradation and violence. However, it is not only modern theorists that would categorize aspects of this literature as pornographic. Scholars have long noted the similarity of the Apocryphal Acts to the Hellenistic romantic novels.[177] It is, therefore, instructive to note that, in antiquity, a medical man, permitted by his medical 'disinterest' to talk about such things, clearly identifies the function of 'romance' as pornographic, as the generation of an erection for a male reader; the doctor links reading texts about sexual activity with achieving an erection.[178] The pornographic and sexual scenes within the *Acts of Paul and Thecla* contain representations of violence, nakedness and voyeurism, and in so doing, they titillate, tantalize and thrill the audience. Diana Russell writes that when women are portrayed as objects, they become depersonalized things, not multifaceted human beings – their bodies are stripped, exposed and contorted in order to bolster masculine esteem; indeed, men get a 'kick and sense of power from viewing females' in this way.[179]

According to Russell, from the power-based masculine perspective, feminine assault and invasion are really quite necessary. She notes that the voyeuristic 'turn on' of most pornography depends on the violation of women's privacy.[180] The picture of a naked Thecla mounting the pyre, the vulnerability of a beautiful woman threatened by rape, the naked figure of a woman in an arena exposed to wild beasts, the picture of a woman in bondage, spread-legged between two bulls: these are all images that violate women, eroticize violence and dominance, bolster male subjectivity and invite the prurient gaze. They contain representations of women's experience of being vulnerable, exposed, threatened and psychologically invaded in a way that men are not.

Analysis and observations thus far

Reading the *Acts of Paul and Thecla* through the lens of pornographic representation highlights and underscores the extent to which the structures of representation sexualize and objectify Thecla. The text represents Thecla being demeaned as the result of the actions of the Governor and others, in front of the audience that is relishing this. In depicting things so graphically, the reading audience is also drawn in to become spectators in the same way as the crowd. Readers are not in Thecla's head, viewing things from her perspective, but viewing her from outside, as if on a seat in the arena, or in a street witnessing actions taking place. Even if the text is attempting to say something positive about this Christian woman and potential martyr, this reading exposes the ambivalent treatment of the woman in this text.

When Thecla displays the manly virtue of ἀνδρεία (making the sign of the cross when mounting the pyre and jumping into the pool of seals to baptize herself), the author is undoubtedly intending to produce a counter-narrative to the usual interpretation of Roman spectacle. The purpose of these scenes is to guide the audience and readers towards a particular Christian interpretative frame. Here, Christian audiences should be 'gazing' with the 'proper' spirit – seeing past the graphic pornographic violence to the more 'spiritually uplifting' narrative that underlies the spectacle.[181] At this point, the spectacle should be working for Christian advantage, as the author attempts to ensure the violent and sexual scenes in the arena are not misread or enjoyed in the 'wrong' way. Thecla is meant to be overturning captivity and domination; a resignification is meant to be taking place.

However, the narratival elements concerning Thecla's manly courageous acts are nominal in comparison to the level of spectacle in the arena. The author could have reinforced Thecla's courageous actions by making them more spectacular and by adding commentary. This would have served to shift the focus away from the voyeuristic, prurient gaze back to the 'proper' uplifting Christian 'spiritual' gaze. However, as it is, the violent, sado-erotic spectacle predominates in both arena scenes escalating and building to the crescendo of a spread-legged image of a naked woman. There is no strong counter-narrative to Roman spectacle here. Thus, even though the sado-erotic spectacle is meant to be read in a particular way, there is no commentary present to correct audience vision. The Christian interpretive frame is minimized, allowing sado-erotic spectacle to dominate.

In this way, the text allows room for multiple layers of signification, without avoiding the prurient, voyeuristic gaze. Castelli notes that Perpetua's performance is also complex in this respect. The narrator's role at critical junctures places the reader in the role of voyeuristic spectator, reminding the reader of the instability of any performance and its openness to multiple interpretations. In concluding her section on martyrdom and spectacle, Castelli highlights that spectacle transforms the reader and consumers into 'uneasy voyeurs'. In this way, 'Christian spectacularization of martyrdom' embodies paradoxes and ambivalence which require 'cautious attention'.[182]

Focusing on the pornographic elements within the *Acts of Paul and Thecla* (elements which have regularly been side-lined and marginalized) brings to the fore the level to which 'spectacle' operates within the text. It also demonstrates how the audience are manipulated into 'uneasy voyeurs' vulnerable to the adoption of the prurient gaze. Furthermore, it draws particular attention to the ambiguous treatment of the heroine within the narrative. No matter who is doing the viewing, eroticism is never far away and cannot be avoided. With every part of her body exposed to audience, narrator and readers alike, Thecla is repeatedly violated. Thecla, therefore, never quite manages to sustain her subjectivity or trespass too far beyond the limits of her feminine gender. Paul is ever present in her mind, and even as the narrative draws to a close, he continues to motivate her actions (*APTh.* 40). Indeed, Thecla works unquestioningly for Paul and a patriarchal God and in so doing cooperates and functions within the very systems of patriarchy which abuse her. Her representation in no way disrupts the patterns of patriarchal gender hierarchy.

Nevertheless, despite Thecla's abuse and objectification, we cannot discount the fact that she evidences the manly quality ἀνδρεία. Furthermore, ultimately she is marked out as completely distinct and atypical in the fact that she repeatedly survives the many attempts to kill her. Salisbury notes that it is the nature of the accounts of martyrs that they close with finality. The stories inevitably end with the death into eternal life of the martyrs and no more needs to be said.[183] Obviously, Thecla does not die; it is, therefore, in surviving her martyrdom that the story of Thecla is exceptional and deviates so clearly from the more 'normal' martyrdoms. Indeed, not only does Thecla survive her martyrdom/s, but no amount of torture or exposure to danger affects this woman either physically or psychologically. Unlike Perpetua, for example, she suffers no pain or injury.[184]

For good reason, Petropoulos calls the *Acts of Paul and Thecla* a 'sacred soap opera' where nudity is forthrightly mentioned. Petropoulos goes on to contrast 'outward exposure' and 'inner integrity'.[185] However, Petropoulos is only partially correct, for although Thecla is exposed, and although she does at times display the inner manly quality of 'ἀνδρεία', Thecla's body also retains an 'outward' integrity. Despite Thecla's bodily exposure, we never hear of her sustaining even a scratch. Thecla's bodily integrity is absolute and extreme.

In this respect, although scholars have argued that the story of Thecla is based upon a historical character, the story of her martyrdom is completely unrealistic.[186] In the account of her martyrdom, therefore, Thecla – the beautiful, eroticized, exposed virgin – has to be a product of male imagination: a literary virgin constructed by men. That this is the case is evidenced by the fact that her body remains impervious and inviolable to any attempts to penetrate it, inscribe upon it and destroy it.

Braun argues that women's pursuit of Christian piety to be 'like men' meant negotiating the complex and tricky connections between a robust manly subjectivity and the female body. Since the female body created one of the greatest obstacles to religious perfection, it became the locus for the *suppression and rejection* of femininity, as well as the site on which to work out the desire.[187] However, in highlighting the pornographic violence within the *Acts of Paul and Thecla*, it becomes evident that no aspect of Thecla's female body is either rejected or suppressed. Rather, her female body is repeatedly flaunted and exposed for all to see, and, in surviving her ordeals, Thecla's virgin body becomes highly privileged. It behaves like the body of a man *ought* to behave: it is inviolable and yet she is a woman. Female virginity and sexuality and masculine bodily integrity emerge as artfully crafted motifs within the text.

Conclusion

Within this chapter, I have focused upon the violent and pornographic elements within the *Acts of Paul and Thecla* in order to gain an appreciation of the ideology and rhetorical techniques that shape the construction of gender. I have also assessed how the pornographic and violent imagery communicates male power, supremacy and dominance. Close examination of the narrative reveals that Thecla is continually objectified. In parading Thecla naked in the arena she is stripped of clothing, subjectivity and personhood. In addition, as a woman who is passed around from man to man and violently abused for attempting to assert her subjectivity, Thecla is affirmed as under male control. The ideological structure within the narrative proclaims Thecla as an object to be owned and desired (meanwhile, the only desire Thecla is permitted is her 'spiritualized' desire for Paul). In this way, Thecla is shown to be at the disposal of powerful men, and this treatment establishes hers (and woman's) place in the world.

Conversely, the text never risks a prolonged viewing of Paul by Thecla, for, in becoming the object of the woman's look, a man's subjectivity would be annulled. Thecla's gaze, therefore, lacks the power to objectify Paul; her eyes gaze into nothingness. The physical description of Paul also establishes his subject status and guards against physical objectification. Instead, his inner integrity and angelic nature is emphasized. Unlike Thecla, who is presented as an insect caught in a trap and who is repeatedly cast as the object of the discourse of others, Paul is also endowed with the power of speech. He emerges as a skilful master of language easily able to persuade and influence others with his words. That Paul's auditory word is emphasized underscores the important masculine signifying system in the text. The representations of Paul and Thecla thus set up a striking inequity between the male and female. Neither in her speech nor in her characterization does Thecla disrupt the pattern of male power and social dominance.

The violent and pornographic elements of the text reach a crescendo in the gratuitous scene where Thecla is tied naked by the legs between two bulls in the midst of the arena. Is this a positive representation of a woman? Such an image is humiliating even for any modern-day woman, and it would have been especially so for a woman steeped in an antique culture of honour and shame. Surely, such representation bears all the hallmarks of patriarchy, of men writing women, and could not be further from affirming female subjectivity. Reading with a hermeneutic of suspicion shows explicitly and unreservedly that there is a need for caution before claiming such a text is female-affirming. No aspect of Thecla's body is veiled from sight; nothing (other than rape) could have been more humiliating for an elite virgin in antiquity. How does such a construct serve to affirm the representation of Thecla and women generally? Is the text empowering for women? The hostile treatment of this woman's beautiful body clearly represents the discourse of patriarchal culture which subjugates and objectifies women.

It is interesting to note that, despite the focus upon Thecla's body and beauty, and in contrast to Paul, we are never given a description of her. Thecla, therefore, has no real identity as such – the reader can know and see Paul but not Thecla. Thecla can, therefore, stand in for any beautiful woman. This aspect of Thecla's representation not only serves to make Thecla less real, an ideal perhaps or especially a metaphor, but also helps audiences to distance themselves from this female. As a woman who is not described, Thecla can justifiably be made an object of fantasy and a victim, with little or no empathy for her suffering, as in the case of the *Damnati ad bestias*.[188] This representation of Thecla is reinforced since no physical or psychological effects of the traumas or ordeals she experiences are ever hinted at, let alone narrated.

In Chapter 4, I noted how the concept of ἀνδρεία disrupted the objectified female representation of Thecla, endowing her with virility and aspects of subjectivity. Here too, it is evident that ἀνδρεία has an important role to play in Thecla's representation. Thus, although reading through a 'pornographic lens' testifies to a woman humiliated, shamed and victimized through naked exposure and sexualized objectification, the ἀνδρεία that Thecla exhibits results in a female body that has complete integrity. And so despite the fact that Thecla does not disrupt patriarchal gender hierarchy, her female body is, nevertheless, endowed with extraordinary fortitude.

Glimmers of subjectivity and manly courage (ἀνδρεία) converge with an inviolable, sexualized, female virgin body to become crucial elements within this text. There is no attempt to suppress or forsake the female form. Indeed, just as in the previous chapter the author ensured that Thecla retained one of the foremost markers of her femininity and womanliness – her long hair – here too, Thecla's femaleness, her female virgin body, forms the nexus around her paradoxical representation, a curious mix of sexual objectification, female victimization and masculine inviolability. It is, of course, the miracles within the arena that ensure Thecla's bodily inviolability. Within the next chapter, I will, therefore, continue to analyse the extent of the female-affirming nature of the text and examine what further light can be shed upon the representation of Thecla.

Notes

1 Nancy Sorkin Rabinowitz, 'Tragedy and the Politics of Containment', in *Pornography and Representation in Greece and Rome*, ed. Amy Richlin (Oxford: Oxford University Press), 38.
2 MacDonald, *Early Christian Women*, 176; see also Gillian Clark, 'Bodies and Blood: Late Antique Debate on Martyrdom, Virginity and Resurrection', in *Changing Bodies, Changing Meanings, Studies on the Human Body in Antiquity*, ed. Dominic Montserrat (London: Routledge, 1998), 103.
3 This is based on the women in Antioch who collaborate together to help Thecla, the lioness who takes her side and Queen Tryphaena who becomes her protector. See e.g. McGinn, 'The Acts of Thecla', 817–18; MacDonald, *Early Christian Women*, 176. See also Dagron, *Vie et Miracles*, 36–8.
4 Since male heterosexual pornography is most relevant to this study, I will not be examining or debating issues concerning gay and child pornography.
5 For modern debates on pornography, see Amy Richlin, ed., 'Introduction' to *Pornography and Representation in Greece and Rome* (Oxford: Oxford University Press, 1992), xiv–xv and references cited there. For arguments concerning violence against women, see Sorkin Rabinowitz, 'Politics of Containment', 36–52. See also Susanne Kappeler, *The Pornography of Representation* (Minneapolis: University of Minnesota Press, 1986), 18–34; Ronald Dworkin, 'Is There a Right to Pornography?' *Oxf. J. Leg. Stud.* (1981): 177–212; Susan M. Easton, *The Problem of Pornography: Regulation and the Right to Free Speech* (London: Routledge, 1994). For a discussion on the abuse of women in the making of pornography and separating the consequences of pornography from the issues of censorship, see Diana E. H. Russell, ed., *Making Violence Sexy: Feminist Views on Pornography* (Buckingham: Open University Press, 1993), 12–14, and the essays contained in Part III of the volume which discuss the harmful effects of pornography. On obscenity, see Catharine A. MacKinnon, *Toward a Feminist Theory of the State* (Cambridge, MA: Harvard University Press, 1989), 196–7.
6 It should be noted that legal usage does not conform to everyday language or to dictionary definitions, see Easton, *The Problem of Pornography*, xii.
7 Russell, *Making Violence Sexy*, 5. For a discussion on pornography and erotica, see Kappeler, *The Pornography of Representation*, 35–48. It should be highlighted that

there is great disagreement among feminists on the issue of pornography. The antipornography movement produced a backlash within feminism, as some feminists argued in defence of pornography. Richlin notes that this debate has generated deep divisions, a huge bibliography, and whole subfields of theory, Richlin, 'Introduction' to *Pornography and Representation*, xiv–xv, and references cited.
8 Andrea Dworkin, *Pornography: Men Possessing Women* (London: Women's Press, 1981), 14–15, 24, 80–106, 200–1.
9 MacKinnon, *Toward a Feminist Theory*, 199.
10 Catharine A. MacKinnon, *Feminism Unmodified: Discourses on Life and Law* (Cambridge, MA: Harvard University Press, 1987), 172.
11 Cited in Easton, *The Problem of Pornography*, xii.
12 MacKinnon, *Toward a Feminist Theory*, 211.
13 John Berger, *Ways of Seeing* (London: BBC & Penguin Books, 1972), 47.
14 Richlin, 'Introduction' to *Pornography and Representation*, xiv.
15 Kappeler, *Pornography of Representation*, 2–8.
16 Richlin, 'Introduction' to *Pornography and Representation*, xvii.
17 Kappeler, *Pornography of Representation*, 2–3.
18 Dworkin, *Pornography*, 24.
19 Catharine A. MacKinnon, 'Feminism, Marxism, and the State: An Agenda for Theory', in *Signs Reader: Women, Gender and Scholarship*, ed. Elizabeth Abel and Emily Abel (Chicago, IL: University of Chicago Press, 1983), 241.
20 Kappeler, *Pornography of Representation*, 49–50.
21 Helen E. Elsom, 'Callirhoe: Displaying the Phallic Woman', in *Pornography and Representation*, ed. Amy Richlin, 214.
22 Cooper, 'A Father, a Daughter', 699.
23 Tac., *Ann.*, 15.44 (Jackson, LCL).
24 Brent Shaw, 'The Passion of Perpetua', *Past and Present* 139 (1993): 10.
25 Clement of Rome, *First Epistle to the Corinthians*, ch. 6, 1–2.
26 Shaw, 'Passion of Perpetua', 18.
27 See e.g. David Potter, 'Martyrdom as Spectacle', in *Theater and Society in the Classical World*, ed. Ruth Scodel (Ann Arbor: University of Michigan Press, 1993), 65–7; see also Donald G. Kyle, *Spectacles of Death in Ancient Rome* (New York: Routledge, [1998] 2001).
28 Potter, 'Martyrdom and Spectacle', 53–5, esp. 54. Because some Christians held such a fanatical attitude to martyrdom, many Romans thought that Christians belonged to a 'death-cult'. Indeed, pagans often regarded Christian attitudes to martyrdom and suicide as identical. Paul Middleton, '"Dying We Live" (2 Cor. 6.9): Discipleship and Martyrdom in Paul', in *Paul, Grace and Freedom: Essays in Honour of John K. Riches*, ed. Paul Middleton, Karen J. Wenell and Angus Paddison (London: T&T Clark, 2009), 82–3. See also Epictetus, *Diatr.* 4.7.6; Lucian, *De mort. Peregr.* 13. However, it should be noted that within the *Acts of Paul and Thecla*, Thecla is not depicted as consciously and actively seeking out martyrdom.
29 Burrus, *Saving Shame*, 8.
30 Ibid., 13.
31 Joyce Salisbury astutely observes that although many Christians thought it inappropriate and indeed harmful to attend the shows in the amphitheatre, they were known to be present as such events. She cites as evidence the martyrdom of Perpetua, a text supposedly written by an eye witness, which would suggest Christians were

present at such events, Joyce E. Salisbury, *Perpetua's Passion: The Death Memory of a Young Roman Woman* (London: Routledge, 1997), 127, 134.
32 See e.g. Tert., *Apol.* 50 and also *De spect.*
33 Tert., *De spect.* 1-13.
34 Ibid., 15.
35 Ibid.
36 Tert., *De virg.* 2.12.
37 Tert., *De spect.* 17.
38 Ibid., 30.
39 Salisbury, *Perpetua's Passion*, 125. See also, Kyle, *Spectacles of Death*, 2-8 and Castelli, *Martyrdom and Memory*, 107-111.
40 Salisbury, *Perpetua's Passion*, 128; see also Castelli, *Martyrdom and Memory*, 107-111.
41 Clem. Al., *Paed.* 3.11. Cyprian, *Ad donatum*, 7, P 4.207A.
42 Salisbury, *Perpetua's Passion*, 131.
43 Elizabeth Castelli, 'The Ambivalent Legacy of Violence and Victimhood: Using Early Christian Martyrs to Think With', *Spiritus* 6 (2006): 18, 19.
44 Clark, 'Bodies and Blood', 105-6.
45 Ibid.
46 See Castelli, who makes this point, *Martyrdom and Memory*, 127.
47 Burrus, *Saving Shame*, 30.
48 John Chrysostom, *Homilies* 18.4 (NPNF vol. 14), cited in Cobb, *Dying to Be Men*, 99.
49 Cobb, *Dying to be Men*, 99.
50 August., *Serm.* 51.2, *NPNF*, vol. 6, cited in Cobb, *Dying to Be Men*, 99, n. 37.
51 August., *Serm.* 280.1, trans. Hill, cited in Cobb, *Dying to Be Men*, 99, n. 38.
52 Nicole Loraux, *Tragic Ways of Killing a Woman*, trans. Anthony Forster (Cambridge MA: Harvard University Press, 1987), vii.
53 Ibid., x.
54 Richard Hawley, 'The Body as Spectacle in Attic Drama', in *Thinking Men: Masculinity and Its Self-Representation in the Classical Tradition*, ed. Lin Foxhall and John Salmon (London: Routledge 1998), 87.
55 Cobb notes that reading in antiquity was 'both public and private, and the term encompassed aural as well as oral presentation'. Cobb goes on to cite Harry Gamble who argues that '[i]n antiquity virtually all reading, public or private, was reading aloud: texts were routinely converted into the oral mode. Knowing this, ancient authors wrote their texts as much for the ear as for the eye ... in the Greco-Roman world virtually all reading was reading aloud; even when reading privately the reader gave audible voice to the text', Harry Gamble, *Books and Readers: A History of Early Christian Texts* (New Haven, CT: Yale University Press, 1995), 30, 203, cited in Cobb, *Dying to Be Men*, 98, n. 34.
56 Burrus, *Saving Shame*, 105, 124.
57 Ibid., 13.
58 Tert., *De spect.* 17.
59 Elizabeth A. Castelli, 'Visions and Voyeurism: Holy Women and the Politics of Sight in Early Christianity', in *Protocol of the Colloquy of the Center for Hermeneutical Studies*, ed. Christopher Ocker (Berkeley, CA: The Graduate Theological Union and the University of California, 1992), 8, my emphasis.
60 Ibid., 11-17.
61 Tert., *De spect.* 30.

62 See Simon Goldhill, 'The Erotic Eye: Visual Stimulation and the Cultural Conflict', in *Being Greek Under Rome: Cultural Identity, the Second Sophistic and the Development of Empire*, ed. Simon Goldhill (Cambridge: Cambridge University Press, 2001), 159.
63 David Frankfurter, 'Martyrology and the Prurient Gaze', *JECS* 17 (2009): 215–45.
64 Ibid., 215–18.
65 Ibid., 227, 231–2.
66 Ibid., 233.
67 Ibid., 239–45.
68 A good image of this painting can be found online at https://culture.pl/en/work/christian-dirce-henryk-siemiradzki.
69 McInerney, *Eloquent Virgin*, 35.
70 Ibid., 36.
71 Burrus, *Saving Shame*, 33.
72 See Chapter 1.
73 Elsom, 'Callirhoe', 213.
74 Ben Witherington III, *The Paul Quest: The Renewed Search for the Jew of Tarsus* (Downers Grove, IL: InterVarsity Press, 1998), 42–4; Abraham J. Malherbe, 'A Physical Description of Paul', *HTR* 79, nos. 1–3 (1986): 170–5.
75 Malherbe, 'A Physical Description', 173–4; Witherington, *The Paul Quest*, 43–4.
76 Witherington, *The Paul Quest*, 43, 44.
77 Malherbe, 'A Physical Description', 173–4.
78 See 2 Cor. 10.10; 13.7-12; Gal. 4.13-16. See Malherbe, 'A Physical Description', 171.
79 Ibid., 175.
80 János Bollók, 'The Description of Paul in the Acta Pauli', in *The Apocryphal Acts of Paul and Thecla*, ed. Jan N. Bremmer (Kampen: Kok Pharos, 1996), esp. 8–9.
81 Ibid., 5–9.
82 Ibid., 6.
83 For the importance of private households as venues of conversion, see Kate Cooper, 'Christianity, Private Power, and the Law from Decius to Constantine: The Minimalist View', *JECS* 19 (2011): 327–43; Cooper, 'Poverty, Obligation'; Kate Cooper, 'The Household as a Venue for Religious Conversion', in *A Companion to Families in the Greek and Roman Worlds*, ed. Beryl Rawson (Oxford: Wiley, 2010), 183–97.
84 Wilson translates the phrase ὡς ἀράχνη ἐπὶ τῆς θυρίδος δεδεμένη as 'who sticks to the window like a spider', NTA, 240. However, there is a point of contention in terms of translating the term ἀράχνη as 'spider' or 'spiders' web'. Janet Spittler points out that 'spider' in the nominative case is not ἀράχνη but ὁ ἀράχνης. Thus, while ἡ ἀράχνη can be used as the feminine form, it is also the proper term for a 'spider's web', whereas ὁ ἀράχνης is the animal. Taking ἀράχνῃ to be the dative case ἀράχνη (given that sometime during the first century BCE, the iota subscript was no longer written thus, there would have been no orthographic difference between ἀράχνη and ἀράχνῃ in the period when the *Acts of Paul and Thecla* was authored, see Spittler, 164, n. 29), Spittler renders the translation: 'and what is more my daughter bound to the window by words as if by a spider's web, is overpowered by a new desire and fearful passion. For the virgin focuses on the words spoken by him and is captured', Janet E. Spittler, *Animals in the Apocryphal Acts of the Apostles* (Tübingen: Mohr Seibeck, 2008), 164.
85 Ibid., 166–7.
86 Aubin, 'Reversing Romance', 264.
87 Berger, *Ways of Seeing*, 9.
88 Aubin, 'Reversing Romance', 264–5.

89 Cooper, 'Apostles, Ascetic Women', 151.
90 Burrus, *Saving Shame*, 33.
91 Sorkin Rabinowitz, 'Politics of Containment', 39 (on these two models, Sorkin Rabinowitz cites Kappeler, *Pornography of Representation*, 51, 90).
92 John Berger, *About Looking* (New York: Pantheon Books, 1980), 4; Kappeler, *Pornography of Representation*, 66. See also 1 Tim. 2.12.
93 Dworkin, *Pornography*, 16; see also Gen. 2.19-20.
94 Berger, *About Looking*, 14.
95 Ibid., 22-6.
96 McInerney, *Eloquent Virgins*, 37–41.
97 Ibid., 42-3.
98 Corrington Streete, *Redeemed Bodies*, 84.
99 Kate Cooper, 'Ventriloquism and the Miraculous: Conversion, Preaching, and the Martyr Exemplum in Late Antiquity', in *Signs, Wonders, Miracles: Representations of Divine Power in the Life of the Church*, vol. 41 of Studies in Church History, ed. Kate Cooper and Jeremy Gregory (Woodbridge, Suffolk: Boydell & Brewer, 2005), 22-3.
100 Methodius, *Symposium*, 11.1.
101 Gregory of Nyssa, *Life of Macrina*, 2; see also his *Homily 14 on the Song of Songs*.
102 Sorkin Rabinowitz, 'Politics of Containment', 50.
103 See Acts 22.25-9.
104 Perkins, 'Fictional Narratives', 51.
105 Castelli, *Martyrdom and Memory*, 64.
106 See Kappeler, *Pornography of Representation*, 90.
107 Ibid., 65.
108 MacKinnon, *Feminism Unmodified*, 130.
109 Laura Mulvey, 'Visual Pleasure and Narrative Cinema', *Screen* 16 (1975): 11.
110 Ibid., 11-17.
111 Ibid.
112 *The Martyrdom of Saints Perpetua and Felicitas* (18) in Musurillo, *The Acts of the Christian Martyrs*.
113 Ann E. Kaplan, 'Is the Gaze Male?' in *Powers of Desire: The Politics of Sexuality*, ed. Ann Snitow, Christine Stansell and Sharon Thompson (New York: Monthly Review Press, 1983), 311, 319.
114 *The Martyrdom of Saints Perpetua and Felicitas* (18-20) in Musurillo, *The Acts of the Christian Martyrs*.
115 Berger, *Ways of Seeing*, 64.
116 Bella Zweig, 'The Mute Nude Female Characters in Aristophanes' Plays', in *Pornography and Representation*, ed. Amy Richlin, 86.
117 Kappeler, *Pornography of Representation*, 52.
118 LSJ 624 (3), BDAG 367.
119 Cobb asserts that she finds no traces of eroticization in the martyrologies within the scope of her study, which includes the *Martyrdom of Felicitas and Perpetua*. However, as argued above, it is certainly possible to interpret aspects of the text as erotic and sexualized, Cobb, *Dying to Be Men*, 7, n. 25. It is informative to note that Burrus also argues that the ancient lives of saints 'are the site of an exuberant eroticism'. Indeed, 'sanctity can be restyled as an erotic art', Virginia Burrus, *The Sex Lives of Saints: An Erotics of Ancient Hagiography* (Philadelphia: University of Pennsylvania Press, 2004), 1.
120 This prurient gaze is also openly invited within a number of the stories contained in the Apocryphal Acts. In the Detorakis edition of the *Acts of Andrew*, e.g., Eucleia

sets two fellow slaves at 'the top of the bed' that they might watch as she has sex with the husband of her mistress (*AA*. 349). This scene is titillating and highly suggestive of people being spied on while having sex. Furthermore, within the *Acts of John*, Callimachus attempts to commit necrophilia with Drusiana in front of his hapless aid Fortunatus (*AJ*. 70). The Berlin Coptic fragment of the *Acts of Peter* similarly narrates a bathing scene which incites lust. Peter's young 10-year-old daughter is spied upon while bathing with her mother (*APt*. 131-5). Further traces of pornographic representation are recounted within the *Acts of Thomas* where women undergo the ordeal of rape and molestation by violating demons (*AT*. 42, 62).

121 Kaplan, 'Is the Gaze Male', 312.
122 This representation is in stark contrast to the Martyrdom of Perpetua where, after being tossed by the mad heifer, Perpetua sits up and pulls down her ripped tunic in order to cover her exposed thighs (20).
123 LSJ 101 (3b), BDAG 61 (3).
124 Richlin, 'Introduction' to *Pornography and Representation*, xix; see also Zweig, 'Mute Nude Female Characters', 74.
125 Richlin, 'Introduction' to *Pornography and Representation*, xix.
126 Kate Cooper, 'Closely Watched Households: Visibility, Exposure and Private Power in the Roman Domus', *Past and Present* 197 (2007): 10.
127 Ibid., 17.
128 Cooper highlights how female vulnerability within martyr texts invites titillation, Kate Cooper, 'The Voice of the Victim: Gender, Representation, and Early Christian Martyrdom', *Bulletin of the John Rylands University Library* 80 (1998): 155.
129 Zweig, 'Mute Nude Female Characters', 74, makes this point in relation to the mute, nude female in Aristophanes' plays.
130 Naomi Wolf, *The Beauty Myth: How Images of Beauty Are Used against Women* (London: Vintage, 1991), 45.
131 See Zweig, 'Mute Nude Female Characters', 87.
132 Tert., *De virg.* 2.4-6.
133 Berger, *Ways of Seeing*, 50.
134 Ibid., 54–5.
135 Tert., *De virg.* 3.10 (*ANF* 4.27-37).
136 Ibid.
137 Tertullian's views are, of course, extreme, and it is difficult to believe that many held such excessive and uncompromising views of virginity.
138 Sorkin Rabinowitz, 'Politics of Containment', 50.
139 On the importance of an inferior individual willingly deferring to a superior and the reciprocity of this hierarchical relationship as affirming a dominant 'in control' male, see Cooper, 'Closely Watched', 7. See also 1 Tim. 1.1-5.
140 Petropoulos, 'Transvestite Virgin', 131.
141 This is discussed in more detail in Chapter 6.
142 BDAG 36-7 (2 and 4).
143 See Chapter 4.
144 See LSJ πειρασμὸς, 1354 (BDAG 793); LSJ χείρων, 1986 (BDAG 1083).
145 LSJ 680, BDAG 389.
146 Dunn, 'The Acts of Paul', 79.
147 Virginia Burrus, 'Word and Flesh: The Bodies and Sexuality of Ascetic Women in Christian Antiquity', *JFSR* 10, no. 1 (1994): esp. 47.
148 Dworkin, *Pornography*, 102.

149 Roman law on rape was ill defined, real cases rarely attested and the victim was blamed, see Amy Richlin, 'Reading Ovid's Rapes', in *Pornography and Representation in Greece and Rome*, ed. Amy Richlin (Oxford: Oxford University Press, 1992), 161; see also Joshel, 'The Body Female', 115–28.
150 Glancy, 'Unveiling Masculinity', 39.
151 Ibid., 39–40.
152 Wolf, *The Beauty Myth*, 14.
153 Dworkin, *Pornography*, 14–15.
154 Berger, *Ways of Seeing*, 9.
155 Liza Cleland, Glenys Davies and Lloyd Llewellyn-Jones, eds, *Greek and Roman Dress from A-Z* (London: Routledge, 2007), 47.
156 Jensen, *Thekla – Die Apostelin*, 89, 36, n. 58.
157 See e.g. *The Martyrdom of Saints Perpetua and Felicitas* (20) where Perpetua, as a woman, is matched in her sex with a mad heifer.
158 McInerney, *Eloquent Virgins*, 41.
159 See Chapter 7, n. 65, for an explanation of the translation of ἀναγκαῖα as 'genitals'.
160 Spittler, *Animals*, 177–8.
161 E.g. A Codex (Parisinum Graecus 520; Paris; eleventh century CE); B Codex (Parisinum Graecus 1454; Paris; tenth century CE); C Codex (Parisinum Graecus 1468; Paris; tenth century CE) and E Codex (Vaticanus Graecus 797; Rome; eleventh century CE) all have minor variants in regard to the word order. While G Codex (Barocciano Graecus 180/Codex Grabe/Recension G, Bodleian Library; Oxford; twelfth century CE) names Thecla and, along with F Codex (Vaticanus Graecus 866; Rome; eleventh century CE), adds the verb κατακαίνω to περίκειμαι. It also specifies that the fire affects the bulls. The Latin Codex Digbaeno 39 (Bodleian Library, Oxford; twelfth century CE) and Recension C also show variants stating that the flame which they were kindling causes the ropes to come untied.
162 Spittler, *Animals*, 177–8.
163 Berger, *Ways of Seeing*, 59.
164 Jeffrey Henderson, *The Maculate Muse: Obscene Language in Attic Comedy* (New Haven, CT: Yale University Press, 1975), 32.
165 Zweig, 'The Mute Nude Female', 84–5.
166 Page duBois, *Torture and Truth* (New York: Routledge, 1991), 36.
167 Virginia Burrus, 'Torture, Truth and the Witnessing Body: Reading Christian Martyrdom with Page duBois', *BibInt* 25 (2017): 5–18.
168 Ibid., 15–17.
169 See the discussion under 'Martyrdom as Spectacle'.
170 Miles, *Carnal Knowing*, 58.
171 Wolf, *The Beauty Myth*, 45.
172 Burrus, *Saving Shame*, 34–5.
173 Ibid., 34.
174 Ibid., 14.
175 Ibid., xi–xii.
176 Jennifer Wright Knust, *Abandoned to Lust: Sex, Slander and Ancient Christianity* (New York: Columbia University Press, 2006), 1.
177 Söder, *Die apokryphen*; Richard I. Pervo, *Profit with Delight: The Literary Genre of the Acts of the Apostles* (Augsburg, MN: Fortress, 1987), has also argued that the Apocryphal Acts should be considered within the genre of historical novel akin to the ancient romances. Other discussions include Perkins, *The Suffering Self*,

124–5 and Cooper, *Virgin and the Bride*, 50–2. See 'The Question of Genre' in Chapter 2 above.
178   Elsom, 'Callirhoe', 215.
179   Russell, *Making Violence Sexy*, 6, 225.
180   Ibid.
181   See e.g. Castelli, *Martyrdom and Memory*, 122.
182   Ibid., 123, 133.
183   Salisbury, *Perpetua's Passion*, 149.
184   We hear that the heifer tossed Perpetua and she fell on her back (20). Perpetua was so affected by this that she needed to be held up by a man (20). Later we are told that 'Perpetua … screamed as she was struck on the bone' (21), *The Martyrdom of Saints Perpetua and Felicitas* in Musurillo, *The Acts of the Christian Martyrs*.
185   Petropoulos, 'Transvestite Virgin', 130–1.
186   See e.g. Jensen, *Thekla – Die Apostolin*.
187   Braun, 'Physiotherapy', 211–12, my emphasis.
188   Shelby Brown rightly observes that the *Damnati ad bestias* consisted of criminals who were considered too low to deserve a fighting chance. Consequently, they were sent unarmed, or bound and helpless, in the arena to die. Their deaths were justified as the annihilation of opponents of the Roman State and of the social good. In seeing them as legitimate victims, audiences distanced themselves, having little or no empathy for their suffering, Shelby Brown, 'Death as Decoration: Scenes from the Arena on Roman Domestic Mosaics', in *Pornography and Representation*, ed. Amy Richlin, 185.

6

Bewitched and bewitching women: Miracles and magical practices

Introduction

Within this chapter, I will explore how the rhetorical and ideological functions of magic and miracles are played out in the text and explore how this impacts upon the constructions of gender and Thecla's body. We have seen how the gender relations of the *Acts of Paul and Thecla* reveal an inherent tendency towards violence, female subjugation and disempowerment: a hierarchical relationship of power with the female situated at the bottom. These features occur despite the fact that Thecla exhibited ἀνδρεία, along with the bodily integrity inherent within that virtue. In the previous two chapters, the subjugation and disempowerment of the heroine have been defined, even though these commingle with glimmers of an unstable subjectivity, manly courage and an inviolable body.

However, one element stands out as needing separate treatment: the miraculous. Given that a type of magic and miracles work continually to save Thecla, can a focus upon these reveal a more 'female empowering' reading of the text? Ann-Marie Korte rightly notes that although women often play a pivotal role in such miracle stories, an in-depth gender perspective has rarely been undertaken, and, when it has, there has been the inevitable link between women's involvement in miracles with stereotypical ideas concerning women's lack of rationality.[1]

Within this chapter, therefore, I aim to investigate what views on gender come to light when we focus on the representation of Thecla in regard to magic and miracles. Given the dissonance between the presentation of a Thecla showing manly integrity and the prurient presentation of Thecla's body, does the miraculous dimension also contain ambiguities and ambivalence related to gender roles – seeking to liberate/empower on the one hand but constraining and disparaging women on the other? Overall, what patriarchal undercurrents can be discerned within the text?

Defining miracle

Before proceeding, we need to clarify exactly what we mean by the term 'miracle' (δύναμις).[2] The question of what exactly constitutes a miracle has been debated and discussed over many years. For example, in his classical work *The Golden Bough*, James Frazer argued that an event is miraculous and not magical if it is contrary to all normal human experience and does not take place using any sort of ritual or instrument; it simply happens.[3] For Frazer, the magician constrains, coerces and forces the divinity to do his will, whereas the religious man meekly submits himself to the will of God.[4] Although this Frazerian dichotomy is no longer adhered to by most, the notion continues to find support within classical scholarship. Benedicta Ward and Caroline Walker Bynum each individually highlight the need for caution in definitions since beliefs and attitudes around the area of magic and miracles are often complex and multifarious.[5] The division between the categories has nevertheless led to wide ranging definitions, some which offer opposing distinctions between magic and miracles and others dismissing the notion of magic as a semantic trap.[6] In an attempt to move beyond this debate to some level of resolution, Fritz Graf surveys a number of prayers in the Greek Magical Papyri (*PGM*) and stresses that magicians not only uttered spells but also prayed to the gods, and like religious prayers, these prayers contained a submissive tone.[7] Graf appropriately concludes that the main distinction of magic lies in the ritual, not in the prayers and not so much in the forms of the ritual (these are shared between magic and religion) as in the function. The function of the magician's rituals put him/her in opposition to ordinary 'religious' ritual and isolates him/her from others. The distinction, then, lies rather in social than in psychological factors. This, of course, would fit perfectly with the social differentiation that made the magician an outsider and the outsider a potential magician, the best known.[8]

Although Korte offers a definition of miracles which includes phenomena that 'go against nature', at the same time she also underscores a particular individual's unique position, power or abilities. Examples of such abilities are precognitive dreams, prophecies and the power to control animals or natural phenomena. These occurrences are amazing and unfathomable because they deviate from what is 'normal' or 'predictable'. The events can be seen as a sign from an alternative or incomprehensible order or reality, and the miracle is understood as an indication or proof that this other realm exists and 'makes a difference'. Korte also looks at the efficacy of miracles and emphasizes their positive effect as events that both meet and fail to meet expectations; what happens exceeds, but does not violate, the witness's 'expectations'. Thus, in some way, a miracle brings salvation or changes things for the better. However, this does not exclude the possibility that a miracle will have a critical, disruptive or even destructive effect on those who are involved.[9]

This helpful analysis may be supplemented by the observations of Gerd Theissen who, in his study of the early Christian miracle stories, similarly notes the element of symbolism and divine revelation present within miracles that are narrated in the New Testament.[10] For Theissen, the revelation always appears with 'pregnant structure', such that an 'ontological fissure' runs through reality, thus ensuring that the forms of the holy stand out sharply from everything profane.[11] Korte and Theissen's approach to defining the miraculous helps to elucidate and clarify the miraculous within the *Acts of Paul and Thecla*. The events within the narrative (a shower of rain and hail to put out a fire; a friendly and protective lioness; a fire which burns through tethers, attaching Thecla to the bull) are not necessarily 'unnatural' or contrary to nature in any way.

However, the things that happen deviate from what is predictable and expected and they also save the life of the heroine; in terms of the timing of the phenomena and the unexpected manifestation of the events 'out of thin air', the audience are meant to assume a divine intervention.

Theissen goes on to classify the different miracle stories within the New Testament into a catalogue of themes which include exorcisms, healings and epiphanies, and rescue miracles, gift miracles and rule miracles. There are within these themes various subdivisions which at times overlap.[12] Theissen notes that any miracle (including rescue miracles) can be regarded as an epiphany, although epiphanies in the narrower sense occur when the divinity of a person becomes apparent not merely in the effects of his actions or in attendant phenomena but in the person himself. For Theissen, an epiphany starts from the human position: divine revelation breaks into this domain and remains a mysterious other. The general characteristic motifs of an epiphany are extraordinary visual and auditory phenomena, the terrified reaction of human beings, the word of revelation and the miraculous.[13] Commonly, such miracles occur spontaneously, and there is no visible miracle worker or invocation. Their origin appears to be 'from heaven'. Nor are the signs necessarily miraculous in the sense of phenomena which is unusual; rather, they are based on the striking: and interpretation requires 'expert knowledge'.[14]

Using Theissen's definitions, some of the miraculous happenings within the *Acts of Paul and Thecla* fall into the category of 'epiphany'. So, for example, within the *Acts of Paul and Thecla*, the first miracle occurs when the heroine is thrown into the arena to be burnt and God miraculously rescues Thecla by 'invisibly' intervening through the manipulation of the weather (*APTh*. 22). Terrified onlookers observe the extraordinary events and many of them perish. More fantastic and exceptional episodes occur when Thecla faces the wild beasts: a sudden bolt of lightning kills the seals that threaten her (once again rescuing her) and a mysterious fire surrounds her (*APTh*. 34). This fire, according to the narrator, eventually ensures Thecla's release from the bulls by burning through the ropes (*APTh*. 35). Finally, at the end of the narrative, only Thecla has the expert 'insider' knowledge as to how her rescues were effected, and she shares this information with the confused Governor, who fails to understand how she survived the ordeals.

Theissen goes on to define a category of rescue miracles in which threatening dangers are averted and a person is plucked from disaster. Within the rescue miracles Theissen includes the overcoming of hostile forces, defeating the power of nature or the state. Here, the miracles are performed on material objects, wind, waves, ships, chains and prison doors. What appeals to us in a rescue miracle is the fact that they give a notion of victory over dull, 'mindless', purely physical violence. Theissen notes that rescue miracles usually involve a striking and visible event, with the rescue brought about by manifestations of numinous power. While epiphanies point to a person or character's divineness or specialness, rescue miracles point to the divine will. However, in both cases, there is a revelation from the divine sphere.[15]

We can see from this that the 'rescue events' within the *Acts of Paul and Thecla* fall very much within the category of the miraculous. Thus, despite the accusation that Paul is a magician, the text vindicates him from such a label (*APTh*. 20). Furthermore, although it is not over emphasized in any way, the fact that Paul, Thecla and Tryphaena actively pray (*APTh*. 24, 29, 30, 31, 34), we are meant to know that the miracles come from God and affect animals and the forces of nature.

Spellbinding thaumaturge and enchanted maiden

The *Acts of Paul and Thecla* would have us believe that Paul bewitches and seduces Thecla with magic. Through closed doors, which are meant to present no obstacle, he casts a spell on the virgin with his words (λόγον λεγόμενον, *APTh*. 7). That the text is insinuating Thecla has been bewitched is evident from the fact that the spell has the intended effect of 'mental disturbance'. This is exactly what spells were meant to achieve. Christopher Faraone notes that the allusions to madness and bondage associated with 'erotic seizure' and love magic are indicative of the ἀγωγή type spells; one of the first symptoms of such spells is 'insanity'.[16] Indeed, the violence and pain inflicted on the victim is so severe, argues Faraone, that it is hard to distinguish the erotic spells from hostile curses used against enemies.[17]

Given this, we see within the *Acts of Paul and Thecla* that on the spot, the virgin goes 'insane' (ἔκπληξιν, *APTh*. 10) with desire and dedicates herself to Paul. The words ἐπιθυμια and πάθος (passion/desire/lust) and their cognates are employed four times in *APTh*. 7-10.[18] However, this is no ordinary passion. It is 'fearful' (δεινός, *APTh*. 9 and 10) and 'terrifying' (ἔκπληκτον, *APTh*. 10). The 'mental disturbance' that has affected Thecla is so bad that her mother describes her as one who is 'deranged' or 'paralysed' (παραπλήξ, *APTh*. 10). The person under this spell has lost all control of their mind. Thecla is 'sorely' or 'grievously troubled' by passion (χαλεπῶς, ἐνοχλεῖται, *APTh*. 8). The fact that the word χαλεπῶς is used mostly of persons who are violent or angry suggests powerful undercurrents of vehemence and wildness; dark forces appear to be at work.[19]

Allusion to magical motifs and practices continue. Thecla sits 'staring' (ἀτενίζω, *APTh*. 8, 9, 10) as in merriment (εὐφρασίαν, *APTh*. 8). The repetition of the word ἀτενίζω reinforces the impact that Paul has upon this young woman: the virgin has 'fallen prey to' (πρόσκειται, *APTh*. 8) 'a strange man' (ἀνδρὶ ξένῳ, *APTh*. 8). The reference to Paul as a stranger (*APTh*. 8, 13, 19 and cf. 12) contains the implicit allegation that Paul is a μάγος. The status of the magician as a 'stranger' was a known concept, which did not represent a xenophobic reaction but corresponded with the social status of the μάγος, who 'is always the other, not us'.[20] Later, Paul is actually described as a μάγος (*APTh*. 15, 20) and his words are 'subtle and deceptive' (ποικίλους, ἀπατηλούς, *APTh*. 8). Thecla is as one 'captured' (ἑάλωται, *APTh*. 9), 'bound' (δεδεμένη, *APTh*. 9) and 'seized' (κρατεῖται, *APTh*. 9 and 10). All Thecla seems capable of doing is 'sitting' (καθεσθεῖσα, *APTh*. 7) and 'staring' (ἀτενίζω, *APTh*. 8, 9 and 10). We are told that Thecla has neither eaten, drunk nor moved for three days (*APTh*. 8); someone in a 'bewitched trance' and someone 'in love' are physically affected in similar ways. Until now, this young woman had been a 'model lady'. Her mother is 'amazed' (θαυμάζειν, *APTh*. 8) how such a 'respectful virgin' (τοιαύτη αἰδὼς τῆς παρθένου, *APTh*. 8) can be affected in this way; and to what is it that Thecla 'stares'? It is 'the Word of Paul' (*APTh*. 10).

All the vocabulary and terminology hint that Thecla has been enchanted and captivated by Paul. Her trance-like state is perfect for someone under a 'binding spell'.[21] The important term 'binding' (δέω, *APTh*. 9) and the related terms (ἀτενίζω, πρόσκειμαι, κρατέω, *APTh*. 8-10) are all meant to underscore the fact that Thecla has fallen prey to an erotic magic spell.[22] Spells are designed to 'bind' the victims in shackles and 'inescapable bonds'.[23] This would explain why Thamyris fears her when he approaches her, lest he too be affected by the spell she is under (*APTh*. 10). Her mother, Thamyris and the whole household mourn. They have lost their daughter, betrothed, and lady of the house; she is no longer a young innocent woman: she has been cast under a powerful spell and is now unrecognizable from the person she was. It creates great 'confusion' (σύγχυσις) in the household. All are at a loss: it is as though Thecla is dead; hence, the entire household mourns (πενθέω). Oblivious to the turmoil and anguish surrounding her, Thecla continues to sit and stare through the window (*APTh*. 10).

Powerful and competing forces are at work: the stranger has defrauded (ξένον καὶ ἀποστεροῦμαι, *APTh*. 13) Thamyris of his rightful bride, causing him much distress and mental anxiety (ἀγωνιῶ, *APTh*. 13). The word ἀγωνιῶ employed here also has the sense of 'contest' or 'to contend for a prize' and serves to intensify the scene and set up the notion of a struggle between rival forces.[24] Faraone notes that in the 'battlefield' of Eros, in the situation of a 'lovers' triangle', for instance, there was intense personal competition and people would regularly resort to κατάδεσμοι or *defixio* when competing for the affections of a woman.[25]

The way in which Thamyris pleads with Thecla to 'turn back to your Thamyris and be ashamed' (αἰσχύνθητι, *APTh*. 10) once again reinforces the notion of an enchantment. Occasionally, spells were meant to directly attack a woman's moral character, resulting in her losing her sense of shame (αἰσχύνω). The idea that erotic magic attacks a woman's 'natural' loyalty and chastity is manifest in classical Greek texts. Faraone notes that many of the extant ἀγωγή spells aim specifically at making the woman forget all those people who make up her moral community.[26] In this respect, the text is portraying Thecla as a model young woman who would not normally worry her parents or tarnish their reputation (*APTh*. 8). However, for now the woman has little volition. She thus continues to sit and stare as one stricken or paralysed (*APTh*. 10).

We then read that θάμυρις μὲν γυναικὸς ἀστοχῶν (*APTh*. 10). Thamyris literally 'misses the mark' or 'aims badly' in regard to a wife. It is quite possible that this is a narrative marker, or double entendre, alerting the reader that Thamyris has not only lost out on his bride but is in fact also 'missing the mark' or 'misunderstanding' what has happened to her. The 'confusion' (σύγχυσις, *APTh*. 10), which overcomes the household, also reinforces this idea. The entire household are failing to understand what has happened to Thecla. To all intents and purposes, Thecla has been enchanted, not by a strange magician or love binding spell, but by a man of God who speaks God's Word.

As a result of all this turmoil and confusion, Paul is eventually led (δεθῆναι) to prison (*APTh*. 17). The theme of 'binding' is again taken up, but this time it is not Thecla who has been 'bound' on a symbolic level but rather Paul who is literally bound and thrown into prison. Meanwhile, Thecla, who until now has been practically catatonic, begins to move and take action (*APTh*. 18). Readers continue to be drawn into the storyline of bewitchment. Thecla, suddenly brazen and degenerate, having lost all sense of shame, leaves her home and family to follow the object of her desire to prison. On the surface level, readers are meant to understand that the ἀγωγή spell has the perfect effect; it maddens the woman with uncontrollable lust and desire, thus severing her attachment to her family and modesty. Unfettered from the web of important relationships, and reverence for her kin, Thecla is now emboldened and free to follow the practitioner, Paul.

The maiden then continues to behave as one enchanted; she removes her bracelets and gives away a silver mirror. Her passion and madness have driven her to spurn and relinquish symbols of her former life. Just as her mother no longer recognizes her, she renounces what defined her previously. In the process, the narrative continues to hint at enchantment. Faraone highlights those spells that sometimes stipulate that the woman be forced to come to the practitioner 'so she will give whatever I tell her to give'. Such wording seems to reflect an active interest in the dowry and property that a woman might bring with her.[27] Although Thecla does not hand her belongings over to Paul but rather uses them to gain access to him, the narrative is exploiting a well-known motif in order to deliberately further convey the idea and illusion of magic.

Once Thecla is in the prison, she continues to behave as one in a daze and appears to worship the object of her devotion, kissing Paul's fetters (καταφιλούσης, *APTh*. 18). However, things are not as straightforward as they might appear. While possibilities beyond magic and binding spells are beginning to present themselves for readers, for the characters within the story, when Thecla's family discovers her disappearance and eventually finds her in the prison with Paul 'bound in affection' (εὗρον αὐτὴν τρόπον τινὰ συνδεδεμένην τῇ στοργῇ, *APTh*. 19), the erotic overtones are once again perfect for someone enchanted by a binding spell. Paul and Thecla are brought before the Governor. For failing to marry Thamyris, Thecla is condemned to be burned while Paul is punished and then set free (*APTh*. 21).[28] We then come to the arena and the site of the first miracle that the crowd and readers will witness.

Up to this point, on the narrative level, Thecla is presented as passive and mute: an easy victim, a stereotypical representation of the 'weak foolish' woman who is unable to resist the charms of a strange and deceitful man. Stories of predatory magicians and virgin women as foolish victims of magic are of a type; the magnitude of the victim's affection results in them becoming raving mad. Jerome, writing near or at the end of the fourth century CE, records how a young man is spurned by a young Christian woman, who chooses to live as a virgin of God. The young man inscribes copper tablets with magic incantations and drawings and buries them under the threshold of the woman's house, with the result that the virgin instantly goes insane. Her parents bring her to a saint who diagnoses the source, an attack through love magic, and helps to re-stabilize the young woman and bring her back to sanity.[29] This was a widespread pattern of representation within Christian literature: it portrayed men as practicing magic and women functioned as their passive and powerless victims.[30]

The *Acts of Paul and Thecla* depicts and exploits this trope beautifully, as do the other Apocryphal Acts which very much hint at women as victims of men's magic, rather than as magicians themselves.[31] In employing this motif, the narrative presents neither a sense of female empowerment nor female agency. Rather, what we are left with is simply the clichéd time-worn ancient patriarchal stereotype of a woman who easily falls prey to a strange exotic man. The text is simply manipulating this ancient female stereotype, along with the motif of enchantment, in order to convey an alternative Christian message. However, although the characters in the story may be buying into the suggestion regarding Thecla's enchantment, readers are left open to the possibility of a different reality. When he is alone with her, Paul uses the time to teach Thecla and refrains from taking sexual advantage of her. Here, the text begins to usher in a dualistic ploy that separates the characters from the readers. The characters are manipulated into believing Thecla has been bewitched by a magician, but readers are open to another alternative. Unfortunately, this alternative does not empower Thecla any more than if she had been bewitched by some magician. Even though Thecla has not been enchanted by a pagan magician who wishes to elope with her, she is instead the captivated victim of a man wielding divine power, a casualty of patriarchy nevertheless.

A baptism of fire: Miracle 1

For choosing not to marry Thamyris, Thecla is condemned to be burned.[32] As a young virgin woman who does not desire marriage and children, Thecla is an aberration.[33] That which is alien and not understood, an unwed virgin, must be suppressed and violently condemned; its destruction must be observed. Therefore, the Governor goes immediately (εὐθέως ὁ ἡγεμὼν, APTh. 21) to the theatre with the whole crowd.

Thecla is described as a lamb in the wilderness who seeks the shepherd Paul (APTh. 21). Although Thecla 'looks around' (περισκοπεῖ, APTh. 21), this is meant in a physically passive sense – she is not physically wandering around. This passivity is stressed further since Thecla is still in a trance-like state and sees an apparition of the Lord as Paul. This vision confirms the fact that Thecla remains 'spellbound' as she continues to 'stare' (ἀτενίζουσα) towards Paul, and he disappears right in front of her. As highlighted in Chapter 5, Thecla does not own an empowered gaze, nor does her gaze possess any mutuality. Thecla then moves beyond her silent trance-like state to speak, 'as if I could not endure Paul has come'. Polymorphism or metamorphosis is a recurring theme in the Apocryphal Acts.[34] Magda Misset-van de Weg notes that metamorphoses is a well-known element of Hellenistic magical belief, and within the *Acts of Paul and Thecla*, the appearance of Jesus in the form of Paul is Thecla's reward for choosing the ascetic lifestyle.[35]

Thecla is then stripped naked (γυμνή, APTh. 22). However, apart from the Governor mourning the loss of such beauty, neither the text nor Thecla make much of her nakedness or exposure. This is contrary to the reaction of the audience when they see Perpetua and Felicitas naked in the arena where '[e]ven the crowd was horrified when they saw that one was a delicate young girl and the other was a woman fresh from childbirth with the milk still dripping from her breasts'.[36] Since the effect of Thecla's shameful exposure is not narrated, it leaves readers no opportunity to identify deeply with the character. This has the effect of making

Thecla's characterization appear one-dimensional. There is also supreme irony in the fact that the very group that was most influenced by Paul's preaching, the virgin women and young men, bring wood and grass in order that Thecla may be burnt (*APTh*. 22). Thecla then stretches out her arms to form the shape of the cross and mounts the pyre. Thecla suddenly radiates strength (δύναμις, *APTh*. 22) and demonstrates a victorious posture,[37] and this is endorsed when God quenches the fire with a great thunderstorm (*APTh*. 22).

Misset-van de Weg argues that Thecla is undergoing a metamorphosis and becoming a Christ-like figure. This, she contends, is reinforced by the betrayal of someone close to her, the almost indifferent Pilate-like attitude of the Governor during the trial, the theme of the lamb and the shape of the cross.[38] However, while the representation of the crucified Christ became a common theme in Christian martyrological texts,[39] and while the idea of a passive 'sacrificial lamb' may be present, there are very important distinctions between two gospel presentations of Jesus' passion and Thecla's experience in the arena.

In Mark and Matthew, for example, Jesus endures physical torture. He is scourged (Mk 15.15; Mt. 27.26) and struck (Mk 14.65; Mt. 27.30), and a crown of thorns is forced on his head (Mk 15.19; Mt. 27.29, cf. also Jn 19.2-3). At no point is Thecla physically harmed in any of her ordeals. Furthermore, the desolation Jesus experiences is evident when he cries out shortly before death, 'My God, my God, why have you forsaken me' (Mk 15.34; Mt. 27.46, NRSV), whereas Thecla after seeing a vision expresses reassurance in her hour of need. In addition, and perhaps most importantly, God does not intervene in the events of the crucifixion – Jesus dies. The fact that in the arena, Thecla, for the first time in the narrative, moves beyond her silent trance-like state to speak, the fact that she takes definitive action in assuming the shape of the cross and mounting the pyre with 'power', a power that is so palpable that the Governor 'marvels' at her, means that Thecla's representation is almost the antithesis of the passion of Jesus. Prior to entering the arena, she was passive and mute, practically comatose, whereas prior to his passion, Jesus was a teacher of words and actions. And, as indicated above, perhaps most importantly, within the *Acts of Paul and Thecla*, God intervenes and spares Thecla from pain, torture and ultimately death.

It, therefore, becomes apparent that Thecla's (not quite) 'martyrdom' diverges in quite fundamental ways from the passion of Christ. Thus, although Thecla at this point in the narrative does begin a metamorphosis, she awakens from a mute trance and passive state and finds instead a voice, strength and fortitude; the resemblance of her experiences in the arena with those of the passion of Christ ought not to be overstated. Within the gospels, Jesus is shown to become introverted, and he appears to lose his power in the events of the passion, whereas Thecla's empowerment begins within the arena. Thus, although the fire is lit, it does not affect her, for God has compassion on her (*APTh*. 22). Thecla's suffering in the arena is, therefore, not a physical one of pain but rather a humiliating one because she is a virgin female who has been stripped naked and publicly exposed. Furthermore, in saving her, God robs Thecla of the ultimate sacrifice of martyrdom. Unfortunately, however, in the process of saving Thecla, other people are violently killed. While Thecla is not sacrificed, God's compassion for her results in alternative victims.

Once Thecla is saved from the fire, the text immediately moves straight to Paul praying and fasting in a tomb. Although it appeared that Paul was absent during Thecla's ordeal, the text assures readers that his absence is not read as desertion or abandonment. In so doing, the text champions the male. Ultimatel,y it was Paul's prayers and fasting that effected God's intervention and Thecla's rescue (*APTh*. 24). Paul is assuaged from the guilt of absenteeism in Thecla's hour of need. Thus, ultimately Paul is the mediator of God's power. This point is underscored when Paul says 'σε ὅτι ὁ ἠρώτησα ἐτάχυνας μοι καὶ εἰσήκοσάς μου' (*APTh*. 24). The invocation of the divine is reserved for the male apostle. The miracle that saved Thecla is ascribed to Paul: it was an answer to his prayer. Thus, despite the 'power' in Thecla, she was merely the passive recipient of a miracle effected by the prayers of a man. As the donor of the miracle, Paul is ensured subject status, while Thecla, the recipient of miraculous favours, remains the object. Thecla's empowerment was short-lived indeed.

Ultimately, God is the Actor who works all miracles, but Paul is clearly marked as his special envoy and Thecla the passive benefactor. Divine intervention could have functioned as a kind of divine signature for female apostleship. However, whereas the miraculous could have been used to strengthen the representation of the feminine, it instead bolsters the presence and power of a patriarchal masculinity.[40] This is commensurate with the other Apocryphal Acts where male apostles perform miracles and women are the passive recipients.[41]

Misset-van de Weg argues that as a result of the miracle and quenching of fire happening through the prayer of Paul the text manoeuvres Paul into a special position since it accentuates that he is a true apostle operating divine sanction.[42] She argues that at the same time a misunderstanding is rectified: Paul is not the kind of magician the Iconians took him for. He is not a *magos* who seduces women but rather a teacher preaching God's word. However, Misset-van de Weg's assessment of Paul is only partially correct; while Paul is not a *magos* but a 'teacher of God', Paul certainly does 'seduce' young women. He may not seduce women for his, or other people's sexual or material gratification, but he does seduce young virgins for Christianity.[43]

The gender stereotyping thus sits comfortably within a patriarchal model; while the virgin is not 'stolen' for an earthly man, she is stolen for a patriarchal God and his work. In the process, she has had to renounce her family, her procreative powers and aspects of her sexuality in order to be fully acceptable to the deity. However, from a male perspective, the more sexualized and desirable aspects of this woman (her physical beauty) have been retained.

Misset-van de Weg speaks of the propagandistic side of the miracle, which is that women are called to choose an ascetic lifestyle and to endure the consequences, because, although they may have to suffer and their family may declare or wish them dead, God will be on their side.[44] The blessings that await them are spelled out in the beatitudes (*APTh*. 6). Misset-van de Weg is right to highlight the underlying doctrine which is aimed at women. This is especially poignant since Paul immediately goes on to speak the word of God concerning continence for both men and women: 'Blessed are they who have kept the flesh holy ... Blessed are the ones having control ... Blessed are they who have wives as if they had them not ... Blessed are the bodies of the virgins' (*APTh*. 5-6). However, the text goes on to focus purely on one specific young female virgin and her body. That the fundamental conviction of chastity is aimed at a woman and encourages her to break social and ideological laws and to suffer the consequences means that ultimately the text is both endorsing and normalizing female isolation and bodily suffering.

Up to this point in the text, the function of the miraculous is fairly ambivalent in terms of gender. On the one hand, the miracle which saves her authorizes Thecla's actions and choices, to leave her family, fiancé and take up chastity and follow Paul.[45] On the other hand, we may observe that the miraculous restricts Thecla as a woman, objectifying her, emphasizing nakedness, dramatic performance and bodily suffering, thus stylizing a specifically female apostolate. Her survival thus appears to be an ambiguous privilege. Although Thecla benefits from the 'miraculous', ultimately she lacks any real religious authority of her own.

This is perhaps underscored by the fact that so little attention is paid to the miracle and its ensuing effects. Since there is no mention of people's reactions to the miracle, we have to assume that no missionary effect is assigned to it either. This is, of course, significant because even punitive miracles (after all, this miracle does not only save but kills as well) usually produce converts or, one might say, frightens people into conversion.

Cooper notes that in late antiquity, the martyr's speech was combined with the miraculous in martyr texts to form a 'preaching' scene that might influence its hearers.[46] However, as noted in Chapter 5, the *Acts of Paul and Thecla* is unusual in that Thecla does not 'speak a martyrdom'. The text thus offers no guidance in how to interpret the miracles. In this respect, the miracles offer a 'missed opportunity' to influence the hearers. The only response to Thecla's miraculous rescue is her expulsion from the city (*APTh*. 26). Thecla's miraculous salvation is dismissed as inconsequential. Neither the miracle nor Thecla's survival is seen as extraordinary or momentous. Instead, the focus of attention is shifted to God's envoy, the person of Paul: it was he who invoked the power of God.

Misset-van de Weg argues that the emphasis in this episode is conversion through the word (*APTh*. 7, 9).[47] She goes on to say that, when all is said and done, Paul's entire mission to Iconium seems to result in one explicit convert only: Thecla.[48] However, this is incorrect. The text, in fact, portrays quite a different picture of Paul's mission. At one point, it is reported that all (πᾶσαι, *APTh*. 9) the virgins and young men of the town have been affected by his preaching. Although this statement may be an exaggeration on the part of Theocleia (especially since some men *and* women do come forward to assist with Thecla's execution, *APTh*. 22), the statement does demonstrate that Paul's preaching had a wide-reaching impact.

In addition, we are also told that Thecla sees 'many' women and young virgins go into hear Paul preach (*APTh*. 7). The downplaying of the miracle and lack of converts may be suggesting that women do not convert the masses. We must not lose sight of the fact that during her ordeal, Thecla was naked. Thus, despite the power (δύναμις) that she displayed, her shameful exposure would diminish how she was ultimately perceived by onlookers. No matter the era, whether modern day or antiquity, it would always be difficult to take a naked woman seriously. Any message communicated by a beautiful naked woman would always be secondary to her physical appearance.

Thus, while in the Christian tradition miracles are usually positive by definition, in this instance, the miraculous interventions surrounding Thecla only seem to benefit her. The miraculous affirms Thecla's vocation, but – by not adding any converts – her apostolate is downgraded. The text validates Thecla on the one hand but devalues her on the other. This ambiguous representation creates a double message. Although it singles Thecla out as extraordinary, her representation still accords well with patriarchal notions of female objectification and subordination. Nevertheless, as the recipient of miraculous intervention, Thecla gains the opportunity to continue on her quest to follow Paul.

On finding Paul (*APTh.* 24), the two of them travel to Antioch where Alexander falls 'in lust' (ἠρασθη, *APTh.* 26) with her. At this point, Paul abandons Thecla, leaving her to fight off Alexander alone. A struggle ensues and Thecla shouts, 'do not force (βιάσῃ) the stranger (ξένην), do not force the handmaid of God' (*APTh.* 26). We move from Thecla's hometown, which condemns and expels her, to Antioch, where Thecla refers to herself as a stranger. Does this description suggest or establish some kind of link between Paul and Thecla as apostles? Are we meant to identify Thecla the 'stranger' with Paul the 'stranger' (*APTh.* 8, 13, 19)? Is the text suggesting there is some likeness between the two characters, and, if so, does this mean that Thecla is beginning to assume the characteristics of a male apostle: one who wanders from town to town unrecognized?

Certainly, at this stage of the narrative, something quite distinct appears to be happening, and this is underscored and borne out in the events that follow. Here, Thecla's representation appears to undergo some positive developments. She could not rely on Paul to protect her; he was more interested in saving himself and, therefore, she takes matters into her own hands in fighting off an important man in public. It is interesting that Thecla's empowerment takes place in Paul's absence. Her display of δύναμις in the arena and her altercation with Alexander happen only when Paul is out of sight. Indeed, in the events that follow, Paul disappears completely from our awareness as women en masse come to the fore. He only returns to our consciousness when Thecla desires to see him at the end of the tale and instigates a search for him.

Bound together: Miracle 2

Meanwhile, once Thecla has been seized by the authorities in Antioch for shaming Alexander, she is forcibly bound to a lioness and processed around the town (*APTh.* 28). However, whereas such enforced proximity to the lioness is meant to instil fear and terror within Thecla, instead the lioness works for her without prayer or incantations: it licks her feet in a show of affection and friendship. This was a well-known motif in hagiographical literature.[49] This is a miracle insomuch as the lioness is behaving contrary to its wild and bestial nature. In antiquity, lions were known along the southern coast of the Mediterranean as well as in Greece and the Middle East. In later classical Greek mythology, the Nemean Lion was portrayed as a people-eating beast; killing it was one of the twelve tasks assigned to Heracles.[50] However, stories of friendly lions also circulated in antiquity.[51] In the story of Androcles, one of Aesop's fables, the hero, a runaway slave, pulls a thorn from a lion's paw; when he is later thrown to the lions as a punishment for escaping, the lion recognizes him and refuses to kill him.[52]

Both Paul and Thecla have episodes with lions in their Acts and both are protected by lions in the arena. The story of Androcles, however, informs Paul's encounter with a lion. In the *Martyrdom of Paul*, as Paul is journeying from Damascus to Jericho, he happens upon a talking lion who asks to be baptized. Although Paul is fearful, he walks the lion down to the river, takes holds of his mane and immerses him three times in baptism. After baptism, the lion shakes off the water, gives thanks and blissfully goes back to the wild, in a chaste state. This chaste state is emphasized when he comes across a lioness but does not mate with her. Later on when in Ephesus, Paul is condemned to fight with the beasts, he is set against the same lion (who has by now been captured) in the arena. The lion immediately recognizes Paul and does not attack him. Paul is, therefore, spared 'death by lion'.[53]

Interestingly, despite the vogue of 'the lion's tale' in antiquity, Paul's episode with the lion made little, if any, impact on material culture.[54] In contrast, Thecla's story of the lion was widely popular as evidenced by the numerous representations of Thecla standing between lions. While images of Thecla and lions abound, one particular category is that of Thecla standing as an orans between two lions;[55] usually one lion is in attack position and another licks Thecla's feet; in one example, the *manus divina* reaches from above with a wreath.[56] A further image is one of Thecla tied to a stake, between a lion and a bear at her feet and wild oxen at her hip (see also Figure 4.1).[57] It is noteworthy that there is no backstory to Thecla's lion encounter, unlike the *Acts of Paul* where the lion's friendly behaviour is explained as a result of a previous encounter.[58] Furthermore, the reader is given no explicit indication of how to interpret this occurrence and no explanation is offered.

Spittler reads the lioness as evidence of divine protection or the animal's ability to recognize something special in Thecla.[59] This point is significant: Braun has also highlighted that in Graeco-Roman physiognomic handbooks, animals were used as an important analogy in gender identification. The lion (both male and female) was seen to exhibit the male type in its most perfect form. It was regarded to have fiery, intelligent, proud traits that were analogically transferable to the ideal male human being. Braun argues that, from the perspective of physiognomic art, the depiction of Thecla and the lioness would suggest a symbolic transfer by literary means of the manly quality from one to the other. Thecla becomes a leonine human being.[60] Given the fact that most women in antiquity, even extremely wealthy women, were praised in stereotypical ways (in references to fathers and sons), thus in ways that posed no threat to the traditional ideology of gender differences, here Thecla receives extraordinary praise.[61]

In antiquity, the power and majesty of a pagan deity was often communicated through wild animals. Surrounded by wild animals, the deity was portrayed as taming these powerful beasts while at the same time the power of the animal was thought to be transferred onto the deity.[62] The lion as king of animals incorporated power, leadership and courage and thus represented the power of the highest Greek deities. With the exception of the sun god Apollo, the lion usually appears as the attribute of female deities (Cybele, Hera and Athena).[63] In ancient myth, Rhea, the wife of Cronus, and mother of Zeus and the other great gods of Olympus, was believed to exercise unbounded sway over the animal creation, especially the lion. Rhea is generally represented with lions crouching at her feet, and she is sometimes depicted sitting in a chariot, drawn by lions.[64] Thecla's encounter with the lioness thus stands out as a significant element of her characterization: she is 'goddess-like'. This is also hinted at in the textual tradition of Thecla's life where in Seleucia, Thecla has to assert her authority over the city's indigenous cult: Athena, virgin goddess.[65]

Pomeroy notes that the goddesses of antiquity were archetypal images of human females, as envisioned by males.[66] The two virgin goddesses that are most pertinent to Thecla's religious and cultural panorama are Artemis and Athena. Pomeroy contends that the most complex of the goddesses was Athena, a masculine, androgynous woman. Although she is female in appearance and was associated with the handicrafts of women, many of the attributes traditionally associated with her, such as wisdom, were considered masculine by the Greeks. She was also a warrior goddess, armed with shield, spear and helmet, and at times she disguised herself as a man.[67] Athena was the archetype of the masculine woman who found success in what was essentially a man's world by denying her own femininity and sexuality.[68] In contrast to Athena, Artemis (Roman Diana) is a huntress who shoots arrows from afar: Amazons are mortal by-forms of Artemis. Like Thecla, both goddess and Amazons wore short tunics, the clothing of men.[69]

Through association, then, Thecla is goddess-like: special and unique. She is affiliated with the lioness; her body is inviolable, she survives events that no human could endure and, at the end of the narrative, she dons a short male tunic like Artemis (and Amazons). Furthermore, just like other virgin goddesses, Thecla is not constrained by familial obligations.[70] Thus, despite her initial 'bewitchment' and passivity, within the Antioch episode, Thecla's representation is certainly developing in the right direction. For becoming physically aggressive toward a powerful, civic man, Thecla is rewarded in being served by a lioness (*APTh*. 26, 28, 33). In a patriarchal culture, this is progress indeed. However, it is not all good news. Despite the text's manoeuvre to empower Thecla, her representation still retains limiting female qualities. She is the embodiment of the pure, inexperienced, sexually unthreatening female, and her devotion to chastity means that essential aspects of her womanliness and sexuality will never be fully integrated. Aspects of her womanhood and female gender, therefore, remain alienated, her 'self' divided.

Dreams can come true: Miracle 3

In the third miracle, Tryphaena has a vision/dream and is visited by her dead daughter, Falconilla, who asks to have Thecla pray for her (*APTh*. 29). At this point, Thecla has not instructed Tryphaena in the faith. This does not take place until later in the narrative (*APTh*. 39). Presumably, then, Tryphaena, at this stage, knows nothing about Christianity or its teaching. Since Tryphaena learns an aspect of Christian teaching from other than earthly realms, this is meant as a sign of revelation from the divine. Giselle de Nie notes that in antiquity, a dream was regarded as a privileged way of perceiving other spiritual realities.[71] Evidence from the *PGM* demonstrates that people in antiquity were convinced that God could reveal his will and counsel in dreams.[72] In this respect, the dream/vision can be counted as a miraculous event.[73] This particular miracle acts as a catalyst for a further miracle since Falconilla is transposed to a 'better place'. The miracle that saved Thecla in Iconium is ascribed to Paul and described as an answer to his prayer. Thecla's prayer is shown to be as effective as Paul's: Falconilla is transferred to the place of the righteous. Like Paul, Thecla's words also have power. God responds to her call, just as he did to Paul's.

However, we soon learn that where prayer is concerned, Thecla is not so extraordinary after all. When Tryphaena asks God to help Thecla (*APTh*. 30), we know from the events that follow, when none of the wild beasts touch her, that God hears the prayer call (*APTh*. 33-36): Thecla is saved. Even though Tryphaena cannot yet be described as a believer or disciple of Christ, her prayers are as effective as Paul's and Thecla's. Since the efficacy of prayer is not reserved for Paul and Thecla alone, this narrative affirms there is equitability among all the characters that support Thecla. All have access to the Divine through prayer: neither gender nor faith necessarily plays a part.

Interestingly, Tryphaena, in losing one child, has temporarily gained another (*APTh*. 30), and Thecla too, having been disowned by her mother, gains a surrogate. Jesus says, '[W]hoever does the will of God is my brother and sister and mother' (Mk 3.34 NRSV). The story echoes Jesus' sentiments in advocating a family of faith rather than kinship through blood relations. In addition to presenting Tryphaena as the ideal 'mother type' figure of faith, there are other aspects of her representation which are also stereotyped. Despite the fact that she is a powerful and well-connected member of society (*APTh*. 36), standard formula of female helplessness and hysteria are attached to her characterization. Thus, when Alexander comes to fetch Thecla (*APTh*. 30), Tryphaena 'cries out' claiming she has no συγγενής (relative/kinsman) to help Thecla; this is despite the fact that she is a relative of Caesar (*APTh*. 36). This representation certainly plays into an antique gender stereotype of female powerlessness and hysteria. This is further reinforced when her loud, vociferous cry frightens Alexander away (*APTh*. 31). One panicked woman and a young female virgin are enough to frighten away the mighty Alexander – so much so that an army needs to be despatched to deal with them. This is a subtle way of depicting female networks as frightening and overwhelming to men.

However, even as Thecla is dragged to the theatre, Tryphaena does not abandon her, and Thecla weeps, not for herself, but for Tryphaena and her impending second loss of a child (*APTh*. 30-32). These two women and the women of Antioch generally seem a more cohesive group. As soon as Thecla is condemned, they cry out 'an evil judgement' (*APTh*. 32). They recognize Thecla's significance and show appreciation of her, while men appreciate her for her beauty and the desire she evokes within them. It is important to note that during Paul's absence, unwavering female bonds are being established. A valuable network is beginning to form, and, as we shall see, when women group together, they can form an effective (albeit temporary) powerhouse.

Animal magic: Miracle 4

Once in the arena, Thecla is treated like any female prisoner; she is stripped and thrown into the arena to the wild beasts (*APTh*. 33). The πικρὰ λέαινα runs towards her, charging at full speed as though to attack (προσδραμοῦσα), but instead licks her feet and lies down. A great bear is then sent into the arena, and as it runs towards Thecla, the lioness meets it and tears it apart (διέρηξεν). In antiquity, the lioness was seen as the keeper of pagan temples, and Esch argues that, in a Graeco-Roman context, the fact that the lioness becomes Thecla's bodyguard demonstrates signs of the deification of the protagonist (APTh. 33). Once again, Thecla's goddess-like quality is underscored. Next, a lion trained to fight people is released; it runs to the lioness and wrestles her and both lion and lioness perish in the fight. Antique fundamentals of gender do not appear to hold sway in the animal kingdom; both male and female are depicted as equally strong. Unfortunately, however, the female cannot master the male outright. The women mourn the death of the lioness because a female ally and defender, one of their number, is lost. The symbolism of lions in an arena is especially important since Christians were fed to the lions as punishment and this was enjoyed as people engaged in spectacle. Thus, the point made by Esch, that in her encounter with the wild animals in the arena Thecla leads the Christians to victory over the pagan gods, is a very powerful one.[74]

A second baptism: Miracle 5a

Once the lioness and the lion die, more beasts are thrown into the arena. At this point, Thecla performs an irregular act of self-baptism, which results in a series of miraculous events. After praying, Thecla turns (ἐστράφη) to see a pit of water, she then throws herself in, crying, 'I baptize myself ... in the name of Jesus Christ' (βαπτίζομαι, APTh. 34).[75] The women and the entire crowd are now on her side; they weep thinking she will be devoured by the seals (APTh. 34). However, the narrator advises us that the seals do not devour her because God sends down a flash of lightning and they float dead on top of the water.[76] The Governor also weeps at this point, but he simply mourns the loss of her beauty.

Following the miraculous event of fire and lightening which kills the seals, a cloud of fire appears around Thecla. Of course, for all we know, Thecla may have been attempting suicide, preferring to be in control of her death rather than being devoured by beasts in the arena (in the martyrdom of Perpetua, e.g., she guides the sword of the executioner).[77] Nevertheless, even though Thecla is active and decisive in the arena, she is not privileged with any miraculous powers. She is, therefore, once again the passive recipient of protection. This, as noted above, is contrary to the way in which male apostles in the Apocryphal Acts are depicted.[78]

Hubble bubble toil and trouble: Miracle 5b

The cloud of fire, which now surrounds Thecla, protects her so that beasts cannot touch her and people cannot see her naked (APTh. 34). Of course, having been exposed to the crowd and readers alike in all her trials, shielding Thecla's nakedness from our sight at this point is illogical. In the reader's minds, Thecla is naked and will remain so. It is, therefore, a gratuitous gesture, and this is especially underscored when towards the end of the story Thecla once again stands naked before the Governor.

As more terrible beasts are let loose, the women unite and take action. They throw petals and spices into the arena and the wild beasts are overpowered or 'held back' by sleep (κατασχεθέντα). We need to ask why, if Thecla is surrounded by fire, this action is even necessary. Surely the fire should protect her from the beasts. This brings into question the efficacy of the fire sent by God. Nevertheless, the women decide to act for Thecla and they take decisive action; and what is this magic they use?

The *PGM* show quite vividly the ordinary and sophisticated command of drug-compounding by the common people: a command not surprising in view of their usual rural upbringing. Pharmaceutical lore was generally accepted and simultaneously intertwined with Greek thinking on magic, religious customs and empirical-practical science. The use of plants, the blend of the rational with the divine, was a characteristic of the so-called scientific levels of Graeco-Roman pharmacy or φάρμακον. John Scarborough underscores the 'fantasies' that men in antiquity created around women and the rituals of root-cutting and the gathering of herbs, even though men were also heavily associated with the practice.[79] Kimberly Stratton similarly highlights the stereotype of the dangerous female sorceress which predominates in Graeco-Roman world where, within Roman Literature, 'magic' clearly emerges as the practice of women.[80]

This use of herbs by women in the *Acts of Paul and Thecla* undoubtedly taps into the ancient female stereotype which associated women with drug lore. Scarborough argues that this particular representation of women demonstrates a deep-rooted fear of females. He notes, for example, how Homer emphasizes a mythological setting of treacherous women who 'know' the plants and drugs.[81] This model or archetype of women, and the fearful knowledge they possess, is a useful trope that is utilized by the text. When women gather together, they possess a power and knowledge which can overcome powerful civic men and even wild beasts. As a woman alone, Thecla does not possess any power as such; she is mostly ineffective against men. However, when women join together, they can act synchronically, to defend against male aggression and violence.

Women's networks can then be both significant and effective. This point is particularly underscored in the Pastoral Epistles where female networks meet with disapproval. Within 1 Tim. 5.3-16, the author attempts to separate out 'real' widows from younger women within the group (vv. 5-12). While there has been much scholarly discussion on the particular emphasis of the group of women, what is markedly striking is that this 'group' is deemed disruptive and troublesome to the church community.[82] One female alone is not problematic; however, a group of women can accomplish something, and this is undoubtedly anxiety provoking for males.

Thus, women en masse resort to a feminine stereotyped defence and use plants and herbs to overcome male violence; they are empowered and a force to be reckoned with. However, this victory against male aggression is but a temporary reprieve. What better way for men to assert their power and strength over the feminine than to usher in two powerful male phallic symbols: bulls.

Raging bulls: Miracle 6

Because Thecla, with God's help, withstands every attempt to annihilate her, the violence against her is escalated and she is eventually bound by the feet between two aggressive bulls. In order to enrage them all the more, the undersides of the bulls are scorched using hot irons. Perhaps this symbolizes the rage contained within the males trying to deal with Thecla; no matter what they do, they seem unable to dispose of this troublesome female. However, a flame burns through the ropes and she is miraculously released. Where did this flame appear from? Presumably, it was not the flame that surrounded Thecla when she threw herself into the pool of water, since this would have prevented her captors from getting close enough in order to tie her by the feet. One possibility is that it was a flame caused by the scorching irons.[83] Nevertheless, at this point, unable to cope with the ensuing drama, Tryphaena passes out and her handmaids declare she is dead (*APTh*. 36). Fear that Caesar, Tryphaena's relative, will seek retribution for her death and invade the city brings the events in the arena to a close: Thecla is released.

Misset-van de Weg contends that since the handmaids do not have access to legitimate power, they use Tryphaena's fainting as an opportunity to manipulate the situation by declaring that she has died. The effect is such that Thecla is not only saved from the wild animals but also released.[84] However, I believe it is unlikely that the handmaids here manipulate the situation. With the violence reaching a climax, the handmaids, like Tryphaena, become hysterical. Hysteria is, after all, infectious. Finding themselves in a frightening situation, unable to manage their emotions or think clearly, especially when their mistress collapses, the handmaids fear the worst and declare Tryphaena dead. Tryphaena's alleged death brings the events in the arena to a close. It is significant that, neither compassion for Thecla, nor the miraculous events associated with her, bring the violence to an end. God's miracles seem almost imperceptible and Thecla's ordeal inconsequential. Only fear of the emperor, the most powerful man, Caesar, brings the events to a halt (*APTh*. 36-37). Thank goodness for an interested relative of Caesar in the crowd.

As an aside, it is interesting to observe that this is only the second time that a Governor acts decisively, the other being when the Governor in Iconium decides not to execute Paul but rather imprison him in order to give him a more attentive hearing at his leisure (*APTh*. 17). It is only when decisions involve men that Governors can think and act resolutely. When they have to make decisions in regard to the beautiful Thecla, they are weak and impotent, allowing themselves to be swayed by other people. For example, Theocleia insists the Governor condemn Thecla to the pyre for refusing to marry (*APTh*. 20). Despite his better judgement, and feeling pity for her, the Governor goes ahead with the punishment anyway (*APTh*. 21). Also in Antioch, when Thecla is in the arena, the Governor disapproves of escalating the violence but agrees to usher in the bulls to tear Thecla apart nevertheless (*APTh*. 35). Are readers to assume that beautiful women adversely affect men's civic power and decision making?

Out of curiosity, the Governor calls Thecla and questions her as to why the beasts had no effect on her (*APTh*. 37). As she stands naked before him, she proclaims that it is her belief in Jesus Christ that found favour with God and he saved her (*APTh*. 37). She then goes on to say that he is a place of refuge for the storm-tossed and relief for the oppressed and shelter for the despairing. Thecla was oppressed and storm-tossed; however, she was never portrayed as despairing.[85] She speaks of her experience and declares her unbending faith in Jesus Christ throughout; this was the key to her survival. When the Governor issues a decree releasing Thecla, the women unite once again: πᾶσσι ἔκραξαν φωνῇ μεγάλῃ καὶ ὡς ἐξ ἑνὸς στόματος ἔδωκαν αἶνον τῷ θεῷ (*APTh*. 38). Now as one, all the women believe in Thecla's God, unlike the Governor or men of the city. Furthermore, while the majority of the maidservants in Tryphaena's house are converted, no men are included in their number (*APTh*. 39).

Despite the fact that God reveals himself in and through the miracles, it mostly escapes the notice of the men. Of course, we need to question why, despite the miraculous interventions, only the women are converted. It is quite possible that this is due to women's stereotypical associations with magic. Indeed, Léon Vouaux argues that the Governor cannot believe there has been no intervention of magic, and this in fact supported in one of the Latin texts which includes Thecla's response '*ego non sum maga.*'[86] However, within this text the men are clearly distanced from any connection and belief in magic.

It is not long before Thecla once again ἐπεπόθει Paul (*APTh*, 40), and so the now empowered Thecla sends people from one place to another (περιπέμπουσα, *APTh*. 40) to look for him. When she receives information about his whereabouts, she takes young men and maidens to go to him whereupon he commissions her to teach (*APTh*. 41). It is significant that after surviving all her ordeals, Thecla now has young men doing her bidding. She eventually returns to Iconium and summons her mother in a commanding voice (προσκαλεσαμένη, *APTh* 43). She has grown in confidence, power and stature, so much so that even Paul marvels at her (ἐθαμβήθη, *APTh*. 40; θαυμάσαι, *APTh*. 41). At the end of the story, she has the crowd of young men and maidens set off with her on her apostolic mission (*APTh*. 40).

Do miracles happen for the female gender?

Misset-van de Weg argues that Thecla/woman, 'unbound' both from the things of the world and in the end from the apostle Paul, is set free and commissioned to pursue her apostolic activities. The most important implication of the relation between women as both performers and beneficiaries of miracles is the validation of Thecla as a τοῦ θεοῦ δούλην (*APTh*. 26) and thus of women's position of (apostolic) authority. For Misset-van de Weg, the miracles demonstrate that the model of Christian miracle workers is mostly one of mediation or a manifestation of the power of God who is the 'true' miracle worker. With this in mind it can, therefore, be established that women are portrayed as important participants in effecting the miracles; they do indeed work miracles. Thecla equals Paul as wonder worker; in fact, she and the women of Antioch outshine him. They resort to their own means-gendered and stereotypical resources to end the injustice taking place in the arena. Their acts, revealing solidarity and wit, are successful and 'divine'. Misset-van de Weg concludes that the success of their actions positively asserts and validates these women and underscores that they are not powerless, but sometimes even divinely empowered: [87] 'wonders never cease!', she exclaims.[88]

In summary, then, Misset-van de Weg claims that women are mediators of divine miracles, and having no direct access to power, they resort to the illegitimate use of power by grouping together and employing wit and cunning. This, Misset-van de Weg argues, culminates in success and a positive outcome for women generally and Thecla specifically. However, as noted above, in demonstrating that God responds to the prayers of men, women and non-believers/disciples (e.g. Tryphaena), the text clearly demonstrates that anyone can be an emissary of God; neither gender nor faith necessarily play a part. The text, therefore, is not saying anything distinct in regard to women (although perhaps unlike the Pastoral Epistles it does include women). Furthermore, although, as argued above, it is doubtful that Tryphaena's servants did manipulate the situation in regard to her fainting, even if that was the case, it is difficult to see how the text is suggesting anything new (or positive) in regard to ancient gender stereotypes. Men in antiquity often spoke of women's cunning and manipulation in a pejorative way.[89] If the text is suggesting this, then it is simply making use of a negative and disparaging stereotype.

Moreover, despite Misset-van de Weg's claim that Thecla and the women of Antioch outshine Paul, again, as noted above, whenever Paul is present in the story, the text 'protects' and excuses him for his crimes of absenteeism. For example, after the first miracle when Thecla is saved from the fire, the text immediately moves to the scene of Paul praying for Thecla's safety in the tomb. Paul may not have been present in the arena, but he does have direct access to the divine and he helps to effect Thecla's miraculous rescue. In addition, when women really come to the fore, uniting as one in meeting masculine aggression head on, Paul is absent both from the narrative and our consciousness. This ensures that his female devotee and her feminine champions never outshine the male apostle. Their temporary victory is only possible because Paul is elsewhere, far from Antioch. Furthermore, while the text depicts female networks as empowering and perhaps threatening, as we noted from Alexander despatching an envoy of soldiers to collect Thecla from the hysterical Tryphaena, and the ushering in of two bulls immediately following the women's use of herbs, ultimately male power can overcome women. Female empowerment within the text is then highly circumscribed.

Nevertheless, while the female heroine is not endowed with anything like the sort of power that is associated with the male apostles in the Apocryphal Acts (Thecla is simply the passive recipient of the miraculous with very little power directly worked through her), the miraculous certainly marks her out as special and distinct and this is especially the case in regard to the behaviour of the lioness. In a Graeco-Roman context, it is usually the female deities who are flanked by lions.[90] Thecla is, therefore, symbolically deified through the behaviour of the lioness after a pagan pattern.[91]

The other crucial aspect of Thecla's representation in regard to the miracles is that ultimately they save her life. Thus, despite the ordeals she faces and the escalation of violence she endures, Thecla does not die in the arena, nor is she injured or wounded in any way. This death-defying quality of the heroine is hardly characteristic of mere mortals and is in complete contrast to other martyrdom stories. The martyrs Perpetua and Felicitas, for example, bear the all-too-human consequence of pain, injury and death in response to the violence that is metered out to them. Although they too undergo eroticized torture and sexualization, their story is more realistic because ultimately no miracles take place to save or protect them.[92]

Furthermore, Thecla's fate also deviates greatly from that of each of the (important) male apostles in the Apocryphal Acts (including Paul), who all meet with an unfortunate end. Thecla's story thus diverges in a very significant way from the usual Christian martyrdom stories that end in death. Thecla's survival makes her 'super human', indestructible and goddess-like. Thus, despite being a passive recipient of miracles, ultimately, the miraculous works for Thecla's representation and establishes and confirms her symbolic uniqueness. Miracles do happen after all!

Conclusion

Within the narrative, Thecla is not bestowed with any powers, neither verbally or doctrinally nor through the power of magic and miracles. This is in contrast to the male apostles in the Apocryphal Acts.[93] Indeed, Korte notes that this paradigm may be traced in both the Old and New Testaments where miracle stories hardly ever overtly refer to miracle-working women. This is even the case with the Virgin Mary, who eventually became an especially important and prominent figure within Christianity. She is never portrayed as personally performing miracles in biblical texts; she is merely a vehicle and mediator of God's actions and serves as an example to women in her virginity and maternity.[94] The representation of Thecla is similarly constructed. While the text sanctions Thecla's decision to follow the ascetic teachings of Paul (perhaps suggesting that women easily fall victim to powerful, persuasive males), the miracles also underscore Thecla's passivity as a woman.

It is, of course, quite possible that given the suspicion that surrounded women generally, any powers emanating directly from a woman would result in the accusation of 'sorceress' (from audience and characters alike) and this may have influenced against granting miraculous powers to Thecla.[95] Too much about women was steeped in suspicion, the good woman was the invisible woman, the silent woman (1 Tim. 2.11-13), not the miracle-wielding, powerful woman; hence, Thecla's representation as a passive recipient of miracles. Any woman who became too prominent, too powerful, too active in religion was open to accusations of transgression. In employing representations of women, therefore, male authors faced a complicated balancing act in stressing extraordinariness on the one hand but their 'normality' in terms of gender on the other. Elizabeth Petroff notes that medieval hagiographers of female saints often struggled with this tension. They tended to get around the problem by emphasizing that the 'power' of the female saint was willed by God.[96]

The overall impression in regard to the wielding of miraculous power in the *Acts of Paul and Thecla* is then of conventional gender patterns. It is dangerous to ascribe miracle-working powers to the heroine; she may appear too powerful and rival the male apostles. Alternatively, she could be accused of using magic and suffer the invective 'sorceress'. Thecla is, therefore, merely the passive recipient of miracles and in this regard she never quite equals the male apostles who all wield miraculous powers. Furthermore, although the miraculous enabled Thecla to reach a level of independence and to practice as a missionary, ultimately she still defers to Paul, thus maintaining the patriarchal norms of hierarchy, while simultaneously undermining her own religious autonomy and authority.

Most notable, perhaps, is the fact that so little is made of the miraculous events that surround Thecla. It becomes quite evident that the miracles are *not* intended to work for conversion of the masses. This would suggest that the function of the miracles serves a purpose other than conversion. Since the miracles ensure that Thecla survives her martyrdom in a way no other martyrs do (not even the male apostles), fundamentally it would suggest that the purpose of the miraculous is to proclaim the female Thecla as inviolable. Thus, despite the conventional gender images that hold sway in regard to the miraculous, the miracles do ultimately work to elevate Thecla's status and representation.

Moreover, since Thecla's actions and decision to remain a virgin direct the story (she refuses to marry Thamyris and is thrown into the arena – she fends off the potential rapist Alexander and again ends up in the arena), the text signifies that female virginity is also of supreme importance. Preserving her virginity provides the catalyst for the miraculous, and the text rewards Thecla by rendering her female virgin body inviolable against any physical assault. Her virginity creates a kind of 'magic' that protects her and transforms her into a goddess-like deity. Thus, although Thecla remains a desirable and sexualized woman, her body carries with it nuances of masculinity, in that it remains impenetrable, as a male body should remain.

This miraculous framework characterizes Thecla as immortal-like. She becomes a woman who can only be emulated by degrees: incomparable to ordinary mortals she is not of this world. Thus, while she becomes an important and saintly figure, Thecla remains distant and untouchable like the gods and goddesses of old. The real woman beneath is camouflaged by the supernatural and miraculous, and the protection she receives leaves her aloof from human society. The text is a utopia-like story that for the audience and readers remains remote and unreal.

We may, therefore, conclude that in order to emphasize her inviolability, Thecla is objectified as her womanly body is given prominence. A nubile virgin body and sado-erotic performance creates a very specific type of female apostle – and while other female martyrs undergo this eroticized torture, they die; Thecla does not: she is unique indeed. The miraculous episodes, along with Thecla's inviolable virgin body, therefore, tend to override and marginalize Thecla's actual apostolic ministry, stressing her utter uniqueness.

This holy woman, sacrosanct as she may be, cannot, however, escape entirely from social and ecclesiastical control, and so she returns to Paul to be officially commissioned. In the *Acts of Paul and Thecla*, the miraculous thus proves to be a 'double-edged' privilege. We have the construction of female apostleship with the heroine elevated to an 'other-worldly' realm, and yet she is sexualized for audience titillation. In this way, the text speaks metaphorically or figuratively the language of a somewhat marginalized woman. However, what is exceptional is that we have here a woman who is neither wife nor mother but who is at the same time presented as an admirable woman: a woman who just will not die.

Working with a hermeneutic of suspicion has then gradually revealed that there is only a vestige of genuine, clear-cut female-affirming facets to Thecla's representation. Little in the text speaks well for her and for women generally. The hostile treatment of this woman's beautiful body clearly represents the discourse of a patriarchal culture which subjugates and objectifies women. The one redeeming element of this text, in favour of women, is that Thecla is endowed with a female body that excels in the arena and cannot be conquered: she is inviolable. No man can penetrate her body.

What is particularly interesting is that, despite the focus upon Thecla's bodily beauty, we are never given a description of her. Her representation thus serves to characterize Thecla as fictional and difficult to identify with. The audience can know and see Paul (note the physical description of Paul, *APTh*. 3) but not Thecla. The result of this representation is that Thecla can stand in for any beautiful woman. In fact, Thecla can now become an ideal, perhaps, or especially a metaphor. This representation is reinforced since no physical or psychological effects of the traumas or ordeals she experiences are ever hinted at, let alone narrated.[97] The pronounced focus upon Thecla's body is quite striking, and it is evident that virginity and bodily inviolability is axiomatic within the text. The female within this story might then be interpreted as a literary device, using conventional gender images. God's intervention and the extraordinary prevent her from being ordinary; her body is sacrosanct and indestructible. Why, when most martyr stories inevitably end in the martyr's death, is there such a focus on this woman's invincible body?

Notes

1 Anne-Marie Korte, ed., 'Introduction' to *Women and Miracle Stories: A Multidisciplinary Exploration* (Leiden: Brill, 2001), 2–3. See also Peter Brown, *The Cult of the Saints: Its Rise and Function in Latin Christianity* (Chicago, IL: University of Chicago Press, 1981), 20, 28.
2 While the question of what constitutes a miracle is relevant to my argument, it is beyond the scope of this investigation to examine the individual theological and philosophical debates on miracles or to enter the various arguments concerning their veracity or otherwise.
3 James G. Frazer, *The Golden Bough: A Study in Magic and Religion* (Hertfordshire: Wordsworth, 1993, originally published in 1890).
4 See e.g. the attempts to discern magical elements in Roman religion, Eli Edward Burriss, *Taboo, Magic, Spirits: A Study of Primitive Elements in Roman Religion* (New York: Kessinger, 1972); see also Howard Hayes Scullard, *Festivals and Ceremonies of the Roman Republic* (London: Thames and Hudson, 1981), 15.
5 Benedicta Ward, *Signs and Wonders: Saints, Miracles and Prayers from the 4th Century to the 14th* (Brookfield, VT: Ashgate, 1992); Carolyn Walker Bynum, 'Wonder', *American Historical Review* 102 (1997): 1–26.
6 See e.g. Olof Petterson, 'Magic-Religion: Some Marginal Notes to an Old Problem', *Ethnos* 22 (1957): 109–19; Jack Goody, 'Religion and Ritual: The Definition Problem',

Br. J. Sociol. 12 (1961): 142–64; Murray Wax and Rosalie Wax, 'The Notion of Magic', *Curr. Anthropol.* 4 (1963): 495–518; Dorothy Hammond, 'Magic – a Problem in Semantics', *Am. Anthropol.* 72 (1970): 1349–56.

7 Fritz Graf, 'Prayer in Magic and Religious Ritual', in *Magika Hiera: Ancient Greek Magic and Religion*, ed. Christopher Faraone and Dirk Obbink (London: Oxford University Press, 1991), 188–213, 188–94.

8 Ibid.

9 Korte, 'Introduction', 7–8.

10 Gerd Theissen, *The Miracle Stories of the Early Christian Tradition* (Edinburgh: T&T Clark, 1983), 35.

11 Ibid., 35–6.

12 Ibid., 85–112.

13 Ibid., 95.

14 Ibid., 98.

15 Ibid., 99, 103, 116.

16 Christopher A. Faraone, *Ancient Greek Love Magic* (Cambridge, MA: Harvard University Press, 1999), 57, 61.

17 Ibid., 51, 55–69. See also Kimberly B. Stratton, 'The Rhetoric of "Magic" in Early Christian Discourse: Gender, Power and the Construction of "Heresy"', in *Mapping Gender in Ancient Religious Discourses*, ed. Todd Penner and Caroline Vander Stichele (Boston, MA: Brill, 2007), 105.

18 These erotic elements were modified and, at times, eliminated altogether by later scribes uncomfortable with the sexual aspects of the text, see Haines-Eitzen, *Gendered Palimpsest*, 97–103.

19 LSJ, BII: 1971; BDAG 1075–6 (2).

20 Fritz Graf, 'How to Cope with a Difficult Life', in Envisioning Magic: A Princeton Seminar and Symposium, ed. Peter Schäfer and Hans G. Kippenberg (Leiden: Brill, 1997), 112. It should, of course, be noted that not every *xenos* was considered a *magos*. For the accusation of '*magos*', see e.g. Gerard Poupon, 'L'accusation de magie dans les Actes Apocryphes', in *Les Actes Apocryphes des Apôtres. Christianisme et monde païen*, ed. F. Bovon and M. Van Esbroeck (Genève: Labor et Fides, 1981), 71–93, 73–6.

21 Archaeological records demonstrate that the vast majority (approximately 86 per cent) of erotic binding spells are performed by men on women, see Faraone, *Ancient Greek Love Magic*, 43, n. 9.

22 See Poupon, 'L'Accusation de Magie', 73; Bremmer, 'Magic, Martyrdom and Women's liberation', 42.

23 Faraone, *Ancient Greek Love Magic*, 62.

24 LSJ 19; BDAG 17.

25 Christopher A. Faraone, 'The Agonistic Context of Early Greek Binding Spells', in *Magika Hiera: Ancient Greek Magic and Religion*, ed. Christopher Faraone and Dirk Obbink (Oxford: Oxford University Press, 1991), 13.

26 Faraone, *Ancient Greek Love Magic*, 168–9.

27 Ibid., 85.

28 In Roman law, the consent of the potential marriage parties was an important condition of marriage. However, consent could be withheld only if the father had selected someone morally undesirable, see Jane F. Gardner, *Women in Roman Law and Society* (Kent: Croom Helm, 1995), 31, 41. Of course, in reality children would have been subject to considerable parental pressure not to object. It is interesting to note that a mother did not have the legal powers a father had, but in the absence of

a father, mothers did, nevertheless, still play a role in marriage and, when there was no agreement between the girl and her mother, the judgement of the Governor of the province could be sought, Judith Evans Grubbs, *Women and the Law in the Roman Empire: A Sourcebook on Marriage, Divorce and Widowhood* (New York: Routledge, 2002), 89, 90.

29 Jerome, *Vita S. Hilarionis Eremitae*, 21.2715-30; 21.2735-65. For similar examples and discussion, see John G. Gager, *Curse Tablets and Binding Spells from the Ancient World* (Oxford: Oxford University Press, 1999), 78-115; and Daniel Ogden, 'Binding Spells: Curse Tablets and Voodoo Dolls in the Greek and Roman Worlds', in *Witchcraft and Magic in Europe: Ancient Greek and Rome*, ed. B. Ankarloo and S. Clark (Philadelphia: University of Pennsylvania Press, 1991), 3-86.

30 In precise contrast to such Christian accounts, which demonize strangers who lure young women away, pagan Greek myths and anecdotes regularly appear to valorize the 'clever men' who use erotic magic to seduce young women, see Faraone, *Ancient Greek Love Magic*, 89-94. Nonetheless, the narrative of the *Acts of Paul and Thecla* evidences the trope of men using magic to seduce young women, one which rarely occurs in Roman or Jewish writings, see Stratton, 'Rhetoric of Magic', 104.

31 See e.g. Jan N. Bremmer, 'Man, Magic, and Martyrdom in the Acts of Andrew', in *The Apocryphal Acts of Andrew*, ed. Jan N. Bremmer (Leuven: Peeters, 2000), 15-24; Bremmer, 'Aspects of the Acts of Peter'.

32 Disregard for parent's wishes was frowned upon, but, as noted earlier, a child who believed parent's motives were unjust could bring a suit against the parents, see Cooper, 'Closely Watched', 27. However, clearly here Thecla has no justifiable grounds not to marry Thamyris.

33 Since Roman jurists saw the well-being of dependents within the household, especially the creation of conditions which fostered the fertility of women, as a matter of civic importance, this would help to explain the judgement against Thecla, Cooper, 'Closely Watched', 26, see also her n. 74.

34 For examples of polymorphism in the Apocryphal Acts, see the *Martyrdom of the Holy and Glorious First-Called Andrew the Apostle* (trans. after Detorakis' edition, see *NTA*, 135), 347; see also APt. 22 (Actus Vercellenses); *AT*. 111; *AJ*. 87. On aspects of metamorphosis in the Apocryphal Acts see P. J. Lalleman, 'Polymorphy of Christ', in *The Apocryphal Acts of John*, ed. Jan N. Bremmer (Kampen: Kok Pharos, 1995), 97-118.

35 Misset-van de Weg, 'Magic, Miracle', 39-40; see also McGinn, 'The Acts of Thecla', 815.

36 *The Martyrdom of Saints Perpetua and Felicitas* (20), in Musurillo, *Acts of Christian Martyrs*.

37 Bremmer, 'Magic, Martyrdom and Women's liberation', 49.

38 Misset-van de Weg, 'Magic, Miracle', 40.

39 See e.g. Richard Valantasis, 'Narrative Strategies and Synoptic Quandaries: A Response to Dennis MacDonald's Reading of Acts of Paul and Acts of Peter', paper presented at the annual meeting of the *SBL* (Atlanta, 1992), 234-9, esp. 238; Bremmer, 'Magic, Martyrdom and Women's liberation', 49.

40 On miracle working as a criterion for sainthood see, e.g., Donald Weinstein and Rudolph M. Bell, *Saints & Society: The Two Worlds of Western Christendom, 1000-1700* (Chicago, IL: University of Chicago Press, 1982), 143-53.

41 E.g., the apostle Andrew can 'put demons to flight' (*AA*. 333 Detorakis edition); he heals Alcames (the servant of Stratocles) from possession (*AA*. 334 Detorakis edition); Andrew is described as stranger who practices mighty works and healing beyond

the power of men (*AA.* 341 Detorakis edition); he is also reported to have healed Maximilla (*AA.* 342 Detorakis edition). Within the *Acts of John*, the apostle heals Cleopatra (*AJ.* 23); strikes down and then resuscitates Lycomedes (*AJ.* 21); heals the sick old women of all diseases (*AJ.* 36); raises the dead (*AJ.* 40, 52); destroys the altar of Artemis, killing the priest then raising him from dead (*AJ.* 42, 47); even the bugs are obedient to John (*AJ.* 60-61). The apostle Paul also heals many (*AP.* 28 P. Heid.) and raises the King's cup-bearer Patroclus from the dead (*AP.* 1 Martyrdom of Paul). The apostle Peter similarly heals many sick (*APt.* 128 Berlin Coptic Papyrus) and plays with the paralysis of his daughter, healing her and then making her lame (*APt.* 130 Berlin Coptic Papyrus); see also the story of the 'Gardener's Daughter'.

42 Misset-van de Weg, 'Magic, Miracle', 41.
43 Whereas in the 'romance' type story the happy ending results in marriage, in the 'magical' account, the story ends with the chaste heroine living happily ever after doing God's work.
44 Misset-van de Weg, 'Magic, Miracle', 42.
45 Misset-van de Weg also makes this point, 'Magic, Miracle', 42.
46 Cooper, 'Ventriloquism and the Miraculous', 30.
47 Misset-van de Weg, 'Magic, Miracle', 42.
48 Ibid.
49 Ibid., 44.
50 See e.g. Robert M. Grant, *Early Christians and Animals* (New York: Routledge, 1999), 17-19.
51 Ibid. Spittler, *Animals*, 161, 172-5. See also the story of Daniel and the lion's den in the Old Testament (Dan. 6:1-28).
52 See Grant, *Early Christians and Animals*, 17-19; Spittler, *Animals*, 172-5.
53 The PH manuscript includes the report of Paul's reunion with a speaking lion in the arena at Ephesus. An English translation of Paul's second encounter with the lion is included in *NTA*, 251-4.
54 The three known variants of the Pauline episode, as well as the resemblance between the lion rescues here and the legendary rescue of Androcles, attest to the popularity of lion scenes in antiquity, see Tamás Adamik, 'The Baptized Lion in the Acts of Paul', in *The Apocryphal Acts of Paul and Thecla*, ed. Jan N. Bremmer, 65-70. It should also be borne in mind that the image of Daniel and the lions was widespread in the Roman catacombs and elsewhere, Weitzmann, ed., *Age of Spirituality*, 371, 377, 386-7, 421, 436. See also Robin Margaret Jensen, *Understanding Early Christian Art* (London: Routledge, 2000), 64-93.
55 These images have been found on a pendant, Coptic comb, ring, miniature of Symeon Metaphrastes and an oil lamp, see Ruth Ohm Wright, 'Rendezvous with Thekla and Paul in Ephesos, Excavating the Evidence', in *Distant Voices Drawing Near: Essays in Honor of Antoinette Clark Wire*, ed. Holly E. Hearon (Collegeville, MN: Liturgical Press, 2004), 227-42, 235.
56 Ohm Wright, 'Rendezvous with Thekla', 234; see also Claudia Nauerth, 'Nachlese von Thekla-Darstellungen', in *Studien zur spätantiken und frühchristlichen Kunst and Kuttur des Orients - Göttinger Orientforschungen*, ed. Guntram Koch (Wiesbaden: Harrassowitz, 1986), 16-17.
57 Here, she is often paired with Saint Menas on pilgrim ampulles which have been found all around the Mediterranean, attesting to the popularity of his cult in the fourth to sixth centuries, Ohm Wright, 'Rendezvous with Thekla', 234. See also Weitzmann, *Age of Spirituality*, 575-8.

58 Spittler makes this point, *Animals*, 176.
59 Ibid.
60 Braun, 'Physiotherapy', 214-15.
61 MacDonald, *Early Christian Women*, 35. See also Pomeroy who points out that for the Greeks, chastity was a virtue only in women, Sarah B. Pomeroy, *Goddesses, Whores, Wives and Slaves: Women in Classical Antiquity* (London: Pimlico, 1994), 5. Womanly behaviour was characterized then, as now, by submissiveness and modesty (98); any reward of the 'good' woman in Rome was likely to be praise in stereotypical type phrases whereas in Athens she won oblivion (228).
62 Elisabeth Esch, 'Thekla und die Tiere. Oder: Die Zähmung der Widerspenstigen', in *Aus Liebe zu Paulus? Die Akte Thekla neu aufgerollt*, ed. Martin Ebner (Stuttgart: Stuttgarter Bibelstudien, 2005), 159-79, 169.
63 Ibid., 170.
64 See e.g. Frazer, *The Golden Bough*, 137; Maarten Jozef Vermaseren, *Mithriaca II: The Mithraeum at Ponza* (Leiden: Brill, 1974), 25.
65 Ohm Wright, 'Rendezvous with Thekla', 235, n. 37.
66 Pomeroy, *Goddesses, Whores*, 8.
67 Ibid., 4.
68 Ibid. In this respect, Athena could be regarded as 'One of the Guys', a rare creature in antiquity, see Taylor, *Jewish Women Philosophers*, 239.
69 Pomeroy, *Goddesses, Whores*, 5-6.
70 Ibid., 5, 9.
71 Giselle de Nie, 'Fatherly and Motherly Curing in Sixth-Century Gaul: Saint Radegund's mysterium', in *Women and Miracle Stories*, ed. Anne-Marie Korte (Leiden: Brill, 2001), 57.
72 Samson Eitrem, 'Dreams and Divination in Magical Ritual', in *Magika Hiera: Ancient Greek Magic and Religion*, ed. Christopher Faraone and Dirk Obbink (Oxford: Oxford University Press, 1991), 181-2; see also Gen. 28.10-22 and 37.5-11.
73 On visions, dreams as miracles, see Misset-van de Weg, 'Magic, Miracle', 45, n. 36.
74 Esch, 'Thekla und die Tiere', 169-70.
75 Note that there is no Trinitarian formula here.
76 It is possible that the author had never encountered seals and was, therefore, unaware that they were unlikely to kill Thecla.
77 *The Martyrdom of Saints Perpetua and Felicitas* (21) in Musurillo, *Acts of Christian Martyrs*.
78 See n. 42 above.
79 John Scarborough, 'The Pharmacology of Sacred Plants, Herbs, and Roots', in *Magika Hiera*, ed. Christopher Faraone and Dirk Obbink, 139, 161.
80 Stratton, 'Rhetoric of Magic', 93.
81 Scarborough, 'Pharmacology of Sacred Plants', 140. Scarborough points out that modern psychology has also demonstrated the strong presence of a generalized masculine fear of women, particularly in the basic consideration of sex, so that the student of ancient erotic magic may be forewarned not to accept the notion of a special feminine expertise in drugs, 162.
82 See discussion on Pastoral Epistles in Chapter 2.
83 See discussion in Chapter 5.
84 Misset-van de Weg, 'Magic, Miracle', 49.

85 Note that Thecla's speech conforms to the 'plain speech', reserved for martyr acts. It consists of staccato sentences that are used to reach audiences with maximum effect, see Cooper, 'Ventriloquism and the Miraculous', 40–1.
86 Two versions of this twelfth-century Latin manuscript include this response, C_c and C_d, Vouaux, *Les Actes de Paul*, 217; Misset-van de Weg, 'Magic, Miracle', 47, n. 39.
87 Ibid., 50–2.
88 Ibid., 52.
89 See MacDonald, *Early Christian Women*, 1–8, 73.
90 As noted earlier, it is, of course, significant that later representations of Thecla repeat these images of Thecla with lions and lionesses.
91 Esch, 'Thekla und die Tiere', 169.
92 Note also the story of the young female martyr Blandina who suffers and dies, Euseb., *Hist. Eccl.*, 5.1 (1.51).
93 See n. 41 above.
94 Anne-Marie Korte, ed., 'Epilogue' to *Women and Miracle Stories*, 326.
95 See e.g. Stratton who discusses this common female stereotype, Stratton, 'Rhetoric of Magic', 90–4.
96 Elizabeth Alvida Petroff, *Medieval Women's Visionary Literature* (Oxford: Oxford University Press, 1986).
97 Unlike the stories of Perpetua, Felcitas and Blandina.

7

Violating the inviolate body

Assessing gender construction in the *Acts of Paul and Thecla*

In the previous chapters, I examined the representation of Thecla in regard to her alleged gender transformation, the sado-erotic violence to which she is subjected and the role that magic and miracles play in relation to gender construction. I concluded that Thecla does not become male. She very much remains female in bodily form; however, elements of manly *andreia* fuse with her passive female representation. This is not a positive, female-affirming representation. As a woman, Thecla is degraded and objectified through sado-erotic violence; nevertheless, she is also heralded as goddess-like, and, despite looking like a woman, her body, in its representation of manly inviolability, receives the ultimate acclamation.

There are thus many irreconcilable tensions within the text, but among the greatest of complexities is the chaste/ascetic message, within a text which simultaneously flaunts Thecla's body in erotically and sadistically charged ways. The three elements of virginity, female sexuality and violence remain paramount throughout the story.

As discussed above, erotic spectacle and public denuding were a calculated move by Romans to strip enemies of the state of dignity and power. Sexual dishonour was an integral part of the shaming process and martyrdom was meant to reverse that shame. However, the story of Thecla has a strange twist because, despite being thrown into the arena on two occasions, the heroine survives totally unscathed. The reversal of shame within this text is, therefore, positioned quite distinctly. Thecla survives two martyrdoms while other martyrs, among them the (highly important) male apostles (Paul, Andrew, Peter, Thomas and John), die. How do we reconcile the adulation of Thecla with the denigration to which her body is subjected? How is it possible to make sense of a text which promotes chastity and virginity on the one hand, but which emphasizes an eroticized female body subjected to pain and violence on the other?

It is evident that virginity and the female body are constant themes that run throughout the narrative. Occasionally endowed with subject status, Thecla displays traits of manliness through some of her actions, but she remains feminine with her long hair and dons a male χιτών. Goddess-like, Thecla survives all her ordeals unharmed. However, nowhere within the story can we find traces of the female protagonist attempting to challenge male dominant norms. The story is not, therefore, a protest against patriarchy. Furthermore, Thecla never breaks away from female corporeality. In the flesh she remains a desirable, beautiful female who pleasures the male gaze and every aspect of her body is flaunted for all to see. So Thecla is not gender-neutral. She has a definite female sexuality about her, so much so that men desire her and want to rape her.

It follows that this erotically charged text contains the inherent violence and misogyny of a patriarchal cultural system. The sexualized violence and humiliation of a woman is intimately linked with reverence for the chaste virgin female body. In addition, unlike other martyr stories, which graphically emphasize the pain borne by martyrs and the precious blood spilt in the arena,[1] Thecla remains completely immune to any physical assaults upon her body. Cooper underscores the importance of a heroine's vulnerability within martyr texts. The heroine's vulnerability stands side by side with her heroism as a means of discrediting her and, by implication, the author's opponents. By presenting a vulnerable heroine in this way, the author could illicit the sympathy and allegiance of his readers.[2] However, as the story of Thecla reaches its crescendo, sympathy for the heroine is far from view.

This lack of sympathy stems from the fact that the narrator never speaks of Thecla's pain or shame. Other than one fleeting reference to her weeping (*APTh*. 31) and her desire for Paul, her point of view is never narrated. In remaining silent on this issue, the narrator misses an opportunity to help readers identify with Thecla, thus winning over sympathy for the heroine: she is simply represented as 'robot-like', moving from one ordeal to the next. Since the narrator tells us nothing of Thecla's thoughts and feelings (he does not even speculate or hypothesize from her perspective), we must assume that he does not know her. However, where the pagan men are concerned, the narrator is more internally focalized. We know of the jealousy of Thamyris (*APTh*. 13, 15) and of Alexander's shame (*APTh*. 27). We know that Hermongenes and Demas felt aggrieved (*APTh*. 4). We know that both Governors were reluctant in their condemnation of Thecla (*APTh*. 21, 34, 35). We even know something of the feelings of the powerful woman Tryphaena (*APTh*. 29, 30). However, where Thecla is concerned, the narrator is more distant: he is unknowing. Thus, despite the occasional shifting perspective of pagan men and others, there is little or no information from Thecla's point of view. Unlike Perpetua, we are not coerced into feeling sympathy for her suffering.[3] Men and women mourn the loss of a beautiful woman (*APTh*. 29, 34), but mostly the narrator remains dispassionate and detached from the heroine's point of view.

A martyr's body was meant to be torn, broken, dismembered and burned. Thecla's body remains unharmed, flawless and impregnable. In surviving such extreme torture and danger, Thecla's body receives the highest accolade possible from a masculine perspective.[4] In this way, her body becomes a means of conveying status and control, and, as far as the construction of masculinity is concerned, it is in this way, more than any other, that Thecla 'becomes male'. Perhaps this is why she dons the male χιτών at the close of the narrative. Even two bulls, symbols of the phallus intended to rip her apart, cannot harm her.[5] Thecla's virgin body is thus highly charged with symbolic meaning. A Christian virgin, who is never free from apostolic male control, has a body that behaves in the way a man's body should and ought to behave: it is impenetrable. No wonder this female (with her flowing locks) may now be cloaked in a manly χιτών.

Clearly, then, bodily inviolability is axiomatic within the text. We are encouraged to gaze upon the symbolic naked Thecla even though she is never described. Again and again, Thecla survives extreme torments. She climbs out of fires unharmed; she is protected against wild beasts; her limbs remain intact even when tethered between two raging bulls, and there are no traces of wounds upon her virgin body. The hyperbolic predominates and leaves a lasting impression, and all of this takes place in the Roman arena. A space that Donald Kyle describes as 'a marginal liminal site where Romans confronted the limits of the human versus the natural world'.[6] The narrative plot encourages us to see this link between a Christian female virgin body and Roman sado-erotic violence. Thecla is immune from bodily harm and her chastity protects her from Roman men, violence and violation.

The story sees bodily inviolability converging with an objectified, subjugated and tortured woman to become crucial elements within the text. Whatever happens in the story, be it female elevation or denigration, be it violence or passivity, the site of exchange always remains Thecla's body. Even at the end of the story when the Governor calls Thecla in order to question her miraculous survival, she stands naked before him. The body of a chaste woman was normally concealed, and a female body on display marked that woman as sexually available,[7] but sexual availability is the last thing that is being communicated here. Within the text, there this clear interplay between a Christian female body and Roman power and society. What is particularly interesting is that despite the focus upon Thecla's body and beauty, we are never given a description of her. This 'anonymous' representation of Thecla is reinforced since no physical or psychological effects of the traumas she experiences are ever hinted at, let alone narrated. I return to the question I posed at the end of the last chapter, why, when most martyr stories inevitably end in the martyr's death, is there such a focus on this woman's invincible body?

Picturing female representation

Until now, the story of Thecla has been read variously as a struggle about gender and authority within the church[8] or as means of subverting the social order of society which promotes marriage and maternity.[9] However, while it is the case that the Apocryphal Acts in general demonstrate the destabilizing nature of a Christian chaste ascetic message upon society, and while this motif is also present within the *Acts of Paul and Thecla*, this particular text is unique in its focus upon one indestructible female protagonist and, therefore, warrants individual attention. Thus, as I begin to draw this study to its conclusion, I want to suggest an alternative way in which this story may have been received by men and women alike. This story envisions the female body as an entity that cannot be annihilated. What I would like to suggest is that Thecla is a constructed body, and by transcending the 'natural' weakness and sub-ordination of her gender, by surviving the physical torments unharmed, Thecla is re-embodied as an image of Christian resistance and resilience that speaks back to the Roman Empire.

In speaking about the ideological function of 'virgins' in early Jewish and Christian martyrologies, Daniel Boyarin and Virginia Burrus argue that both Rabbis and Church

Fathers 'identified' with female virgins as a way of 'dis-identification' with Rome, and this is especially because Rome's power was stereotyped as a highly sexualized penetrative male.[10] Both Boyarin and Burrus contend that female virgins in antiquity reflected an ego identification, on the part of male writers, with the vulnerable but chaste female bodies over against the invasive violence of Rome.[11] The virgin thereby serves as a trope for early Christian writers to locate themselves and their communities in opposition to Rome's power and violence, imagined in terms of sexualized masculinity and aggression.

This approach would help to explain the significant focus upon female virginity within the text of the *Acts of Paul and Thecla* and the importance of an inviolable body. Such a reading would see our character Thecla embody and dramatize issues and concerns that deeply affected male Christians.[12] Thus, within the *Acts of Paul and Thecla*, Thecla the virgin represents the vulnerable male Christians. The civic males Alexander, Thamyris and the Governor (highly sexualized males in the story) represent the invasive might of Rome and stand over and against the virgin. The female virgin's body communicates conceptions of inviolability against the invasive and phallic Rome. This is a contest between the aggressive threatening masculinity of Imperial Rome and the vulnerable body of the Church.

How does ego identification work?

That the virgin girl is a topos in both Judaism and Christianity for thinking about male bodies and their relationship to God has, as noted above, been usefully argued by both Boyarin and Burris. Drawing on the citation from Prov. 5.8 ('Keep your way far from her, and do not go near the door of her house', NRSV), Boyarin notes that the Talmudic exploration of the text closely associates the three themes, heresy, collaboration and prostitution: 'Sectarian heresy, prostitution, and collaboration with Roman power had become associated in the cultural "unconscious" of rabbinic Judaism, no doubt at least in part simply because all three are seductive and dangerous.'[13] Thus, men should be wary of the sexual lure of the 'strange woman' figured as collaboration with 'other' secular worldly powers or interests: all of which are gendered as female. By transposing on to themselves the attributes of a woman, men could transform their nature, thus destroying lust and other sensual drives. In short, imitating a woman meant a man could begin to behave like a woman. Eventually, the transformation of the chaste Jewish male into female virgin becomes the one most fit to resist these sexualized enticements. This development can be seen throughout the Talmud. Ego identification with a woman – or becoming 'female' – meant Jewish men could transcend their own sexual desire to be with a woman, that is, to stray either to a foreign power or alternative cult.[14]

Burrus similarly argues that the figure of the female virgin performed symbolically for contemporary Christians such as the fourth-century Bishop Ambrose of Milan. As will be seen below, just like the Rabbis, Ambrose encouraged Christian men to feminize themselves in order to resist male weaknesses and temptations. Burrus notes, 'post-Constantinian Christianity lays claim to the power of classical male speech; yet at the same time late ancient Christian discourse continues to locate itself in paradoxical relation to classical discourse through a stance of feminizing ascesis that renounces public speech.'¹⁵ This process is all part of the move to resist the dominant Roman discourse of masculinity and of masculine sexuality in particular, and forms a crucial aspect of the ancient construction of maleness itself, a construction which becomes ever more complex when set in the context of an 'imperial' Christian discourse. What is particularly interesting for our purposes is that Burrus highlights the way in which Ambrose uses the figure of Thecla for this process of female gender identification.¹⁶ Ambrose rewrites the story of Thecla in a way which conflates the male and female lions that she encounters into one. The two lions within the Thecla story (the female lion which protects Thecla and the male lion which is sent into the arena to devour her) are collapsed into a single male lion. The lion represents the sexual violence and 'rage' of Thamyris and the lust of the men who gaze upon her nakedness as she performs in the arena. Ambrose then develops the story further.

When faced with the attacking lion, Thecla presents her vital parts (*vitalia ipsa*) to the lion. In a feminizing gesture, the lion averts its gaze, becomes tame and honours Thecla by licking her feet (*Virg.* 2.7).¹⁷ Offering her vital parts to the lion symbolizes and enacts a sort of erotic displacement of her sexual parts to her rejected fiancé. Male sexuality is equated with the devouring of a woman and the lion represents the predatory, ravaging desire of husband/empire. The desire to eat the virgin's flesh is seen as commensurate with the lust of her would be husband/empire. However, in the presence of the virgin, the lion is led to transform its bestial and violent sexual male nature, and instead yields to Thecla.

Burrus argues that since the female martyr, as virilized woman, subverted categories of sexuality and gender, she could function as an ego ideal for Christian women. However, as passive virgin (mirrored by the feminized male lion), Thecla is no longer primarily a figure for the virilized female but rather for the feminized male, who upon perceiving her is inspired, like the lion, to a complete renunciation of his 'natural' violent, male sexuality. In this way, the male audience identify with the male lion and the victim.¹⁸

Thus, in both late ancient Christianity and Judaism, via cross-gender identification, the figure of the virgin becomes an ideologically charged symbol through which ideal male identity was secured. This process of male identification with virgins is an important one for understanding the *Acts of Paul and Thecla* as it helps to explain why Thecla maintains her femininity throughout the text, never becoming fully male. Thecla needs to remain a virgin and a woman for this mechanism of ego identification to work.

Of course, it is possible to argue that the embellishments added by Ambrose are not present in the second-century text (i.e. Thecla does not exhibit her private parts to the lion, nor does the male lion change its behaviour and become passive). However, the narrative, as it stands, still contains elements which allow for cross-gender identification, for both men and women. Although Burrus maintains that the passive elements of the text emerge through the particular components added by Ambrose, as has been argued throughout this study, Thecla's representation continually exhibits elements of passivity.¹⁹ The passive submissiveness is manifest from the beginning of the narrative in the Iconium episode. Thecla has a male owner (Thamyris) and she is transfixed by Paul's preaching. A mere passive object, she listens intently to

Paul's word, 'night and day', and does not turn away from the window (*APTh*. 7). As discussed above, she is also compared to an insect that has been captured by the apostle (*APTh*. 8). She is owned, motionless and very much given over to desire for a strange man (*APTh*. 18). When brought before the Governor, Thecla remains unresisting, unassertive and silent, simply 'looking steadily at Paul. And ... she did not answer' (*APTh*. 20). Thecla is portrayed as the passive victim of a powerful man. She has no agency as such. Rather, as noted in Chapter 6, we simply have here the clichéd time-worn ancient patriarchal stereotype of a woman who easily falls prey to a strange exotic man. This passivity spills over into the first arena scene as she seems to be in a trance-like state and sees an apparition of the Lord as Paul (*APTh*. 21). She is also described as a lamb (*APTh*. 21), a vulnerable follower of Paul. Thecla is a mere passive listener and a passive victim.

The theme of passivity continues throughout the narrative in the presentation of a woman who is passed around from man to man (Thamyris, Paul, the Governor, Alexander) and is also evident in the second arena trial where Thecla initially relies on the lioness to protect her (*APTh*. 33) and then the women's herbal magic (*APTh*. 34): she is the passive recipient of miraculous favour; no power is ever worked through her. She never cries out and passively endures sadistic torture and punishment. She is a mute and easy victim. Indeed, for the most part, the text characterizes her as a passive virgin who exhibits only traces of *andreia*, and these more empowered components only loom large at specific points in the text. Thus, while the elements of virility offer the opportunity for women to identify with her, the passive components of her behaviour (which are present throughout the narrative and in the arena scenes) provide the medium through which Christian (possibly ascetic) men could identify with her.

Of course, Thecla's passivity is particularly heightened at the point where she is tied naked by the legs between the two bulls (*APTh*. 35). Although Thecla here is forced to have her vital parts displayed, she nevertheless remains passive and 'intact', both in body (i.e. she is unharmed) and as a virgin. The two raging bulls, metaphorical symbols of the phallus, remain impotent, and she survives unhurt, unblemished and undefiled. As men project their look onto the passive woman and as she withstands the violence, and remains impenetrable, she gives a satisfying sense of omnipotence to those identifying with her. At this point, although her naked body is on display, Thecla has transcended her femaleness as it were. As men identify with her, she is no longer the beautiful female icon, titillating the male audience and possessed by male characters within the narrative. However, she has not escaped male control or possession entirely since she is now instead possessed by male spectators, as a type of castrated male.

Despite the fact that Boyarin and Burrus situate their discussion in late antiquity, there is precedent, very early within Judaism, for this process of 'feminizing' men. The nation of Israel was unique in the ancient world because Yahweh had no female consort. Instead, God's close companion was the nation herself. This imagery is most poignantly described by the prophets Hosea and Ezekiel. The covenant between Israel and Yahweh was imaged as a marriage between God and his people Israel (see, e.g., Ezek. 16.7-14). In addition, Israel's continual interest in foreign deities and cults was depicted as the actions of a whore or loose woman (see, e.g., Ezek. 16.15-26, 28-29, 33-38; 23). Similarly, Hosea attacked the people of Israel for their interest in other cults and accused them of adultery (Hos. 1.2). His accusation led to the symbolic action of marrying a whore. This was meant to imply that just as he could continue to love an unfaithful wife, so too God would always continue in his faithfulness to the people of Israel, despite their infidelity. This image of Israel as God's wife is found throughout the prophetic literature (see, e.g., Isa. 49.18; Jer. 2.2-3.1).[20] If God's unfaithful people could be depicted or identified with a whore, then those who are faithful to God can be likened to a virgin woman. This process of religious men identifying with the feminine is also explored by Eilberg-Schwartz who argues that a consequence of male worshippers relating to a male god results in a homoerotic relationship. One of the ways in which Jewish men negotiated this difficulty, and the resultant loss of manly status, was through feminization.[21]

There are, then, early antecedents for this process of religious men identifying with women or female figures. Indeed, Beverley Roberts Gaventa has brought to light the way in which Paul uses a female metaphor to depict himself as a 'mother' to his communities.[22] Paul also 'feminizes' himself by identifying with defeated nations under Roman rule (Gal. 4.19; 1 Thess. 2.7). He employs gendered imagery in order to portray himself as vulnerable. In this way, he models a masculinity that opposes that of the Romans, thus challenging the dominant paradigm of the period.[23]

The fact that the *Acts of Paul and Thecla* has at its very core the dominant figure of a young female virgin woman prompts further consideration on the use of this topos within the narrative. The absolute insistence upon virginity is introduced almost from the moment Paul begins to preach in the opening of the narrative. Thus, the second beatitude promises that the ones keeping their 'flesh holy' (ἁγνὴν) shall become temples of God (*APTh*. 5). Paul then reinforces this in the next beatitude, stating that God will speak to those who have 'control' (ἐγκρατεῖς, *APTh*. 5) over their bodies. After momentarily turning his attention to the ones who have renounced this world, Paul, in the fifth beatitude, again returns to the theme of chastity to bless those who have wives as if they did not have them (*APTh*. 5). Three of the five opening beatitudes thus firmly set in place the theme of the text: chastity is of supreme importance. Out of the thirteen beatitudes, almost a quarter of them (four) are concerned with this theme, and, having opened up his sermon in this way, Paul returns to the established theme in the final beatitude as he proclaims, 'Blessed are the bodies of the virgins, for they shall be well pleasing to God, and shall not lose the reward of their chastity. For the Word of the Father shall be for them a work of salvation' (*APTh*. 6). The concept of virginity is further reinforced when immediately in the next verse we are told that a young 'virgin' sits listening intently to Paul preaching concerning the pure or holy word (ἁγνείας λόγον) and that many women and 'virgins' go to hear him (*APTh*. 7). Virginity is thus a central and significant motif.

There is also an emphasis, throughout the text, on Thecla remaining a virgin. When Alexander attempts to rape her, she moves out of one of her regular passive states to fight back (*APTh*. 26), and when she is condemned for shaming an important and powerful man, she asks for protection of her chastity (*APTh*. 27). In remaining a virgin, Thecla allows Christians to reconfigure their world in gendered terms and in a way that stands in polarized contrast to the dominant Roman gender paradigm of the period. The contest between the Christians and Rome takes place in the Roman arena where the might of Rome is met with resistance and resilience; it is here that the Christian virgin body challenges and rejects Rome's imperial power. The fact that Rome represented captured lands as the subjugation of women makes this particular representation of the female virgin body more compelling since Christians are employing Roman imagery that many in antiquity will have been familiar with.[24] Through the 'virgin body', the embattled Christians demonstrate the subversive power of God against that of *polis*, civic authority and Roman Empire.

Roman visual representation

Davina Lopez looks at three specific representations of how the Roman Empire communicated their ideology of world rule through the use of gendered imagery in personification of ἔθνη: the Judaea Capta coin; the cuirassed statue of Augustus at Prima Porta, and reliefs from the Sebasteion, the Roman Imperial cult complex at Aphrodisias.[25] These examples all represent male and female bodies in hierarchical relation to one another. They demonstrate not only how Roman Imperial ideology is depicted as thoroughly patriarchal but also how Romans are 'rendered as victorious "super-men" and defeated nations are consolidated into dejected, racially specific, women's bodies'.[26] The Roman Empire was then represented as a conquering man standing over female ethnic personifications. In this way, Roman visual representation affirmed imperial ideology in distinctly gendered ways.

Natalie Boymel Kampen observes that the ideological task of representation is to 'reconfigure the world' and in the process to 'challenge or to reproduce social arrangements in such way as to make institutions and practices seem completely natural, so inevitable and universal'.[27] These images, utilized for visual communication, thus convey sexual status and deliver a gendered Imperial Roman message. They naturalize ideas about Roman hegemony and domination among both elites and the wider population. As Lopez highlights, all who could see and walk past a victory monument would be able to 'read' it. In this way, public art formed a 'symbolic system' or 'grammar' that articulated and naturalized power relationships.[28] The use of such visual images would thus establish the 'proper' Roman power relationship, defining and maintaining the norms of Roman masculinity, state and power.

The Judaea Capta coin type noted by Lopez (Figure 7.1) provides a prime example of the gendered visual propaganda imagery employed by Rome.

This commemorative coin series was issued to celebrate the capture and destruction of Jerusalem in 70 CE and was much reissued. The coin shows a veiled female figure seated on the ground under a palm tree, weeping and looking dejected. The woman symbolizes the Jewish people. The narrow stalk supporting the heavy upper part of the tree transforms the image into a kind of trophy.[29] Standing next to the woman is a victorious Roman soldier who has a very large body in comparison to her. He holds a staff upright in his right hand and a *parazonium* scabbard in his left. The representation highlights the difference between conquered and conqueror. The woman looks

Figure 7.1 'Judaea Capta' coin issued following the destruction of Jerusalem.
Image courtesy of www.romancoins.info, copyright Andreas Pangerl.

crestfallen while the Roman soldier in contrast looks powerful. The imagery on the coin communicates very clearly the idea that Roman forces have defeated and feminized the people of Judaea. The unsubtle positioning of the *parazonium* scabbard in the Roman soldier's groin, with its distinctive shape, is meant to allude to notions of phallic penetration, domination and submission. Antique notions of gender relations and hierarchy are utilized to represent territorial conquest.

The second image (Figure 7.2) of the cuirassed statue of Augustus from Prima Porta similarly reveals this same use of gendered imagery to communicate the conquering of lands.

The statue depicts the emperor dressed in full military parade costume. Such statues were erected throughout the Roman world in honour of reigning and deceased emperors and functioned as an important form of honorific dedication that would have been recognized as such in Rome and its provinces.[30] They belonged to a pattern of triumphal art identifiable in most areas of the Roman Empire and provided a rich visual medium for celebrating the military victories of Rome. They also documented the course of Roman territorial expansion throughout the Mediterranean world. There are more than 600 known cuirassed statues from the Roman Imperial period, of which some 150 depict conquered peoples and nations.[31]

This particular statue depicts the emperor Augustus as a powerfully built 'Herculean' type figure who is well proportioned with tame hair and sturdy-looking legs. He has a muscular body and an athletic physique. The lean and toned body image conveys an ideal Roman masculinity and impenetrable stability: here stands a 'real' man. The images on the cuirass combine history and mythology in order to convey a certain 'story' to the viewers. In the centre, a representative of Rome (either Mars or Tiberius)[32]

Figure 7.2 Emperor Augustus in military dress: marble figure from the Prima Porta.
Image courtesy of the Vatican Museums, Vatican State.

flanked by gods, goddesses and various personifications receives the military standard from the Parthian king (see Figure 7.3).

The scene depicts Rome's 'victory' over the Parthians.[33] The Roman male mirrors the self-same masculinity depicted by the statue of Augustus. He wears a helmet and cuirass, bearing a *paludamentum* (cloak or cape fastened at one shoulder, worn by military commanders) clasped to his shoulder and a dagger at his side. He is a dominant male and a victor. In complete contrast, the Parthian represents a foil to this perfected masculinized image. He has unruly, uncut hair and a big beard and wears loose-fitting trousers that the Romans associated with barbarian peoples who have not achieved their level of masculinity.[34] This representation serves to effeminize the Parthian and by association the entire nation.

The manliness of Augustus and the Roman figure on his cuirass are particularly accentuated by the figures of two women seated at the right and left, just under his

Figure 7.3 Cuirass of Augustus from Prima Porta, Hispania and Gaul.
Image courtesy of the Vatican Museums, Vatican State.

armpits. These allegorical female figures represent the conquered Roman provinces, probably Gaul and Spain, and imply that Roman borderlands have been brought under control (see Figure 7.3).[35] Each woman is shown to be crouching and is depicted in traditional dress with attributes of the ethnic group that she personifies. The cuirass and idealized images promote a manly Augustus and portray Rome's military prowess. Powerful representations communicate Roman ideology. The images serve to enhance the domineering masculinity and submissive femininity at the core of Roman Imperial consciousness. As with the Judaea Capta coin, sexual overtones come to the fore to communicate Rome's victory over conquered nations, represented as women.

The third image to be discussed comes from the relief from the Sebasteion at Aphrodisias (see Figure 7.4).

This particular image represents Claudius overpowering a personified Britannia. Claudius is nude apart from a sword strap and a cape which billows behind him. He looks heroic and masterful and stands over Britannia pulling her head back by her hair. His right knee presses down on Britannia's thigh in order to pin her down. Britannia struggles to defend herself by raising her right hand, her right breast is clearly exposed and with her left hand she tries to stop her dress slipping off the other shoulder. The scene is overtly suggestive of sexual assault. The bare breast is a popular motif in depictions of women as violently defeated (and it is interesting to note that in the later iconography that developed around the Thecla cult, she is depicted more often naked than usual, with many of the representations displaying her partially nude

Figure 7.4 Relief of Emperor Claudius triumphing over Britannia.
From the Sebasteion at Aphrodisias.
Image courtesy of the Aphrodisas Excavations, New York University.

with her breasts clearing showing).³⁶ Britannia, with her long, loose, barbarian hair is dressed in a short χιτών (strikingly this image very much resembles how the heroine Thecla would appear, with her long hair and a masculine χιτών). The representation portrays the vulnerability of Britannia and is meant to evoke the military might of Rome and their ability to subjugate foreign countries. The iconography clearly depicts sexual imagery and is full of strong innuendo of rape. Britannia is poised to be sexually conquered by Claudius, illustrating his impenetrability and her vulnerability.

This relief is one of a number at the Sebasteion in Aphrodisias that depict representations of captured women alongside victorious Roman emperors. Another representation which portrays this drama of vanquished territories shows Nero brutally subduing the nation of Armenia. A muscular Nero helmeted and, like Claudius, nude, wearing only a *paludamentum* draped over his shoulders and a sword strap, is depicted reaching down to the personified Armenia to raise her to her feet. Armenia is slumped on the ground between his legs and, apart from a soft eastern hat, she is revealed as fully naked with her arms spread-eagled by Nero. The nudity expresses the patriarchal discourse of a dominant military order: nude female bodies are displayed in postures of humiliation. The discourse of sexuality and phallic aggression is implicit in these images. The north portico of the relief at Aphrodisias contains around fifty personified female ἔθνη featured as life-size single female bodies. Each female in these relief panels are shown in varying shades of uncivilized femininity. There is variation in their dress, which indicates differences in status, and all are unified in their deference to Roman rule.[37]

Other images may also be added, and, while it is not my purpose to review them all, it may be noted that this representation is evident, not only in public works of art, but also in private collections. The Gemma Augustea, a seven by nine inch engraved sardonyx cameo housed in Vienna's Kunsthistorisches Museum, is a further example of a famous Augustan work of art which similarly constructs the stance of manly victory and an elevated Roman status.[38] It consists of an upper and lower register. The upper level depicts Augustus, naked to the waist and enthroned. He is surrounded by several gods and is being crowned by a personification of *Oikoumene* (the inhabited world) amid symbols of world rule. Within this scene, Roman men communicate control and military prowess through their uniforms and flowing capes.

This victory scene is juxtaposed with the lower register beneath which displays the defeat of people (lands) in varying degrees of subjugation. They are bound, stricken and vanquished, hair is dishevelled and women in state of undress. A woman is shown to be mourning with her hands in her head while the man, much like the Parthian figure on the cuirass of Augustus with his unruly hair, beard and barbarian clothes, has his hands bound behind his back. The figures that surround them show Roman legionary soldiers erecting a trophy pole (a tree trunk adorned with the enemies captured arms and armour). Towards the lower right of the register, two soldiers are shown pulling a captive man and a woman by their hair toward the trophy pole.[39] The symbolism of the hair is significant. The image is intended to present a metaphor of Roman conquest by rape. The theme of gender domination is closely associated with military conquest and the upper register serves to express control over those who are depicted below. Once again, emperors are shown to be vanquishing enemies portrayed as naked figures personifying subject nations and peoples.

Through this representation, Roman military success is advertised in a spectacular way while foreign nations, depicted as individual women or effeminized men, are shown captured, conquered and subjugated. The confrontation between two nations – Rome and Other – is depicted as a struggle between an individual man and an individual woman, or a feminized man. The Roman man is always the victor and the female, or feminized, is the vanquished. We can see the use of representation to communicate social and political mastery. These images invite and draw observers to participate in a narrative of superior Roman masculinity. They demonstrate that gender is a fundamental part of Roman Imperial ideology and its representations. Gender is correlated with ethnicity and social status and utilized in a way that clearly communicates power relationships and hierarchies. Women are shown as dejected, captured and subdued while the Roman male bodies, by contrast, display an erect, virile and stable stance.

If we now consider the *Acts of Paul and Thecla*, the image of the naked Thecla appears in some ways to conform to this pattern of iconography. However, in the use of the virgin body the *Acts of Paul and Thecla* employs this image as a public display of power and resistance. Thus, when Thecla is tied naked between two bulls, despite scorching irons being applied to their genitals to enrage them, she survives. The symbolism of the bulls, owned by the male Alexander, with their red-hot genitals is, as Corrington Streete highlights, 'not difficult to read'.[40] The scene is overtly in line with the lustful and penetrative masculinity of Imperial Rome. The narrative utilizes the virgin body as a visual and textual device that serves the writer's rhetoric.[41] The text becomes a written witness. The virgin body, as spectacle, is a visible symbol of God's power as it was imagined to exist over earthly opposing powers. Thus, Thecla's Christian body is sacrosanct and indestructible. Her inviolate body is a metaphor and a means of conveying status and control.

Christians versus Empire, really?

Here it is important to bear in mind that the story and dating of the text (second century CE) is set in the period of Imperial Rome. The battle between the heroine and beasts in the arena testifies to the cultural realities of Christians living in the Roman Empire. The Christian presbyter writing in second-century Asia Minor about the 'games' and torture of Christians bears witness to the far-reaching influences of the Roman Empire and the clash between colonizer and culture.[42] Just as Christians used prose narratives to tell the story of Jesus in the gospels, they did the same with the acts of the martyrs and the lives of the saints; they too were subjects of a cruel and oppressive regime. Furthermore, the period between 192 and 280 CE was a particularly troubled time for the Roman Empire. Emperor Commodus was assassinated in 192 CE and this saw Septimus Severus come to the fore. During the role of the Severans, there was a marked increase in the importance of the provinces. Politically, Italians were becoming less important as provincials took on more and more of the key positions.[43] Roman power was undoubtedly relevant and very much felt by the locals in the provinces. In a context where Greek and Roman culture intersected, local elites found themselves in various unstable positions with respect to changing social structures. With the erection of imperial images in temples and city centres, one could never escape the body politic of Rome.

Roman Imperial context cannot then be removed from the culture in the Hellenistic Roman world. In addition, it should also be borne in mind that in antiquity, religion and political life were inseparable. The political dimensions of life were deeply enmeshed with the religious and there was no separation between religion and state/political power.[44] It has, in fact, been argued that the imperial cult was the very medium through which imperial power relations were constituted.[45] In this respect, recent studies of Paul have highlighted the importance of situating his letters within a Roman Imperial context and in particular his opposition to the Roman Imperial ideology.[46] This trend in scholarship moves beyond new perspectives on Paul to consider the way in which his letters critique Rome's tyrannical power and instead contemplate a world free from the violence of the Roman order.[47] Within the *Acts of Paul and Thecla*, there is not so much a coded signification as a very clear binary opposition set up between Roman (evidenced by the arena) men and a Christian virgin woman.

However, despite this discussion which contextualizes the narrative, Horsley has noted that by the end of the New Testament era, 'Christian' writers had begun to emphasize that they were not a serious threat to the established Roman Imperial order. He contends that later Christian apologists and martyrs about to face execution asserted that Christians were patriotic and loyal to Caesar despite their allegiance and faithfulness to the one God.[48] Given that the *Acts of Paul and Thecla* does manifest this deference to Caesar (after all, both Governors are shown to be sympathetic towards Thecla despite agreeing to her execution [*APTh*. 21, 22, 35, 38], and ultimately Thecla's persecution is halted due to fear of Caesar, [*APTh*. 36]), how does loyalty to Caesar sit with a text which, I claim, appears to oppose Rome's might?

The point is that although the text does, quite clearly, manifest a contraposition to Roman masculinity, representation and the societal order it is not anti-Empire in the sense of wanting to overthrow Rome, depose Caesar and conquer the world. Rather, the text is asserting that Christians, as the people of God, are impervious and immune to the might of Rome; the masculinity of Christian men can withstand Roman domination. Thus, situated within an Imperial Roman frame of reference, something very specific is being communicated in a text which tells the story of a virgin female Christian who remains impenetrable to imperial violence. As discussed in Chapter 4, Roman society placed an inordinate amount of importance on an inviolable body. This concept was closely associated with masculine Roman identity and formed an integral part of the composite culture of the period. It is the idea that those who control the body are the ones possessing ultimate authority and control.

Dunn has also underscored the unequivocal encratic nature of the *Acts of Paul and Thecla*.[49] He defines 'encratism' as 'any form of Christianity which not simply encourages but requires a rigid asceticism, manifested chiefly by the total abstinence from sexual intercourse'.[50] By this understanding, encratism is, therefore, chiefly concerned about the struggle for power and dominance over the sexual inclinations of the body. Through chaste practice, the body can be harnessed as a source of power. As the discussion on virginity above has highlighted, the narrative of the *Acts of Paul and Thecla* states, very early on, the importance of self-control and virginity:

Blessed are those who have kept the flesh holy (*APTh*. 5)
Blessed are the ones having control (ἐγκατεῖς) (*APTh*. 5)
Blessed are they who have wives as if they had them not (*APTh*. 5)
Blessed are the bodies of the virgins (*APTh*. 6)

There is clearly, then, a bodily discourse embedded within the text of the *Acts of Paul and Thecla*. Furthermore, and again as noted in the discussions above, Thecla's bodiliness is stressed over and over again, and, although powerful civic men appear to control her body, it is nonetheless inviolable against all forms of Roman attack. Conversely, the pagan male characters display evidence of a violent, sexually aggressive Roman masculinity. Meanwhile, Thecla as a chaste virgin has an inviolable, protected body. Impenetrability is a Roman, masculine quality, and as highlighted above, gender was not a given but an acquired and proven state, an on-going process. Bearing in mind that gender and sexual difference operate firmly within the structures of power, and the fact that categories of male and female, masculinity and femininity, are performatively produced, it follows that through the mechanism of ego identification, Christians could claim to be impervious to Roman power and control. Within the text, the virgin body becomes the primary site by which to establish personal and corporate identity. The social relationship between ruler and ruled is enacted and renegotiated and thus reconfigured anew.

Caroline Vander Stichele and Todd Penner helpfully underscore the fact that Christians redeployed various tropes against imperial agendas and in the process created distinctive identities and discourses.[51] The shifting balance of political and social power in the ancient world was regularly mediated and modified through language and literature. In this way, narrative fiction can play a role in resistance against repressive authorities. That texts were utilized in this way and formed a crucial element in the formation of Christian identity has been argued by Lieu, Castelli, Boyarin and Shaw, and this seems to be right here.[52] Christian martyr acts, in particular, were seen to play an important role in this respect. Castelli, for example, notes that early Christian writers used martyrs 'to think with' in order to both construct identity and 'turn around' the spectacle of violence and passivity to their own ends.[53] She asserts, 'One might even go so far as to argue that they did not simply preserve the story of persecution and martyrdom but, in fact *created* it.'[54] Castelli reminds us that early Christian texts are intensely rhetorical in their character and, therefore, 'require approaches that treat them in their textuality rather than approaches that presume their documentary status'.[55] The reading and hearing of such narratives helped to inspire a largely non-literate audience and 'trained' early Christians, in shaping their perceptions of the Christian way of life, thus cultivating a particular subjectivity.[56] In this way, the Christian church not only reinterpreted martyrdom as the triumph of a faithful spirit over a vulnerable body but also supplied a history and dominant image of what it meant to be Christian.

As noted in Chapter 5, Cobb similarly argues that the martyrologies were written to reveal the strength, resolve, power and solidarity of Christianity as a social group. The texts helped to create social identities not only for the community experiencing persecution but also for subsequent generations of Christianity, a process essential to group survival.[57]

Perhaps more importantly, Cobb highlights the fact that scholars rarely consider the importance of the physical location where Christian identity formation took place, the Roman amphitheatre: one of Rome's most famous structures. As noted above, the Roman arena was not simply about entertainment; it was a potent symbol of power, rife with political meaning. In this respect, the amphitheatre is not incidental to the story of the martyrs.

Cobb draws attention to the pertinent quote from Keith Hopkins who states that for Romans, the amphitheatre was 'their parliament'.[58] Associated with complex discourses, it is where Romans assembled to make their voices heard. This is evidenced by the fact that sometimes participants, as well as spectators, could influence the results of the games.[59] It was, therefore, a place where, on occasion, the authority of Rome and its emperor would be challenged. It was this which made the arena a place for the negotiation for power rather than the exertion of it.[60] The amphitheatre thus became valuable to the story of the martyrs because it was a place where the possession of power was contested and where masculinity and masculine *virtus* was displayed, even by female martyrs.[61]

Since the arena was a highly contested site, a place of constant struggle between emperor and people as to how power was to be distributed and where sovereignty lay, it was also a culturally productive site for the negotiation of power and a prized location for Christian authors to appropriate and reimagine that power and its dynamics. Locating Christian martyrdom in the amphitheatre thus had great potential for the formation of Christian identities that were based on the possession of strength and power, an ideal setting for Christians to use in the construction of their social identities.[62]

We can certainly see this interplay of shifting political and social power within the *Acts of Paul and Thecla*. What we have in this text is a bodily discourse, set alongside the theme of virginity. A Christian virgin woman is stripped naked and exposed within a Roman arena. She is also subjected to horrific violence and abuse. However, this martyrdom story has a strange twist because each time the virgin is brought naked into the arena, events take an unexpected turn and the balance of power is overturned as the heroine survives all forms of assault. From a Roman perspective, as Thecla is stripped naked and thrown into the arena, she is being shamed, controlled and subjugated, put in her place by the dominant masters. However, rather than cowering and showing fear and terror, Thecla emerges from a regular state of passivity and instead displays power (δύναμιν, *APTh*. 22), so much so that the Governor weeps and marvels at her. Thecla continues in this powerful vein throughout the arena scenes. She stretches her arms out to the sides and makes the sign of the cross as she mounts the pyre (*APTh*. 22). Thecla thus persists in resisting the image of a subjugated and shamed woman. This imagery contravenes the representations of captured women in Roman art and iconography. Here, women's naked bodies and captured state demeans and humiliates them: they are conquered, powerless, pulled by the hair, weeping and desperate. The figure of a naked woman exhibiting power in the midst of a Roman arena, however, tells a different story.

These counter images are reinforced throughout the text. As Paul and Thecla travel to Antioch, there is, once again, an attempt to subjugate the woman and put her in her place. When Alexander's attempt to buy Thecla is unsuccessful, he decides to take her by force (*APTh*. 26). The obvious outcome to any encounter between a powerful, lust-crazed man and a vulnerable woman is usually rape. However, here again there is an unforeseen outcome, not because Thecla escapes, but because she manages to completely turn the tables on her assailant. Rather than having her clothes ripped off when Alexander attacks her, Thecla manages to tear off his manly cloak. She also pulls the crown (στέφανον) from his head, making him a laughing stock (*APTh*. 26). How could any woman, in reality, overpower such a man and shame him? The point is that the male is being depicted as impotent, feeble and vulnerable while the female is shown to be inviolable – gender roles are reversed. Roman masculinity represents the man as the conquering, impenetrable hero and the female his subjugated victim. The *Acts of Paul and Thecla*, however, depicts the complete antithesis to this representation.

It could also be argued that allusion to Rome is reflected in the mention of Alexander's crown which Thecla pulls off his head. Scholars have long noted that since Thecla is charged with being sacrilegious (Ιερόσυλος, *APTh*. 28; ἱερόσλον, *APTh*. 32), she is punished in the arena for damaging the imperial image on Alexander's crown.[63] Based on the earliest Syriac versions of the text, Simon Price has argued that the crown was almost certainly that of a priest of the imperial cult who would also have been responsible for the games in the arena. The crown will have carried an imperial image and was an important expression of imperial ideology.[64] This would help to make sense of the accusation against Thecla: she is a woman 'Guilty of Sacrilege' (*APTh*. 28, 32). This entire scene is, therefore, significant in its allusions to Imperial Rome and Thecla clearly stands over and against the 'dominant' masters.

With a further mention of her crime, the 'sacrilegious one' (*APTh*. 32) is again brought to the arena for a second time. Once again, she is stripped naked and put in her place (*APTh*. 33). However, Thecla continues to defy Rome's power with her dynamism and action. After a confrontation with the wilds beasts, she defies all odds to survive and then jumps into a pit of water to baptize herself (*APTh*. 34). An important and symbolic Christian rite (albeit irregular) serves to bring attention to this woman's religious affiliation in the midst of a Roman setting. All ideas of a subjugated and dejected female are countered. Instead, Thecla is a resistant and unyielding Christian who cannot be overpowered. There is no taming this inviolate virgin: she cannot be vanquished. As a result, the violence directed towards Thecla is escalated. What better way to conquer this woman than to forcibly pull her legs apart (as would be the case in any violent rape) and tether her between two powerful (and enraged) masculine symbols: bulls (*APTh*. 35). Just as bulls represent the phallic, so too do the red-hot irons that are applied to their bellies. In all likelihood, this description refers to their private parts, which are now torturously branded (*APTh*. 35).[65] It is difficult to escape the symbolism of the male (phallus) inflamed with desire, with Thecla as the passive recipient, suffering what is done to her. The fact that there are here *two* phallic symbols intensifies the nature of this display. The two bulls represent Roman phallic aggression; they are the substitute penises intended to rip her apart.

Dworkin argues that one of the tenets of male supremacy is that sexual power authentically originates in the penis, and indeed the sexual power of the phallus dominates in this scene. Dworkin goes on to note that force and violence confirms the male in his masculinity and is seen as the essential purpose of the penis, its animating principle as it were. The penis must embody the violence of the male in order for him to be male. Throughout male culture, the penis is seen as a weapon, especially a sword; in fact, the word 'vagina' literally means 'sheath'.[66] As noted above, the Judaea Capta coin employs this exact imagery to communicate the capture and subjugation of the Jewish people (see Figure 7.1). The representation on the coin very graphically depicts a Roman soldier standing over a pacified and conquered female Judaea, with a provocatively positioned and distinctively shaped *parazonium* scabbard in the groin area. The sword overtly emphasizes the Roman soldier as both victorious/violent conqueror and phallic penetrator.

Robert Sutton, in an examination of sexually explicit vase paintings, which appear primarily on the cups and bowls intended for men's symposia in antiquity, similarly notes that sexual violence was an integral part of the symposium and that this served in part to develop male supremacist behaviour in young men.⁶⁷ The majority demonstrate a propensity towards representations of female debasement, torture and violence.⁶⁸ Like the imagery on the Judaea Capta coin, the representations convey the idea that women need to be violently conquered and subjugated. The scene which recounts Thecla's voyeuristic ordeal in the arena displays Roman sadistic male supremacy. Violence and degradation are an integral part of Thecla's punishment in the arena. However, as an inviolable Christian virgin, Thecla cannot be penetrated by Rome's phallic might. Through miraculous intervention she escapes – intact and unharmed.

Following her triumph in the arena, the Governor summons Thecla and questions her as to her survival (*APTh.* 37). Upon her response it becomes evident that, even now, she stands naked before him (*APTh.* 38). Whereas public nakedness was meant to humiliate and mortify women, emphasizing their powerlessness and subjugation, as land and peoples, here there is defiance: Thecla stands proud and valiant. She demonstrates a boldness and bravado that challenges Roman gender power relationships and, as a result, she eventually dons a male χιτών (*APTh.* 40). A virgin Christian woman has been involved in not one contest, but two, with Rome. She has also made a mockery of the imperial image and yet she emerges intact, unharmed and proud. The contest ultimately results in a kind of equitability: the virgin is impervious to Roman brutality and assault. These motifs and themes parallel and correspond to Roman representation and the importance of impenetrability for men in the Roman world.

When all of this is set beside religious men's propensity to feminize themselves and the importance of literature in creating a distinctive Christian identity, a new reading of the text begins to emerge. Here, Christians produce a superior, stable identity for themselves. However, at the same time they produce a 'fiction' in regard to the story of the martyr Thecla. Furthermore, in terms of fostering their identity over and against Roman masculinity, they produce a fiction in regard to their own masculinity. They are not, in reality, the powerful ones.

Candida Moss has seriously questioned what she calls the 'myth' of martyrdom and persecution in early Christianity. She argues that in the first 250 years of Christianity, Christians were regarded with superstition, as irritants, and that Roman persecution was never prolonged or systematic.⁶⁹ She notes that when Christians were persecuted, it was not for their faith, as such, but because they stubbornly refused to participate in the public cults and it was this that led to their deaths and execution.⁷⁰ Moss is not alone in pointing out that Christians were not systematically persecuted. The sporadic and more localized persecution that Christians are likely to have suffered has been highlighted previously.⁷¹ However, even if Christians were not subjected to systematic and prolonged persecution, they were still regarded with mistrust and suspicion. Paula Fredriksen notes, for example, the rumours that were associated with Christians who were thought of as a sect involved in cannibalism and incest. She also notes, like Moss, that once a Christian was in court, they were expected to show respect to the authorities in the form of honouring the emperor's image or eating meat dedicated to the gods, and sometimes they refused to comply and met with the consequences.⁷²

Christians were, then, seen to be difficult and disrespectful and were consequently viewed, in the eyes of the Romans and society, as antisocial. Thus, even if Christians were not systematically persecuted over long periods of time, the fact that they were a small, nonconformist, unorthodox sect means not only that they were prosecuted (as opposed to persecuted) but also that they would have been subject to prejudice by locals and members of their communities. Such treatment would have had an impact. Moss also strongly indicates that it is more the 'belief' that people are 'persecuted' that empowers them to fight back. The 'rhetoric' of persecution alone 'legitimates and condones' a response. When 'disagreement' between groups is viewed as 'persecution', people who regard themselves as innocent sufferers feel provoked and want to fight back – rhetorically and literally – to defend themselves.[73]

Christians, viewed as mavericks, were subjected to prosecution for breaking the law. They would have been subject to bias and discrimination, resulting in a mindset where they saw themselves as separate and downtrodden: different to 'others'. This would have had an impact upon their sense of self and their identity but not, necessarily, in a negative way. In looking at the psychological effects of prejudice on early Christians, Paul Holloway highlights research which has confounded the view that prejudice is inevitably psychologically damaging. Indeed, the opposite has, repeatedly, been shown to be the case. Social stigma can result in people becoming 'remarkably resilient' and

> [f]ar from mechanically internalizing stigma they [the stigmatized] regularly exhibit levels of esteem equal to if not greater than their non-stigmatized counterpart … Targets of prejudice exhibit a wide variety of coping strategies.[74]

Writing and reading narratives in which Christians depicted themselves as having 'power' and being 'manly' and 'in-control' may well have been cathartic while also functioning as a coping strategy at the same time. Thus, whether or not Christians were systematically persecuted, the fact that they were regarded with misgiving and behaved in ways that subverted the norms of society would have culminated in a 'persecuted' mindset which was psychologically 'processed' through narrative.

Burrus and Rebecca Lyman have argued that ideas of persecution simultaneously also created the context for the emergence of practices and ideologies of martyrdom that placed Christianity in a public stance of political resistance to empire.[75] This is surely right. Clearly, within the *Acts of Paul and Thecla*, the female Christian martyr story responds – there is ultimately no contest in the battle between the Kingdom of God and the earthly empire of Rome – any attempt by Rome to triumph over the Christian 'nation' symbolized by Thecla's body is rendered futile.[76]

This narrative then reveals how Thecla functions as a trope in early Christian discourse. The depiction of Thecla relies on the existing stereotype of woman as weak and vulnerable – much like the early Christians who are victimized and stigmatized within the Roman Empire. The text seeks to redress this balance of power – through the tropes of chastity and the miraculous virgin body – to demonstrate that Christians are not without power against the imperial might of Rome.

The community, or ἐκκλσηία, of Christ made up the body of 'the church'. It is quite relevant that in early Christian iconography, the church is often represented as a chaste woman, the 'Bride of Christ' (Rev. 19.7).[77] For example, the fourth-century mosaic of Santa Pudenziana in Rome shows the 'Church of the Gentiles' and the 'Church of the Circumcision' as two nun-like figures. More specifically, Monika Peshty has highlighted the unpublished *Cathedral Homily* 97 of Severus of Antioch, the Syrian Orthodox patriarch from 512 to 518, which was dedicated to Saint Thecla. Thecla is explicitly defined as being representative of the church, the bride of Christ: 'Examine in the case of Thecla what I have said and you will understand at once that through the person of the church and through what I have said, the martyr has been depicted and represented in advance,'[78] states Severus, and, as Catherine Burris and Lucas van Rompay note, '[f]or Severus ... Thecla is above all an image of the church'.[79] The representation of Thecla within the text of the *Acts of Paul and Thecla* may also be read in this way. By transcending the 'natural' weakness and subordination of her gender, by surviving the physical torments unharmed, Thecla is re-embodied as an image of the church itself. Her story defines a Christian resistance and resilience, on behalf of the ἐκκλσηἰα, that speaks back to the Roman Empire.

Authorial intention: Do I know something others don't?

Ultimately, of course, a reading such as this impacts upon authorial intention. Given that authorial intention is a highly contested area, how is it possible to reconcile this reading with claims that we can never truly ascertain an author's intention?

Since all texts are intrinsically multivalent, I am putting this interpretation forward as just one way in which the representation within the narrative may have been received by audiences and/or readers alike. Jacques Derrida has argued that appealing to authorial intention as the locus of meaning is a political claim, functioning to authorize or privilege certain interpretations and readings over others.[80] However, my aim is not to privilege this as the only reading and the author's only true intended meaning. I am aware of the difficulty of attempting to ascertain authorial intention. Roland Barthes's symbolically entitled essay, 'The Death of the Author', demonstrates that authorial intention soon becomes inaccessible to subsequent readers, if it is indeed ever accessible. Along with Derrida, Roland Barthes argues against traditional literary criticism's practice of incorporating the intentions of an author in an interpretation of a text and instead maintains that writing and creator are unrelated.[81] Derrida underscores the fact that an author can never have complete control or mastery over what he or she writes, and neither can control be exercised in how texts are received by readers.[82] Since authors have little or no effect on the way texts are subsequently read by various readers, it follows that there are many possible ways to interpret a text and no one specific approach or interpretation is the 'correct' reading. There can then be several legitimate interpretations of a text, and the reader's interpretation is just as valid as that of the author's intended meaning.

Thus, although I put this particular reading forward, I do not claim that it is the only legitimate one. Since texts are multivalent, their interpretation is also many and varied. I simply offer one (further) possible exploration of how this text may have been received by men and women alike. For example, from as early as the second century, the writings of Tertullian demonstrate that the Thecla tradition was subject to various interpretations. Tertullian not only provides us with the 'alleged' authorial intention of the *Acts of Paul and Thecla* (i.e. in order to add to Paul's honour) but also demonstrates at least two possible ways in which the text was received or read by audiences.[83] First, according to Tertullian, it appears that women read this text in a way which gave them authority to teach and baptize. Second, due to his views on women, Tertullian received the text in a way which led him to regard it as completely spurious and misguided. If we can take Tertullian's reference at face value, that a presbyter in Asia Minor penned the *Acts of Paul and Thecla*, it also demonstrates very clearly that even if we can get to authorial intention once texts are in the public domain, we lose control of them. In this particular case, a Christian male wrote the story to add to Paul's reputation, but some women interpreted the story (and possibly also informed by wider traditions) in ways which empowered them to teach and preach.

Modern interpretations have also varied in their approach to the text, some reading it as proof of women's active Christian ministry and authority in antiquity, and others viewing the stories more a type of Christian novel.[84] Within this milieu of interpretation, I offer a new and alternative perspective. As a feminist in the twenty-first century, I struggled to identify with this particular female character that many viewed as 'empowered'. By assessing gender construction within the text and contextualizing the narrative, I have, therefore, attempted to make sense of some of the contradictions that present within the story. I have argued that the text represents a struggle between minority Christians and Roman power structures. From this perspective, the text presents a rhetorical strategy in a particular power struggle and, through a process of ego identification, men and women read it, identify with the heroine and find a sense of identity, dignity and empowerment.

The effect of Thecla's gender-bending (i.e. her partial masculinization) along with the representations of both passivity and *andreia* allowed men to identify with her. Penetration, for Romans, is equated with domination and at the top of the social ladder stood the impenetrable penetrator. Jonathan Walters has highlighted that the impenetrable boundaries of the social body are drawn around those of the adult male, physical body.[85] As Thecla's body is protected from intrusion, assault and penetration, social relationships of power are re-inscribed and rewritten. As someone who remains impenetrable, the virgin Thecla is shown to stand at the top of the social pyramid, all the while paying deference to Caesar and Rome. She is not, then, female-affirming, in any simple way: she is a female body which remains feminine and is only partially masculinized in order to serve male ends. Ultimately, her purpose is to be male-affirming, a symbol of the church for men, who 'looked' at her voyeuristically on the one hand and identified with her on the other.

Conclusion

As Cooper highlights, women provided an excellent literary tool for storytellers to think with.[86] In this respect, it is vital that all early Christian texts be examined with a view to establishing their rhetorical strategy and their tendency to tailor both fact and fiction to rhetorical ends.[87] The *Acts of Paul and Thecla* stands out in contrast to the other Apocryphal Acts in its single-minded focus upon a young virgin protagonist. It also stands out in contrast to most other martyrdom stories since the heroine has a body that is immune to Roman power and brutality. In the case of emerging Christianity, the execution and prosecution of Christians as criminals, by the Roman Imperial government, was an attempt in a literal and immediate way to exercise power over the bodies of Christians, as an inherently rebel group.

Roman Imperial representation employed gendered bodies and sexual difference to communicate, both visually and symbolically, that Romans are the dominant masters, 'on top' and 'in control'. Sexual conquest was an effective tool of state control. It was employed as a metaphor for expansionism in the history of imperial politics, colonialism and nation-building because it effectively communicated dominant power relationships.[88] Those who do the penetrating are 'male' and the land is 'female' and vulnerable to penetration. This construction ensures that inhabitants are effeminized by the masculine conquerors.

Christians, as inhabitants of the empire, will have been exposed to Roman Imperial representation. Such imagery would provide a strong impulse and impetus to reconfigure that representation in ways that helped them contest Roman domination. I believe that it is particularly significant that the story of the *Acts of Paul and Thecla* is embedded in the *Acts of Paul*, the apostle to the 'nations' (Rom. 11.13). This also explains the emphasis upon Thecla's naked body and why she is never fully masculinized. Thecla has to remain female in order for the imagery to work. Indeed, with her long hair and her short manly χιτών, she resembles the Amazonian type figure of Britannia found on the relief in Sebasteion. The arena thus becomes a gendered space where the female virgin body resists and speaks back to the Roman Empire. The Roman masculine empire has no power over this new Christian ἔθνος, featured as a virgin woman. Indeed, Richard Valantasis has cogently argued that Christians identified themselves as a separate race.[89]

Much has been made of a Christian martyr's willingness to bear physical pain and to suffer death for their faith with dignity as a way of subverting the humiliation of Roman torture and death.[90] As noted by Kate Cooper,

> the spectacular enactments of social power undertaken in the arena were not merely *reflections* of the social order: by requiring – and generally obtaining – the humiliation of those who stood out of place, they brought the social order into being. For a martyr to best his executors by dying with dignity, his message intact, was more than a symbolic gesture: it struck at the heart of the social contract.[91]

The story of Thecla takes that subversion a number of steps further. In the struggle for dominance within the arena, the *Acts of Paul and Thecla* completely rewrites the social contract in a way which leaves Christianity impervious to Roman power. Christians redeployed various tropes against imperial agendas and in the process created distinctive discourses and identities. The representation of Thecla in the *Acts of Paul and Thecla* demonstrates one of the ways in which Christians reconfigured their identity over and against Roman masculinity and power. Such a reading certainly helps to make sense of Thecla's contradictory representation. Engaging with an inviolable virgin body within the arena resists and destabilizes Rome's power, while Christian men remain intact and impenetrable. They are now the 'real' men.

Notes

1. See e.g. Clark, 'Bodies and Blood', 108. See also, Joyce E. Salisbury, *The Blood of Martyrs: Unintended Consequences of Ancient Violence* (London: Routledge, 2004).
2. See Cooper, 'Voice of the Victim', 155–7.
3. See *The Martyrdom of Saints Perpetua and Felicitas* (20) in Musurillo, *The Acts of Christian the Martyrs*.
4. Walters, 'Invading the Roman Body', 30; Skinner, 'Ego Mulier', 134–6.
5. 'The ταῦρος, bull … is the phallus', Henderson, *The Maculate Muse*, 127; see also Rabinowitz, 'Politics of Containment', 48.
6. Kyle, *Spectacles of Death*, 10.
7. Clark, 'Bodies and Blood', 103.
8. See e.g. Davies, *Revolt of the Widows*; Burrus, *Chastity*; MacDonald, *Legend*.
9. See e.g. Cooper, *Virgin and the Bride*; Perkins, *The Suffering Self*; Aubin, 'Reversing Romance'. See also Chapter 1.
10. Daniel Boyarin, *Dying for God: Martyrdom and the Making of Christianity and Judaism* (Redwood, CA: Stanford University Press, 1999), 67–92, 79; Virginia Burrus, 'Reading Agnes: The Rhetoric of Gender in Ambrose and Prudentius', *JECS* 3 (1995): 25–46.
11. Boyarin, *Dying for God*, 67–92; Burrus, 'Reading Agnes', 28–9.
12. See Cooper's book, *Virgin and the Bride*, which provides an extended exploration of the ways in which male authors in antiquity utilize female representation in rhetorical struggles for prestige and power.
13. Boyarin, *Dying for God*, 68.
14. Ibid., 69–74.
15. Burrus, 'Reading Agnes', 44.
16. Ibid., 30–3.
17. 'Docuerunt etiam castitatem, dum virgini nihil aliud nisi plantas exosculantur, demersis in terram oculis, tamquam verecundantibus, ne mas aliquis vel bestia virginem nudam videret', cited in Burrus, 'Reading Agnes', 32–3.
18. Burrus, 'Reading Agnes', 44–6.
19. See e.g. Chapters 4 and 5.
20. See Rev. 21.2, 9, where Jerusalem is depicted as God's bride. See also Rev. 17.1-6 where Rome is depicted as a whore.
21. Howard Eilberg-Schwartz, *God's Phallus and Other Problems for Men and Monotheism* (Boston, MA: Beacon Press, 1994), see esp. 97–105, 163.
22. Beverly Roberts Gaventa, *Our Mother Saint Paul* (Louisville, KY: Westminster John Knox Press, 2007). See also Beverly Roberts Gaventa, 'Our Mother St. Paul: Toward the Recovery of a Neglected Theme', *PSB* 17 (1996): 29–44.
23. See also Davina C. Lopez, 'Before Your Very Eyes: Roman Imperial Ideology, Gender Constructs and Paul's Inter-Nationalism', in *Mapping Gender*, ed. Todd Penner and Caroline Vander Stichele, 154–61, who discusses how Paul presents himself as a man who was formerly impenetrable, a paradigm of Roman Imperial masculinity but, after his conversion, moves from a masculine identity to a feminized, dominated, one.
24. As highlighted in n. 20 above, in the book of Revelation, the cities of Jerusalem and Rome are gendered female.
25. Lopez, 'Before Your Very Eyes', 115–62.
26. Ibid., 118.

27 Natalie Boymel Kampen, 'Epilogue, Gender and Desire', in *Naked Truths: Women, Sexuality and Gender in Classical Art and Archaeology*, ed. Ann Olga Koloski-Ostrow and Claire L. Lyons (London: Routledge, 1997), 267.
28 Lopez, 'Before Your Very Eyes', 118.
29 Steven Fine, *Art and Judaism in the Greco-Roman World: Toward a New Jewish Archaeology* (Cambridge: Cambridge University Press, 2005), 143.
30 Cornelius C. Vermeule, *Roman Imperial Art in Greece and Asia Minor* (Cambridge, MA: Harvard University Press, 1968), 41–6.
31 See Richard A. Gergel, 'Costume as Geographic Indicator: Barbarians and Prisoners on Cuirassed Statue Breastplates', in *The World of Roman Costume*, ed. J. Sebesta and L. Bonfante (Madison: University of Wisconsin Press, 2001), 191–208.
32 Karl Galinsky, *Augustus: Introduction to the Life of an Emperor* (Cambridge: Cambridge University Press, 2012), 76.
33 On the prima porter, see Paul Zanker, *The Power of Images in the Age of Augustus*, trans. Alan Shapiro (Ann Arbor: University of Michigan Press, 1998), 188–92.
34 Gergel, 'Costume as Geographic Indicator', 195.
35 John Dominic Crossan, 'Roman Imperial Theology', in *In the Shadow of Empire: Reclaiming the Bible as a History of Faithful Resistance*, ed. Richard A. Horsley (Louisville, KY: Westminster John Knox Press, 2008), 59–73, 69.
36 Beth Cohen, 'Divesting the Female Breast of Clothes', in *Naked Truths: Women, Sexuality and Gender in Classical Art and Archaeology*, ed. Ann Olga Kolski-Ostrow and Claire L. Lyons (London: Routledge, 1997), 72, 74, 77. Dagron, *Vie et Miracles*, 37.
37 See Lopez, 'Before Your Very Eyes', 140–1.
38 Fred S. Kleiner, *A History of Roman Art* (Boston, MA: Clark Baxter, 2010), 106–7.
39 On the Gemma Augustea, see Zanker, *The Power of Images*, 230–2.
40 Corrington Streete, *Redeemed Bodies*, 88.
41 Corrington Streete makes this point about martyr's bodies, ibid., 15.
42 Tert., *De bapt.* 17.5.
43 See e.g. Pat Southern, *The Roman Empire from Severus to Constantine* (New York: Routledge, 2001), esp. p. 2.
44 Honours and festivals for the emperor were widespread and pervaded public life, particularly in Greece and Asia Minor, see Simon R. F. Price, *Rituals and Power: The Roman Imperial Cult in Asia Minor* (Cambridge: Cambridge University Press, 1984).
45 Richard A. Horsley, ed., *Paul and Empire: Religion and Power in Roman Imperial Society* (Harrisburg, PA: Trinity, 1997), 4.
46 Dieter Georgi, *Theocracy in Paul's Praxis and Theology*, trans. David E. Green (Augsburg, MN: Fortress, 1991); Neil Elliott, *Liberating Paul: The Justice of God and the Politics of the Apostle* (New York: Orbis, 1994).
47 Scholars who examine the counter imperial aspect of Paul's writings include e.g. Richard A. Horsley and Neil A. Silberman, *The Message and the Kingdom: How Jesus and Paul Ignited a Revolution and Transformed the Ancient World* (Augsburg, MN: Fortress, 2002); John Dominic Crossan and Jonathan L. Reed, *In Search of Paul: How Jesus' Apostle Opposed Rome's Empire with God's Kingdom* (San Francisco, CA: Harper, 2004); N. T. Wright, *Paul: In Fresh Perspective* (Augsburg, MN: Fortress, 2005). It should be noted, however, that not all scholars agree with this view of Paul. John Barclay, e.g., argues that although Paul's gospel could be read as an analogy to counter the imperial cult it is neither how Paul meant nor intended it. He contends that Paul's theology is deeply political but in a way that makes Rome far less central and more of a marginal consideration. See e.g. John M. G. Barclay, *Pauline Churches*

and *Diaspora Jews* (Grand Rapids, MI: Eerdmans, 2016), esp. his chapter 'Why the Roman Empire Was Insignificant to Paul', 363–88.
48 Horsley, *Paul and Empire*, 1.
49 Dunn, 'The Acts of Paul', 77.
50 Ibid., 70.
51 Caroline Vander Stichele and Todd Penner, *Contextualizing Gender in Early Christian Discourse: Thinking Beyond Thecla* (London: T&T Clark, 2009), 81.
52 Lieu, *Christian Identity*; Castelli, *Martyrdom and Memory*; Boyarin, *Dying for God*; Brent Shaw, 'Body, Power, Identity: Passions of the Martyr', *JECS* 4 (1996): 269–312. See also Perkins, *The Suffering Self*.
53 Castelli, 'The Ambivalent Legacy'.
54 Castelli, *Martyrdom and Memory*, 25.
55 Ibid.
56 Nicole Kelley, 'Philosophy as Training for Death: Reading the Ancient Christian Martyr as Spiritual Exercises', *Church History* 75, no. 4 (2006): 724. Kelley rightly notes that not all Christians believed martyrs were to be emulated (p. 727). Paul Middleton defines that, by the end of the second century, there were mainly three established views among Christians when it came to martyrdom: those who scorned martyrdom completely; those who rushed headlong into it; and those who did not actively seek it out but who accepted it when the opportunity presented itself, see Middleton, 'Dying We Live', 82.
57 Cobb, *Dying to Be Men*, 16.
58 Keith Hopkins, *Death and Renewal: Sociological Studies in Roman History* (Cambridge: Cambridge University Press, 1983), 16; see Cobb, *Dying to Be Men*, 38.
59 Cobb, *Dying to be Men*, 38–40, where she cites evidence of both gladiators and spectators challenging the emperor and thus influencing the outcome of the spectacles. It should also be noted that an example of spectator influence manifests within the *Acts of Paul of Thecla* with the women's herbal magic (*APTh*. 34).
60 Cobb, *Dying to Be Men*, 40.
61 Ibid., 57.
62 Ibid., 40–4.
63 See e.g. MacDonald, *Legend*, 41.
64 Price, *Rituals and Power*, 170–1.
65 Spittler similarly agrees that ἀναγκαῖα is most likely meant to indicate 'genitals'. She notes that the astrologer Vettius Valens uses the phrase τοὺς ἀνακαίους τόπους, literally 'the necessary places' to refer to genitals (*Anthologiae* 2.37.133), Spittler, *Animals*, 178, esp. her n. 90; see also 1 Cor. 12.22.
66 Dworkin, *Pornography*, 24, 55–6.
67 Robert Sutton, 'Pornography and Persuasion on Attic Pottery', in *Pornography and Representation in Greece and Rome*, ed. Amy Richlin (Oxford: Oxford University Press, 1992), 3–35.
68 Ibid., 9–12, 32; see also Eva C. Keuls, *Reign of the Phallus: Sexual Politics in Ancient Athens* (Berkeley, CA: University of California Press, 1985), 176, 180–2.
69 Candida Moss, *The Myth of Persecution: How Early Christians Invested a Story of Martyrdom* (London: Harper Collins, 2013), 14–16.
70 Ibid., 14–15, 163–5.
71 See e.g. P. A. Holloway, *Coping with Prejudice: 1 Peter in Social and Psychological Perspective* (Tübigen: Mohr Seibeck, 2009), 41–66, esp. 65–6. Judith Lieu, 'Jews, Christian and "Pagans" in Conflict', in *Critique and Apologetics: Jews, Christian*

and *Pagans in Antiquity*, ed. A. C. Jacobsen, Jörg Ulrich and David Brakke (Frankfurt: Lang, 2009), 43–58.
72 Paul Frediksen, 'Christian in the Roman Empire in the First Three Centuries CE', in *A Companion to the Roman Empire*, ed. David S. Potter (West Sussex: Blockwell, 2010), 602. Moss, *The Myth of Persecution*, 14, 163–4.
73 Moss, *The Myth of Persecution*, 3, 9.
74 Holloway, *Coping with Prejudice*, 114.
75 Virginia Burrus and Rebecca Lyman, 'Introduction' to *Late Ancient Christianity: A People's History of Christianity*, ed. Burrus (Augsburg, MN: Fortress, 2005), 7.
76 For the possibility that Christians identified themselves as a different race, see Valantasis, 'Question of Early Christian Identity', 60–76.
77 See also Eph. 5.25-27; 2 Cor. 11.2.
78 Pesthy, 'Thecla among the Fathers', 174.
79 Catherine Burris and Lucas van Rompay, 'Thecla in Syriac Christianity: Preliminary Observations', *Hugoye: JSS* 5, no. 2 (2002): 20, online at https://hugoye.bethmardutho.org/article/hv5n2burrisvanrompay.
80 Jacques Derrida, 'Biodegradables: Seven Diary Fragments', trans. Peggy Kamuf, *Critical Inquiry* 15 (1989): 821, 840–1.
81 Roland Barthes, 'The Death of the Author', in *Image Music Text*, ed. and trans. Stephen Heath (New York: Hill & Wang, 1977), 185–9; See also Michel Foucault, 'What Is an Author?', in *Textual Strategies: Perspectives in Post-Structuralist Criticism*, ed. and trans. Josué V. Harari (London: Methuen, 1979), 141–60. William K. Wimsatt and Monroe C. Beardsley, 'The Intentional Fallacy', in *The Verbal Icon: Studies in the meaning of Poetry*, ed. W. K. Wimsatt (Lexington: University of Kentucky Press, 1954), 3–20.
82 Jacques Derrida, *Of Grammatology*, trans. Gayatri Chakravorty Spivak (Baltimore, MD: John Hopkins University Press, 1976), 158.
83 Tert., *De bapt.* 17.5.
84 See Chapter 2.
85 Walters, 'Invading the Roman Body', 37.
86 Cooper, *Virgin and the Bride*, 3–4, 13–14, 55.
87 See Cooper, 'Apostles, Ascetic Women', 149.
88 See Richard Trexler, *Sex and Conquest: Gendered Violence, Political Order and the European Conquest of the Americas* (Ithaca, NY: Cornell University Press, 1995).
89 See n. 76 above.
90 See Cooper, 'Voice of the Victim', 151–2; see also Shaw, 'The Passion of Perpetua', esp. 6; Maureen Tilley, 'The Ascetic Body and the (Un)making of the World of the Martyr', *JAAR* 59, no. 3 (1991): 467–79.
91 Cooper, 'Voice of the Victim', 152.

8

Conclusion

Thecla: This is my body

I was winning the game of Anagrams and I loved it! I could feel my mind working like a powerful machine as I easily outdistanced the boy who faced me across the small table. I felt like Atlanta, a Greek heroine I admired at that time. She could run faster than anyone, man or woman, and I wanted to be just like her. But our mothers passed the room in which we were playing and, as they looked inside, they could see what was happening. My mother called me aside and whispered to me in a conspiratorial voice: 'Let him win, dear, it will make him feel good. You know, boys don't like to lose to girls.' So I went back to our game of Anagrams, and I dutifully lost it. My mother, in all good faith, was teaching me the subtle rules I would be expected to follow for the remainder of my life. She was helping to create my inner patriarch, who would rule over my behaviour as a woman.[1]

I began this study questioning whether the *Acts of Paul and Thecla* is designed to be a text promoting female empowerment, or whether, as Cooper has suggested about the Apocryphal Acts generally, it is more of a complex literary entity that represents a power struggle between men and that ultimately has very little to do with women at all. Given that the text contains highly pornographic and misogynistic representations of a virgin woman who is repeatedly stripped bare and punished, I was interested to learn the text's message. In particular, I was sceptical in regard to how a text of this nature can be 'about women, for women'. My overall aim was to understand the relationship of power and discourse and the underlying rhetoric in a text which promotes female virginity and sado-erotic violence at the same time. This meant an examination of how gender and the representation of Thecla are constructed by the text, along with the social forces at work in this construction. Rather than seeing Thecla as a positive construct of a woman, I chose to resist what Stichele and Penner class as 'the rhetorical tactics and ideological games' of a text which, on the surface, presents a chaste Christian female heroine who chooses to assert her independence.[2] As a feminist, I therefore attempted to problematize features of the text that, in my mind, speak against women.

In order to address these questions, I considered three main areas of the text. The first of these was Thecla's apparent 'manly' transformation, the second was the representations of sado-erotic violence and the third was the role that magic and miracles play in the narrative. The reason I chose to focus on these three particular areas was because, first, when it comes to Thecla's gender construction, the majority of scholars argue that since Thecla cuts her hair short and dons a manly cloak (*APTh*. 25, 40), she becomes male. In this respect, the *Acts of Paul and Thecla* has been regarded as the quintessential text which displays an early manifestation of the notion of the female becoming male. My aim within Chapter 4 was therefore to challenge this common assumption since nowhere within the second-century text does it incontrovertibly state that Thecla cuts her hair. I examined the implications of Thecla retaining her feminine characteristics in order to assess what this would reveal about her representation and the construction of masculinity.

Second, despite the fact that many scholars have given extensive consideration to the text of the *Acts of Paul and Thecla*, very little attention has been focused upon the sado-erotic violence to which Thecla is subjected. The pornographic violence within the text forms a substantial component of the narrative. My aim within Chapter 5 was to explore the impact of sexualized violence within a text that has been viewed as containing a positive representation of a woman.

Third, it was important to examine the role of magic and miracles. This is because the magic and miracles that take place ensure that Thecla survives two attempts of painful execution unscathed, and from this perspective, it would seem that the text is trying to say something quite positive about Thecla; she must be special to survive these ordeals unharmed. However, despite this positive portrayal (in terms of Thecla surviving her trials), I was interested to learn to what extent she is empowered in relation to the magic and miracles. Chapter 6, therefore, examined where exactly power is located in terms of gender relations?

In Chapter 4, entitled 'Female Beheadings', I argued that despite donning male apparel at the end of the narrative, Thecla's gender transformation is greatly impeded because she never cuts her hair (*APTh*. 25). She never becomes fully male as this could threaten to unmake men and expose a fragile masculinity. If she cuts her hair, she becomes a tomboy, confuses gender boundaries and threatens the binary nature of gender. Her long hair thus ensures that she remains feminine-looking, which is why Alexander falls in love with her on first sight and attempts to rape her. Nevertheless, although Thecla is never fully masculinized, there are aspects of virility present in her representation. She displays manly courage in fighting off Alexander, transgressing spatial boundaries and showing bravery in the arena. However, ultimately in donning a male χιτών at the close of the narrative, with her long hair and legs on display, Thecla is transformed into a feminine sexualized cross-dresser, and this ensures that she continues to be an object of the male gaze. That she has been sexualized in this way is evidenced by the fact that, at times, prostitutes wore short tunics and masculine dress.[3] Even if becoming male could be seen as a positive construct for women, it is clear that Thecla never fully becomes male. There is no attempt to suppress or forsake the female body. A haircut may well have helped to consolidate her transformation, but such an action is considered 'inappropriate/shameful' (*APTh*. 25). In body, therefore, Thecla remains a woman. Since long hair is one of the foremost markers of her femininity and since the explicit detail of a haircut could quite easily have been added to complete her masculine transformation, one has to assume that, within this narrative, it is essential that Thecla remains female in body.

I then assessed, in Chapter 5, how the pornographic and violent imagery shapes the construction of gender within the text. I concluded that a close examination of the narrative reveals that Thecla is continually objectified. Despite the ascetic message, the text regales in a woman's sexualized body, which is voyeuristically displayed. However, in parading Thecla naked in the arena, she is stripped of clothing, subjectivity and personhood. In addition, as a woman who is passed around from man to man and violently abused for attempting to assert her subjectivity, Thecla is affirmed as under male control. The ideological structure within the narrative proclaims Thecla as an object to be owned and desired (meanwhile, the only desire she is permitted is her 'spiritualized' desire for Paul). In this way, Thecla is shown to be at the disposal of powerful men, and this treatment establishes hers (and woman's) place in the world. The violent and pornographic elements of the text reach a crescendo in the gratuitous scene where Thecla is tied naked by the legs between two bulls. No aspect of her body is veiled from sight. In a culture of honour and shame, Thecla bears the ultimate humiliation through the exposure of her body.

This sado-erotic treatment of Thecla clearly represents the discourse of a patriarchal culture which subjugates and objectifies women. Furthermore, despite the focus upon her bodily beauty, and in contrast to Paul, we are never given a description of her. Thecla, therefore, has no real identity as such. This aspect of Thecla's representation not only serves to make her less real but also encourages the audience/reader to view her as some kind of metaphor. This representation is further reinforced since no physical or psychological effects of the traumas or ordeals she experiences are ever hinted at or narrated.

Nevertheless, although reading through a 'pornographic lens' testifies to a woman humiliated and shamed, Thecla does exhibit ἀνδρεία and she has complete bodily integrity (in that her body is never harmed). Thecla's female body thus forms the nexus around her paradoxical representation: a curious mix of sexual objectification, female victimization and masculine inviolability. Glimmers of subjectivity and bodily inviolability weave in and out of a story which objectifies, eroticizes and pummels at the body of a heroine. It would seem that the ever-increasing sado-erotic violence and abuse which she endures, without a murmur, serves its purpose in proving the (masculinized) perfection of Thecla's body. The Roman concept of *virtus* is reconfigured in favour of this one particular virgin woman. Although Thecla does not disrupt the patriarchal gender hierarchy, in this way her female body is endowed with extraordinary status. It is, of course, the miracles within the arena that ensure Thecla's bodily inviolability.

In Chapter 6, I concluded that Thecla is not personally bestowed with any powers as such: neither verbally, doctrinally nor directly through the use of powerful magic. This is in contrast to the male apostles in the Apocryphal Acts. While the miracles sanction Thecla's decision to follow the ascetic teachings of Paul (perhaps suggesting that women easily fall victim to powerful, persuasive males), they also serve to underscore her passivity as a woman. It is, of course, quite possible that, given the suspicion that surrounded women generally, any powers emanating directly from a woman would result in the accusation of 'sorceress' (from audience and characters alike) and this may have influenced against granting miraculous powers to Thecla. Any woman who became too prominent, too powerful or too active in religion was open to accusations of transgression. Thecla is, therefore, represented as a passive recipient of miracles. Overall, my assessment in regard to the wielding of miraculous power in the *Acts of Paul and Thecla* concluded that conventional patriarchal gender patterns and biases obtain within the narrative. It is dangerous to ascribe miracle-working powers to the heroine; she may appear too powerful and rival the male apostles.

Most notable, within Chapter 6, was the fact that so little is made of the miraculous events that surround Thecla. It becomes quite evident that the miracles are *not* intended for the purposes of promulgation of the Christian message and conversion. However, the miracles do ensure that Thecla, goddess-like, survives her martyrdom in a way no other martyrs do (not even the male apostles). This would suggest that the purpose of the miraculous is to proclaim the female Thecla as inviolable. Thus, despite the conventional gender images that hold sway, the miracles ultimately work to elevate Thecla's status and representation. They bring to the fore the more empowering elements of her representation.

Moreover, since Thecla's actions and decision to remain a virgin direct the story (she refuses to marry Thamyris and is thrown into the arena; she then fends off the potential rapist Alexander, which results in her facing the wild beasts in a second arena scene) indicates that female virginity is of supreme importance. Preserving her virginity provides the catalyst for the miraculous, and the text rewards Thecla by rendering her female virgin body inviolable against any physical assault. Her virginity creates a kind of 'magic' that protects her and transforms her into a goddess-like deity. Although Thecla remains a desirable and sexualized woman, her body carries with it nuances of masculinity, in that it remains impenetrable, as a Roman male body should remain. Thecla's inviolable body prevails and renders her victorious. Commissioned by Paul, she is sent out into the male realm. Somehow, a sadistic journey of shame and exposure has given her the necessary credentials to carry out the orders of a male apostle. In the meantime, Paul is continually characterized as a man of virtue. Clearly then, the text, as it stands, packages things in a male-dominant, androcentric way, perhaps indicating both male redactions and ambivalent attitudes to women.

Given these findings and the fact that (as concluded in Chapter 1) this text is probably male-authored, as indicated by Tertullian (*De bapt.* 17.5), I went on to consider how such a text might function as an expression of male contemplation and problem-solving within an Imperial Roman context. Taking into account the predilection of men in antiquity to identify with, and use virgins to 'think with', and the fact that texts formed a crucial element in the formation of Christian identity, I went on to argue that Thecla's virgin body becomes the primary site through which Christians establish a new personal and corporate identity over and against Rome.

Thecla: The Church

As highlighted in Chapter 7, the language and iconography of empire is full of violent sexual imagery. Gender is overtly and conspicuously correlated with ethnicity and utilized to portray hierarchy and power relationships. Women are shown as captured and subdued while male Roman bodies, by contrast, are shown to be powerful, domineering and in control. Within the *Acts of Paul and Thecla*, the social relationship between Imperial Rome (and Roman masculinity) and those that it ruled (in this case, Christians) is enacted, renegotiated and reconfigured anew. Thus, despite being objectified and framed as a sexual object, Thecla's virgin body is presented as the epitome of idealized Roman masculinity: she is inviolable and impenetrable. Moreover, it is interesting that some centuries later, her virginity remains paramount to her representation. As discussed in Chapter 4, in the longer ending manuscript of the *Acts of Paul and Thecla*, doctors attempt to rape Thecla in the hope that, without her virginity, she would lose her power to heal.

The ideological function of Thecla is thus as a constructed body that transcends its 'natural' feminine weakness. Thecla is linked to the self-identity of male Christians that communicates conceptions of inviolability of the church against an invasive and phallic concept of Rome. As discussed in Chapter 7, in early Christian writing and iconography, the church is often represented as a chaste woman, the 'Bride of Christ' (Rev. 19.7). The fourth-century mosaic of Santa Pudenziana in Rome also shows the 'Church of the Gentiles' and the 'Church of the Circumcision' as two nun-like figures. Valantasis has also highlighted the way in which Christians identified themselves as a separate race.[4] Reading Thecla as representative of Christian ἔθνος and a symbol of the church that is impervious to Roman Imperial power is one way of making sense of an ascetic message which, paradoxically, utilizes sexualized representations of the female body. I thus revisit the text to provide a completely fresh perspective and interpretation. Ultimately, I conclude that Thecla has been appropriated by a male author/s and that the narrative represents an ancient male power struggle and contest against an idealized, dominant Roman masculinity. Thecla's body becomes the site by which Christian men establish and reconfigure their personal and corporate identity within a context of Imperial Rome.

We need to bear in mind that, even though people in antiquity had a different frame of reference in regard to their world view, they were neither stupid nor credulous. They knew that a fire burns human flesh, that wild animals rip people to pieces and that a person tied between two bulls would be split in two. In this respect, other martyrdom stories tell a more authentic tale.[5] The text does not, therefore, only strain the credulity of contemporary readers. Audiences in antiquity will have similarly received this tale on a more metaphorical/didactic level. Cooper notes, 'One of the distinctive features of early Christian writers was their interest in the reader's experience.' Here she highlights how many of the early Christian sources invite the readers to project themselves into the narrative as a kind of 'shadow protagonist' and that this identity strategy 'reflected the sometimes perilous position of Christians as representatives of a minority faith.'[6] A close analysis of gender construction within the story brings to the fore the rhetorical purpose of the narrative. There is interplay within the text between chastity and naked exposure, faith and Roman aggression/violence; these elements are juxtaposed and meet head-on in a contest within the Roman arena. The text testifies to a Christian resistance against a dominant Roman ideology.

Thecla: A man within and a man on top

This understanding of the text does not mean that there are no alternative voices in the narrative. The text does engage with opposing positions. Thus, as noted in Chapters 5 and 6, in Antioch, there is the powerful woman Tryphaena, closely associated with Caesar, who protects Thecla. The women of the city are also closely allied to Thecla and protest against her judgement. They eventually intervene with herbal magic to keep the wild beasts at bay. A female lioness also befriends Thecla and does what she can to protect her.

It is possible to read these female representations positively, depicting women en masse as empowered. Jointly and collaboratively as a body, women can act synchronically to defend their kind against the aggressive and violent power of men. These 'all female' alternative voices may well testify to an earlier oral tradition emanating from women. However, as discussed previously, they are ultimately contained by patriarchy; female networks are shown to be ineffective against Roman male power, although – as noted – due deference is still given to Caesar (*APTh*. 36). Thus, despite the protests of the women in the city, Thecla is thrown into the arena, an army is sent to deal with the hysterical Tryphaena, raging bulls answer to women's herbal magic and, finally, despite the furore over Tryphaena fainting, Thecla's torture is ultimately only brought to end due to fear of reprisals from Caesar. Female power and networks are easily quieted and contained by the 'very masculine' Roman order.

These alternative voices, which emerge only in the second arena scene, should, therefore, not be overemphasized. Furthermore, it should be borne in mind that in Iconium, women too collude in Thecla's punishment (women and men bring wood to burn her and women are included in the baying crowd, *APTh*. 22), and it is her own mother who heartlessly and coldly cries 'burn the lawless one' (*APTh*. 20). This is far removed from the text of Perpetua's martyrdom, which more naturally shows a parent (in this case, the father) pleading with his child to turn away from the Christian faith so that she may be spared execution.[7] Why would an author choose to represent Thecla's mother in such an unnaturally, cold and unsympathetic light? One can only hypothesize, but the representation may speak poignantly of a deep held fear and suspicion of women (see, e.g., 1 Tim. 4.7; 5.11-14; 2 Tim. 3.6-8), and it once again underscores the androcentric nature of the text. Overall, then, a conventional sense of gender relations can be detected between the females encountered in the story and the powerful men narrated. Clearly, Roman men have power and this is never fundamentally challenged, except in the fact that Thecla's body remains immune to it.

The entire story presents against this traditional, male-dominated, background. Thus, even though Thecla appears to challenge the social values of antiquity (she transgresses physical boundaries moving into public spaces and she also refuses marriage), there are complex dynamics at work because she is still, very much, under the authority of patriarchy. In line with the quote which began this chapter, Thecla has a strong 'inner Patriarch' that ensures that she continually seeks Paul out. No matter what she experiences, Thecla always returns to Paul. It is as though she has an internal 'homing' device. When Paul is led off to prison, Thecla bribes the doorkeeper and jailor in order to gain access to him. After she is rescued by miraculous intervention from the fire, she sets off in search of Paul, and, following the trials in Antioch, she once again longs for him and pursues him. This representation ensures that Paul never loses his status or importance: he remains 'on top' of events and in charge of Thecla. So although Thecla moves from cloistered, veiled, secure space into the public domain, her boundary crossing is shown to have negative consequences. On one occasion, she finds herself in prison and then condemned to die, and on the second occasion, she is attacked and threatened with rape. In each case, the boundaries she transgresses are re-established because she is punished and contained. Masculine power and authority speak back to a woman's boundary crossing and ultimately, of course, she returns to Paul. Thus, although the text appears to deconstruct boundary markers, they are re-established through her punishment, eventual containment and then finally through Paul's commission: she is under male apostolic authority. The relationship between bodies, boundaries and empire are, therefore, multifaceted, but Thecla never escapes from the hold of patriarchy.

Obedient to God and to Paul, Thecla is, therefore, secondary to Paul, the male apostle and leader. Even when Thecla does demonstrate dynamism and subjectivity, the text renders Paul absent, thus protecting his status, ensuring he is never in her shadow: there is no breach in conventional gender relations. The same constellation of relations is presented between Paul and Thecla as would be presented between any male and female couple in antiquity except, when he ought to, he does not protect her in Antioch. Although Paul's absenteeism allows the plot to develop and gives the opportunity for Thecla to shine, ultimately, female religious ministry is carefully stylized to match established cultural codes and is thus kept within firm boundaries. Thus, although Thecla, the would-be masculinized, female martyr, is a useful representation to demonstrate the superiority of Christians over and against the pagan Romans, as Cobb has highlighted, when it comes to intragroup relations, Christians are far more conservative.[8] Within the Christian community, the masculinized woman is a far less useful trope: she needs to be tamed. The patriarchal preoccupation of putting and keeping a woman in her place outweighs all else. Thecla is, like most women in antiquity, defined in relation to a man.

The text is, therefore, devoid of any critical attitude to gender relations and reflects nothing more than androcentric story telling. In desiring Paul and actively seeking him out, allowing him to commission her apostleship, Thecla adapts herself to the dominant gender division without protest or criticism. The story, then, along with the sado-erotic violence and voyeurism to which Thecla is subjected, reveals the struggles for a woman in a man's world. Thecla operates within patriarchal structures and surrenders herself to masculine authority. Nowhere do we find traces of a female protagonist's strategy to challenge male dominant norms. The text is not trying to promote women or female independence per se. The hierarchical oppositions which underpin patriarchy, which guarantee the superiority of the male over the female, are very much alive and kicking. Rather, the story of Thecla is one where the fantastical, the miraculous, the shameful and sadistic predominate. The emphasis is instead upon Thecla's stoic virginity. We have a creative narrative of virginity and sado-erotic violence – a voyeur's dream; what reader can resist this spectacle?

Thecla: Imagine my body

This focus on Thecla's body may appear to speak well for women and their bodies; after all, her body displays control and she is impervious to penetration – completely inviolable – no matter what she does. However, it needs to be remembered that Thecla's body remains in the grip of male power, and basically, in reality, the concept of woman here merely constitutes a 'body'. Thecla may have a body that endures, but she has not escaped her corporeality. Nevertheless, the fact that her body behaves in an idealized masculinized way does open up the binary pair male/female to slippage and uncertainty. Is this progress?

While Thecla becomes an important and saintly figure, the focus on her (unrealistic) inviolable body means that she is simply a prototype of sorts. She is a one-off model who remains distant and untouchable like the gods and goddesses of old. The heightened 'staging' of Thecla's performance results in a purely imaginary body – she is a fiction. Thecla's superhuman body completely veils the real woman beneath. What woman would not bear the psychological scars of such terrible and debasing exposure? Thus, although the text heaps accolades upon the body of a beautiful virgin woman, it is at the expense of real women who suffer humiliation and who also bleed and die. The text thus gives voice, not to a female heroine or communities of women, but rather to a fictional – Terminator-like – heroine who reveals the struggles and ideology of the text's male author/s. It verbalizes men's and the church's vulnerability and resistance to the Roman world. A tradition about the woman Thecla has been appropriated by male authors for their own ends, to critique a violent and invasive Rome and, ultimately, to help them to feel 'good'.

Within this process, in depicting sado-eroticized attacks upon a woman, although the author is supposedly countering Rome, he simultaneously colludes with Rome in debasing and exposing the heroine. Even though the spectacle is meant to be abhorrent, it still privileges the male gaze and results in shaping a specific female gender identity which emphasizes objectification. Cobb writes that producing such graphic visual images of female martyr bodies is one of the most effective ways authors feminize the female martyrs.[9] How is it possible to truly empower a heroine (and women) through such debasing treatment?

Although, like stage performances, the point of martyr stories was to enact an all-pervasive truth, to show that what is done to the body cannot affect the soul, the author merely replicates the kinds of stereotypical generalizations about women that typify misogynism. In its very writing, the text participates in propagating not only faith but also the erotic violence done to women; and as readers we all become involved – we all participate in the spectacle and perpetuate it, along with the author.

If Thecla is to be held up as a challenge to patriarchal apostolic hierarchy in the ancient world, then it is important, at the same time, to give voice to those aspects of the text which reflect men's sadistic prurient gaze and to ask what is being done to real women by such violent representations of female bodies. Tertullian suggested this was a dangerous text, and maybe it was. We should not turn a blind eye to the dangers inherent within it for women. Fundamentally, the text displays a woman for voyeuristic titillation and a concern for control and authority over her body. Although Thecla is, in the eyes of some, held up as a female exemplar, it needs to be remembered that there is a fine line to be drawn between adulation and disparagement.

I am aware that there are many who read these narratives as historical, sacred accounts of women in early Christianity, and an approach such as mine may be seen to risk damaging the sanctity of these hallowed and beloved martyrdoms. I may also be criticized, as a feminist, for presenting a very 'negative' interpretation of a text that has regularly been seen to provide hopeful glimmers of women's activity in nascent Christianity. However, we should heed the words of Burrus, who writes,

> Heroines of ancient romances are notorious for their improbable acts of resuscitation ... With a little help from romance, might not a martyrology already subtly shifted out of the context of the persecution of Christians now also be transmuted into a literary Life for a woman?[10]

As noted above, there is now general agreement among scholars that martyrologies contain highly rhetorical and stylized elements. Furthermore, they contain what Burrus describes as a 'disturbingly sadistic strain of violence ... which simultaneously replicates and subverts the explosive pressures of empire'.[11] For female martyrs, this 'disturbing sadistic strain of violence' inevitably involves sexualized, sado-erotic violence. These motifs, the intersection of explicit sado-erotic violence and gender, beckon scholarly attention and closer scrutiny.

However, it has regularly been stated that it is always a good idea to end on a hopeful note; therefore, as I draw this study to a close, I will say that the text does betray some progress for women because historically women have been associated with the role of 'mother'. This is in contrast to men who are associated with culture and subjectivity. While women can become subjects if they assimilate to male subjectivity, a separate subject position for women in antiquity has rarely existed. From this perspective, the *Acts of Paul and Thecla* does evidence a shift of sorts. Unlike Perpetua and Felicitas, Thecla is not maternal. She is instead, unlike other females, impenetrable (like a 'proper' man) and, therefore, stands for resistance and power.

The traditional association between the female body and the domestic sphere is thus removed. Thecla does not have a maternal body but the body of a female Olympian athlete. In antiquity, a female Olympic athlete may have more in common with a male Olympic athlete than with a wife/mother. And, by the close of the narrative, as she once again goes in hot pursuit of Paul, Thecla's representation has developed to the point that Paul marvels at her ἐθαμβήθη (*APTh*. 40) θαυμάαι (*APTh*. 41). Thecla also has a crowd of young men and maidens with her as she sets off on her apostolic mission (*APTh*. 40). A beautiful woman, dressed sexily in a short χιτών, is permitted both male and female followers and to teach the Word of God. Patriarchy affirms and confirms a sexy τοῦ θεοῦ δούλην (*APTh*. 26). There is, therefore, a certain legitimating of female autonomy. Ultimately, in surviving her ordeals with an inviolate body, the representation of Thecla really resists male power: that is male *Roman* power but not male *apostolic* power.

Thecla: The myth of the perfect female body

The goal of most martyrdoms is death, and Thecla never dies. In light of the reading that has been presented within this study, it becomes clear that the story of Thecla does not fit the mould of other martyr texts. As it stands, the text evokes a multitude of complexities. One way of making sense of a superhuman female heroine and an eroticized discourse embedded alongside chaste ascetic practice is to read this as a text about men and the formation of male Christian identity. Inviolability positively defined Roman men and the masculine gender. The text of the *Acts of Paul and Thecla* depicts the heroine as impervious to penetration of any sort. Relationships of power are explored through the engagement of gender. Utilizing a virgin body, Roman ideology is subverted and rendered totally ineffective. Through the virgin body, Christian males can assert their masculine subjectivity and resist Roman masculine ideology. By identifying with Thecla, they can regard themselves in the dominant role within this scenes narrated. The virgin body demonstrates that the church as virgin is an impenetrable 'superman'. The Roman Empire has no power over this new Christian ἔθνος. The female body is used to speak for Christianity against the Roman subjection of the church; however, as noted above, it does not speak against patriarchy.

As noted in Chapter 7, extant literature, such as the unpublished *Cathedral Homily* 97 of Severus of Antioch which explicitly defines Thecla as being representative of the church, the bride of Christ, demonstrates that Christians of the first centuries understood this rhetorical purpose of texts. The representation of Thecla is then a startling instance of the use of a woman's body as a signifier for Christian self-definition and a critique of Roman Imperial hegemony. But her portrayal does not represent a real woman. We have the voyeuristic exposure of a young, beautiful virgin woman, as an object of male lust. Within the text, her role as leader, teacher and healer is either repressed or understated. Nor is she depicted as true companion and co-apostle to Paul.

Whether Thecla existed in reality or not, within this text, she is presented as an impenetrable, inviolable virgin, surrounded by a kind of magic. Her representation is both guarded and censored. Despite the wider tradition of Thecla, here the focus is only on her beautiful, inviolable body. That it is exposed and tortured should serve as a warning to any who might use this text as a positive example of women's subjectivity in antiquity. Always in the grip of some male power, Thecla-as-female-body is constrained and acted upon by external forces. She is exposed and tortured by one set of male (Romans) and appropriated by a Christian author for his own ends: to present her as the church for the nations in the story he tells out of love for Paul.

None of this is to say that women could not, or did not, identify with the story, or that the story could not be received or interpreted in other ways. Indeed, the reference in Tertullian (*De bapt.* 17.5) testifies to the fact that women found a message for themselves within the text. However, reading Thecla's inviolate body as a challenge to Roman Imperial culture helps to make sense of some of the more contradictory elements within the narrative.

Thus, in applying the hermeneutic of suspicion and advancing the insights of Cooper, who reads the female figures within the Apocryphal Acts as ideological constructs of masculine identity, we have gained new insights and offered a completely fresh perspective and reading of the text. Analysing how gender is constructed and intertwined with power and the representation of the female body has fully brought out of the shadows the highly androcentric and patriarchal nature of a text which appears to take a special interest in a woman. Despite its focus on one female protagonist who rebels against societal norms, and despite the apparent interest in what, on the surface, seems to be a strong heroine who is 'raised up' in God's cause, this project has truly exposed the extent to which the *Acts of Paul and Thecla* is the literature of men. Rethinking factors that have, until now, been taken for granted or neglected, and taking into consideration the Roman Imperial aspect, the project has unravelled the androcentricism that surrounds Thecla. Ultimately, this exploration has identified how a victimized female representation creates a meaningful image of the church for male Christian writers within a Roman Imperial context.

At the beginning of the *Acts of Paul and Thecla*, Paul proclaims, 'Blessed are the bodies of the virgins (τὰ σώματα τῶν πρθένων) for they shall be well pleasing to God, and shall not lose the reward of their purity' (ἁγνείας *APTh*. 6). Despite the violent treatment she receives, ultimately Thecla's body is blessed; indeed, she is truly inviolable. The preservation of intactness may be read as a divine intervention on the side of women. Haines-Eitzen notes that in the Syriac palimpsest from Saint Catherine's Monastery in Sinai, the *Acts of Paul and Thecla* is written on top of Mark's gospel.[12] The text of Thecla 'on top' of one of the earliest Christian texts to be written! Not only may Thecla's imaginary body be seen to 'win', but in this particular case, so too does the text.

Notes

1 Sidra Stone, *The Shadow King: The Invisible Force That Holds Women Back* (Lincoln, NE: iUniverse, 2000), xv.
2 Vander Stichele and Penner, *Contextualizing Gender*, 201.
3 See Chapter 4.
4 Valantasis, 'Question of Early Christian Identity'.
5 See, e.g., *The Martyrdom of Saints Perpetua and Felicitas* in Musurillo, *The Acts of Christian the Martyrs*, 106–31, and the martyrdom of Blandina which is presented in Euseb., *Hist. eccl.* 5.1.
6 Kate Cooper, 'The Bride of Christ, the "Male Woman," and the Female Reader in Late Antiquity', in *The Oxford Handbook of Women and Gender in Medieval Europe*, ed. Judith Bennett and Ruth Mazo Karas (Oxford: Oxford University Press, 2013), 33.
7 See *The Martyrdom of Saints Perpetua and Felicitas* in Musurillo, *The Acts of Christian the Martyrs*.

8 Cobb, *Dying to Be Men*, 126–7.
9 Ibid., 111.
10 Burrus, *Sex Lives of Saints*, 56.
11 Ibid., 13.
12 Haines-Eitzen, *Gendered Palimpsest*, 131.

Bibliography

Aageson, James W. *Paul, the Pastoral Epistles and the Early Church*. Peabody, MA: Hendrickson, 2008.
Adamik, Tamás. 'The Baptized Lion in the Acts of Paul'. In *The Apocryphal Acts of Paul and Thecla*, edited by Jan N. Bremmer, 60–72. Kampen: Kok Pharos, 1996.
Adamik, Tamás. 'The Influence of the Apocryphal Acts on Jerome's Lives of the Saints'. In *The Apocryphal Acts of John*, edited by Jan N. Bremmer, 171–82. Kampen: Kok Pharos, 1995.
Adams, Sean A. *The Genre of Acts and Collected Biography*. Cambridge: Cambridge University Press, 2013.
Anson, John. 'The Female Transvestite in Early Monasticism: The Origin and Development of a Motif'. *Viator* 5 (1974): 1–32.
Aubin, Melissa. 'Reversing Romance? The Acts of Thecla and the Ancient Novel'. In *Ancient Fiction and Early Christian Narrative*, edited by Ronald F. Hock, J. Bradley Chance and Judith Perkins, 257–72. Atlanta, GA: Scholars Press, 2003.
Aymer, Margaret P. 'Hailstorms and Fireballs: Redaction, World Creation and Resistance in the Acts of Paul and Thecla'. *Semeia* 79 (1997): 45–61.
Barclay, John M. G. *Pauline Churches and Diaspora Jews*. Grand Rapids, MI: Eerdmans, 2016.
Barrier, Jeremy M. *The Acts of Paul and Thecla: A Critical Introduction and Commentary*. Tübingen: Mohr Siebeck, 2009.
Barthes, Roland. 'The Death of the Author'. In *Image Music Text*, edited and translated by Stephen Heath, 185–9. New York: Hill & Wang, 1977.
Bassler, Jouette M. 'Limits and Differentiation: The Calculus of Widows in 1 Timothy 5.3-16'. In *A Feminist Companion to the Deutero-Pauline Epistles*, edited by Amy-Jill Levine, 122–46. London: T&T Clark, 2003.
Bassler, Jouette M. *1 Timothy, 2 Timothy, Titus*. Nashville, TN: Abingdon Press, 1996.
Bassler, Jouette M. 'The Widows' Tale: A Fresh Look at 1 Tim 5.3-16'. *Journal of Biblical Literature* 103 (1984): 23–41.
Bauer, Walter, Frederick W. Danker, William F. Arndt and F. Wilbur Gingrich. *A Greek-English Lexicon of the New Testament and Other Early Christian Literature*. 3rd ed. Chicago, IL: University of Chicago Press, 2000.
Bedale, Stephen. 'The Meaning of κεφαλη in the Pauline Epistles'. *Journal of Theological Studies* 5 (1954): 211–15.
Berger, John. *About Looking*. New York: Pantheon Books, 1980.
Berger, John. *Ways of Seeing*. London: BBC & Penguin Books, 1972.
Betz, Hans Dieter. *Galatians*. Philadelphia, PA: Fortress Press, 1979.
Bloch, R. Howard. *Medieval Misogyny and the Invention of Western Romantic Love*. Chicago, IL: University of Chicago Press, 1991.
Blundell, Sue. 'Clutching at Clothes'. In *Women's Dress in the Ancient Greek World*, edited by Lloyd Llewellyn-Jones, 143–69. London: Duckworth, Classical Press of Wales, 2002.

Bollók, János. 'The Description of Paul in the Acta Pauli'. In *The Apocryphal Acts of Paul and Thecla*, edited by Jan N. Bremmer, 1–15. Kampen: Kok Pharos, 1996.
Bonfante, Larrisa, and Eva Jaunzems. 'Clothing and Ornament'. In *Civilization of the Ancient Mediterranean: Greece and Rome*, edited by Michael Grant and Rachel Kitzinger, 1385–413. New York: Charles Scribner, 1988.
Booth, Wayne C. *The Rhetoric of Fiction*. Chicago, IL: University of Chicago Press, 1983.
Boughton, Lynne C. 'From Pious Legend to Feminist Fantasy: Distinguishing. Hagiographical License from Apostolic Practice in the Acts of Paul/Acts of Thecla'. *Journal of Religion* 71 (1991): 362–83.
Bovon, Francois. 'Canonical and Apocryphal Acts of the Apostles'. *Journal of Early Christian Studies* 11 (2003): 165–94.
Bowie, Ewen. 'The Readership of Greek Novels in the Ancient World'. In *The Search for the Ancient Novel*, edited by James Tatum, 435–95. Baltimore, MD: John Hopkins University Press, 1994.
Boyarin, Daniel. *Dying for God: Martyrdom and the Making of Christianity and Judaism*. Redwood, CA: Stanford University Press, 1999.
Boyarin, Daniel. *A Radical Jew: Paul and the Politics of Identity*. Berkeley: University of California Press, 1994.
Boymel Kampen, Natalie. 'Epilogue, Gender and Desire'. In *Naked Truths: Women, Sexuality and Gender in Classical Art and Archaeology*, edited by Ann Olga Koloski-Ostrow and Claire L. Lyons, 267–77. London: Routledge, 1997.
Braun, Willi. 'Physiotherapy of Femininity in the Acts of Thecla'. In *Text and Artifact in the Religions of Mediterranean Antiquity: Essays in Honour of Peter Richardson*, edited by Stephen G. Wilson, 209–29. Waterloo, ON: Wilfrid Laurier University Press, 2000.
Bremmer, Jan N., ed. *The Apocryphal Acts of John*. Kampen: Kok Pharos, 1995.
Bremmer, Jan N., ed. *The Apocryphal Acts of Paul and Thecla*. Kampen: Kok Pharos, 1996.
Bremmer, Jan N. 'Aspects of the Acts of Peter: Women, Magic, Place and Date'. In *The Apocryphal Acts of Peter: Magic, Miracles and Gnosticism*, edited by Jan N. Bremmer, 1–20. Leuven: Peeters, 1998.
Bremmer, Jan N. 'Drusiana, Cleopatra and Some Other Women in the Acts of John'. In *Feminist Companion to the New Testament Apocrypha*, edited by Amy-Jill Levine, with Maria Mayo Robbins, 77–87. Cleveland, OH: Pilgrim, 2006.
Bremmer, Jan N. 'Magic, Martyrdom and Women's liberation in the Acts of Paul and Thecla'. In *The Apocryphal Acts of Paul and Thecla*, edited by Jan N. Bremmer, 36–59. Kampen: Kok Pharos, 1996.
Bremmer, Jan N. 'Man, Magic and Martyrdom in the Acts of Andrew'. In *The Apocryphal Acts of Andrew*, edited by Jan N. Bremmer, 15–24. Leuven: Peeters, 2000.
Bremmer, Jan N. 'Women in the Apocryphal Acts of John'. In *The Apocryphal Acts of John*, edited by Jan N. Bremmer, 37–56. Kampen: Kok Pharos, 1995.
Brock, Sebastian P., and Susan Ashbrook Harvey. *Holy Women of the Syrian Orient*. Berkeley: University of California Press, 1987.
Brooten, Bernadette J. *Love between Women: Early Christina Responses to Female Homoeroticism*. Chicago, IL: University of Chicago Press, 1996.
Brown, Lucinda A. 'Asceticism and Ideology: The Language of Power in the Pastoral Epistles'. *Semeia* 57, *Discursive Formations, Ascetic Piety and the Interpretation of Early Christian Literature*, part 1 (1991): 77–94.
Brown, Peter. *The Body and Society: Men, Women and Sexual Renunciation in Early Christianity*. London: Faber, 1990.

Brown, Peter. *The Cult of the Saints: Its Rise and Function in Latin Christianity*. Chicago, IL: University of Chicago Press, 1981.
Brown, Shelby. 'Death as Decoration: Scenes from the Arena on Roman Domestic Mosaics'. In *Pornography and Representation in Greece and Rome*, edited by Amy Richlin, 180–211. Oxford: Oxford University Press, 1992.
Burnett McInerney, Maud. *Eloquent Virgins from Thecla to Joan of Arc*. New York: Palgrave MacMillan, 2003.
Burridge, Richard A. *Four Gospels, One Jesus?* London: SPCK, 1994.
Burridge, Richard A. *What Are the Gospels: A Comparison with Graeco-Roman Biography*. Grand Rapids, MI: Eerdmans, 2004.
Burris, Catherine, and Lucas van Rompay. 'Thecla in Syriac Christianity: Preliminary Observations'. *Hugoye: Journal of Syriac Studies* 5, no. 2 (July 2002): 225–36.
Burriss, Eli Edward. *Taboo, Magic, Spirits: A Study of Primitive Elements in Roman Religion*. New York: Kessinger, 1972.
Burrus, Virginia. *Chastity as Autonomy: Women in the Stories of the Apocryphal Acts*. Lewiston, NY: Edwin Mellen, 1987.
Burrus, Virginia. 'Chastity as Autonomy: Women in the Stories of the Apocryphal Acts'. *Semeia* 38 (1986): 101–17.
Burrus, Virginia, ed. *Late Ancient Christianity: A People's History of Christianity*. Vol. 2. Augsburg, MN: Fortress, 2005.
Burrus, Virginia. 'Mimicking Virgins: Colonial Ambivalence and the Ancient Romance'. *Arethusa* 38 (2005): 49–88.
Burrus, Virginia. 'Reading Agnes: The Rhetoric of Gender in Ambrose and Prudentius'. *Journal of Early Christian Studies* 3 (1995): 25–46.
Burrus, Virginia. 'Response'. *Semeia* 38 (1986): 133–5.
Burrus, Virginia. *Saving Shame: Martyrs, Saints and Other Abject Subjects*. Philadelphia: University of Pennsylvania Press, 2008.
Burrus, Virginia. *The Sex Lives of Saints: An Erotics of Ancient Hagiography*. Philadelphia: University of Pennsylvania Press, 2004.
Burrus, Virginia. 'Torture, Truth and the Witnessing Body: Reading Christian Martyrdom with Page duBois'. *Biblical Interpretation* 25 (2017): 5–18.
Burrus, Virginia. 'Word and Flesh: The Bodies and Sexuality of Ascetic Women in Christian Antiquity'. *Journal of Feminist Studies in Religion* 10, no. 1 (1994): 27–51.
Burrus, Virginia, and Rebecca Lyman. 'Introduction' to *Late Ancient Christianity*. In *Late Ancient Christianity*, edited by Virginia Burrus, 1–26. Augsburg, MN: Fortress, 2005.
Calef, Susan A. 'Thecla "Tried and True" and the Inversion of Romance'. In *Feminist Companion to the New Testament Apocrypha*, edited by Amy-Jill Levine, with Maria Mayo Robbins, 163–85. Cleveland, OH: Pilgrim, 2006.
Cameron, Averil. 'Early Christianity and the Discourse of Female Desire'. In *Women in Ancient Societies: An illusion of the Night*, edited by Leonie S. Archer, 152–68. Basingstoke: Macmillan Press, 1994.
Cameron, Averil. 'Virginity as Metaphor: Women and the Rhetoric of Early Christianity'. In *History as Text: The Writing of Ancient History*, edited by Averil Cameron, 181–205. London: Duckworth, 1989.
Campbell, Douglas A. *The Quest for Paul's Gospel*. London: T&T Clark, 2005.
Carson, Anne. 'Putting Her in Her Place: Woman, Dirt and Desire'. In *Before Sexuality: The Construction of Erotic Experience in the Ancient Greek World*, edited by David M. Halperin et al., 135–70. Princeton, NJ: Princeton University Press, 1990.

Cartlidge, David R., and J. Keith Elliot. *Art and the Christian Apocrypha*. London: Routledge, 2001.
Castelli, Elizabeth A. 'The Ambivalent Legacy of Violence and Victimhood: Using Early Christian Martyrs to Think With'. *Spiritus: A Journal of Christian Spirituality* 6 (2006): 1–24.
Castelli, Elizabeth A. 'I Will Make Mary Male: Pieties of the Body and Gender Transformation of Christian Women in Late Antiquity'. In *Body Guards: The Cultural Politics of Gender Ambiguity*, edited by Julia Epstein and Kristina Straub, 29–49. London: Routledge, 1991.
Castelli, Elizabeth A. *Martyrdom and Memory, Early Christian Culture Making: Gender Theory and Religion*. New York: Columbia University Press, 2004.
Castelli, Elizabeth A. 'Romans'. In *Searching the Scriptures: A Feminist Commentary*, edited by Elisabeth Schüssler-Fiorenza, with Ann Brock and Shelly Matthews, 272–300. New York: Crossroad, 1994.
Castelli, Elizabeth A. 'Virginity and Its Meaning for Women's Sexuality in Early Christianity'. *Journal of Feminist Studies in Religion* 2 (1986): 61–88.
Castelli, Elizabeth A. 'Visions and Voyeurism: Holy Women and the Politics of Sight in Early Christianity'. In *Protocol of the Colloquy of the Center for Hermeneutical Studies*, edited by Christopher Ocker, 1–12. Berkeley, CA: The Graduate Theological Union and the University of California, 1992.
Chatman, Seymour B. *Story and Discourse: Narrative Structure in Fiction and Film*. New York: Cornell University Press, 1978.
Clark, Elizabeth. *Ascetic Piety and Women's Faith, Essays on Late Ancient Christianity*. New York: Edwin Mellen, 1986.
Clark, Elizabeth. 'Holy Women, Holy Words: Early Christian Women, Social History and the "Linguistic Turn" '. *Journal of Early Christian Studies* 6 (1998): 413–30.
Clark, Elizabeth. 'Ideology, History and the Construction of 'Woman' in Late Ancient Christianity'. *Journal of Early Christian Studies* 2 (1994): 155–84.
Clark, Elizabeth. *Jerome, Chrysostom and Friends: Essays and Translations*. New York: Mellen, 1979.
Clark, Gillian. 'Bodies and Blood: Late Antique Debate on Martyrdom, Virginity and Resurrection'. In *Changing Bodies, Changing Meanings: Studies on the Human Body in Antiquity*, edited by Dominic Montserrat, 99–115. London: Routledge, 1998.
Cleland, Liza, Glenys Davies and Lloyd Llewellyn-Jones, eds. *Greek and Roman Dress from A-Z*. London: Routledge, 2007.
Cobb, L. Stephanie. *Dying to Be Men: Gender and Language in Early Christian Martyr Texts*. New York: Columbia University Press, 2008.
Cohen, Beth. 'Divesting the Female Breast of Clothes in Classical Sculpture'. In *Naked Truths: Women, Sexuality and Gender in Classical Art and Archaeology*, edited by Ann Olga Kolski-Ostrow and Claire L. Lyons, 66–92. London: Routledge, 1997.
Cole, S. G. 'Could Greek Women Read and Write'. In *Reflections of Women in Antiquity*, edited by H. Foley, 219–45. New York: Gordon & Breach, 1981.
Conybeare, Frederick C. *The Apology and Acts of Apollonius and other Monuments of Early Christianity*. London: Swan Sonnenschein, 1894.
Conzelmann, Hans. *I Corinthians*. Translated by James W. Leitch. Philadelphia, PA: Fortress, 1975.
Cook, Zeba. 'Honour, Shame and Social Status Revisited'. *Journal of Biblical Literature* 128, no. 3 (2009): 591–611.

Cooper, John M., ed., and D. Hutchinson, associate ed. *Plato: Complete Works*. Indianapolis, IN: Hackett, 1997.

Cooper, Kate. 'Approaching the Holy Household'. *Journal of Early Christian Studies* 15 (2007): 131–42.

Cooper, Kate. 'Apostles, Ascetic Women and Questions of Audience: New Reflections on the Rhetoric of Gender in the Apocryphal Acts'. *Society of Biblical literature Seminar Papers* 31 (1992): 147–53.

Cooper, Kate. *Band of Angels: The Forgotten World of Early Christian Women*. London: Atlantic, 2013.

Cooper, Kate. 'The Bride of Christ, the "Male Woman," and the Female Reader in Late Antiquity'. In *The Oxford Handbook of Women and Gender in Medieval Europe*, edited by Judith Bennett and Ruth Mazo Karas, 529–44. Oxford: Oxford University Press, 2013.

Cooper, Kate. 'Christianity, Private Power and the Law from Decius to Constantine: The Minimalist View'. *Journal of Early Christian Studies* 19 (2011): 327–43.

Cooper, Kate. 'Closely Watched Households: Visibility, Exposure and Private Power in the Roman Domus'. *Past and Present* 197 (2007): 3–33.

Cooper, Kate. 'A Father, a Daughter and a Procurator: Authority and Resistance in the Prison Memoir of Perpetua of Carthage'. *Gender and History* 2 (2011): 685–702.

Cooper, Kate. The Household as a Venue for Religious Conversion'. In *A Companion to Families in the Greek and Roman Worlds*, edited by Beryl Rawson, 183–97. Oxford: Wiley, 2010.

Cooper, Kate. 'Insinuations of Womanly Influence: An Aspect of the Christianization of the Roman Aristocracy'. *Journal of Roman Studies* 82 (1992): 150–64.

Cooper, Kate. 'Poverty, Obligation and Inheritance: Roman Heiresses and the Varieties of Senatorial Christianity in Fifth Century Rome'. In *Religion, Dynasty and Patronage in Early Christian Rome*, edited by Kate Cooper and Julia Hillner, 165–87. Cambridge: Cambridge University Press, 2007.

Cooper, Kate. 'A Saint in Exile: The Early Medieval Thecla at Rome and Meriamlik'. *Hagiographica* 2 (1995): 1–24.

Cooper, Kate. *The Virgin and the Bride: Idealized Womanhood in Late Antiquity*. Cambridge, MA: Harvard University Press, 1996.

Cooper, Kate. 'Ventriloquism and the Miraculous: Conversion, Preaching and the Martyr Exemplum in Late Antiquity'. In *Signs, Wonders, Miracles: Representations of Divine Power*. Vol. 41 of *Life of the Church: Studies in Church History*, edited by Kate Cooper and Jeremy Gregory, 22–45. Woodbridge, Suffolk: Boydell & Brewer, 2005.

Cooper, Kate. 'The Voice of the Victim: Gender, Representation and Early Christian Martyrdom'. *Bulletin of the John Rylands University Library* 80 (1998): 147–57.

Cooper, Kate, and Conrad Leyser. 'The Gender of Grace: Impotence, Servitude and Manliness in the Fifth Century West'. *Gender and History* 12 (2000): 536–51.

Corrington, Gail P. 'The "Divine Woman?" Propaganda and the Power of Celibacy in the New Testament Apocrypha: A Reconsideration'. *Anglican Theological Review* 70 (1988): 207–20.

Corrington, Gail P. 'The Divine Woman, Propaganda and the Power of Chastity in the New Testament Apocrypha'. *Helios* 13 (1987): 151–62.

Corrington Streete, Gail P. 'Authority and Authorship: The Acts of Paul and Thecla as a Disputed Pauline Text'. *Lexington Theological Quarterly* 40 (2005): 265–76.

Corrington Streete, Gail P. 'Buying the Stairway to Heaven: Perpetua and Thecla as Early Christian Heroines'. In *Feminist Companion to the New Testament Apocrypha*, ed. Amy-Jill Levine, with Maria Mayo Robbins, 186–205. Cleveland, OH: Pilgrim, 2006.

Corrington Streete, Gail P. 'Of Martyrs and Men, Perpetua, Thecla and the Ambiguity of Female Heroism in Early Christianity'. In *The Subjective Eye, Essays in Culture, Religion and Gender in Honor of Margaret R. Miles*, edited by Richard Valantasis, 254–64. Eugene, OR: Pickwick, 2006.

Corrington Streete, Gail P. *Redeemed Bodies, Women Martyrs in Early Christianity.* Louisville, KY: Westminster John Knox, 2009.

Crossan, John Dominic. 'Roman Imperial Theology'. In *In the Shadow of Empire: Reclaiming the Bible as a History of Faithful Resistance*, edited by Richard A. Horsley, 59–73. Louisville, KY: Westminster John Knox, 2008.

Crossan, John Dominic, and Jonathan L. Reed. *In Search of Paul: How Jesus' Apostle Opposed Rome's Empire with God's Kingdom.* San Francisco, CA: Harper, 2004.

Crusemann, Marlene. 'Irredeemably Hostile to Women: Anti-Jewish Elements in the Exegesis of the Dispute about Women's Right to Speak, 1 Cor 14.34-45'. *Journal for the Study of the New Testament* 79 (2000): 19–36.

Culler, Jonathan. *Structuralist Poetics: Structuralism, Linguistics and the Study of Literature.* London: Routledge & Kegan Paul, 1975.

D'Angelo, Mary Rose. '(Re)Presentations of Women in the Gospel of Matthew and Luke-Acts'. In *Women and Christian Origins*, edited by Ross Shepard Kraemer and Mary Rose D'Angelo, 171–95. Oxford: Oxford University Press, 1999.

D'Angelo, Mary Rose. 'Veils, Virgins and the Tongues of Men and Angels: Women's Heads in Early Christianity'. In *Off with Her Head! The Denial of Women's Identity in Myth, Religion and Culture*, edited by Howard Eilberg Schwartz and Wendy Doniger, 131–64. Berkeley: University of California Press, 1995.

D'Angelo, Mary Rose. 'Women in Luke-Acts: A Redactional View'. *Journal of Biblical Literature* 109 (1990): 441–61.

Dagron, Gilbert, and Marie Dupré de la Tour. *Vie et Miracles de Saint Thècle. Texte Grec. Traduction et Commentaire.* Brussels: Société des Bollandistes, 1978.

Davies, Stevan L. *The Revolt of the Widows: The Social World of the Apocryphal Acts.* Carbondale: Southern Illinois University Press, 1980.

Davies, Stevan L. 'Women, Tertullian and the *Acts of Paul*'. *Semeia: The Apocryphal Acts of the Apostles in Intertextual Perspective* 38 (1986): 139–44.

Davis, Stephen J. 'Crossed Texts, Crossed Sex: Intertextuality and Gender in Early Christian Legends of Holy Women Disguised as Men'. *Journal of Early Christian Studies* 10 (2002): 1–36.

Davis, Stephen J. *The Cult of Saint Thecla: A Tradition of Women's Piety in Late Antiquity.* Atlanta, GA: Oxford University Press, 2001.

de Nie, Giselle. 'Fatherly and Motherly Curing in Sixth Century Gaul: Saint Radegund's *Mysterium*'. In *Women and Miracle Stories: A Multidisciplinary Exploration*, edited by Anne-Marie Korte, 53–86. Leiden: Brill, 2001.

Derrida, Jacques. 'Biodegradables: Seven Diary Fragments'. Translated by Peggy Kamuf. *Critical Inquiry* 15 (1989): 812–73.

Derrida, Jacques. *Of Grammatology.* Translated by Gayatri Chakravorty Spivak. Baltimore, MD: John Hopkins University Press, 1976.

Döpp, S., and W. Geerlings, eds. *Lexikon der antiken christlichen Literatur.* Vienna: Herder Verlag, 1998.

duBois, Page. *Torture and Truth.* New York: Routledge, 1991.

Dunn, Peter W. 'The Acts of Paul and the Pauline Legacy in the Second Century', PhD diss., University of Cambridge, 1996. Online at: http://www.actapauli.files.wordpress. com/ 2009/01/pwdunn1996.pdf.

Dunn, Peter W. 'Women's Liberation, the Acts of Paul and Other Apocryphal Acts of the Apostles: A Review of Some Recent Interpreters'. *Apocrypha* 4 (1993): 245-61.

Dworkin, Andrea. *Pornography: Men Possessing Women*. London: Women's Press, 1981.

Dworkin, Ronald. 'Is There a Right to Pornography?' *Oxford Journal of Legal Studies* 1 (1981): 177-212.

Easton, Susan M. *The Problem of Pornography: Regulation and the Right to Free Speech*. London: Routledge, 1994.

Ehrman, Bart D., ed. and trans. *The Apostolic Fathers I, I Clement, II Clement, Ignatius, Polycarp, Didache*. Cambridge, MA: Harvard University Press, 2003.

Eilberg-Schwartz, Howard. *God's Phallus and Other Problems for Men and Monotheism*. Boston, MA: Beacon Press, 1994.

Eilberg-Schwartz, Howard. 'The Spectacle of the Female Head'. In *Off with Her Head! The Denial of Women's Identity in Myth, Religion and Culture*, edited by Howard Eilberg Schwartz and Wendy Doniger, 1-14. Berkeley: University of California Press, 1995.

Eilberg-Schwartz, Howard, and Wendy Doniger, eds. *Off with Her Head! The Denial of Women's Identity in Myth, Religion and Culture*. Berkeley: University of California Press, 1995.

Eitrem, Samson. 'Dreams and Divination in Magical Ritual'. In *Magika Hiera: Ancient Greek Magic and Religion*, edited by Christopher A. Faraone and Dirk Obbink, 175-87. Oxford: Oxford University Press, 1991.

Elliott, J. K. *The Apocryphal New Testament*. Oxford: Oxford University Press, 1993.

Elliott, Neil. *Liberating Paul: The Justice of God and the Politics of the Apostle*. New York: Orbis, 1994.

Elm, Susanna. *Virgins of God: The Making of Asceticism in Late Antiquity*. Oxford: Clarenden Press, 1994.

Elsom, Helen E. 'Callirhoe: Displaying the Phallic Woman'. In *Pornography and Representation in Greece and Rome*, edited by Amy Richlin, 180-211. Oxford: Oxford University Press, 1992.

Epstein, Julia, and Kristina Straub, eds. *Body Guards: The Cultural Politics of Gender Ambiguity*. London: Routledge, 1991.

Epstein, Julia, and Kristina Straub. 'Introduction to *Body Guards*'. In *Body Guards: The Cultural Politics of Gender Ambiguity*, edited by Julia Epstein and Kristina Straub, 1-28. London: Routledge, 1991.

Esch, Elisabeth. 'Thekla und die Tiere. Oder: Die Zähmung der Widerspenstigen'. In *Aus Liebe zu Paulus? Die Akte Thekla neu aufgerollt*, edited by Martin Ebner, 159-79. Stuttgarter: Bibelstudien, Stuttgart, 2005.

Esch-Wermeling, Elisabeth. *Thekla—Paulusschülerin wider Willen? Strategien der Leserlenkung in den Theklaakten*. Münster: Aschendorff, 2008.

Evans Grubbs, Judith. *Women and the Law in the Roman Empire: A Sourcebook on Marriage, Divorce and Widowhood*. London: Routledge, 2002.

Faraone, Christopher A. *Ancient Greek Love Magic*. Cambridge, MA: Harvard University Press, 1999.

Faraone, Christopher A. 'The Agonistic Context of Early Greek Binding Spells'. In *Magika Hiera: Ancient Greek Magic and Religion*, edited by Christopher A. Faraone and Dirk Obbink, 3-32. Oxford: Oxford University Press, 1991.

Faraone, Christopher A., and Dirk Obbink, eds. *Magika Hiera: Ancient Greek Magic and Religion*. Oxford: Oxford University Press, 1991.
Fee, Gordon D. *1 and 2 Timothy, Titus*. Peabody, MA: Hendrickson/Paternoster, 1995.
Fee, Gordon D. *The First Epistle to the Corinthians*. Grand Rapids, MI: Eerdmans, 1987.
Ferguson, John, trans. *Clement of Alexandria, Stromateis, Books One to Three*. Washington, DC: Catholic University of America Press, 1991.
Fine, Steven. *Art and Judaism in the Greco-Roman World: Toward a New Jewish Archaeology*. Cambridge: Cambridge University Press, 2005.
Foucault, Michel. *The History of Sexuality. Vol. 1, An Introduction*. Translated by Robert Hurley. New York: Vintage Books, 1990.
Foucault, Michel. *The History of Sexuality. Vol. 2, The Use of Pleasure*. Translated by Robert Hurley. England: Penguin Books, 1984.
Foucault, Michel. *The History of Sexuality. Vol. 3, The Care of the Self*. Translated by Robert Hurley. England: Penguin Books, 1984.
Foucault, Michel. 'What Is an Author?' In *Textual Strategies: Perspectives in Post-Structuralist Criticism*, translated and edited by Josué V. Harari, 141–60. London: Methuen, 1979.
Fowler, Alistair. *Kinds of Literature: An Introduction to the Theory of Genres and Modes*. Oxford: Oxford University Press, 1982.
Fowler, Alistair. 'The Life and Death of Literary Forms'. In *New Directions in Literary History*, edited by Ralph Cohen, 77–94. London: Routledge & Kegan Paul, 1974.
Foxhall, Lin. 'Pandora Unbound: A Feminist Critique of Foucault's *History of Sexuality*'. In *Rethinking Sexuality: Foucault and Classical Antiquity*, edited by D. H. J. Larmour, P. A. Miller and C. Platter, 122–37. Princeton, NJ: Princeton University Press, 1998.
Frankfurter, David. 'Martyrology and the Prurient Gaze'. *Journal of Early Christian Studies* 17 (2009): 215–45.
Frazer, James G. *The Golden Bough*. 3rd ed. Cambridge: Cambridge University Press, 2012.
Frediksen, Paul. 'Christians in the Roman Empire in the First Three Centuries CE'. In *A Companion to the Roman Empire*, edited by David S. Potter, 587–606. West Sussex: Blockwell, 2010.
Frey, Jörg, Jens Herzer, Martina Janssen and Clare K. Rothschild, eds. *Pseudepigraphic und Verfasserfiktion in frühchristlichen Briefen*. Tübingen: Mohr Siebeck, 2009.
Fulton, John. *Index Canonum: The Canons Called Apostolical, the Canons of the Undisputed General Councils and the Canons of the Provincial Council of Ancyra Neo-Caesarea, Gangra, Antioch and Laodicea*. New York: Pott, Young, 1872.
Gager, John G. *Curse Tablets and Binding Spells from the Ancient World*. Oxford: Oxford University Press, 1999.
Galinsky, Karl. *Augustus: Introduction to the Life of an Emperor*. Cambridge: Cambridge University Press, 2012.
Gamble, Harry. *Books and Readers: A History of Early Christian Texts*. New Haven, CT: Yale University Press, 1995.
Gardner, Jane F. *Women in Roman Law and Society: Women's Life in Greece and Rome*. London: Midland, 1995.
Gentili, Bruno, and Giovvani Cerri. *History and Biography in Ancient Thought*. Translated by L. Murray. Amsterdam: Gieben, 1988.
Georgi, Dieter. *Theocracy in Paul's Praxis and Theology*. Translated by David E. Green. Augsburg, MN: Fortress, 1991.

Gergel, Richard A. 'Costume as Geographic Indicator: Barbarians and Prisoners on Cuirassed Statue Breastplates'. In *The World of Roman Costume*, edited by J. Sebesta and L. Bonfante, 191-208. Madison, WI: University of Wisconsin Press, 2001.

Girard, Rene. *Violence and the Sacred*. Translated by Patrick Gregory. London: Baltimore, 1977.

Glancy, Jennifer A. 'Unveiling Masculinity: The Construction of Gender in Mark 6.17-29'. *Biblical Interpretation* 1 (1994): 34-50.

Gleason, Maud W. *Making Men, Sophists and Self-Presentation in Ancient Rome*. Princeton, NJ: Princeton University Press, 1995.

Gleason, Maud W. 'The Semiotics of Gender: Physiognomy and Self-Fashioning in the Second Century CE'. In *Before Sexuality: The Construction of Erotic Experience in the Ancient Greek World*, edited by David M. Halperin, John D. Winkler and Froma I. Zeitlin, 389-415. Princeton, NJ: Princeton University Press, 1990.

Goldhill, Simon. 'The Erotic Eye: Visual stimulation and the Cultural Conflict'. In *Being Greek under Rome: Cultural Identity, the Second Sophistic and the Development of Empire*, edited by Simon Goldhill, 154-94. Cambridge: University of Cambridge Press, 2001.

Goldhill, Simon. *Foucault's Virginity: Ancient Erotic Fiction and the History of Sexuality*. Cambridge: Cambridge University Press, 1995.

Goody, Jack. 'Religion and Ritual: The Definition Problem'. *British Journal of Sociology* 12 (1961): 142-64.

Graf, Fritz. 'How to Cope with a Difficult Life'. In *Envisioning Magic: A Princeton Seminar and Symposium*, edited by Peter Schäfer and Hans G. Kippenberg, 93-114. Leiden: Brill, 1997.

Graf, Fritz. 'Prayer in Magic and Religious Ritual'. In *Magika Hiera: Ancient Greek Magic and Religion*, edited by Christopher A. Faraone and Dirk Obbink, 188-213. Oxford: Oxford University Press, 1991.

Graham Brock, Ann. 'Genre of the *Acts of Paul*: One Tradition Enhancing Another'. *Apocrypha* 5 (1994): 119-36.

Grant, Robert M. *Early Christians and Animals*. London: Routledge, 1999.

Grossman, Maxine L. 'Reading for Gender in the Damascus Document'. *Dead Sea Discoveries* 11, no. 2 (2004): 212-23.

Grudem, Wayne. 'Appendix I: Does kephale ("head") Mean "Source" or "Authority Over" in Greek Literature? A Survey of 2,336 Examples'. In *The Role Relationship of Men and Women: New Testament Teaching*, edited by George W. Knight, 49-80. Chicago, IL: Moody, 1985.

Grudem, Wayne. 'Appendix 1: The Meaning of Kephale ("Head"): A Response to Recent Studies'. In *Recovering Biblical Manhood*, edited by John Piper and Wayne Grudem, 425-68. Wheaton, IL: Crossway, 2006.

Gryson, Roger. *The Ministry of Women in the Early Church*. Translated by Jean Laporte and Mary Louise Hall. Collegeville, MN: Liturgical Press, 1976.

Hagg, Thomas. *The Art of Biography in Antiquity*. Cambridge: Cambridge University Press, 2012.

Haines-Eitzen, Kim. 'Engendering Palimpsests: Reading the Textual Tradition of the Acts of Paul and Thecla'. In *The Early Christian Book*, edited by William E. Kingshirn and Linda Safran, 177-93. Washington: DC: Catholic University of America Press, 2007.

Haines-Eitzen, Kim. *The Gendered Palimpsest: Women, Writing and Representation in Early Christianity*. Oxford: Oxford University Press, 2012.

Hallett, Judith P., and Marilyn B. Skinner, eds. *Roman Sexualities*. Princeton, NJ: Princeton University Press, 1997.
Halperin, David M. *One Hundred Years of Homosexuality and Other Essays on Greek Love*. London: Routledge, 1990.
Halperin, David M., John J. Winkler and Froma I. Zeitlin, eds. *Before Sexuality: The Construction of Erotic Experience in the Ancient Greek World*. Princeton, NJ: Princeton University Press, 1990.
Hammond, Dorothy. 'Magic – a Problem in Semantics'. *American Anthropologist* 72 (1970): 1349–56.
Hanson, Ann Ellis. 'The Medical Writers' Woman'. In *Before Sexuality: The Construction of Erotic Experience in the Ancient Greek World*, edited by David M. Halperin et al., 309–38. Princeton, NJ: Princeton University Press, 1990.
Hawley, Richard. 'The Body as Spectacle in Attic Drama'. In *Thinking Men: Masculinity and Its Self-Representation in the Classical Tradition*, edited by Lin Foxhall and John Salmon. London: Routledge 1998.
Hays, Hoffman R. *The Dangerous Sex: The Myth of Feminine Evil*. London: Methuen, 1966.
Hays, Richard B. *First Corinthians*. Louisville, KY: John Knox Press, 1997.
Henderson, Jeffrey. *The Maculate Muse: Obscene Language in Attic Comedy*. New Haven, CT: Yale University Press, 1991.
Hennecke, Edgar. *Neutestamentlichen Apokryphen in deutscher Übersetzung*, edited by Wilhelm Schneemelcher. Tübingen: Mohr Siebeck, 1964.
Hennecke, Edgar. *New Testament Apocrypha II*. Rev. ed., edited by Wilhelm Schneemelcher. Translated by R. McLean Wilson. Louisville, KY: James Clarke, John Knox, 1992.
Herter, Hans. 'The Sociology of Prostitution in Antiquity in the Context of Pagan and Christian Writings'. In *Sex and Difference in Ancient Greece and Rome*, edited by Mark Golden and Peter Toohey. Translated by Linwood DeLong, 57–113. Edinburgh: Edinburgh University Press, 2003.
Hilhorst, A. 'Tertullian on the Acts of Paul'. In *The Apocryphal Acts of Paul and Thecla*, edited by Jan N. Bremmer, 150–63. Kampen: Kok Pharos, 1996.
Hock, Ronald F., J. Bradley Chance and Judith Perkins, eds. *Ancient Fiction and Early Christian Narrative*. Atlanta, GA: Scholars Press, 2003.
Holloway, P. A. *Coping with Prejudice: 1 Peter in Social and Psychological Perspective*. Tübingen: Mohr Seibeck, 2009.
Hopkins, Keith. *Death and Renewal: Sociological Studies in Roman History*. Cambridge: Cambridge University Press, 1983.
Horn, Cornelia B. 'Suffering Children, Parental Authority and the Quest for Liberation?: A Tale of Three Girls in the Acts of Paul (and Thecla), the Act(s) of Peter, the Acts of Nerseus and Achilleus and the Epistle of Pseudo-Titus'. In *Feminist Companion to the New Testament Apocrypha*, edited by Amy-Jill Levine, with Maria Mayo Robbins, 118–45. Cleveland, OH: Pilgrim, 2006.
Hornblower, Simon, and Antony Spawforth, eds. *The Oxford Companion to Classical Civilization*. 2nd ed. Oxford: Oxford University Press, 2014.
Horsley, Richard A., ed. *Paul and Empire: Religion and Power in Roman Imperial Society*. Harrisburg, PA: Trinity, 1997.
Horsley, Richard A., and Neil A. Silberman. *The Message and the Kingdom: How Jesus and Paul Ignited a Revolution and Transformed the Ancient World*. Augsburg, MN: Fortress, 2002.

Howe, Margaret E. 'Interpretations of Paul in the Acts of Paul and Thecla'. In *Pauline Studies Essays Presented to Professor F.F. Bruce on His 70th Birthday*, edited by Donald A. Hagner and Murray J. Harris, 33-49. Exeter, Devon: Paternoster, 1980.

Hurtado, Larry W. 'Who Read Early Christian Apocrypha?'. In *Oxford Handbook to Early Christian Apocrypha*, edited by Christopher Tuckett and Andrew Gregory, 153-66. Oxford: Oxford University Press, 2015.

Hylen, Susan E. *A Modest Apostle: Thecla and the History of Women in the Early Church*. Oxford: Oxford University Press, 2015.

James, M. R. *The Apocryphal New Testament*. Oxford: Clarendon Press, 1924.

Jensen, Anne. 'Die Theklageschichte. Die Apostolin zwischen Fiktion und Realität'. In *Compendium Feministische Bibelauslegung*, edited by L. Schottroff and M. T. Wacker, 742-7. Darmstadt: Wissenschaftliche Buchgesellschaft, 1999.

Jensen, Anne. *Thekla – Die Apostelin: Ein apokrypher Text neu entdeckt*. Freiburg: Herder, 1995.

Jensen, Robin M. 'Baptismal Rites and Architecture'. In *Late Ancient Christianity*, edited by Virginia Burrus, 117-44. Augsburg, MN: Fortress, 2005.

Jensen, Robin M. *Understanding Early Christian Art*. London: Routledge, 2000.

Joshel, Sandra R. 'The Body Female and the Body Politic: Livyis Lucretia and Verginia'. In *Pornography and Representation in Greece and Rome*, edited by Amy Richlin, 112-30. Oxford: Oxford University Press, 1992.

Joshel, Sandra R. 'Female Desire and the Discourse of Empire: Tacitus's Messalina'. *Signs* 21 (1995): 50-82.

Judith, Perkins. 'The Apocryphal Acts of the Apostles and Early Christian Martyrdom'. *Arethusa* 18 (1985): 211-30.

Junod, Eric. 'Les vies des philosophes et les actes apocryphes: Un dessein similarie?' In *Les Acts Apocryphes de Apôtres: Christianisme et Monde Paien*, edited by F. Bovon, 209-19. Geneva: Labor et Fides, 1981.

Kaestli, Jean-Daniel. 'Fiction littéraire et réalité sociale: que peut-on savoir de la place des femmes dans le milieu de production des Actes apocryphes des Apôtres?' *Apocrypha* 1 (1990): 279-302.

Kaestli, Jean-Daniel. 'Les Actes Apocryphes et la reconstitution de l'histoire des femmes dans le christianisme ancient'. *Cahiers bibliques de Foi et Vie* 28 (1989): 71-9.

Kaestli, Jean-Daniel. 'Response'. *Semeia: The Apocryphal Acts of Apostles* 38 (1986): 119-31.

Kaplan, Ann E. 'Is the Gaze Male?' In *Powers of Desire: The Politics of Sexuality*, edited by Ann Snitow, Christine Stansell and Sharon Thompson, 309-27. New York: Monthly Review Press, 1983.

Kappeler, Susanne. *The Pornography of Representation*. Minneapolis: University of Minnesota Press, 1986.

Kelley, Nicole. 'Philosophy as Training for Death: Reading the Ancient Christian Martyr as Spiritual Exercises'. *Church History* 75 (2006): 723-48.

Keuls, Eva C. *Reign of the Phallus: Sexual Politics in Ancient Athens*. Berkeley: University of California Press, 1985.

King, Karen L. 'Prophetic Power and Women's Authority: The Case of the Gospel of Mary Magdalene'. In *Women Preachers and Prophets through Two Millennia of Christianity*, edited by Beverly M. Kienzle and Pamela Walker, 21-41. Berkley: University of California Press, 1998.

Klauck, Hans-Josef. *The Apocryphal Acts of the Apostles: An Introduction.* Waco, TX: Baylor University Press, 2008.
Kleiner, Fred S. *A History of Roman Art.* Boston, MA: Clark Baxter, 2010.
Koloski-Ostrow, Ann Olga, and Claire L. Lyons, eds. *Naked Truths: Women, Sexuality and Gender in Classical Art and Archaeology.* London: Routledge, 1997.
Konstan, David. 'Acts of Love: A Narrative Pattern in the Apocryphal Acts'. *Journal of Early Christian Studies* 6 (1998): 15–36.
Korte, Anne-Marie. 'Epilogue' to *Women and Miracle Stories: A Multidisciplinary Exploration.*, edited by Anne-Marie Korte, 325–40. Leiden: Brill, 2001.
Korte, Anne-Marie. 'Introduction' to *Women and Miracle Stories: A Multidisciplinary Exploration*, edited by Anne-Marie Korte, 1–28. Leiden: Brill, 2001.
Korte, Anne-Marie, ed. *Women and Miracle Stories: A Multidisciplinary Exploration.* Leiden: Brill, 2001.
Kraemer, Ross Shepard. 'The Conversion of Women to Ascetic Forms of Christianity'. *Signs* (1980): 298–307.
Kraemer, Ross Shepard. *Her Share of the Blessings: Women's Religions among Pagans, Jews and Christians in the Greco-Roman world.* Oxford: Oxford University Press, 1992.
Kraemer, Ross Shepard. *Unreliable Witnesses, Religion, Gender and History in the Greco-Roman Mediterranean.* New York: Oxford University Press, 2011.
Kraemer, Ross Shepard. 'Women's Authorship of Jewish and Christian Literature in the Greco-Roman Period'. In *'Women Like This': New Perspectives on Jewish Women in the Greco-Roman World*, edited by Am-Jill Levine, 221–42. Atlanta, GA: Scholars Press, 1991.
Kraemer, Ross Shepard, ed. *Women's Religions in the Greco-Roman World: A Sourcebook.* Oxford: Oxford University Press, 2004.
Kyle, Donald G. *Spectacles of Death in Ancient Rome.* London: Routledge, 2001.
Lalleman, P. J. 'Polymorphy of Christ'. In *The Apocryphal Acts of John*, edited by Jan N. Bremmer, 97–118. Kampen: Kok Pharos, 1995.
Lalleman, Pieter J. *The Acts of John: A Two Stage Initiation into Johannine Gnosticism.* Leuven: Peeters, 1998.
Lane Fox, R. 'Literacy and Power in Early Christianity'. In *Literacy and Power in the Ancient World*, edited by A. K. Bowman and G. Woolf, 126–48. Cambridge: Cambridge University Press, 1994.
Lang, Karen. 'Shaven Heads and Loose Hair: Buddhist Attitudes toward Hair and Sexuality'. In *Off with Her Head! The Denial of Women's Identity in Myth, Religion and Culture*, edited by Howard Eilberg Schwartz and Wendy Doniger, 32–52. Berkeley: University of California Press, 1995.
Laquer, Thomas. *Making Sex: Body and Gender from the Greeks to Freud.* Cambridge, MA: Harvard University Press, 1990.
Lefkowitz, Mary R. 'Did Ancient Women Write Novels?' In *'Women Like This': New Perspectives on Jewish Women in the Greco-Roman World*, edited by Am-Jill Levine, 199–219. Atlanta, GA: Scholars Press, 1991.
Levine, Amy-Jill. 'Introduction' to *A Feminist Companion to the Deutero-Pauline Epistles*, edited by Amy-Jill Levine, 1–13. London: T&T Clark, 2003.
Levine, Amy-Jill, ed. *'Women Like This': New Perspectives on Jewish Women in the Greco-Roman World.* Atlanta, GA: Scholars Press, 1991.
Levine, Amy-Jill, with Marianne Blickenstaff, eds. *A Feminist Companion to the Deutero-Pauline Epistles.* London: T&T Clark, 2003.

Levine, Amy-Jill, with Maria Mayo Robbins, eds. *A Feminist Companion to the New Testament Apocrypha.* Cleveland, OH: Pilgrim, 2006.
Liddell, G., and R. Scott. *Greek-English Lexicon.* Oxford: Clarendon Press, 1996.
Lieu, Judith M. 'The "Attraction of Women" into Early Judaism and Christianity: Gender and the Politics of Conversion'. *Journal for the Study of the New Testament* 72 (1998): 5–22.
Lieu, Judith M. *Christian Identity in the Jewish and Graeco-Roman World.* Oxford: Oxford University Press, 2004.
Lieu, Judith M. 'Jews, Christian and "Pagans" in Conflict'. In *Critique and Apologetics: Jews, Christian and Pagans in Antiquity*, edited by A. C. Jacobsen, Jörg Ulrich and David Brakke, 43–58. Frankfurt: Lang, 2009.
Lipsett, Diane B. *Desiring Conversion: Hermas, Thecla, Aseneth.* Oxford: Oxford University Press, 2001.
Lipsius, Richard Adelbert, and Maximillianus Bonnet, eds. *Acta Apostolorum Apocryphra, Post Constantinum.* Hildesheim: Georg Olms, [1852] 1990.
Lopez, Davina C. 'Before Your Very Eyes: Roman Imperial Ideology, Gender Constructs and Paul's Inter-Nationalism'. In *Mapping Gender in Ancient Religious Discourses*, edited by Todd Penner and Caroline Vander Stichele, 115–62. Boston: Brill, 2007.
Loraux, Nicole. *Tragic Ways of Killing a Woman.* Translated by Anthony Forster. Cambridge, MA: Harvard University Press, 1987.
MacDonald, Dennis R. 'Corinthian Veils and Gnostic Androgynes'. In *Images of the Feminine in Gnosticism*, edited by Karen L. King, 276–92. Philadelphia, PA: Fortress, 1988.
MacDonald, Dennis R. 'From Audita to Legenda: Oral and Written Miracle Stories'. *Forum, Foundation and Facets* 2 (1986): 15–26.
MacDonald, Dennis R. *The Legend and the Apostle: The Battle for Paul in Story and Canon.* Philadelphia, PA: Westminster, 1983.
MacDonald, Dennis R. *There Is No Male and Female: The Fate of a Dominical Saying in Paul and Gnosticism.* Philadelphia, PA: Fortress, 1987.
MacDonald, Margaret Y. *Early Christian Women and Pagan Opinion: The Power of the Hysterical Woman.* Cambridge: Cambridge University Press, 1996.
MacDonald, Margaret Y. *The Pauline Churches: A Socio-Historical Study of Institutionalization in the Pauline and Deutero-Pauline Writings.* Cambridge: Cambridge University Press, 1988.
Mackay, Thomas W. 'Response'. *Semeia* 38 (1986): 145–9.
MacKinnon, Catharine A. 'Feminism, Marxism and the State: An Agenda for Theory'. In *Signs Reader: Women, Gender and Scholarship*, edited by Elizabeth Abel and Emily Abel, 227–56. Chicago, IL: University of Chicago Press, 1983.
MacKinnon, Catharine A. *Feminism Unmodified: Discourses on Life and Law.* Cambridge, MA: Harvard University Press, 1987.
MacKinnon, Catharine A. *Toward a Feminist Theory of the State.* Cambridge, MA: Harvard University Press, 1989.
Malherbe, Abraham J. 'A Physical Description of Paul'. *Harvard Theological Review* 79 (1986): 170–5.
Marshall, Howard I. *A Critical and Exegetical Commentary on the Pastoral Epistles.* London: T&T Clark, 2004.
Martin, Dale B. *The Corinthian Body.* New Haven, CT: Yale University Press, 1995.
Martin, Dale B. 'Hererosexism and the Interpretation of Romans 1.18-32'. *Biblical Interpretation* 3 (1995): 332–55.

Matthews, Shelly. 'Thinking of Thecla: Issues in Feminist Historiography'. *Journal of Feminist Studies in Religion* 12 (2002): 39–54.
McGinn, Sheila E. 'The Acts of Thecla'. In *Searching the Scriptures: A Feminist Commentary*, edited by Elisabeth Schüssler-Fiorenza et al., 800–28. New York: Crossroad, 1994.
McInerney, Maud Burnett. *Eloquent Virgins from Thecla to Joan of Arc*. New York: Palgrave MacMillan, 2003.
McKitterick, Rosamond. *The Carolingians and the Written Word*. Cambridge: Cambridge University Press, 1989.
McNamara, Jo-Ann. *A New Song: Celibate Women in the First Three Christian Centuries*. New York: Harrington Parks Press, 1983.
Meeks, Wayne A. 'The Image of the Androgyne: Some Uses of a Symbol in Earliest Christianity'. *History of Religions* 13, no. 3 (1974): 165–208.
Meeks, Wayne A., and John T. Fitzgerald, eds. *The Writings of St. Paul*. New York: Norton, 2007.
Methuen, Charlotte. 'The "Virgin" Widow: A Problematic Social Role for the Early Church?' *Harvard Theological Review* 90 (1997): 285–98.
Metzger, M. *A Textual Commentary on the Greek New Testament*. New York: United Bible Societies, 1971.
Middleton, Paul. '"Dying We Live" (2 Cor 6.9): Discipleship and Martyrdom in Paul'. In *Paul, Grace and Freedom: Essays in Honour of John K. Riches*, edited by Paul Middleton, Karen J. Wenell and Angus Paddison, 82–93. London: T&T Clark, 2009.
Miles, Margaret R. *Carnal Knowing*. Eugene, OR: Wipf & Stock, 1989.
Misset-van de Weg, Magda. 'Magic, Miracle and Miracle Workers in the Acts of Thecla'. In *Women and Miracle Stories: A Multidisciplinary Exploration*, edited by Anne-Marie Korte, 29–52. Leiden: Brill, 2001.
Moss, Candida. *The Myth of Persecution: How Early Christians Invested a Story of Martyrdom*. London: Harper Collins, 2013.
Mounce, William D. *Pastoral Epistles*. Vol. 46 of *Word Biblical Commentary*. Nashville, TN: Thomas Nelson, 2000.
Mulvey, Laura. 'Visual Pleasure and Narrative Cinema'. *Screen* 16 (1975): 6–18.
Murphy-O'Connor, Jerome. 'Sex and Logic in 1 Corinthians 11.2-16'. *Catholic Biblical Quarterly* 42 (1980): 482–500.
Musurillo, Herbert. *The Acts of the Christian Martyrs: Introduction Texts and Translation*. Oxford: Clarendon Press, 1972.
Myerowitz Levine, Molly. 'The Gendered Grammar of Ancient Mediterranean Hair'. In *Off with Her Head! The Denial of Women's Identity in Myth, Religion and Culture*, 76–130. Berkeley: University of California Press, 1995.
Nauerth, Claudia. 'Nachlese von Thekla-Darstellungen'. In *Studien zur spätantiken und frühchristlichen Kunst and Kuttur des Orients – Göttinger Orientforschungen*, edited by Guntram Koch, 14–18. Wiesbaden: Harrassowitz, 1986.
Nauerth, Claudia, and Rüdiger Warns. *Thekla. Ihre Bilder in der frühchristlichen Kunst: Göttinger Orientforschungen, Studien zur spätantiken und frühchristlichen Kunst*. Wiesbaden: Harrassowitz, 1981.
Ng, Esther Yue L. 'Acts of Paul and Thecla: Women's Studies and Precedent'. *Journal of Theological Studies* 55 (2004): 1–29.
Ogden, Daniel. 'Binding Spells: Curse Tablets and Voodoo Dolls in the Greek and Roman Worlds'. In *Witchcraft and Magic in Europe: Ancient Greek and Rome*, edited by B. Ankarloo and S. Clark, 38–86. Philadelphia: University of Pennsylvania Press, 1991.

Ohm Wright, Ruth. 'Rendezvous with Thekla and Paul in Ephesos: Excavating the Evidence'. In *Distant Voices Drawing Near: Essays in Honor of Antoinette Clark Wire*, edited by Holly E. Hearon, 227–42. Collegeville, MN: Liturgical Press, 2004.

Olson, Kelly. *Dress and the Roman Woman: Self-Presentation and Society*. New York: Routledge, 2008.

Oseik, Carolyn. 'The Widow as Altar: The Rise and Fall of a Symbol'. *Journal of Early Christian Studies* 3 (1983): 159–69.

Pao, David W. 'The Genre of the Acts of Andrew'. *Apocrypha* 6 (1995): 179–202.

Parker, Holt N. 'The Teratogenic Grid'. In *Roman Sexualities*, edited by Judith P. Hallett and Marilyn B. Skinner, 47–65. Princeton, NJ: Princeton University Press, 1997.

Patterson, Stephen J., and James M. Robinson, with a New English Translation by Hans-Gebhard Bethge. *The Fifth Gospel: The Gospel of Thomas Comes of Age*. Harrisburg, PA: Trinity Press International, 1998.

Payne, Philip B. 'Fuldensis, Sigla for Variants in Vaticanus and in 1 Corinthians 14:34-35'. *New Testament Studies* 41 (1995): 240–62.

Penner, Todd, and Caroline Vander Stichele, eds. *Mapping Gender in Ancient Religious Discourses*. Boston, MA: Brill, 2007.

Perkins, Judith. 'The Apocryphal Acts of the Apostles and Early Christian Martyrdom'. *Arethusa* 18 (1985): 211–30.

Perkins, Judith. 'Fictional Narratives and Social Critique'. In *Late Ancient Christianity*, edited by Virginia Burrus, 46–69. Augsburg, MN: Fortress, 2005.

Perkins, Judith. *Roman Imperial Identities in the Early Christian Era*. London: Routledge, 2009.

Perkins, Judith. 'The Social World of the Acts of Peter'. In *The Search for the Ancient Novel*, edited by James Tatum, 296–307. Baltimore, MD: John Hopkins University Press, 1994.

Perkins, Judith. *The Suffering Self: Pain and Narrative Representation in the Early Christian Era*. London: Routledge, 1995.

Pervo, R. *Profit with Delight: The Literary Genre of the Acts of the Apostles*. Philadelphia, PA: Fortress, 1987.

Pervo, R. 'Early Christian Fiction'. In *Greek Fiction: The Greek Novel in Context*, edited by J. Morgan and R. Stoneman, 239–54. London: Routledge, 1994.

Pervo, R. 'The Ancient Novel Becomes Christian'. In *The Novel in the Ancient World*, edited by G. Schmeling, 685–711. Leiden: Brill, 1996.

Pesthy, Monika. 'Thecla among the Fathers of the Church'. In *The Apocryphal Acts of Paul and Thecla*, edited by Jan N. Bremmer, 164–78. Kampen: Kok Pharos, 1996.

Peterson, Peter M. *Andrew, Brother of Simon Peter*. Leiden: Brill, 1963.

Petroff, Elizabeth Alvida. *Medieval Women's Visionary Literature*. Oxford: Oxford University Press, 1986.

Petropoulos, John C. B. 'Transvestite Virgin with a Cause: The Acta Pauli et Thecla and Late Antique Proto-"Feminism"'. In *Greece and Gender*, edited by Brit Berggreen and Nanno Marinatos, 125–39. Athens: Norwegian Institute, 1995.

Petterson, Olof. 'Magic-Religion: Some Marginal Notes to an Old Problem'. *Ethnos* 22 (1957): 109–19.

Pilarski, Ahida E. 'The Past and Future of Biblical Feminist Hermeneutics'. *Biblical Theology Bulletin* 1 (2011):16–23.

Pliny the Elder. *Natural History*, 10 vols. Translated by W. H. S. Jones. Loeb Classical Library. Cambridge: Harvard University Press, 1963.

Pomeroy, Sarah B. *Goddesses, Whores, Wives and Slaves: Women in Classical Antiquity*. London: Pimlico, 1994.

Portefaix, Lilian. '"Good Citizenship" in the Household of God: Women's Position in the Pastorals Reconsidered in the Light of Roman Rule'. In *A Feminist Companion to the Deutero-Pauline Epistles*, edited by Amy-Jill Levine, 147–58. London: T&T Clark, 2003.

Potter, David. 'Martyrdom as Spectacle'. In *Theater and Society in the Classical World*, edited by Ruth Scodel, 53–88. Ann Arbor: University of Michigan Press, 1993.

Poupon, Gerard. 'L'accusation de magie dans les Actes Apocryphes'. In *Les Actes Apocryphes des Apôtres. Christianisme et monde païen*, edited by F. Bovon and M. van Esbroeck, 71–93. Genève: Labor et Fides, 1981.

Price, Simon R. F. *Rituals and Power: The Roman Imperial Cult in Asia Minor*. Cambridge: Cambridge University Press, 1984.

Prieur, Jean Marc. 'Le genre Littéraire du récit biographique', *Acta Andreae* II: *Praefaitio – Commentarius*. Brepols: Turnhout, 1989.

Radford Ruether, Rosemary. 'Mother of the Church: Ascetic Women in the Late Patristic: Age'. In *Women of Spirit: Female Leadership in the Jewish and Christian Traditions*, edited by Rosemary Radford Ruether and Eleanor McLaughlin, 71–98. New York: Simon & Schuster, 1998.

Rehmann, Luzia Sutter. 'German-Language Feminist Exegesis of the Pauline Letters: A Survey'. *Journal for the Study of the New Testament* 79 (2000): 5–18.

Rhoads, David. 'Narrative Criticism of Gospel of Mark 9–11'. *Journal of the American Academy of Religion* 50 (1982): 411–34.

Richlin, Amy, ed. *Pornography and Representation in Greece and Rome*. Oxford: Oxford University Press, 1992.

Richlin, Amy. 'Reading Ovid's Rapes'. In *Pornography and Representation in Greece and Rome*, edited by Amy Richlin, 158–79. Oxford: Oxford University Press, 1992.

Ricoeur, Paul. *Freud and Philosophy: An Essay on Interpretation*. Translated by Denis Savage. New Haven, CT: Yale University Press, 1970.

Roberts, Alexander, and James Donaldson, eds. Vol. 4 of *The Ante-Nicene Fathers*. Cleveland, OH: Hendrickson, 1995.

Roberts Gaventa, Beverly. 'Our Mother St. Paul: Toward the Recovery of a Neglected Theme'. *Princeton Summary Bulletin* 17 (1996): 29–44.

Roberts Gaventa, Beverly. *Our Mother Saint Paul*. Louisville, KY: Westminster John Knox Press, 2007.

Robertson, A. T. *A Grammar of the Greek New Testament in the Light of Historical Research*. New York: Hodder & Stoughton, 1914.

Rordorf, Willy. 'Tertullien et les Actes de Paul (a propos de bapt. 17.5)'. In *Autour de Tertullien. Hommage a Rene Braun, II*. Nice, Paris: Les Belles Lettres, 1990.

Rordorf, Willy. 'Tradition and Composition in the *Acts of Thecla*'. *Semeia* 80 (1986): 43–53.

Rordorf, Willy in collaboration with Pierre Cherix and Rudolphe Kasser. 'Actes de Paul'. In *Écrits apocryphes chrétiens*, edited by François Bovon and Pierre Geoltrain, 1115–77. Bibliothèque de la Pléiade, Saint Herblain: Gallimard, 1997.

Rousselle, Aline. *Porneia: On Desire and the Body in Antiquity*. New York: Basil Blackwell, 1988.

Russell, Diana E. H., ed. *Making Violence Sexy: Feminist Views on Pornography*. Buckingham: Open University Press, 1993.

Salisbury, Joyce E. *The Blood of Martyrs: Unintended Consequences of Ancient Violence*. London: Routledge, 2004.

Salisbury, Joyce E. *Church Fathers, Independent Virgins*. London: Verso, 1991.

Salisbury, Joyce E. *Perpetua's Passion: The Death Memory of a Young Roman Woman*. London: Routledge, 1997.

Scarborough, John. 'The Pharmacology of Sacred Plants, Herbs and Roots'. In *Magika Hiera: Ancient Greek Magic and Religion*, edited by Christopher A. Faraone and Dirk Obbink, 38–174. Oxford: Oxford University Press, 1991.
Schmidt, Carl, and Wilhelm Schubart. Πράξεις Παύλου, *Acta Pauli nach dem Papyrus der Hamburger*. Glückstadt, Hamburg: Staatsund Universitäts-Bibliothek, 1936.
Schneemelcher, Wilhelm, ed. *New Testament Apocrypha II*. Rev. ed. Translated by R. McLean Wilson. Cambridge: James Clarke; Louisville, KY: Westminster John Knox Press, 1992.
Schneiders, Sandra M. *The Revelatory Text: Interpreting the New Testament as Sacred Scripture*. Collegeville, MN: Liturgical Press, 1999.
Schottroff, Luise. 'Non-Violence and Women's Resistance in Early Christianity'. In *The Pacifist Impulse in Historical Perspective*, edited by Harvey L. Dyke, 79–89. Toronto: University of Toronto Press, 1996.
Schreiner, Thomas R. 'Head Coverings, Prophecies and the Trinity'. In *Recovering Biblical Manhood and Womanhood: A Response to Evangelical Feminism*, edited by J. Piper and W. Grudem, 117–32. Wheaton, IL: Crossway, 1991.
Schüssler-Fiorenza, Elisabeth. *Bread Not Stone: The Challenge of Feminist Biblical Interpretation*. Boston, MA: Beacon, 2002.
Schüssler-Fiorenza, Elisabeth. *But She Said: Feminist Practices of Biblical Interpretation*. Boston, MA: Beacon, 1992.
Schüssler-Fiorenza, Elisabeth. *In Memory of Her: A Feminist Theological Reconstruction of Christian Origins*. London: Crossroad, 1994.
Schüssler-Fiorenza, Elisabeth. 'Text and Reality-Reality as Text: The Problem of a Feminist Historical and Social Reconstruction Based on Texts'. *Studia Theologica* 43 (1989): 19–34.
Schüssler-Fiorenza, Elisabeth. *Wisdom Ways: Introducing Feminist Biblical Interpretation*. Maryknoll, NY: Orbis, 2001.
Schüssler-Fiorenza, Elisabeth, with Ann Brock and Shelly Matthews, eds. *Searching the Scriptures: A Feminist Commentary*. Vol. 2. New York: Crossroad, 1994.
Scullard, Howard H. *Festivals and Ceremonies of the Roman Republic*. London: Thames & Hudson, 1981.
Seim, Turid Karlsen. 'Ascetic Autonomy? New Perspectives on Single Women in the Early Church'. *Studia Theologica* 43 (1980): 125–40.
Shaw, Brent. 'Body, Power, Identity: Passions of the Martyr'. *Journal of Early Christian Studies* 4 (1996): 269–312.
Shaw, Brent. 'The Passion of Perpetua'. *Past and Present* 139 (1993): 3–45.
Shepardson, Nikki. *Burning Zeal: The Rhetoric of Martyrdom and the Protestant Community in Reformation France 1520–1570*. Cranbury, NJ: Rosemont, 2007.
Skinner, Marilyn B. 'Ego Mulier: The Construction of Male Sexuality in Catullus'. In *Roman Sexualities*, edited by Judith P. Hallett and Marilyn B. Skinner, 129–50. Princeton, NJ: Princeton University Press, 1997.
Skinner, Marilyn B. *Sexuality in Greek and Roman Culture*. Oxford: Blackwell, 2005.
Söder, Rosa. *Die apokryphen Apostelgeschichte und die romanhafte Literatur der Antike*. Stuttgart: W. Kohlhammer, 1932.
Sorkin-Rabinowitz, Nancy. 'Tragedy and the Politics of Containment'. In *Pornography and Representation in Greece and Rome*, edited by Amy Richlin, 36–52. Oxford: Oxford University Press, 1992.
Southern, Pat. *The Roman Empire from Severus to Constantine*. London: Routledge, 2001.

Spittler, Janet E. *Animals in the Apocryphal Acts of the Apostles*. Tübingen: Mohr Seibeck, 2008.

Stone, Sidra. *The Shadow King: The Invisible Force That Holds Women Back*. Lincoln, NE: iUniverse, 2000.

Stratton, Kimberly B. 'The Rhetoric of "Magic" in Early Christian Discourse: Gender, Power and the Construction of Heresy'. In *Mapping Gender in Ancient Religious Discourses*, edited by Todd Penner and Caroline Vander Stichele, 89–114. Boston, MA: Brill, 2007.

Straub, Kristina. 'The Guilty Pleasures of Female Theatrical Cross-Dressing and the Autobiography of Charlotte Charke'. In *Body Guards: The Cultural Politics of Gender Ambiguity*, edited by Julia Epstein and Kristina Straub, 142–66. London: Routledge, 1991.

Sutter Rehmann, Luzia. 'German-Language Feminist Exegesis of the Pauline Letters: A Survey'. *Journal for the Study of the New Testament* 79 (2000): 5–81.

Sutton, Robert. 'Pornography and Persuasion on Attic Pottery'. In *Pornography and Representation in Greece and Rome*, edited by Amy Richlin, 3–35. Oxford: Oxford University Press, 1992.

Swan, Laura. *The Forgotten Desert Mothers: Sayings, Lives and Stories of Early Christian Women*. Mahwah, NJ: Paulist Press, 2001.

Swancutt, Diana M. 'Greek Androgyny, the Roman Imperial Politics of Masculinity and the Roman Invention of the *Tribas*'. In *Mapping Gender in Ancient Religious Discourses*, edited by Todd Penner and Caroline Vander Stichele, 11–61. Boston, MA: Brill, 2007.

Szesnat, Holger. 'Mostly Aged Virgins, Philo and the Presence of the Therapeutrides at Lake Mareotis'. *Neotestamentica* 32 (1998): 191–201.

Tate, W. Randolph. *The Handbook for Biblical Interpretation: An Essential Guide to Methods, Terms and Concepts*. Grand Rapids, MI: Baker, 2012.

Tatum, James, ed. *The Search for the Ancient Novel*. Baltimore, MD: John Hopkins University Press, 1994.

Taylor, Joan E. *Jewish Women Philosophers of First Century Alexandria: Philo's 'Therapeutae' Reconsidered*. Oxford: Oxford University Press, 2003.

Taylor, Joan E. 'The Woman Ought to Have Control over Her Head Because of the Angels, 1 Corinthians 11.10'. In *Gospel and Gender: A Trinitarian Engagement with Being Male and Female in Christ*, edited by Douglas A. Campbell, 37–57. London: T&T Clark, 2003.

Taylor, Joan E. 'The Women 'Priests' of Philo De Vita Contemplativa: Reconstructing the Therapeuta'. In *On the Cutting Edge: The Study of Women in the Biblical World*, edited by Jane Schaberg, Alice Bach and Esther Fuchs, 102–22. New York: Continuum, 2004.

Theissen, Gerd. *The Miracle Stories of the Early Christian Tradition*. Edinburgh: T&T Clark, 1983.

Thomas, Christine M. *The Acts of Peter, Gospel Literature, and the Ancient Novel*. New York: Oxford University Press, 2003.

Thomas, Christine M. 'Stories without Texts and without Authors: The Problem of Fluidity in Ancient Novelistic Texts and Early Christian Literature'. In *Ancient Fiction and Early Christian Narrative*, edited by Ronald F. Hock, J. Bradley Chance and Judith Perkins, 272–91. Atlanta, GA: Scholars Press, 2003.

Tilley, Maureen. 'The Ascetic Body and the (Un)making of the World of the Martyr'. *Journal of the American Academy of Religion* 59 (1991): 467–79.

Todorov, Tzvetán. *Introduction à la literature fantastique*. Paris: Swuil, 1970. Translated by Richard Howard into *The Fantastic: A Structural Approach to Literary Genre*. New York: Cornell University Press, 1975.

Torjesen, Karen Jo. 'Reconstruction of Women's Early Christian History'. In *Searching the Scriptures: A Feminist Commentary*, vol. 2, edited by Elisabeth Schüssler-Fiorenza, with Ann Brock and Shelly Matthews, 290–310. New York: Crossroad, 1994.

Torjesen, Karen Jo. *When Women Were Priests: Women's Leadership in the Early Church and the Scandal of Their Subordination in the Rise of Christianity*. San Francisco, CA: Harper, 1993.

Trexler, Richard. *Sex and Conquest: Gendered Violence, Political Order and the European Conquest of the Americas*. Ithaca, NY: Cornell University Press, 1995.

Trible, Phyllis. *God and the Rhetoric of Sexuality*. Philadelphia, PA: Fortress Press, 1978.

Valantasis, Richard. *The Gospel of Thomas*. London: Routledge, 1997.

Valantasis, Richard. 'Narrative Strategies and Synoptic Quandaries: A Response to Dennis MacDonald's Reading of Acts of Paul and Acts of Peter'. *The Society of Biblical Literature 1992 Seminar Papers* (Atlanta, 1992).

Valantasis, Richard. 'The Question of Early Christian Identity: Three Strategies Exploring a Third Genos'. In *Feminist Companion to the New Testament Apocrypha*, edited by Amy-Jill Levine, with Maria Mayo Robbins, 60–76. Cleveland, OH: Pilgrim, 2006.

Vander Stichele, Caroline, and Todd Penner. *Contextualizing Gender in Early Christian Discourse: Thinking beyond Thecla*. London: T&T Clark, 2009.

Vermaseren, Maarten Jozef. *Mithriaca II: The Mithraeum at Ponza*. Leiden: Brill, 1974.

Vermeule, Cornelius C. *Roman Imperial Art in Greece and Asia Minor*. Cambridge, MA: Harvard University Press, 1968.

Vorster, Johannes N. 'Construction of Culture through the Construction of Person: The Construction of Thecla in the Acts of Thecla'. In *Feminist Companion to the New Testament Apocrypha*, edited by Amy-Jill Levine with Maria Mayo Robbins, 98–117. Cleveland, OH: Pilgrim, 2006.

Vouaux, Léon. *Les Actes de Paul et ses lettres apocryphes*. Paris: Letouzey et Ané, 1913.

Walker Bynum, Carolyn. *Holy Feast and Holy Fast: The Religious Significance of Food to Medieval Women*. Berkeley: University California Press, 1987.

Walker Bynum, Carolyn. *Fragmentation and Redemption: Essays on Gender and the Human Body in Medieval Religion*. New York: Zone Books, 1991.

Walker Bynum, Carolyn. 'Wonder'. *American Historical Review* 102 (1997): 1–26.

Walters, Jonathan. 'Invading the Roman Body: Manliness and Impenetrability in Roman Thought'. In *Roman Sexualities*, edited by Judith P. Hallett and Marilyn B. Skinner, 29–43. Princeton, NJ: Princeton University Press, 1997.

Ward, Benedicta. *Signs and Wonders: Saints, Miracles and Prayers from the 4th Century to the 14th*. Hampshire: Variorum, 1992.

Warner, Lyndan. *The Ideas of Man and Woman in Renaissance France: Print, Rhetoric and Law*. Surrey: Ashgate, 2011.

Wax, Murray, and Rosalie Wax. 'The Notion of Magic'. *Current Anthropology* 4 (1963): 495–518.

Wehn, Beate. 'Blessed Are the Bodies of Those Who Are Virgins: Reflections on the Image of Paul in the Acts of Thecla'. *Journal for the Study of the New Testament* 79 (2000): 149–64.

Weinstein, Donald, and Rudolph M. Bell. *Saints & Society: The Two Worlds of Western Christendom, 1000–1700*. Chicago, IL: University of Chicago Press, 1982.

Weitzmann, Kurt, ed. *Age of Spirituality*. New York: Museum, 1977.

Weitzmann, Kurt, ed. *Age of Spirituality: Late Antique and Early Christian Art, Third to Seventh Century. Catalogue of the Exhibition at the Metropolitan Museum of Art*,

November 19, 1977, through February 12, 1978. New York: Metropolitan Museum of Art in association with Princeton University Press, 1979.

Wenham, J. W. *The Elements of New Testament Greek.* Cambridge: Cambridge University Press, 2003.

White, Cynthia. *The Emergence of Christianity.* Westport, CT: Greenwood, 2007.

Wilkinson, John. *Egeria's Travels.* Warminster: Aris and Philips, 1981.

Wills, Lawrence M. *The Jewish Novel in the Ancient World.* Ithaca, NY: Cornell University Press, 1995.

Wilson, Brittany E. *Unmanly Men: Refigurations of Masculinity in Luke-Acts.* New York: Oxford University Press, 2015.

Wilson, Nigel Guy, ed. *Encyclopedia of Ancient Greece.* New York: Routledge, 2006.

Wilson, R. MacLachlan. *The Gospel of Philip, Translated from the Coptic Text, with an Introduction and Commentary.* London: Mowbray, 1962.

Wilson, R. McLachlan, and George W. MacRae. 'The Gospel of Mary'. In *The Coptic Gnostic Library, Nag Hammadi Codices V, 2-5 & VI with Papyrus Berolinensis 8502, 1 and 4*, edited by Douglas M. Parrott, 453–72. Leiden: Brill, 1979.

Wimsatt, William K., and Monroe C. Beardsley. 'The Intentional Fallacy'. In *The Verbal Icon: Studies in the Meaning of Poetry*, edited by W. K. Wimsatt, 3–20. Lexington: University of Kentucky Press, 1954.

Witherington III, Ben. *The Paul Quest: The Renewed Search for the Jew of Tarsus.* Leicester: InterVarsity, 1998.

Wolf, Naomi. *The Beauty Myth: How Images of Beauty Are Used against Women.* London: Vintage, 1991.

Wright Knust, Jennifer. *Abandoned to Lust: Sex, Slander and Ancient Christianity.* New York: Columbia University Press, 2006.

Wright, N. T. *Paul: In Fresh Perspective.* Augsburg, MN: Fortress, 2005.

Zanker, Paul. *The Power of Images in the Age of Augustus.* Translated by Alan Shapiro. Ann Arbor: University of Michigan Press, 1998.

Zweig, Bella. 'The Mute Nude Female Characters in Aristophanes' Plays'. In *Pornography and Representation in Greece and Rome*, edited by Amy Richlin, 73–89. Oxford: Oxford University Press, 1992.

Ancient sources

Ambrose	*Virg. De Virginibus*
Arist.,	*Gen. an.* Aristotle, *De generatione animalium*
Arist.,	*Rh.* Aristotle, *Rhetorica*
August.,	*Serm.* Augustine, *Sermones*
Cic.,	*Inv. Rhet.* Cicero, *De inventione rhetorica*
Cic.,	*De or.* Cicero, *De oratore*
Clem. Al.	*Strom.* Clement of Alexandria, *Stromateis*
Clem. Al.	*Paed.* Clement of Alexandria, *Paedagogus*
Clement of Rome	*First Epistle to the Corinthians*
Cyprian	*Ad donatum*
Diog. Laert.	Diogenes Laertius, *Vitae Philosophorum*
Epictetus,	*Diatr.* Epictetus, *Diatribe*
Euseb.,	*Hist. eccl.* Eusebius, *Historia ecclesiastica*
Gregory of Nyssa	*Life of Macrina*
Gregory of Nyssa	*Homily 14*
Hom.,	*Il.* Homer, *Iliad*
Ignatius,	*Smyrna.* Ignatius, *Letter to the Smyrnaeans*
Jer.	Jerome, *Vita S Hilarionis Eremitae*
Jer.,	*Ep.* Jerome, *Epistulae*
Lactant.,	*Div. inst.* Lanctantius, *Divinae institutiones*
Lucian,	*De mort. Peregr.* Lucian, *De morte Peregrini*
Methodius	*Symposium*
Origen,	*Princ.* Origen, *De Principiis*
Pl.,	*Ti.* Plato, *Timaeus*
Philo,	*Quaest. in Exod.* Philo, *Quaestiones et Solutiones in Exodum*
Philo,	*Vit. Cont.* Philo, *De vita contemplativa*
Philo,	*Spec. Leg.* Philo, *De specialibus legibus*
Polycarp,	*Phil.* Polycarp, *Philippians*
Quint.,	*Inst.* Quintilian, *Institutio oratoria*
Severus of Antioch	*Cathedral Homily 97*
Tac.,	*Ann.* Tacitus, *Annales*
Tert.,	*Apol.* Tertullian, *Apologeticum*
Tert.,	*De spect.* Tertullian, *De spectaculis*
Tert.,	*De bapt.* Tertullian, *De baptismo*
Tert.,	*De cul. Fem.* Tertullian, *De cultu feminarum*
Tert.,	*De virg.* Tertullian, *De virginibus velandis*

Rabbinic works

b. Menah. Babylonian Talmud, tractate Menahot
y. Ber. Jerusalem Talmud, tractate Berakot
t. Ber. Tosefta, tractate Berakot

Index

action 115, 116, 117
Acts of Paul 3-4, 7, 8, 20, 33, 39, 43-4
   and political authority 19, 36
Acts of Paul and Thecla
   and *Acts of Paul* 20, 39
   audience 38-9
   authorship 38-40, 44, 59-61, 181-2
   genre 33, 36-7, 135
   history and dating of text 37-8
   manuscripts and translations of 38-40, 178
adultery 84, 166-7
Alexander of Antioch 72-3, 77, 109, 115-17, 143
   crown of 116, 177, 178
Amazons 145
Ambrose, bishop of Milan 164, 165
Androcles 143
androgyny 66, 67, 69, 87 n.15
Apocryphal Acts 2-5
   Acts of Andrew 129 n.120
   Acts of John 19, 36, 156n41
   Acts of Peter 19, 36, 130 n.120
   Acts of Thomas 130 n.120
   authorship 7-8, 39
   chastity 3, 4-6, 18
   eroticism 129 n.119, 129 n.120
   gender roles 6, 15, 141
   genre 17-19, 33-6, 121
   patriarchy 6-7, 12, 22, 138, 141
   see also Acts of Paul; Acts of Paul and Thecla
apostolic heroes 6
arenas, Roman 163
   arena scenes 135
      bulls 118, 166, 174
      eroticism 95, 113, 114-15, 117
      masculinization of Thecla 115, 177, 178
      nakedness 117, 118, 119, 120-1, 139, 147-8, 179

      wild beasts miracle 135, 146-7, 148, 165, 166, 194
   and martyrdom 99, 100, 103
   and power 176-7, 183, 186 n.59
Aristotle 35, 67
Armenia 172
Artemis, goddess 145
asceticism, female 3, 13, 16, 23, 41-2, 66, 80, 141-2, 163
asceticism, male 166
Athena, goddess 145
Augustine 101
Augustus, emperor 169-71, 173
authorship
   Acts of Paul and Thecla 38-9, 59-61
   Apocryphal Acts 7-8, 39
   authorial intention 181-2
   female 7-8
   male 54-6, 60

baptism 144
   baptism of Thecla 72, 78, 117, 139, 147, 178
   Paul's refusal 74, 115
barbarians 170, 172, 173
beauty, Thecla's 71, 73-4, 116, 154, 198
   comeliness 74, 82
biographies 34-5, 36-7
Britannia 171-2, 183
Buddhism 80-1
bulls 118, 149-50, 162, 166, 174, 178

Caesar, emperor 146, 149, 175, 182, 194
celibacy *see* chastity
chastity
   Apocryphal Acts 3, 4-6, 18
   female 3, 4-5, 38, 142, 163, 164
      and patriarchy 10, 14, 42, 162
   male 164-5
   Paul on 41, 43, 141, 167, 175
chiton (χιτῶνα) 76-7

'Christian Dirce' (Henry Siemiradzki), painting 104
Christianity
    Christian identity 15, 177, 179–81, 192–3, 198
        and martyrdom 83, 176, 186 n.56
        and shame 99, 120
        and gender roles 41–2, 54–5, 66, 67–8, 152–3
        and martyrdom/persecution 99–101, 102, 119, 121–2, 126 n.31, 179–80
        and identity 83, 176, 186 n.56
        and Roman Empire 164–5, 174–5, 179–80, 183
        and inviolability 175, 176–7, 192–3, 198–9
        and virginity 163, 168, 183
    Thecla as symbol of 180–1, 182, 192–3
    and virginity/chastity 38, 54, 81, 163–5, 180–1
        and Roman Empire 163, 168, 183
        and voyeurism 118, 122, 182
Chrysostom, John 101
Cicero 35
Claudius, emperor 171–2
Clement (II) homily 68
Clement of Alexandria 100
Clement of Rome 99
clothing, male
    Alexander of Antioch 116, 177, 178
    Thecla 76–80, 86, 162
Codex Trecensis 523 40
comeliness 74, 82
conquest 169, 173, 183
Corinthians, First Epistle to
    1 Cor. 11 42, 71, 73, 74, 81
    1 Cor. 14.34–35 42, 49 n.92
    1 Cor. 7. 41, 43
counterculture 15
courage 77, 86, 115, 122, 123, 177, 178, 179, 190
covenant between God and Israel 166
cross, making the shape of 140
crowns 116, 177, 178
Cyprian, bishop of Carthage 100

Damnati ad bestias 124, 132 n.188
Decretum Gelasianum 5 37
degradation of women 99, 119, 121, 179

deification of Thecla 144–5, 147, 151, 152, 153–4, 196
divine intervention 135, 140, 141, 156 n.41, 199
domination, male
    and patriarchy 110, 138–9, 172–3, 189
    and Paul 6, 105, 115, 194–5
    and power 98, 105, 108, 111
    and Roman Empire 172–3, 183, 193
    and sado-erotic violence 113–15, 117, 118–21, 123–4
    and voyeurism 113, 116–17, 121, 179, 182, 191, 195–6
    see also masculinity; patriarchy
dowries 138
dreams 79, 145–6

emperors, Roman 169–72, 173, 174
    Caesar 146, 149, 175, 182, 194
empowerment, female 22, 23–4, 51–61, 124–5, 139, 194
    female power 146, 148, 151, 152–3, 158 n.81
    and Thecla 104–5, 141, 143, 182, 197–8
    and voyeurism 1, 121, 197, 198
encratism 175
enslavement/bondage 107, 108
epiphanies 135
Eros 137
erotic substitution 5
eroticism 79, 118–19, 161
    Apocryphal Acts 129 n.119, 129 n.120
    arena scenes 95, 113, 114–15, 117
    and hair 80, 82
    Martyrdom of Saints Perpetua and Felicitas 113, 129 n.119
    voyeurism 111–12, 113, 129 n.119, 129 n.120
    see also sado-erotic violence
ethnicity 168, 171, 173, 192–3
Eugenia of Alexandria 73
Eusebius 8
executions, public 99
Ezekiel, book of 166, 167

Falconilla, Pompeia Sosia 40, 145, 146
fear, male 148, 158 n.81
femininity
    characteristics of 83, 145, 151

Index

beauty/comeliness 71, 73–4, 82, 116, 154, 198
   modesty 83, 108
   passivity 78, 108, 112, 139, 147, 152, 165–6, 191
   silence 92, 93 n.143, 106–9, 114–15
   submissiveness 16, 77, 83, 96, 165, 171
   vulnerability 75, 77, 119, 121, 164, 172, 177
   female inferiority 11–12, 58, 65, 67, 105
objectification of women
   and sado-erotic violence 111–19, 196–7
   Thecla 82, 85–6, 110, 113, 116, 123–4, 142, 190–1
   and voyeurism 53, 77, 82, 85–6, 98, 117, 121
   and patriarchy 12–13, 21, 23–4, 29 n.97, 122, 161–2
   and Roman society 11, 23–4, 163, 172–3
   stereotyping of 11, 69, 138–9, 144, 146, 148, 150–1
   subordination of women 16, 92 n.121, 98
   and Paul 7, 13, 49 n.91
   and Thecla 13, 108, 115
   Thecla 75–6, 123–5, 145
   and virginity 86, 123
   see also objectification of women; Thecla
feminism 7, 21, 51–4, 96, 126 n.7, 182
feminization 164, 165, 166, 167, 168–9
fire, cloud of 117, 118, 147–8, 149
flogging 110
folk culture/oral history 4–5, 17–18, 25 n.18, 41, 43, 48 n.75

Galatians (Gal. 3.28) 66
gaze
   of the imagination 100–3, 104, 112, 127 n.55
   male 97, 112–15
   Thecla's 107, 111, 112–13, 124
   see also eroticism; sado-erotic violence; voyeurism
Gelenius 40
Gemma Augustea, sardonyx cameo 173
gender roles 54–8

   and Christianity 41–3, 54–5, 66, 67–8, 152–3
   and Graeco-Roman society 9, 10, 13–14, 56–7, 66–7, 79
   see also femininity; masculinity
gender transformation *see* feminization; masculinization of Thecla
genre 33–7, 135
   biographies 34–5, 36–7
   Hellenistic novel 17–19, 33, 121
Gospel According to Mary 68
Gospel of Philip 68
Gospel of the Egyptians 68
Gospel of Thomas 67
gospels, canonical 33, 34
Governors 78, 106, 110, 114, 120–1, 149–50
Grabe, Ernestus 37
Graeco-Roman culture 56–8, 101, 174
   femininity 11
   and gender roles 7–8, 9, 10, 13–14, 56–7, 66–7, 79
   Hellenistic novel 17–19, 121
   and lions 144, 147
   see also Roman Empire
Greek literature 7–8
Greek Magical Papyri (PGM) 134, 145, 148
Greek Tragedy 101
Gregory of Nyssa 110

hair 79, 80–2, 173
   and eroticism 80, 82
   icons of 75, 91 n.91, 91 n.94
   and Paul 69, 70, 71, 72, 81
   Thecla's 68–76, 80–1, 86, 190
Hamburg Papyrus (PH) 38, 157 n.53
head, female 82
Hellenistic novel 17–19, 33, 121
Heracles/Hercules 105, 143, 169
herbal magic 148, 166, 194
'hermeneutics of suspicion' 51–4, 85
heroine, sympathy for 162
heroization of Paul 105–6
Homer 7, 148
honour 14, 71, 77, 81
   see also shame
Hosea, book of 166, 167
humiliation 172, 177, 183
   of Thecla 1, 95, 108, 124, 140, 162, 191
hysteria 100, 146, 149

identity
    Christian identity 15, 177, 179–81,
        192–3, 198
    and martyrdom 83, 176, 186 n.56
    and shame 99, 120
    ego identification 164–8, 175–6
    gender 56–8, 82
    male 19, 23–4, 165, 175;
        (*see also* femininity; masculinity)
    social 83, 176, 177
Ignatius, *Smyrna* 42
imagery/representation of women 168–74
    rape in 171–2, 173
    of Thecla 75–6, 144, 157 n.55,
        157 n.57
imprisonment/bondage 107, 108, 137–8
inferiority, female 11–12, 58, 65, 67, 105
insanity 136
integrity 54, 123, 124–5, 191
interpretation, reader 181–2
inviolability, bodily 161–83
    and Christianity and the Roman Empire
        175, 176–7, 192–3, 198–9
    Thecla 123, 162, 191, 192, 196, 198–9
    and virginity 125, 153–4, 164, 174
Israel 166–7

Jerome 65, 138
Jesus 34–5, 67, 139, 140, 146, 150
Jewish people, feminization of 168–9
Judaea Capta coin 168–9, 178
Judaism 66, 164, 166–7
Judgement Day 100

lamb, sacrificial 77, 111, 140, 166
leadership of women 42, 43
liberation of women 3, 5, 12, 21, 65
Life and Miracles of Saint Thecla 44,
    50 n.100, 74, 77
lions 117, 143–5, 147, 165
literary tools, women as 54–6, 176
Luke-Acts 12

Macrina the Younger 110
magic 133–54
    female 148, 150, 152–3
    herbal magic 148, 166, 194
    paganism 138, 156 n.30
    and Paul 136–7, 139

as seduction tool 136–7, 138, 156 n.30
and Thecla 136–7, 138, 139, 190, 191–2
see also miracles
Mark's Gospel 140, 199
marriage
    between God and man 166, 180–1
    rejection of 18, 95
    and Roman society 156 n.28, 156 n.32,
        156 n.33
    and Thecla 95, 138, 139
martyrdom
    and *Acts of Paul and Thecla*
        36–7, 104–21
    and Christianity 99–101, 102, 119,
        121–2, 126 n.31, 179–80
    and identity 83, 176, 186 n.56
    female 36, 37
        masculinization of 83–4, 165
        and Roman Empire 195, 196
        and sado-erotic violence 102, 103,
            104, 119–20, 196, 197
    and paganism 99, 126 n.28
    Perpetua 78–9, 112, 113, 122, 129 n.119,
        152, 194
    and Roman Empire 119, 176, 183, 195
    and arenas 99, 100, 103
    and sado-erotic violence 99–121,
        196, 197
    Thecla 20, 109
        inviolability 153, 162
        survival 85, 104, 122–3, 151–2, 153–4
Martyrdom of Paul 144
Martyrdom of Saints Perpetua and Felicitas
    78–9, 112, 113, 129 n.119
martyrologies 36–7, 83, 99–104, 176, 196–7
    and voyeurism 101–4, 129 n.119,
        129 n.120
masculinity
    characteristics of 84, 86
        action 115, 116, 117
        courage 77, 86, 115, 122, 123, 177,
            178, 179, 190
        strength 120, 140, 177, 178
        virility 84, 85, 86, 165, 190;
            (*see also* inviolability, bodily; speech,
            power of)
    feminization of 164, 165, 170, 173, 177
    and patriarchy 97, 141
    and Paul 105–6, 116, 124

and pornography/eroticism 96–7,
    98, 116–17
and power 23–4, 141, 168–71
and domination 98, 105, 111
and Roman Empire 169–71, 173, 175–8,
    183, 193
    and Roman culture/society 84,
        164–5, 168–9
    stereotyping of 84, 105, 164
    see also domination, male
masculinization of Thecla 10–12, 65–86,
    122–3, 161–2, 182, 189–91
    actions 115, 116, 117
    arena scenes 115, 177, 178
    courage 77, 86, 115, 122, 123, 177, 178,
        179, 190
    cutting of hair 68–76, 80–1
    male clothing 76–80
    as masculine symbol 144, 162
    metamorphosis 69, 140
    and speech 82, 93 n.143
    strength 77, 120, 140, 177, 178
    virility 86, 165, 190
masculinization of women 65–86, 165
Matthew's Gospel 140
Medusa 80, 113
memory, collective 15
Mesnartius manuscript 39–40
metamorphosis
    Paul into Jesus 139, 166
    Thecla 69, 140
metaphor, women as 54, 61 n.19
Methodius, bishop of Olympus and
    Patara 110
miracles 23, 34, 133–54
    and *Acts of Peter* 19, 36
    bulls 118, 149–50, 162, 166, 174, 178
    burning of Thecla 77, 113–15, 139–43
    cloud of fire 117, 118, 147–8, 149
    definition 133–6
    dreams miracle 145–6
    lions miracle 117, 143–5, 147, 165
    and magic 190, 191–2
    New Testament miracles 135
    and prayer 134, 146, 151
    rescue miracles 135
    self-baptism 72, 78, 117, 139, 147, 178
    wild beasts miracle 135, 146–7, 148, 165,
        166, 194

by women 152
modesty 83, 108
Mombritian manuscript 38
motherhood 197
mounting 113

nakedness 171–3
    nudity 113, 114
    Thecla 113–14, 117, 118, 119, 120–1,
        139, 147–8, 179
narrative 35, 59–61
Nero, emperor 172
New Testament
    canonical gospels 33, 34
    Corinthians
        1 Cor. 11 42, 71, 73, 74, 81
        1 Cor. 14.34–35 42, 49 n.92
        1 Cor. 7 41, 43
    Galatians (Gal. 3.28) 66
    Mark's Gospel 140, 199
    Matthew's Gospel 140
    miracles 135
    Pastoral Epistles 3–4, 8, 41–2, 43–4,
        48 n.80, 148
    Timothy
        1 Tim. 2 4, 42, 43
        1 Tim. 2.11–15 4

objectification of women 98
    and sado-erotic violence 111–19, 196–7
    Thecla 82, 85–6, 110, 113, 116, 123–4,
        142, 190–1
    and voyeurism 53, 77, 82, 85–6, 98,
        117, 121
Old Testament
    Ezekiel 166, 167
    Genesis 1.27 66
    Hosea 166, 167
    Proverbs 5.8 164
'oneness' 66, 68, 87 n.15
Onesiphoros 108
oral history *see* folk culture/oral history
otherness 102, 103, 109, 180
Oxyrhynchus papyrus 38

paganism 54–5, 147, 175
    and magic 138, 156 n.30
    and martyrdom 99, 100, 126 n.28
Palatine, L manuscript 38

Papyrus No 1 (P. Heid.) 38, 39
Paris manuscripts, 1 and K 38
Parisinum Graecus (Paris. Gr.) 520 37,
    131 n.161
Parthians 170
passivity 78, 112, 139, 147, 152, 165–6, 191
Pastoral Epistles 3–4, 8, 41–2, 43–4,
    48 n.80, 148
patriarchy 51–4, 95
    Apocryphal Acts 6–7, 12, 22, 138, 141
    and femininity 12–13, 21, 23–4,
        29 n.97, 122
    Thecla 122, 161–2
    and male domination 110, 138–9,
        172–3, 189
    and masculinity 97, 141
    and Paul 7, 115, 139, 194–6
    in Roman society 172–3, 194, 198
    and sado-erotic violence 53, 118–20,
        162, 191
    and virginity/chastity 10, 14, 42,
        162, 195–6
Paul
    appearance 105–6
        as an angel 105, 106, 116, 124
    as envoy of God 141, 142
    and gender identity 66, 87 n.15, 87 n.17
        Paul's 105–6, 116, 124, 167
    and hair 69, 70, 71, 72, 81
    heroization of 105–6
    imprisonment/bondage 107, 108, 137–8
    and lions 144
    as magician 136–7
    metamorphosis 139, 166
    and patriarchy 7, 115, 139, 194–6
    and prayer 115, 141, 146
    preaching 106, 140, 141, 142, 167
    and Roman Empire 174, 185 n.47
    as seduction tool 108, 136, 141–2
    and speech 106–8, 124
    and subordination of women 7, 13,
        49 n.91
    and Thecla
        absence of Paul 143, 151, 195
        attracted to Paul 78, 106–8, 194–5
        baptism of Thecla 74, 115
        disowning of Thecla 77, 115–16
        gazing at Paul 85, 94 n.156, 111, 124
        and hair 69, 70, 71, 72

    and magic 136–7, 139
    and male domination 6, 115, 194–5
        passivity 141, 165–6
    and virginity/chastity 41, 43, 81, 105,
        141, 167, 175, 199
Pauline tradition 41–4, 71
Pelagia, prostitute 73
Perpetua 78–9, 112, 122, 152, 194
persecution of Christians 100–1, 102,
    176, 179–80
phallic symbols 113, 169
    bulls 148, 178
    swords 178
Philo 66, 77
piety 38, 65, 66, 67, 68, 123
Plato 66
Plutarch 81
pornography 95–125
    and feminism 96, 126 n.7
    see also eroticism; sado-erotic violence;
        voyeurism
power
    female 146, 148, 151, 152–3, 158 n.81
        Thecla 144–5, 177, 178;
        (see also empowerment, female)
    and male domination 98, 105, 108, 111
    and masculinity 23–4, 98, 105, 111,
        141, 168–71
    and Roman Empire 99, 168–73
    in arenas 176–7, 183, 186 n.59
prayer 115, 134, 141, 145, 146, 151
preaching
    Paul 106, 140, 141, 142, 167
    Thecla 42, 57, 109–10
prisons, access to 55
prostitutes 77
Proverbs 5.8 164
public/private domain 77, 119
punishment 95–6, 110–11

Quintilian 35

rape 114, 116, 117, 131 n.149, 178
    in Roman imagery 171–2, 173
representation, female see imagery/
    representation of women
Rhea, goddess 144
rhetoric 54–6, 176, 189, 193
ritual 134

Roman Empire
    arenas 99, 100, 103, 163, 176-7, 183, 186 n.59
    and Christianity 163, 164-5, 174-5, 179-80, 183
        and inviolability 175, 176-7, 192-3, 198-9
        and virginity 163, 168, 183
    and conquest 169, 173, 183
    emperors 169-72, 173, 174
        Caesar 146, 149, 175, 182, 194
    and femininity 11, 23-4, 163, 172-3
    and gender roles 9, 10, 13-14, 66-7, 79
    images/representation of 168-74, 183
        rape in 171-2, 173
    and male domination 172-3, 183, 193
    and marriage 156 n.28, 156 n.32, 156 n.33
    and martyrdom 119, 176, 183
        and arenas 99, 100, 103
        female 195, 196
    and masculinity 168-71, 173, 175-8, 183, 193
        in Roman society 84, 164-5, 168-9
    patriarchy in 172-3, 194, 198
    and Paul 174, 185 n.47
    power 99, 168-73
        in arenas 176-7, 183, 186 n.59
    Roman provinces 171, 174
    and Thecla 178, 193, 198-9

'sacred soap opera' 123
sacrilege 178
sado-erotic violence 23, 99-121, 190
    and *Acts of Paul and Thecla* 104-21
    and male domination 113-15, 117, 118-21, 123-4
    and martyrdom 99-121, 196, 197
        female 102, 103, 104, 119-20, 196, 197
    and objectification of women 111-19, 196-7
    and patriarchy 53, 118-20, 162, 191
    see also eroticism
Saint Catherine's Monastery, Sinai 199
Santa Pudenziana, Rome 180-1, 193
seals 135, 147, 158 n.76
Sebasteion relief, Aphrodisias 171-3, 183
seduction tools
    magic as 136-7, 138, 156 n.30

Paul as 108, 136, 141-2
Severan dynasty 174
Severus of Antioch 181, 198
sexual desire, male 164
sexual violence *see* sado-erotic violence
sexuality *see* femininity; gender roles; masculinity
shame 14, 78-9, 119
    and Christian identity 99, 120
    Thecla 104, 108, 137, 138, 161, 177, 178
    see also honour
silence of women 82, 93 n.143, 106-9, 114-15
slaves 119
social status 6-7, 19, 38-9, 73, 84
    and punishment 111, 113
solidarity, female 117-18, 146, 148, 150-1, 194
Spartans 81
spectacle 99-104, 122
    see also sado-erotic violence; voyeurism
speech, power of 142
    Paul 106-7, 124
    Thecla
        as martyr/preacher 109-10, 115, 150, 159 n.85
        silence 82, 93 n.143, 106-7, 108-9
spiderwebs 106-7, 128 n.84
stereotyping
    of men 84, 105, 164
    of women 11, 69, 144, 146, 148, 150-1
    Thecla 138-9, 180
strength 77, 120, 140, 177, 178
subjugation of women 42, 133, 178-9, 193
submissiveness 16, 77, 83, 96, 165, 171
subordination of women 16, 92 n.121, 98
    and Paul 7, 13, 49 n.91
    and Thecla 13, 108, 115
survival 85, 104, 151-2, 153-4
Synod of Gangra 65, 71, 74
Syriac manuscripts 38, 178

Tacitus 99
teachers, women as 4, 42, 110
temptation 69, 72
Tertullian 4, 81, 197
    on authorship of *Acts of Paul and Thecla* 39-40, 44, 59-60, 181-2
    De baptismo 14, 39

    and martyrdom 100, 102, 103
    on virginity/chastity 42, 114
    and women's roles 42, 54–5
Thamyris 110, 137
thaumaturgy *see* magic
Thecla
    and Alexander 72–3, 177
    baptism of 72, 78, 117, 139, 147, 178
        Paul's refusal 74, 115
    cult of Saint Thecla 44
    deification of 144–5, 147, 151, 152, 153–4, 196
    female empowerment 104–5, 141, 143, 182, 197–8
    femininity 75–6, 123–5, 145
        beauty/comeliness 71, 73–4, 82, 116, 154, 198
        masculinization of 11, 78–9, 123, 161–2
        objectification of 82, 85–6, 110, 113, 116, 123–4, 142, 190–1
        passivity 78, 108, 112, 138–9, 147, 152, 165–6, 191
        patriarchy 122, 161–2
        silence 82, 93 n.143, 106–9, 114–15
        subordination of women 13, 108, 115
        vulnerability 75, 77, 162, 177
    gaze of 107, 111, 112–13, 124
    icons/images of 75–6, 144, 157 n.55, 157 n.57
    integrity 54, 123, 124–5, 191
    inviolability 153–4, 161–83, 191, 192, 196
        and virginity 125, 153–4, 164, 174
    and magic 136–7, 138, 139, 190, 191–2
    marriage 95, 138, 139
    martyrdom 20, 109
        and humiliation 1, 95, 108, 124, 140, 162, 191
        and inviolability 153, 162
        survival 85, 104, 122–3, 151–2, 153–4
    masculinization of 10–12, 22–3, 57, 65–86, 122–3, 182, 189–91
        action 115, 116, 117
        arena scenes 115, 177, 178
        courage 77, 86, 115, 122, 123, 177, 178, 179, 190
        cutting of hair 68–76, 80–1, 86, 190
        male clothing 76–80, 86, 162
        as masculine symbol 144, 162
        metamorphosis 69, 140
        and speech 82, 93 n.143
        strength 77, 120, 140, 177, 178
        and virginity 123, 192
        virility 86, 165, 190
    and Paul
        absence of Paul 143, 151, 195
        attracted to Paul 6, 78, 106–8, 194–5
        baptism of Thecla 74, 115
        disowning of Thecla 77, 115–16
        gazing at Paul 85, 94 n.156, 111, 124
        and hair 69, 70, 71, 72
        and magic 136–7, 139
        and male domination 6, 115, 194–5
        passivity 141, 165–6
    power 144–5, 177, 178
    power of speech
        as martyr/preacher 109–10, 115, 150, 159 n.85
        silence 82, 93 n.143, 106–7, 108–9
    and prayer 145, 146
    as role model 1, 6, 12
    and Roman Empire 178–9, 193, 198–9
    and sexuality 77, 82–5, 198
    shame 104, 108, 137, 138, 161, 177, 178
    as symbol of Christianity 180–1, 182, 192–3
    and virginity 9, 86, 167–8, 192, 195–6, 199
        inviolability 125, 153–4, 164, 174
        and masculinity 123, 192
    see also miracles
Theocleia, Thecla's mother 110, 111, 194
thunderstorms 140
Timothy (1 Tim 2) 4, 42, 43
torture 119
    see also sado-erotic violence
transvestism 11, 65, 67, 69, 85, 86 n.3
truth 119
Tryphaena of Pontus, Queen 4, 110, 117, 145, 146, 149, 194

Vatican manuscript, F 38
victimization of women 111, 124, 180, 191, 199
violence *see* sado-erotic violence
Virgin Mary 152
virginity 3, 114, 161–8

and Christianity 38, 54, 81, 163–5, 180–1
    and Roman Empire 163, 168, 183
    and femininity 86, 123
    and patriarchy 162, 195–6
    Paul on 81, 141, 167, 175, 199
    Thecla 9, 86, 167–8, 195–6, 199
        inviolability 125, 153–4, 164, 174
        and masculinity 123, 192
virility 84, 85, 86, 165, 190
virtue 66, 108–9
voyeurism 99–104
    and Christianity 118, 122, 182
    and eroticism 111–12, 113, 129 n.119, 129 n.120
    and female empowerment 1, 121, 197, 198
    and male domination 113, 116–17, 121, 179, 182, 191, 195–6
    and martyrologies 101–4, 129 n.119, 129 n.120
    and objectification of women 53, 77, 82, 85–6, 98, 117, 121
    see also sado-erotic violence
vulnerability 119, 121, 164, 172
    Thecla 75, 77, 162, 177

widows 3, 4, 41–2
wild beasts miracle 135, 146–7, 148, 165, 166, 194

Yahweh 166

www.ingramcontent.com/pod-product-compliance
Lightning Source LLC
Chambersburg PA
CBHW072148290426
44111CB00012B/2005